Statistical Panic

STATISTICAL PANIC

Cultural Politics and Poetics of the Emotions

KATHLEEN WOODWARD

DUKE UNIVERSITY PRESS

Durham and London 2009

Printed in the
United States of America
on acid-free paper ∞

Designed by Jennifer Hill
Typeset in Scala by
Keystone Typesetting, Inc.

Cataloging information for this title
is available from the Library of Congress.

ISBN 978-0-8223-4354-7 (cloth : alk. paper)
ISBN 978-0-8223-4377-6 (pbk. : alk. paper)

"At the End of the Line" by J.-B. Pontalis appears in *Love of Beginnings* by J.-B. Pontalis, which was originally published in French under the title *L'amour des commencements* (Éditions Gallimard, 1986). The English translation by James Greene with Marie-Christine Réguis was published by Free Association Books, Ltd. (London: 1993). "At the End of the Line" is reproduced here with permission of Free Association Books, Ltd., Great Britain.

To Herbert Blau

CONTENTS

ACKNOWLEDGMENTS

As director of the Simpson Center for the Humanities at the University of Washington and, before that, as director of the Center for Twentieth Century Studies at the University of Wisconsin, Milwaukee, I have had many, many welcome occasions to introduce visiting speakers. It is a task I love because it offers the opportunity to refer to the important work that scholars are doing and to thank them for it. Thus it seems altogether appropriate to mention here that the mode of debate has never been as temperamentally congenial to me as the mode of acknowledgment itself. To me it is simply a given that my own work represents a collaboration with other lives and with many texts (I am first and foremost a reader, after all), and thus the space granted to me here seems strangely constricted and insufficient, amenable only to enumeration and the alphabetical making of lists, whereas I am far more at home in the world of adjectives—almost always inflected positively, as in brilliant, astute, deft, and generous. Everyone named below should imagine their name paired with such words. I mean it. I have many people to thank, including those I have never met whose work has helped shape my own feeling and thought. In fact I regard the notes and the bibliography as a continuation of the deeply felt acknowledgments here.

I am altogether privileged to count as friends—and intellectual partners —Gabriele Schwab and Carolyn Allen. Both of these wonderful women read the entire manuscript and offered invaluable suggestions. I want to thank Ken Wissoker, the legendary editor at Duke University Press, and the readers he secured whose fine intelligence, excellent advice, and warm counsel have served me well. I am indebted to them. Regarding the individual chapters, many people contributed welcome comments and precious bibliographies (to my mind, one of the greatest gifts of all), including Karyn Ball, Anne Basting, Dick Blau, Lothar Bredella, Paul Brodwin, Thomas Cole, Cecelia Condit, Diane Driver, Susan Dunn, Julie Ellison, Pamela Gilbert, Sandra Gilbert, Tina Gillis, Herbert Grabes, Margaret Gullette, Lane Hall, Steven Katz, Sharon Kaufman, Teresa Mangum, Andrew Martin, Susan Miller, Patrice Petro, Larry Polivka, John Rodriguez-Luis, Nigel Rothfels, Maura Spigel, Michael Warner, and Anne Wyatt-Brown. I would also like to acknowledge my colleagues at the University of Washington, including Eva Cherniavsky, Tom Foster, Gillian Harkins, Chandan Reddy, and Nikhil Singh, as well as Jodi Melamed, who was in residence at the Simpson Center for the Humanities for two years as a Woodrow Wilson National Fellowship Foundation postdoctoral scholar.

I am grateful to have been given the opportunity to present embryonic versions of this work at the École des Hautes Études en Sciences Sociales where I taught a month-long seminar. I thank the audiences at Brown University, Michigan State University, Moscow University, Pacific Lutheran University, Pennsylvania State University, Texas A&M University, Trent University, University of British Columbia, University of Buffalo, University of Copenhagen, University of California at San Diego, University of Greifswald, University of Michigan, University of Pennsylvania, and Wayne State University, as well as a special cross-disciplinary audience at the University of Washington, which was destined at that point to become my intellectual home. I have also presented versions of this work at conferences and annual meetings of professional associations, including the conference "Culture and the Unconscious 2" at the University of East London, several incarnations of the European-American Conference on Literature and Psychoanalysis, the German-American Studies Association, the International Psychogeriatrics Association, the Modern Language Association, a series of conferences on postmodernism held in Germany, and the Society for Literature and Science. I extend my grateful thanks to the people who made this possible—among them, Corey Creekmur, Michael Davidson, Joan DeJean, Mary Ann Doane, Julie Ellison, John Frow, Heike Hartung, Jean Heffer, Veronica Hollinger, Gerhard Hoffmann, Alfred Hornung, Fedwa Malti-Douglas, Ellen McCallum, Peter Madsen, Ellen Pollack, Helen Powell, James Rosenheim, Judy Segal, Susan Squier, Barbara Temple-Thurston, Andrew Wernick, Inge Crosman Wimmers, James Winn, and Ewa Plonowska Ziarek.

I would like especially to single out the centers for the humanities, which have been the fertile incubators of so much cross-disciplinary and interdisciplinary work. I am thankful for their very existence and for their intellectual hospitality in encouraging such work, including my own on the emotions. My greatest debt is to the Center for Twentieth Century Studies (now the Center for Twenty-First Century Studies) at the University of Wisconsin, Milwaukee, which devoted a year of research to the emotions in 1989–1990, thereby offering me the prized opportunity to invite people from a wide variety of disciplines to participate in this area of study over the course of the year. This work culminated in an extraordinary conference titled "Discourses of the Emotions." Among the gifted people present were Mitchell Breitwieser, Virginia Carmichael, Rey Chow, Ed Cohen, Valie Export, Jane Gallop, Marjorie Garber, Liz Grosz, Gloria-Jean Masciarotte, Robin Pickering-Iazzi, Pat Mellencamp, Michael Moon, Meaghan Morris, Juliana Schiesari, Murray Schwartz, Eve Kosofsky Sedgwick, Madelon Sprengnether, Susan Stewart, Calvin Thomas, Lynn Worsham, and my partner in life, Herbert Blau. Is there such a feeling as intellectual nostalgia? I can testify that there is. Happily, in 2003–2004 the Simpson Center for the Humanities at the University of Washington supported a research cluster on the emotions, for which Lauren Berlant, Emily Martin, and Rukmini Bhaya Nair gave unforgettable presentations.

I want in addition to thank the Centre for the Study of Theory, Culture and Politics at Trent University, the Cogut Center for the Humanities at Brown University, the Doreen B. Townsend Center for the Humanities at the University of California at Berkeley, the Glasscock Center for Humanities Research at Texas A&M University, the Humanities Institute at the University of Buffalo, the Institute for the Humanities at the University of Michigan, and the Obermann Center for Advanced Study at the University of Iowa, as well as the Consortium of Humanities Centers and Institutes, to which, at its annual meeting in Brisbane in 1999, I was honored to present my work.

It is a warm pleasure to thank the many graduate students in my seminars on the emotions at the University of Washington and the University of Wisconsin in Milwaukee. In particular I have benefited enormously from conversations with Scott Barr, Jamie Carlaccio, Margareta Dancus, Maura Danforth, Jennifer Driscoll, JoAnn Kelly, Tom Kerr, Ralitsa Lazarova, Suzanne Leonard, Nancy Levy, Nancy Mayer, and Gretchen Papazian.

I thank Ellen Kaisse, the University of Washington's divisional dean in the Arts and Humanities, who generously arranged for me to devote the winter quarter of 2006 to this book. I am exceedingly grateful to Miriam Bartha, the assistant director of the Simpson Center, who with aplomb assumed my responsibilities during that period. To Kristy Leissle and Linda Wagner, research assistants at the Simpson Center, I cannot begin to express my appreciation for their creativity, conceptual astuteness, and can-do spirit as well as for their impeccable attention to detail, a quality I treasure.

I have been inspired by Feel Tank, founded by Lauren Berlant (among other scholars and activists), which is devoted to the study of feeling as it relates to political life. The Feel Tank conference, organized by Berlant and sponsored by the University of Chicago in October 2007, afforded me the opportunity to meet new colleagues in the study of the emotions, including Heather Love and Kathleen Stewart, as well as to acquire a T-shirt I have already worn to great effect. It is black (of course), with the single-word question "DEPRESSED?" inscribed across the front in red block letters. On the back we find the answer to this pertinent question: "IT MIGHT BE POLITICAL." I also treasure the tongue-in-cheek T-shirt given to me by Jane Gallop and Lynne Joyrich. The word "EMOTIONS" is inscribed on it, along with Paul Ekman–like emotion faces.

Much of the material in this book took shape in various journals and edited collections, and I am grateful to Justine Coupland, Marilyn Hacker, Gordon Hutner, Rob Mitchell, Liubava Moreva, John O'Neill, and Phillip Thurtle for their support of my work.

Perhaps my greatest debt is to the world of literature itself—to literature as an evocative object, in the psychoanalyst Christopher Bollas's sense, and to literature that makes us feel more alive, as Lisa Ruddick has put it. A few weeks ago I read Annie Dillard's luminous novel *The Maytrees,* a story of a man and a woman and how the love between them changes over the course of their long life both together and apart, together and apart. In inhabiting the world created by reading Dillard's words, reading in the dark on the plane from Washington, D.C. back to Seattle, I resolved to be a better wife, although I was under no illusion that under the pressure of everyday life this feeling or even the resolution would last. I dedicate my own book with love to Herbert Blau, who knows how to tease me, whose fierce devotion to blooded thought has been an inspiration, and who long ago promised me that he would never die.

THINKING FEELING, FEELING THINKING

It's rare nowadays to hear words which, belonging to no
one in particular, can be the property of anyone, words that
are solid and inexhaustible like "grief" or "hatred."
                    —J.-B. Pontalis, *Love of Beginnings*

Critical reflection on emotion is not a self-indulgent
substitute for political analysis and political action. It is itself a
kind of political theory and political practice, indispensable for
an adequate social theory and social transformation.
                    —Alison Jaggar, "Love and Knowledge"

Stories are much bigger than ideologies. In that is our hope.
                    —Donna Haraway, *The Companion Species Manifesto*

The Year of Magical Thinking. I picked up Joan Didion's book by chance one
night (I couldn't sleep, no surprise there) and didn't put it down until I was
finished. The next day I realized it offered me a perfect prism with which
to open this book. For Didion's narrative uncannily echoes many of my
own concerns in the pages to follow, not least of which is the signal
importance of understanding our emotional experience through literature. For those who haven't read the book, Didion writes about her devastating grief in the wake of the altogether unexpected death of her husband
of forty years. At first she turns to reading—a form of research for her, as it
is for me—to help her understand what she was feeling and why. There is
Freud's seminal essay "Mourning and Melancholia," poetry and fiction
and journals, self-help books and professional literature. But precious
little makes a difference to her. The professional literature in particular
seems peculiarly inapt—*unfeeling*. It is poetry with its distinctive vocabulary and rhythm that provides something illuminating to grasp and hold
close. Surprisingly perhaps, the advice she finds in the redoubtable Emily
Post's book of etiquette, published in 1922, also provides comfort through

its delineation of protocols. Why is she moved by *Etiquette in Society, in Business, in Politics, and at Home?* Because at that point in American culture, Didion realizes, death had not yet been rendered unspeakable. The perspective of history offers her understanding and thus consolation. An important truth.

As I read *The Year of Magical Thinking* I thought of my own experience years earlier. I too had lost my partner to an altogether unexpected death. It was as if my own life—half of my body—had been ripped from me. I too did what others would find demented but to me seemed quite sensible at the time. I asked his doctor if it were possible to extract sperm from his body (we hadn't had children together). I became obsessed with his identical twin brother (this did not prove to be a good idea). I went to see my first husband (we had divorced some seven years earlier and had intermittently kept in touch) in an effort to establish a sense of continuity in my life in the wake of the gaping wound that had appeared. I too turned to reading and research about grief, and it seemed to me too that virtually nothing clarified my extreme confusion.

But isn't loss a common experience? Why was there no department at my university devoted to the study of the emotions? Why did the department of philosophy focus only on the history of thought, on logic and rationality, on the forms of analytic and dispassionate reason? Why didn't it dedicate attention to the forms of feeling?[1] How could such an important dimension of life receive so little consideration from the academy?[2] I didn't understand then what now seems so self-evident that it doesn't even require elaboration: that reason and emotion have long been constructed as antimonies in western culture, with reason exalted as the preferred term, figured as masculine, and emotion denigrated as feminine.[3] I consider myself a reader by profession as well as by temperament, and I don't remember anything I read being especially enlightening or consoling. But then it's also true that I remember very little from that year. So I wasn't surprised to see that Didion, remarking on the large gaps in her memory, devotes much of her book to simply trying to *remember* what happened in the year after her husband died.

Thus the genesis of this book—a collection of essays on the emotions written over the course of several years—can be found in my desire to comprehend the turmoil I felt as well as my bewilderment at the reactions of some people (they were my friends) to my state of grief. "It's been three months now since his death," I heard someone say at a party. "Why isn't she over it?" To which I silently returned these questions: Why didn't they understand? And more to the point, why was my experience considered *inadmissible* in what seemed a social court of emotion law? Later I found myself studying the emotions—academically.

I read Freud's essay "Mourning and Melancholia" and found myself wishing from Freud something that wasn't in his temperament or professional passion to give—a description of the phenomenology of grief (indeed we don't even find the word "grief" in his essay). But his theoretical explanation of the process of mourning I found spellbinding. Freud insists we must call up all of our memories binding us to the person we have lost and "test" them in order to come to understand that the person is in fact no longer *there*. It is excruciating. Perhaps even more daunting, we must also detach ourselves from the memories of the prospects and plans—*all* of them—we had imagined for the future together. *Each memory* of the past *and* of the future. It is a painful process, this cutting off of our very selves from those to whom we have been intimately bound. It is anguishing work and it takes time. For as Freud so profoundly understood, we never willingly give up what means everything to us and has given our life its very shape and meaning.[4] Didion quotes the very passage from Freud that so fascinates me: "Every single one of the memories and expectations in which the libido is bound to the object is brought up and hypercathected, and detachment of the libido is accomplished in respect of it" (*SE* 14: 245).[5] She also tells us how she tried to short-circuit this process by avoiding places of memory—where they had lived, eaten, shopped, taken their daughter Quintana. "There were many such traps," she writes. Falling into what she calls the vortex means experiencing "a sudden rush of memories" (118). They are overwhelming.

I wrote about "Mourning and Melancholia" in my last book, where I reproached Freud for not offering us (*me*) a more expressive vocabulary for grief. I still wish he had, but I understand it now as a self-interested wish on my part. I can look elsewhere in the psychoanalytic literature—to Julia Kristeva, for example, who combines both expressive and analytical modes in her work, and to J.-B. Pontalis, whose work as he has grown older has become increasingly autobiographical and poetic.[6] For Freud is not interested in offering a poetics of the emotions but rather in theorizing our psychic processes. Furthermore his focus is on the investigation of pathologies, most famously of repressed desire.

In *Studies on Hysteria* Freud formulates a theory of affect that rests on the notion of repressed desire, resonating with the dominant tradition in western culture of the emotions as negative: the emotions are associated with women—hysterical women—and the emotions are something to be purged. Affect, unable to speak in its own language, is transcribed into another language, the bodily symptoms of hysteria that Freud describes later in *Five Lectures on Psychoanalysis* as "precipitates" of emotional experience (*SE* 11: 14). It is as if affect, located deep inside, is so strong that it has to push against the body, forcing itself out into the performative gestures of hysteria. Freud understands affect as "cut off" from the memory to which it is attached, as "strangulated" (*SE* 2: xviii). Affect is often "paralyzing" (*SE* 2: 11). It is something that needs to be discharged or, in that strange Freudian word, *abreacted* through the work of analysis. The goal of psychoanalysis in Freud's hands is not so much to give affect voice as to rid ourselves of it once it has been remembered. Freud's basic model of the functioning of the mental apparatus—not the *emotional* apparatus—is thus homeostatic, quietistic, and economic: the mental apparatus works to free itself from excitation and disturbance, both of which are associated with scenes of emotional trauma.

Given Freud's theory of the emotions, it might not come as a surprise that I also judged him to be acutely insensitive to the fact that it might be preeminently "reasonable" to hold onto one's grief.[7] If we still feel the pain of grief intensely, then perhaps the person we have lost will somehow return through the force of our refusal of the irreversibility of time. (This was my fervent wish.) Here is Didion on the ritual of disposing of her late husband's clothes:

> I was not yet prepared to address the suits and shirts and jackets but I thought I could handle what remained of the shoes, a start.
> I stopped at the door to the room.
> I could not give away the rest of his shoes.
> I stood there for a moment, then realized why: he would need shoes if he was to return.
> The recognition of this thought by no means eradicated the thought.
> I have still not tried to determine (say, by giving away the shoes) if the thought has lost its power. (36–37)

As she lives through the year following his death, Didion doesn't want to come to the end of her book, for the writing itself keeps her memories sharp and alive. If her magical thinking exposes the "shallowness of san-ity," at the same time her writing—she began *The Year of Magical Thinking* nine months into that year—gives her the perspective to understand her deranged experience (7). (I understand this. Remember, I wanted to follow the identical twin brother of the man I had lost.) Paul Monette remarks in *Borrowed Time: An AIDS Memoir*, to which I turn later in this book, that mourning is a form of self-compassion. In contrast Didion is hard, very hard on herself, insisting on judging herself severely for the self-pity that at times overtakes her.

It is a truth undeniable that what we once dismissed when younger we may understand—indeed value—when we are older. This is a good thing. Our place in the world in terms of age and experience powerfully shapes our views of everything, including the emotions, and hopefully growing older will give rise to both conviction and humility. In *The Year of Magical Thinking* Didion acknowledges exactly this: "I remember despising the book Dylan Thomas's widow Caitlin wrote after her husband's death, *Leftover Life to Kill*. I remember being dismissive of, even censorious about, her 'self-pity,' her 'whining,' her 'dwelling on it.' *Leftover Life to Kill* was published in 1957. I was twenty-two years old. Time is the school in which we learn" (198). She understands, now, the need to apologize for judging far too harshly the sentiments of the widow of Dylan Thomas. In the end Didion concludes that "if we are to live ourselves there comes a point at which we must relinquish the dead, let them go, keep them dead" (225–26). She is wiser than I was, it seems to me now. But she is also older than I was when my partner died. And if personally (of course) and theoretically (this may be more difficult to understand) I wanted to hold onto the pain of his loss, I also married within two years of his death. My husband—we have been married for twenty-eight years—*promised me* before we married that he will never die, and at some level I find myself reassured by this, magically so.

Although this is not a book about psychoanalysis and the emotions, Freud casts a large shadow over it because he provided me with my first sustained reading about what is called affect in psychoanalysis.[8] "Affect" names a crucial theoretical category in psychoanalytic theory and, more recently, in cultural studies.[9] I will generally not use the term in this book; I want instead to focus on specific emotions and to offer more texture to our emotional experience. (I will sometimes use the term "affective," as in "affective experience," because the analogous phrase "emotional experience" can carry the unfortunate connotation of being overwrought.) I engage Freud at length in my chapter on anger, and I return to grief, psychoanalytically, at the end. I draw on psychoanalytic theory at various points, and I adopt a view of the structuring of the emotions that could be said to be Freudian (I will comment on this in a moment). Freud has also provided me with an important path to approaching the emotions, and that is the study of autobiography. Famously he turned to self-analysis in *The Interpretation of Dreams*, a book that can be understood as autobiography, plumbing his own experience, narrating it, and reading his dreams as keys to repressed desires and anxieties. Didion does this too, in fact, although not in as monumental a register. In *The Year of Magical Thinking* she turns to her dreams as a form of knowledge, albeit with a decided difference. She had, she tells us, a long-standing habit of telling her dreams to her husband. But after he died, she stopped dreaming completely. I find it fascinating that in the absence of her own night-time dreams she remembers a dream she had given to a character—Elena—in one of her novels, *The Last Thing He Wanted*. In her moment of intense need Didion turns to her own consciously-crafted dream from a decade earlier, one that had come uncannily to speak to her own anxieties in the present:

> Elena's dreams were about dying.
> Elena's dreams were about getting old.
> Nobody here has not had (will not have) Elena's dreams.
> We all know that.
> The point is that Elena didn't.
> The point is that Elena remained remote most of all to herself, a clandestine agent. (159–60)

With a shock of recognition Didion understands that Elena's dream is her own, it belongs to her. Her husband's life had protected her against the threat of her own mortality, and with his death she grows old in her own eyes, stunned into fear of frailty and into frailty itself. "I realize," she writes, "that Elena's situation is my own" (160). (This is chilling.) If her dream was created deliberately, it has waited for her, stored in her own fiction, safeguarded in what we might call her *writing unconscious* until she was ready to hear its message. "Elena's dreams were about getting old. Nobody here has not had (will not have) Elena's dreams." Didion understands this now with the force of feeling. The death of her husband, combined with her own gaunt fragility, transforms her into an old woman who has at that point no palpable sense of a foreseeable future.

Thus particularly important to me is the elaboration and analysis of autobiographical experience understood in an expanded field. This is one of the ways we learn not only about the emotions but also about the world, for the two are of course intimately related. We consult our emotions—they may be literary emotions as in Joan Didion's case—as a way of disclosing our relation to the world around us. My primary textual touchstone in this book is a marvelous scene in Virginia Woolf's *A Room of One's Own* where the narrator attends to the emotional experience of her own spontaneous anger, which is—and this is where she and Freud definitively part company—transparently available to her. (This scene, which is in and of itself a short story, surfaces in three of the chapters to follow.) Woolf, moreover, honors her narrator's experience. She doesn't consider her anger "hysterical" or a screen for something else but rather values it and seeks to understand the reasons for it. Her anger has an epistemological edge, one that the philosopher Alison Jaggar calls attention to in her seminal essay "Love and Knowledge: Emotion and Knowledge in Feminist Epistemology."[10] Anger is both a "personal" and a "political" emotion, one that discloses the unequal relations of power in which Woolf's character is enmeshed. At stake is a cultural politics of the emotions.

My concern overall in this book is the cultural politics of the emotions in America since the 1950s, with an emphasis on texts from the late 1960s to the late 1990s. By cultural politics I mean to suggest two overlapping areas of inquiry that correspond to the two major parts of the book. Part 1, which contains four chapters, is titled "Cultural Politics, Communities of Feeling." I focus on the cultural politics of the emotions with gender, age, and race as my primary interests, and I place under analysis the psychological emotions of anger, shame, and compassion. Indeed anger, it turns out, is the emotion of choice in this book, although grief receives pride of place. But a cultural politics of the emotions is not limited to identity politics or the politics of difference. Part 2, composed of three chapters, is called "Structures of Feeling, 'New' Feelings." Here I place more pressure on feelings as sensitive and telling sensors that register emerging shifts in social and cultural formations. I turn to three "new" feelings (or categories of feeling) associated with changes in the culture of postmodernity—an increasing sympathy for nonhuman cyborgs; what I call bureaucratic rage; and the potent feeling I call statistical panic. Underwriting part 2, then, is technological and institutional change—the emergence of robo sapiens, the mammoth medical bureaucracies that characterize the consumer society in which we are all considered potential patients, and the social technology that is statistics. It is not a coincidence that in all three chapters in this section I consider narratives of illness, most of them autobiographical.

Also underwriting this book is the conviction that we live in a time of the rapid circulation of the emotions. Indeed a new economy of the psychological emotions has been emerging in terms of gender. Receiving its impulse in great part from the youthful energy of the 1960s, the possibilities of an individual's emotional repertoire are expanding even as a culture of intensities, or sensations, is increasing. If anger is the feminist emotion of choice from the 1960s onward (and if in recent years anger is being embraced by older women too), we are also witnessing the emergence of the man of sentiment, as I observe in my chapter "Liberal Compassion, Compassionate Conservatism." The display of the emotion of grief, long considered unmanly, has been embraced by many men. As I suggest in my chapter on nonhuman cyborgs, the notion of sympathy, long understood to have the potential to knit together the human body politic (in particular across sites of bodily suffering), is being extended in our cultural imagination to nonhuman beings made in our own image, thereby bridging a divide between the organic human world and the technological lifeworld. We live in a time of the vertiginous emergence of new sensations. The panic that many of us feel, for example, at the pronouncement of a certain statistic (it may feel ominously like a verdict—I will turn to this in a moment) was simply not a possibility before the invention of the science, practice, and omnipresent deployment of statistics themselves. As this so clearly reveals, emotions and feelings have histories. Thus if my overall focus is on the latter part of the twentieth century, three chapters in this volume offer larger temporal frames by counterpointing texts from the first part of the twentieth century with texts from the latter part of the twentieth century.

One of my major points is this: we all have experience of the emotions and shouldn't hesitate to draw on it—reflecting on it, turning it over in our minds, watching when a certain emotion subsides and is replaced by another, and placing it in perspective in the arc of our own personal lives and in the context of social constraints, commands, and controls as well as larger historical change. As Jaggar has written, "Time spent in analyzing emotions and uncovering their sources should be viewed . . . neither as irrelevant to theoretical investigation nor even as a prerequisite for it" (164). This is one of the reasons why quite a few of the texts discussed in this work are memoirs. Some are long and some are short, but all are telling reflections on emotional experience that makes a difference. For that is what a memoir is—a reflection on experience and a shaping of that experience into a narrative, a discovery of meaning and a creating of meaning that can rise to a poetics of expression and understanding through the plot of a story and the texture of words, yielding thought inextricably intertwined with feeling. In my chapter on the cultural politics of anger and aging, for example, I turn to *Look Me in the Eye* by the lesbian activist Barbara Macdonald. In the important tradition of *A Room of One's Own*, Macdonald interrogates the flaring rage she felt as an older woman at the unintended ageist gesture of a younger woman. This method—the reading of emotional experience—mirrors an assignment I gave in a recent graduate seminar on the cultural politics and poetics of the emotions. I asked the participants each to choose an emotion to research, with the further request that rather than bracketing their own affective experience of the emotion they should consult it. My point was not to solicit confessional material but to refuse the firewall that has been erected between what is erroneously understood to be only "personal" experience (for of course it is socially inflected and shaped) and "impersonal" or "objective" academic research on the emotions. It is correctly considered an academic virtue to interrogate our thinking. Self-reflexive thought is honored. Analogously we should do so as well with our feelings.

I have also attended to my own experience. But for the most part the traces are invisible except for here and there a few small stories cast predominantly in a lighthearted vein or observations offered in a more solemn register. This choice is no doubt a matter of temperament. While I am a serious person given to reading books in solitude (*anywhere*—at home, on the bus and airplanes, in airports, you name it) and have also had my own singular share of experience, in the company of others I tend to be high-spirited and sociable, expressing a comic view of life.

Still, here it seems important to explain that the chapter entitled "Statistical Panic" began to take shape as I puzzled over the fast-moving sequence of feelings I had while reading the draft of a chapter about Social Security in a book manuscript by one of our country's most distinguished and beloved gerontologists. In an alternately galvanizing, numbing, and reassuring enumeration of national statistics about the increasing proportion of the population in the United States that is sixty-five and older and the concomitant necessity to strengthen Social Security (with which I heartily agree), I suddenly found myself in a panic when I read a sentence describing how much money "one" would need in retirement. In today's financial terms the sentence would go something like this: "If one needs $80,000 per year from savings (not counting social security or a pension), has $100,000 in investments, saves $5,000 a year, and plans to retire in five years at the age of sixty-five, one would need $1,655,220 in *after-tax* dollars on the last day of work; this amount would have to earn eight percent, but about 3.5 percent would disappear with inflation . . ." WHAT? I remember instantly snapping alert. In a split second "one" turned into "I." I was singled out. I would need *what* in personal savings if I were to *retire* (what does that mean anyway?) and wanted to generate $80,000 a year in constant dollars? How, if I were sixty, could I possibly save $1,555,220 in *five* years? What possibly—impossibly—could that mean I would need fifteen years from now? I felt myself targeted as a reader, impaled on what seemed to me to be an astronomical figure, panicked at my financial future (and in the United States women live on the average five and a half years longer than men—that's the good news and the bad news).[11] What I would call my *economic* panic had infinitely more to do with an anxiety about the future than it did the avidity of greed. It signaled the financialization of everyday life that the cultural critic Randy Martin has so astutely identified. (How did I allay that anxiety? Among other things I formulated, mordantly, a "rational" response to these financial figures, calculating against my self-interest that I could save a lot of money by simply dying earlier!)

I conceived my notion of statistical panic as I reflected on this telling experience of financial panic in tandem with reading the historian Alice Wexler's book *Mapping Fate* and seeing the independent filmmaker Yvonne Rainer's film *MURDER and murder*, both of which deal with statistics about disease. Thus, methodologically, at certain starting points in this book I draw on what might be called a critical phenomenology of the emotions and feelings, attending to them and placing them in social and historical contexts, much as did Virginia Woolf in *A Room of One's Own*.

1

This book takes its title from the chapter "Statistical Panic," crucial to which is Raymond Williams's elastic notion of "structures of feeling," a conceptual lever that also informs the other chapters in part 2. I thus turn here to elaborating the ways in which I understand "structures of feeling" through the prism of that chapter. Notoriously difficult to define, Williams's notion of "structures of feeling"—indeed the very phrase itself—insists on the vital interpenetration of social structures and subjectivity, one mediated by forms of culture.[12] In the seven-page section devoted to "Structures of Feeling" in *Marxism and Literature*, Williams's concern is to find a way to feel the pulse of social change, to grasp what is emerging, to reveal it in its "generative immediacy," to preserve it, and above all, not to reduce it (133). For Williams, literature and art offer openings onto our always emerging world. They are themselves structures that embody forms of feeling—in tone and rhythm, color and diction, nuance and detail. At stake is a cultural poetics as well as a politics of the emotions. Literature and art serve as witness, as it were, to the ongoing process of social change. What is altogether important to Williams is to find a way to hold onto the intangible texture and force—the *presence*, which is for him a form of life itself. In using an analogy familiar from high school chemistry, Williams explains that "structures of feeling can be defined as social experiences in solution" as opposed to social experiences that have been struck into their "precipitants" or catalogued according to their separate components. In these forms of apprehension, feeling and thought are not divided from each other but are interrelated. What is at issue, Williams insists, is "specifically affective elements of consciousness and relationships: not feeling against thought, but thought as felt and feeling as thought: practical consciousness of a present kind, in a living and interrelating continuity" (132). "Methodologically, then, a 'structure of feeling' is a cultural hypothesis," he proposes, "actually derived from attempts to understand such elements and their connections in a generation or period" (132–33).

If some fifteen years ago it could be said that the concept of "structures of feeling" had not been taken up by others, this is assuredly not the case in recent years where it has enabled much work on the emotions in literary, cultural, and performance studies.[13] It is perhaps because of its very ambiguity that it has proven so suggestive, albeit in different ways. For some it provides a crucial theoretical lever for taking up the general project of the cultural politics of the emotions. For others it offers an understanding of experience as simultaneously cultural, discursive, and embodied, with feeling a site for insight into social control. For still others it articulates the connection between a particular genre or mode of performance and the politics of emotions in a certain historical moment or period.

There are three overlapping ways in which the notion of "structures of feeling" underwrites "Statistical Panic." The first is epistemological and returns us to Virginia Woolf's *A Room of One's Own* and Alison Jaggar's essay "Love and Knowledge." For in retrospect it's clear to me that I have read Williams's notion of "structures of feeling" through Woolf's dramatic scene in which the writer questions the anger she felt as the target of male anger—and vice versa. Woolf's important piece, cast in a mode that is both narrative and analytical, merges the two such that feeling is the ground of thought and thought is profoundly felt, thereby providing us with a sense of the lived experience of the emergence of feminism at that particular point in history and offering us the model that thinking originates in a subjectivity that is embodied. Indeed Woolf also refers in *A Room of One's Own* to what I have called "new" feelings in a way that would have pleased, I think, Raymond Williams. In articulating a sense of social history as expressed through comparative poetics, Woolf compares poetry that is altogether familiar and conveys "old" feelings (she is thinking of Tennyson and Christina Rossetti) with the modern poetry of her place and time: "The living poets express a feeling that is actually being made and torn out of us at the moment," she writes. "One does not recognize it in the first place; often for some reason one fears it; one watches it with keenness and compares it jealously and suspiciously with the old feeling that one knew" (14). Williams has been severely criticized for his "literary exceptionalism," for elevating literature to this position of privilege.[14] But it is certainly worth repeating that Williams's emphasis is on a certain form or way of knowing, one that brings together feeling and thought and does not separate them; there is thus an implicit epistemology of feeling at stake in his very idea of literature and art.

It's also evident to me that I have read Woolf's literary piece through

Jaggar's philosophical essay, further underscoring the epistemological edge of emotion that, in a dialectical relation to thought, can serve to disclose the structures of the world in which we are situated. As Jaggar writes, "Rather than repressing emotion in epistemology it is necessary to rethink the relation between knowledge and emotion and construct conceptual models that demonstrate the mutually constitutive rather than oppositional relation between reason and emotion" (157). Jaggar's excellent essay is complex and I can't address the many issues that it raises here. But central to it is her notion of "outlaw" emotions: "People who experience conventionally unacceptable, or what I call 'outlaw,' emotions often are subordinated individuals who pay a disproportionately high price for maintaining the status quo. The social situation of such people makes them unable to experience the conventionally prescribed emotions: for instance, people of color are more likely to experience anger than amusement when a racist joke is recounted, and women subjected to male sexual banter are less likely to be flattered than uncomfortable or even afraid" (160). Jaggar concludes that being in a subordinate position offers the possibility of epistemological privilege and that therefore we would do well to consult our feelings, reflecting critically on them, to reveal these imbalances of power. As she writes, "Only when we reflect on our initially puzzling irritability, revulsion, anger, or fear may we bring to consciousness our 'gut-level' awareness that we are in a situation of coercion, cruelty, injustice, or danger" (161). The extent to which this is possible—and when—I take up in my chapters on anger and shame in particular.

Jaggar is concerned with the politics of difference, as am I in several of the chapters of this book. But we can enlarge her analysis beyond the intersecting politics of difference. Indeed situations of coercion or danger may prove more intangible and difficult to identify when they are more diffuse or distributed seemingly innocuously in virtually every dimension of everyday life to the point of disappearance. Thus in my chapter on statistical panic I attend to the feelings of fear voiced in Rainer's film about breast cancer, including her own contraction of the disease and her mastectomy. I also attend to the feelings of confusion that Wexler reports in her book about Huntington's disease. Both Rainer and Wexler were haunted, if not stalked, by statistics of disease, and both women provide us with the palpable sense of the lived experience of statistical panic, as well as offer reflections upon it. They thus call our attention in striking ways to the dominating hold this experience can have on us. For statistical panic is not limited or confined to a particular class or age group, gender or race. It is an equal-opportunity experience.

The second way in which the notion of "structures of feeling" underwrites statistical panic is as an intimation of new and emerging social formations. As Williams provocatively suggests, "Methodologically, then, a 'structure of feeling' is a cultural hypothesis, actually derived from attempts to understand such elements and their connections in a generation or period" (132–33). Our generation or period? Statistical panic discloses the society of the statistic, one underwritten by the sense of omnipresent risk. In my chapter on statistical panic the focus is on risks to the body from disease, the ground of which is the medicalized, mediatized, and marketized world in which we live. But this is just one sign of what we might call the statistical hegemony in which we find ourselves in the twenty-first century, where statistical probabilities—about the effects of global warming, of avian flu, or the probability of hurricanes hitting our coasts—bombard our everyday life. Of course it goes without saying that since September 11, 2001, risk has taken on another altogether potent dimension by adding the politics of the everyday fear of terrorism to the volatile mix. Moreover the society of the statistic is but one "element," to use Williams's word, of postmodernity: a world increasingly characterized by a pervasive sense of precariousness—of insecurity, uncertainty, and what the critical sociologist Zygmunt Bauman has called "unsafety."[15]

Finally, I also understand "structure of feeling" in the sense suggested by an example Williams offers in *Politics and Letters: Interviews with New Left Review*, in which he describes the dominant middle-class structure of feeling in the British 1840s as "an anxious oscillation between sympathy for the oppressed and fear of their violence" (166). What interests me here is the idea of an emotional spectrum anchored by two related—and opposite—feelings about something. These feelings are themselves embedded in a structure; in this sense a "structure of feeling" does not have one emotion or feeling at stake, but fundamentally two that are interrelated. In the instance mentioned by Williams, fear and sympathy are involved. In "Statistical Panic" I suggest that the "structure of feeling" is characterized by statistical panic at one extreme and statistical boredom at the other (or alternatively, in another scenario, I could imagine statistical panic and statistical hope). Further, I contrast the shock and boredom linked with modernity at the turn of the twentieth century with the statistical panic and statistical boredom I associate with the postmodern consumer society at the turn of the twenty-first century. In so doing I historicize feelings of panic and boredom by relating them to the emergence of different kinds of technologies. Given my debt to Freud, it is not surprising that this view of the emotions is itself profoundly Freudian, with feelings understood as related in terms of opposites or in terms of their "logical" sequence.[16] Thus at certain points in this book my aim is to trace linked sequences of the emotions.

I understand statistical panic not as a psychological emotion (anger, jealousy, and grief are notable examples of psychological emotions), but rather as a sensation or intensity, one that is at base a charged anxiety. At the other pole of this structure of feeling is statistical boredom, a state characterized by *lack* of emotion—one *devoid* of sensation or intensity. Enter Fredric Jameson's essay "Postmodernism, or The Cultural Logic of Late Capitalism," which appeared in 1984 and is still resonant today. In this seminal essay he suggests that postmodern culture is characterized by "the waning of affect." By this Jameson means that the psychological depth that distinguished the culture of modernism (the deep anxiety of alienation is an example) has been succeeded in postmodern culture by an insistence on flatness and on surfaces, an insistence that is reinforced by the extreme penetration of commodification in our everyday lives. Jameson calls our attention to the postmodern aesthetic of surfaces and fragments found in the work of Andy Warhol and John Cage, Samuel Beckett and Robert Wilson, Nam June Paik and William Gibson, work I would argue is characterized by intensities on the one hand and boredom on the other, a structure of feeling endemic—if not epidemic—to postmodern culture. "As for expression and feelings or emotions, the liberation, in contemporary society, from the older *anomie* of the centered subject may also mean not merely a liberation from anxiety but a liberation from every other kind of feeling as well" (15), Jameson writes, with such psychological emotions being replaced by "intensities" (16).[17]

This passage has been often quoted and commented upon. But we should remember that in this essay Jameson doesn't engage at any length the question of the emotional styles or experience of actual people. In referring to postmodern culture as marked by the "waning of affect," Jameson doesn't mean of course that we no longer experience feelings of love and hate, jealousy and shame: emotions that bind us to others. His concern is to identify the culturally dominant aesthetic of postmodernism related to the emergence of global capitalism. Indeed he deplores what he refers to as "culture-and-personality diagnosis" of society and art (26). I do not think, however, it is a mere accident that Jameson's periodizing distinction between modernism and postmodernism in terms of the emotions, with his emphasis on *affectlessness* in contemporary culture, resonates with work that appeared in the late 1980s and mid-1990s in such disparate fields as history, psychoanalysis, and neurology, work to which I now briefly turn.

In *American Cool: Constructing a Twentieth-Century Emotional Style*, the historian Peter Stearns argues that between 1920 and 1950 a cultural preference for "coolness" emerged in the United States. The strength of the emotions so prized in American Victorian culture became suspect in and of itself, and psychological emotions (Stearns devotes attention in particular to grief, jealousy, and anger) came to be perceived—and experienced—not only as "bad" but at the extreme as pathogenic. Over the three decades he examines Stearns shows that a progressive diminution— or cooling—of the emotions took place and that ultimately this kind of psychological emotional intensity itself came to be seen as "a barrier rather than a bond" in the maintenance of relationships between people (199); "It was often the emotional individual," he concludes, "not the object of his or her emotion, who was seen as requiring remediation" (230). While Stearns attributes this development to multiple forces, he insists that our expanding consumer culture required the suppression of the emotions and the cultivation of impersonality, and he rues the loss of what he calls the intensity of the psychological emotions associated with Victorian culture, a kind of intensity so unlike the "intensities" Jameson identifies as key to postmodern culture.

If Stearns regrets our culture's devaluation of strong feelings that connect us both to others and to ideals, then Christopher Bollas in his book *The Shadow of the Object: Psychoanalysis of the Unthought Known* has given this cultural phenomenon a name—"normotic illness." As a psychoanalyst he is primarily concerned with the childhood roots of normotic illness. But Bollas also connects the emergence of this disorder to the demands of today's commodity culture. He describes a person who suffers from normotic illness as betraying a *lack of subjectivity*—in particular, a lack of self-regarding feelings. A normotic person is one who is "abnormally normal"

(136), who "lives contentedly among material objects and phenomena" but doesn't experience subjective states within the self (137). A normotic is a person whose life is organized in terms of activity and routines, who seems consistently stable and outgoing, who is surrounded by material objects sought not for symbolic purposes—they hold no subjective or symbolic meaning—but for purely functional reasons. There is a sense in which normotic illness can be described in terms of interior emptiness. But as understood by Bollas, the anguish and stupor associated with depression as theorized by Julia Kristeva in *Black Sun* and described by Andrew Solomon in *Noonday Demon* are not at all at stake. Indeed in a very real sense, *there is no interior.* In normotic illness we see the incarnation of the emotional style required by society that Stearns has called "American cool." It is not just that a person psychologically invests more in material objects than in relationships with other people. Rather, it is that *the self is conceived of as an object,* a material object, or, as Bollas puts it, as "an object with no subject" (156).

What would be the extreme manifestation of this emotionless individual? The neurologist Antonio Damasio offers an answer. In *Descartes' Error: Emotion, Reason, and the Human Brain,* Damasio recounts the case history of his patient Elliot, a former businessman who undergoes surgery to remove a frontal lobe brain tumor. He emerges retaining his mental abilities and memory, but he displays no emotions whatsoever and is no longer able to make any decisions regarding anything, himself included.[18] I imagine Elliot as a computer complete with every conceivable variable but with no program for reaching a conclusion, calculating endlessly in terms of contemporary culture's hyper values of costs and benefits, taking into account every possible factor but remaining paralyzed until he does what someone else tells him to do or blurts into action. His "process" of making a decision is a tragic parody of economic rationality, one that does not involve his own interests at all. As Damasio writes, "The cold-bloodedness of Elliot's reasoning prevented him from assigning different values to different options, and made his decision-making landscape hopelessly flat," as flat as his emotions (51). A person like Elliot will report that he feels fine and yet experiences no emotional life whatsoever. His ability to identify even with his own suffering has been destroyed. We could put it this way: he is no longer capable of telling his own story or, in psychoanalytic terms, of speaking his own desire, for it no longer exists. Unlike Virginia Woolf's writer in *A Room of One's Own,* his disastrous standpoint on his own life is that of "a dispassionate, uninvolved specta-tor" (44). Elliot thus serves Damasio as a parable of the potential tragic consequences of our culture's devaluation of the emotions, in particular of our lack of understanding of the interaction of emotion and reason as grounded in the body.

Thus if at the turn of the twentieth century Freud theorized the emo-tions as negative, as something to be gotten rid of, we might say that at the end of the twentieth century attention has turned to the *lack* of what I have been calling the psychological emotions as something seriously to regret. What we call mental or emotional illness has a cultural history, with dif-ferent kinds of illnesses dominant in certain periods. We identify the hysteric with the Victorian repression of sexuality and with turn-of-the century Freudian psychoanalysis. We associate what is called the border-line personality with a person in whom a lack of feeling and a feeling of nothingness predominates; dissociation is one of the symptoms.[19] The midcentury appearance of the category of the borderline patient, Stearns argues in *American Cool*, is connected to the growing emphasis in the United States on the negative value of the strong emotions and the corre-sponding injunction to control them—to ventilate them, as he puts it. (Lest we think this is an exaggeration and no longer characteristic of our moment we need only consider the medicalization of the emotions in the pamphlet *Post-Traumatic Stress Disorder: A Real Illness* issued in 2005 by the National Institutes of Mental Health; here we learn that everyday anger and fear can be read as symptoms of the omnipresent disorder of PTSD, one virtually *everyone* seems to be suffering from, and that these emotions need to be excised.)[20] As Nancy K. Miller and Jason Tougaw insist in *Extremities: Trauma, Testimony, and Community*, "If every age has its symptoms, ours appears to be the age of trauma" (1). In a lighter vein, consider a cartoon that appeared in 2007 in the *New Yorker*: a man lying on the therapeutic couch says to the analyst behind him, "Could we up the dosage? I still have feelings."[21]

What disease could be said to characterize the first decade of the twenty-first century? It is, I would suggest, the phenomenon of autism that has taken our cultural imagination by storm. An illness commonly under-stood as characterized by the tragic inability to read the emotions of others and to establish affective bonds, autism is a disorder that confines people to a world of intensities, uncannily resonating with our media-crazed cul-ture of sensation.[22]

In *New Maladies of the Soul*, Julia Kristeva insists that "the end of the possibility of *telling a story*" is characteristic of contemporary culture, dominated as it is by a market-and-image economy (43). I too am concerned about the psychic impoverishment that our media-saturated culture underwrites by promoting high-speed intense sensation at the expense of the psychological dimension of our lives. Thus in this book a cultural poetics of the emotions is also at stake for me. This is one of the reasons I have adopted a more literary and less argumentative mode at the outset of this introductory chapter. This is why I have been threading passages from Didion's *The Year of Magical Thinking* throughout these opening pages, understanding that my own thought and feeling is an irresistible collaboration between other lives and other texts.[23] This explains my admiration in the pages that follow for the expressive and reflective force of literary work in different modes, including (to give just three examples) Toni Morrison's evocative prose in her short novel *The Bluest Eye*, Michael Cunningham's science fiction novella *Like Beauty* in his eloquent book *Specimen Days*, and the moving autobiographical prose poem entitled "At the End of the Line" by the French psychoanalyst J.-B. Pontalis.

A potent antidote to the hectoring intensity of statistical panic is the *story*, a narrative that both expresses that feeling and reflects upon it or, to refer once again to Raymond Williams, a narrative in which a "practical consciousness" is involved, "not feeling against thought, but thought as felt and feeling as thought" (132). I am a person who loves literature, and so it may not come as a surprise that here I understand one genre as providing commentary on another genre. One kind of narrative—here an autobiographical one—serves as a self-reflexive commentary on another kind of narrative, what in the chapter on bureaucratic rage I call the "information-story"—that is, a narrative that has been reduced to an unfeeling fragment. Thus countering a fragment, or providing nuanced context for an information-story, is a more ample narrative—a story.[24] I also agree with Donna Haraway, in her comments in *The Companion Species Manifesto*, that "stories are much bigger than ideologies. In that is our hope" (17).

As Michelle Rosaldo, one of the founding figures of the anthropology of the emotions, wrote in a landmark essay, "Affects, whatever their similarities, are no more similar than the societies in which we live"; "the life of feeling is an aspect of the social world" (145). Her research was on the Ilongot people of the Philippines, specifically how they experienced and practiced anger (many would find it a surprising challenge to the western notion that we should not "repress" our anger lest it escape in explosion). Rosaldo's concern was to underscore the ways in which cultures shape our emotional lives. "Feelings are not substances to be discovered in our blood," she insisted, "but social practices organized by stories we both enact and tell" (143).[25] Although she was referring to large cultural narratives about the emotions, I want to take her at her literal word and place the emphasis on the word "stories." For as many people have pointed out, we learn emotions through the medium of stories. The kinds of stories I am privileging here—many of them are book length, others are stories so short they might be called anecdotes—embody for me feeling as thought and thought as feeling.[26] In part 1 many of these stories rewrite dominant cultural scenarios of the emotions; in part 2 many draw attention to what I am calling "new" feelings—sympathy for nonhuman cyborgs, bureaucratic rage, and statistical panic.

As I write this I realize how much I have missed the very telling of stories in cultural studies and literary criticism. I miss the life that a story brings to discussion and analysis. I miss the intertwining of the two. What might be termed professional affect has a dominant style at any given point in time.[27] Notwithstanding the practice of what came to be called personal criticism in feminist literary studies during the 1980s and 1990s, the prevailing tone in cultural and literary studies is what I would call *professional cool*. The expository argument has assumed center stage, and I have come to feel an emptiness and insufficiency and colorlessness in the reduction of our work to argument. I suspect in fact that one of the reasons so much research on the emotions has appeared in the academy over the past twenty years is that it has served as compensation for the anesthetization of the emotions in academic life, a profession saturated with stringent rules of emotionless rationality in relation to research itself and to writing. Thus it is that I am interested in the literary emotions.[28]

In lieu of strict definitions I offer these thoughts about my "emotional" vocabulary. Research by anthropologists, historians, and literary critics over the past twenty years has shown us that the emotions have fascinating histories and that emotional experience varies in remarkable ways across cultures.[29] I have been referring to what I call the psychological emotions as binding emotions—those that connect us to other people (either positively or negatively), with anger, shame, and compassion (or sympathy) as the prime instances that I take up in the chapters to follow. Thus for me these psychological emotions are social emotions. They may attach us to members of the nonhuman world as well, as I suggest in "Sympathy for Nonhuman Cyborgs."

I am, of course, well aware that histories have been written of the emergence of the very category of the "psychological" emotions. Indeed in *Marxism and Literature* Williams himself calls attention to the "psychological" as one the "great modern ideological systems" in the West (129).[30] One of many points of departure is Freud's own conceptualization of affect as profoundly private and often so deeply hidden in our interior spaces that it is unknown even to ourselves. In response feminists, among others, have shown how the emotions, shaped by cultural norms and practices, can be collective as well as personal, thus underscoring the mutually constitutive nature of subjectivity and sociality. An important case in point is the sociologist Arlie Hochschild's pioneering work in *The Managed Heart: Commercialization of Human Feeling,* her classic study of the commodification of the emotions that, in a service economy populated predominantly by women, are themselves for sale and performed as part of the job, thereby creating the possibility of alienation from one's "own" feelings. Focusing on flight attendants (most of them women), Hochschild coined the important term "emotional labor," arguing that feelings "are not stored 'inside us,' and they are not independent of acts of management" (17).[31] (What does it tell about me that for years now I have been consistently mistaken in airports and on airplanes for a flight attendant?)

Similarly, poststructuralist theorists have insisted on the decisive role that language plays in shaping our world, a role in which we are spoken by language and not the other way around. Literary and rhetorical critics of earlier historical periods as well as historians have discovered other forms of feeling at work. Adela Pinch in her book *Strange Fits of Passion: Epistemologies of Emotion, Hume to Austen,* for example, asks of her period and place, where do feelings come from? What she finds is that in England in the late eighteenth century and early nineteenth, feelings were often understood as extravagantly wayward—transpersonal and seemingly autonomous in and of themselves, coming from other people and, wonderfully, from books. This is a strong view of the emotions at odds with that of the psychological view of the emotions as originating in a deep interior.[32] In *How Novels Think: The Limits of Individualism from 1719–1900*, Nancy Armstrong basically picks up where Pinch leaves off, arguing that the very form of the British novel provides the ground for the emergence of the self-possessed individual, one whose interiority offers a way of exceeding the constraints that characterized their social position.[33] Armstrong provocatively suggests that the strategies adopted by the novel at various points in time—ambivalence, repetition, and displacement, among them —were transformed by Freud into the theoretical figures by which unconscious desire expresses itself. The rhetorician Susan Miller, drawing on the long tradition of commonplace books, traces across nineteenth-century America the emergence of the discourse of the privatized and interiorized emotions—what we can call the aesthetic of psychological realism.[34] Accounts of our experience are never transparent. They are always shaped by cultural values and codes. I understand the contingency and critique of the psychological self. But I do not therefore wish to give up the psychological emotions.

That we must choose one view over the other—either the emotions arise within us or they come from outside of us—has characterized recent research, with an emphasis on the latter view. In *The Cultural Politics of Emotion*, for example, Sara Ahmed rejects the Freudian model. "Rather than emotions being understood as coming from within and moving outwards, emotions are assumed to *come from without and move inward*," she explains. "An 'outside in' model is also evident in approaches to 'crowd psychology,' where it is assumed that the crowd *has* feelings, and that the individual gets drawn into the crowd by feeling the crowd's feelings as its own" (9).[35] Emile Durkheim's book *The Rules of Sociological Method*, published in 1895, is for Ahmed a key paradigm of the generation of affect from within a crowd and not the individual; contagion is the metaphor at work. The late Teresa Brennan also challenges the Freudian notion of the bounded individual as the source of the affects and drives. "My theory," she writes, "is an alternative to psychoanalytic theory or metapsychology in that it postulates an origin for affects that is independent of the individual experiencing them. These affects come from the other, but we deny them" (13).[36] Like Ahmed, she too draws on theories of the crowd, although her reference points are the French social psychologist Gustave Le Bon, whose book on the psychology of the crowd also appeared in 1895, and the British psychoanalyst Winfred Bion whose work on groups appeared at midcentury.

It can be no coincidence that both Freudian depth psychology and the psychology of crowds took shape at the turn of the twentieth century.[37] These two paradigms of the emotions that emerged in modernity—the psychological and the sociological—are two sides of the same coin. Accepting the category of the psychological emotions is not incompatible with the view that emotions can also originate outside the self. As we see in the case of feminist anger, emotions that have their origins in social experiences *become* psychological emotions. Such social emotions can be strategic, as I have already mentioned. In referring to Durkheim, among other thinkers, Mette Hjort in *The Strategy of Letters* also takes up the question of the strategic value of the emotions. "The main point is that social emotions," she concludes, "tend to produce a very particular form of interdependence, namely *reciprocal interdependence*" (185–86). Notwithstanding her debt to Durkheim, Hjort associates the social emotions with the strategic generation of positive feeling and with what she calls "positive freedom" (186).[38] Thus in the chapters that follow I admit no necessary contradiction between the psychological emotions that have their origin in the self (grief would be such an example) and the social emotions that have their origin in a group (feminist anger would be an example).[39]

At the same time I understand, in the spirit of Brennan's *The Transmission of Affect*, that unwanted emotions can circulate far and wide. It can be a heavy burden to carry other people's psychological emotions for them, as Brennan explains, in stressing the cultural division of emotional labor according to gender (women, for example, as unfortunate repositories of men's anger, a dynamic in Woolf's *A Room of One's Own*). But it is my temperament to accentuate the positive, not the negative, and I admit to being partial to the psychological emotions. It need hardly be said that they lend depth and tone and nuance to our lives. They are expressions of what is meaningful to us. Indeed it may very well be that today's suspicion in cultural studies of the very notion of the psychological emotions—the view that the belief in a meaningful interior life is a telltale symptom of the neoliberal conception of the autonomous individual whose emotions are a fetishized form of private property—is itself a *symptom* of the expanding global capitalism of media culture. I'm reminded of the heart-rending words of one of the psychoanalyst Marion Milner's patients who longed for the experience of interiority. Diagnosed with schizophrenia, she was twenty-two years old when she experienced *for the first time* the feeling of being in the world and in her body. For the first time she felt—this is how she expressed it—that her emotions were "inside her," endowing her with a sense of vibrancy and coherence between the inside world and the outside world (this feeling tragically disappeared in the wake of shock therapy, which left her empty, with no inner world or inner perceptions).[40] To repeat my epigraph from Pontalis, "It's rare nowadays to hear words which, belonging to no one in particular, can be the property of anyone, words that are solid and inexhaustible like 'grief' or 'hatred' " (103). What a shame that today a psychoanalyst, of all people, finds these words in short supply. Grief. Anger. Compassion. We need to hear these words and claim them as our own. As Didion writes, "Grief turns out to be a place none of us know until we reach it" (188). She is right.

My project thus departs from—but at certain points also joins—that of Brian Massumi who in *Parables for the Virtual: Movement, Affect, Sensation* theorizes a philosophy of "affect," where affect is similar to what Jameson calls intensities, not a signifying practice. Massumi is following Deleuze (who was following Spinoza). "There seems to be a growing feeling within media, literary, and art theory that affect is central to an understanding of our information- and image-based late capitalist culture," Massumi writes, but "emotion and affect—if affect is intensity—follow different logics and pertain to different orders" (27). As he explains: "An emotion is a subjective content, the sociolinguistic fixing of the quality of an experience which is from that point onward defined as personal. Emotion is qualified intensity, the conventional, consensual point of insertion of intensity into semantically and semiotically formed progressions, into narrativizable action-reaction circuits, into function and meaning. It is intensity owned and recognized" (28). I agree that affect is key to understanding our information and image culture. I agree that intensities and psychological emotions follow different logics. Indeed that is an assumption in this book. But I do not dismiss the psychological emotions as, in Massumi's words, "owned emotions" that are "old surprises to which we have become more or less accustomed" (220–21). In my chapters on bureaucratic rage and statistical panic (both of which name what I would call affects or intensities), my point is that reflecting feelingly on our experience helps us *recognize*—I borrow Massumi's word here—the assault to which we are being submitted.[41] We live in a mixed economy of feelings, one characterized by both the psychological emotions and intensities, and my point is that they often stand in *dialectical relationship* to each other, with the narration of our experience a crucial capacity. *Emotion* can be *intensity* recognized, redescribed, and owned, understood as if for the first time.

We have witnessed a waning of the psychological emotions and are subjected to an increase in sensations, or intensities, in postmodernity, characterized as it is by a rampant consumer culture of manufactured and simulated excitement (one that is also boring), ever-expanding channels of mass-mediated information, exploding networks of digital communication, and new and multiple forms of visual entertainment. In fact it could certainly be said that the affect of the crowd at the turn of the twentieth century has been succeeded by the affect of media culture at the turn of the twenty-first century. The media could be said to abet affective epidemics, where anger is one of the emotions of choice.[42] The film critic David Denby, writing in the *New Yorker* about Quentin Tarantino's *Kill Bill Vol. 2*, describes the film's "anger" as a "mock" emotion (he uses scare quotes around anger to make sure it is understood as a flat version of in-depth, intense emotion). Television, radio, and the Internet present us with what my colleague Nikhil Singh, referring to the likes of Ann Coulter, Bill O'Reilly, Nancy Grace, and Howard Stern, has called "talk show affect," where, in pelletlike quotas of angry affect, anger is distributed scattershot as intensities.

Grief too can be stunted by the media, with the critical dimension of duration foreshortened to virtually zero. In the wake of the deadly attack by a student at Virginia Polytechnic Institute in April 2007 in which thirty-two people were killed by gunshot, media anchors and news reporters began talking about beginning the healing process even *before* the number of the dead had been determined. I call this TV grief. In the crosshairs of the media the depth of shame can be turned inside out, twisted into a hollow and preening exhibitionism presenting us with reality-TV feelings. Conversely, the paparazzi voyeurism of multiple screens may target ordinary individuals with mock feelings igniting murderous rage, an example of which I take up in my chapter on shame. At the same time we are urged to get over our feelings.

Video games hardwire us to seek ever-increasing violent thrills, and commercials—compressed to seconds—are downloaded on our cell phones. In postmodern culture the large-scale narrative has been compressed to an image fragment.[43] Sound bites and image fragments are *affect bites*. I take up these issues in my chapter on statistical panic where I identify intensities as short-lived feelings that attach us not to *people* but rather suture us to the task—it is a form of work—of avoiding risk in our society of ever-increasing risk.[44] Here the affect bite that is statistical panic is countered by the psychological emotion of anger—or better, outrage—an anger that is analytical. It has a cognitive edge.

Didion too articulates this phenomenon in *The Year of Magical Thinking*. In the aftermath of her husband's death she finds herself worrying, worrying about medication statistics:

> I fretted for example over a Bayer commercial for a low-dose aspirin that was said to "significantly reduce" the risk of heart attack. I knew perfectly well how aspirin reduces the risk of heart attack: it keeps the blood from clotting. I also knew that John was taking Coumadin, a far more powerful anticoagulant. Yet I was seized nonetheless by the possible folly of having overlooked low-dose aspirin. I fretted similarly over a study done by uc-San Diego and Tufts showing a 4.65 percent increase in cardiac death over the fourteen-day period of Christmas and New Year's. I fretted over a study from Vanderbilt demonstrating that erythromycin quintupled the risk of cardiac arrest if taken in conjunction with common heart medications. I fretted over a study on statins, and the 30 to 40 percent jump in the risk of heart attack for patients who stopped taking them.
>
> As I recall this I realize how open we are to the persistent message that we can avert death. (205–6)

In order to avoid death, the unmistakable message is that we must reduce our risk by consuming these products. If we don't, the result is what I call statistical guilt, and it is one that Didion counters—she has come to understand how it works—by embedding it in her larger story.

Finally, throughout this book at times I also use the word "feelings," as we do in everyday life, to refer either to the psychological emotions or to intensities (such as the sensations—and lack thereof—that can be said to characterize modernity and postmodernity). The matter of mood I take up in my last chapter, where I focus on the poetic power of a literary mood. As Lawrence Grossberg has explained, if desire is focused on an object and is goal-oriented, then mood arises out of a situation and gives to it a distinctive tone or atmosphere. A mood is an affective space, a state of body and mind, one in which thought and feeling can be indistinguishable from each other.[45] Christopher Bollas theorizes the generative power of moods as a psychic process akin to dreaming. In my discussion of the piece by Pontalis with which I close this book, it is the process of writing that is akin to dreaming. It is writing that creates for us an evocative object in and of itself, one that speaks of an elegiac hope and in its small and treasured way may help to reshape our culture's politics of the emotions through a poetics of the emotions.[46]

Thus to the Coda I give the subtitle "Inexhaustible Grief" in homage to the sentiments of Pontalis. If my first chapter focuses on Freud and takes an analytic approach to his own analysis of anger over an almost forty-year period, my last words embrace this poetic piece of prose by Pontalis that offers us what Freud could not in "Mourning and Melancholia"—the feeling of the grief to come and the moving impulse to repair broken bonds in a fragile world.[47] This book concludes on the note of feeling, albeit one marked by analysis, reflecting my honoring of analysis that is literary but also my growing sense of its increasing lack of connection to our lives— my conviction that much of it, like the professional literature that Didion read in her search for understanding her grief, is *unfeeling.*

CULTURAL POLITICS, COMMUNITIES OF FEELING

In *An Archive of Feelings: Trauma, Sexuality, and Lesbian Public Cultures*, Ann Cvetkovich probes the issue of "how affective experience can provide the basis for new cultures"—namely, cultures that are determinedly public cultures (7). Her book itself serves as an archive of feelings (her wonderful phrase), and it is one I imagine will itself generate new communities, or publics. With the memoir in various modes (including interviews) as her preferred genre, Cvetkovich examines the legacies not of catastrophic trauma but of trauma of everyday life. I am especially interested in her articulation of the relationship between the intimacy of feeling engendered in the process of caring for others (for people with AIDS in particular) and the complex emotional politics of activism—or lack of it—that emerges from this work. Understanding the burden that despair and conflict can bring, Cvetkovich also recognizes "the feelings of hope and survival that activism promotes in the face of trauma," and thus her book itself provides an intellectual plot of the emotions by moving from despair to hope (231). Douglas Crimp explores a related question in his brilliant essay from the late 1980s "Mourning and Militancy." He insists, against Freud, that mourning and activism, the private psychic act of bereavement and the collective rituals of mourning in public, are not antithetical but crucially interrelated—indeed critically so, given the virulent fear in the 1980s that AIDS was a distinctly gay disease. It was imperative that mourning be undertaken collectively and in public, and that the many emotions associated with it—outrage, anger, fear, guilt, and shame, among others—be voiced. Finally, moving back in historical time, Glenn Hendler, in his far-reaching book *Public Sentiments: Structures of Feeling in Nineteenth-Century American Literature*, astutely historicizes the practice of reading, showing that the reading of sentimental literature in the nineteenth century was understood to promise more than a merely private experience limited to an individual. Drawing on Habermas, Hendler argues for the mutual constitution of affective psychological categories (such as sympathy and sentiment) and social and political categories (such as the public sphere and the citizen), with the emergence of a black public sphere in America serving as a prime example. Cvetkovich, Crimp, and Hendler, then, all identify publics that have formed in great part around affective experiences. At stake for them is a cultural politics of the emotions.

In the four chapters that constitute the first part of this book I explore the cultural politics at work in the way the emotions are conceptualized and experienced, contained and deployed. I am interested in the connection between affective experience and the understanding of relationships of power. I ask when and how certain kinds of emotional experience can lead to such knowledge and to the creation of new communities, which I understand may be imagined communities only, yet powerful nonetheless. I also look at the ways in which rhetorics of the emotions are used strategically to shape and proscribe ways of being in the world. I consider how second-wave feminism was constellated in great part around the emotion of anger, and I show how across twentieth-century America anger on the part of the elderly was outlawed, thereby contributing, I argue, to their marginalization. With my focus on race, among other things, I also examine the traumatic modalities of shame and the use of narratives of compassion .in both its liberal and conservative guises.

"Containing Anger, Advocating Anger: Freud and Feminism," my first chapter, is devoted to a study of anger from the conflicting and gendered perspectives of Freud and academic feminism, with work drawn from literary studies and philosophy in the late 1970s and in the 1980s. Freud's world is that of depth psychology, and he understands anger as a predominantly interiorized affect. In contrast, the very word "anger" in the feminist work I discuss serves as a site for those who hold similar views (and within feminism, dissimilar views). Understood as a collective emotion, anger is also understood as an interior emotion, one that can in fact be *created retrospectively*. In this chapter I am interested also in the sequencing of the emotions. I trace the evolution of Freud's thinking about anger over the course of his career, with anger ultimately linked to guilt, which he theorizes functions in psychological stealth to exert a preemptive strike against anger. Freud doesn't historicize the emotions. But we can read a narrative of the emotions over the arc of his life, one that is virtually ontological in nature. As Freud grows older he finds ways to contain anger. By contrast, for feminists the challenge is to move from a state of confusion and inchoate anger to an articulate anger. The challenge is also to evaluate the expiration date on anger in given historical situations.

Thus the deployment of the rhetoric of anger can be a conscious political strategy, one I myself advocate in the next chapter. Entitled "Against Wisdom: Aging and Anger," it focuses on older women. Age is one of the most important psychic dimensions of our lives as well as one of the most significant social categories in our culture, and yet age has received scant attention from scholars in cultural and literary studies. Here I look at the way wisdom is conceptualized as antithetical to anger, with the central part of the chapter devoted to two books on aging—one by the psychologist G. Stanley Hall and the other by the feminist activist Betty Friedan. I argue that the attribution of wisdom to older people is a subtle screen for denying to them a meaningful social role. I also argue that the denial of a rich emotional palette to older people—anger in particular—is an index of the ageism of our culture and a loss to all of us. In this chapter, which is a manifesto on behalf of aging and anger, I question the extent to which there can be a politics based on the category of older age (especially since it is a commonly held view that older people are "hyperindividualized"), a politics animated by protest and consolidated around the discursive site of anger. I also look at the relationship between anger (and rage) and depression.

In the third chapter I explore shame through multiple models, among them racial shame (both traumatic and chronic), mass-mediated shame, and mutual shame. Here as well I take up the question of the relation of age to the emotions, with the sequencing of the emotions as a key concern. Can shame provide the epistemological advantage that Alison Jaggar theorizes for the emotions of the oppressed, and if so under what conditions? What is the relation of shame to knowledge? When can shame be converted into anger? When does it turn into rage? When does it devolve into depression? When can it be transformed into pride? What is the relation of shame to states of confusion? By looking at different models of shame (drawing on the work of Jean-Paul Sartre, Virginia Woolf, and Eve Kosofsky Sedgwick, as well as Sandra Bartky), we see that generalizations are meaningless—that is, in some cases communities of feeling may be possible (if only for a given historical moment) and in others utterly impossible. In this chapter I consider the politics and poetics of racial shame as read through Toni Morrison's *The Bluest Eye*. Here shame is presented as a psychological emotion, one that also circulates as a social emotion within communities and is transmitted intergenerationally. But I look, in addition, at the circulation of shame in the mass media, drawing on three accounts from the mid-1990s. Here the shame of celebrities is paraded self-importantly and converted as if instantaneously by the media into a vacuous and preening pride. Here shame and pride are not so much psychological emotions as intensities. Here ordinary people are submitted to brutal shaming in—and by—the media, a shock tactic used to sell TV programs that is itself shameful. It is all only infinitely more so today.

In the final chapter in part 1, I consider compassion through a double lens: the liberal narrative of compassion, which has a long tradition in American literary studies (*Uncle Tom's Cabin* is the touchstone historical text) and focuses on the suffering body (in particular the African American body), and the compassionate conservatism advocated by the George W. Bush administration, which focused on the economic body, with the individual understood as driven by economic emotions. I take up the books *Compassionate Conservatism* and *The Compassionate Conservative*, both published in 2000. I also take up the work of academics from the late 1980s to the late 1990s, who simultaneously champion and critique the possibilities for emotional understanding—and action—across difference offered by narratives (sentimental and otherwise) that call forth compassion in the face of suffering. The strongest indictment is reserved for the aesthetic of the sentimental, which, it is argued, privatizes the reader as a consumer of suffering and thus offers no possibility of the creation of a community. But while I understand the cautionary note sounded by critique, I consider the intention of illuminating suffering and injustice through narrative to be a noble one. For we should not cede the uses of compassion to the ideologues on the Right. The circulation of the rhetoric of compassion was a carefully crafted strategy in presidential politics in the United States in 2000 and 2004. Here the politics of the emotions and the politics of the nation coincided, with compassion deployed in the George W. Bush presidential campaigns and administrations as a national emotion. It has, however, lost its meaning and circulates as an word empty of emotion. If the liberal narrative of compassion identifies social suffering at the hands of racism and other prejudices, compassionate conservatism is an ideology, not a feeling—one that attempts to create the illusion of community when it is in reality an appeal to the "base" of voters, with individual economic gain being the shameful goal.

Finally, these four chapters are largely animated by an interest in identity politics, which has itself spawned feelings that taken together can be understood to constitute a structure of feeling, one that has for some decades been institutionalized within the academic structure of the university.

one

CONTAINING ANGER, ADVOCATING ANGER: FREUD AND FEMINISM

I had early discovered . . . that passions often lead to sorrow.
—Freud, *The Interpretation of Dreams*

The streets of London have their map; but our passions are uncharted.
—Virginia Woolf, *Jacob's Room*

We need to acknowledge that experiments in creating a new social order, a social movement, create not only spaces of new ethics but also new emotions.
—Sarita Srivastava, "You're Calling Me a Racist?"

Hysterical rage. Annihilating anger. Frozen wrath. Disabling guilt. I open this chapter on Freudian and feminist anger by tracing this trajectory in Freud's thought about the strong emotion of anger. By "strong emotions" I mean those such as fear, hate, triumph, jealousy, horror, greed, and *l'amour fou*—most of which could also be referred to as the "passions", (disgust and shame, however, are strong emotions we would not identify as passions). In their intensity, duration, and focus, the strong emotions differ from what I call the quiet emotions (nostalgia, sadness, and tranquility, for example), the chafing emotions (annoyance, irritation), and the expansive emotions (oceanic feeling, amusement, sympathy).[1]

The Freudian passages I've chosen with the strong emotion of anger in view are drawn from *Studies on Hysteria* (1895), *The Interpretation of Dreams* (1900), "The Moses of Michelangelo" (1914), and *Civilization and Its Discontents* (1930), and as such cover a span of thirty-five years. I've selected these works in great part because, with the exception of *Civilization and Its Discontents*, they focus on what could be termed "professional" relations between people rather than on erotic wishes, for so long familiar to us in Freud. The path traced through these four texts leads from feminized hysterical anger to grandiose annihilating anger, from frozen wrath to guilt. It defines a trajectory of emotional development in Freud's work that culminates in the containment of the drive of aggressivity—and anger, its emotional representative—by guilt, the quintessential Freudian emotion.

I don't want to be understood as suggesting that Freud didn't value the emotions. On the contrary, as he asserted in "Delusions and Dreams in Jensen's *Gradiva*," the emotions are the only valuable things in psychic life.[2] But in general for Freud, the strong emotions are explosive, volatile, dangerous. Or perhaps it would be more accurate to say that Freud was ambivalent about the strong emotions (it would certainly be more "Freudian" to put it this way). At each and every point we'll find that for Freud a different mechanism *inhibits* the expression of the strong emotions. Each mechanism is a *defense* mechanism, similar to what the American psychologist Silvan Tomkins calls an affect management script.[3] Over the course of his life Freud considers in turn the inhibition of anger by repression, the suppression of anger through the dream-work, and the containment of anger by self-control. Ultimately Freud concludes in *Civilization and Its Discontents* that fire must be fought with fire, emotion with emotion. In the final analysis, the controlling emotion—guilt, which is a passion for Freud—is a chilling and paralyzing one.

I'm drawn to this subject by my interest in theories, discourses (or emotional standards), and the experience of the emotions, but more specifically by what may seem at first to bear a far-flung relation to Freud: the value placed on the emotion of anger in the writing of American feminists in the 1970s and 1980s. During this period anger was the emotion of choice for academic feminists (and thus "professional" relationships were very much at stake, among them the relation between students and professors).[4] I'm fascinated by this emphasis on anger, which finds a historical touchstone in the work of Virginia Woolf and is indisputably one of the prime examples of the general redistribution of the emotions in terms of gender taking place in contemporary culture. Long associated with men, anger was now being appropriated by women. What is entailed by this feminist valorization of anger? At whom or what should it be directed? What tone or shape should it take? What assumptions about anger are contained in this work? What are the limits of anger? I take this opportunity to address at least some of these questions at the end of this chapter. By returning to Freud I hope to provide a contrasting perspective from which to do so. Thus my purpose in this chapter is to understand more clearly the bases of both Freudian and feminist views of anger through their differences, as well as to underline the distinctly different historical projects they served.[5]

1

What does Freud have to say about anger? In the index to the *Standard Edition* I was surprised to find virtually no subentries under the heading "anger." The index does refer to *Studies on Hysteria*, published in 1895, but all of the references there are to sections authored by Josef Breuer, Freud's coauthor. The single exception is "Preliminary Communication," the one essay attributed to both Breuer and Freud. I will turn to this piece in a moment, but first I need to insist on a distinction between anger and aggressivity, one signaled by the index itself: if "anger" has few entries, "aggressiveness" has many. Anger is an *emotion*, what in modern western culture we understand primarily as an interiorized affective state (there are other cultures, as anthropologists point out, that conceive of emotion as something that exists *between* people, not as something *in* individuals). Aggressivity is a *drive* to action, to behavior. In his work as a whole Freud placed much more emphasis on a theory of the drives than he did on the emotions. In fact he devoted remarkably little attention to the emotions in comparison, say, to Melanie Klein, whose work is a veritable theoretical atlas of the strong emotions of psychoanalysis. What, then, is the relationship between emotion and aggressivity? Certainly the two are linked, but not indissolubly so. We can imagine angry feelings that don't eventuate in aggressive behavior toward others. Indeed Freud astutely theorized the conversion of aggressivity toward others into self-aggressivity—in the form of an emotion. With these observations in mind I turn to *Studies on Hysteria* and feminized hysterical anger.

Hysteria is associated overwhelmingly with women and with the repression of sexual desire, which I understand as a drive, not an emotion. But in *Studies on Hysteria* Freud does report one case that deals explicitly with the repression of the emotion of anger. I call it the case of the hysterical employee. It is, as we will see, a case with a distinctly contemporary flavor. Given the traditional understanding of anger as a male emotion and hysteria as associated with women, it may come as a surprise to us that this hysterical patient is a man, one feminized by his hysteria as the result of his repressing his rage. What has enraged him? He is furious at his employer who has mistreated him physically, and he is furious at the legal justice system that has accorded him no redress. What is the outcome of his repression of anger? It erupts hysterically in the guise of "a frenzy of rage" as if its repression had compressed it into a denser, more volatile force. Here is the entire passage devoted to the scenario:

> An employee who had become a hysteric as a result of being ill-treated by his superior, suffered from attacks in which he collapsed and fell into a frenzy of rage, but without uttering a word or giving any sign of a hallucination. It was possible to provoke an attack under hypnosis, and the patient then revealed that he was living through the scene in which his employer had abused him in the street and hit him with a stick. A few days later the patient came back and complained of having had another attack of the same kind. On this occasion it turned out under hypnosis that he had been re-living the scene to which the actual onset of the illness was related: the scene in the law-court when he failed to obtain satisfaction for his maltreatment. (*SE* 2: 14)

For Freud and Breuer this case is an illustration of a hysterical attack that consists only of "motor phenomena" (that is, it doesn't exhibit a hallucinatory phase). Like other forms of hysteria, the root or precipitating cause is a memory of a psychical trauma, a memory that has been repressed. But what is the memory of? An event? An emotion? A desire?

Although Freud doesn't say anything more about this case, we can assume he understands it the way he does other cases of hysteria: a person afflicted with hysteria must remember and rehearse either their desire or affect (allow me to repeat that here I am associating desire with a drive, affect with an emotion). The psychical trauma, signaled by the symptom of hysterical rage, must be "disposed of by abreaction or by associative thought-activity" (*SE* 2: 15). But there is a significant difference between this case of hysterical anger and a case of hysterical erotic desire. In the latter, Freud counsels the recognition and acceptance of sexual desire, which is the manifestation of what he will later understand as the libidinal drive. In effect he approves of it. In the case of the hysterical employee, on the other hand, it appears to be the emotion itself—the employee's anger, indeed rage, at the legal justice system and at his employer—that is the precipitating factor of the illness. Repressed anger, in other words, may not be a mere symptom of the illness but its very root. Thus it is the anger itself that should be "abreacted," released as it were into the air.

In his essay "The Unconscious" Freud explains the relation between memory, representation, and emotion this way: "Affects and emotions correspond to processes of discharge, the final manifestations of which are perceived as feelings," while "ideas are cathexes—basically of memory-traces" (178). The psychoanalyst James Hillman, glossing this passage in *Emotion*, offers the following analogy, one that perfectly captures Freud's view of anger as a violent and destructive emotion: "Let us conceive of these 'cathexes—ultimately of memory-traces' as bombs. The bombs 'exist' in the unconscious, but the affect has the quantitative explosive potential of the bombs" (53).

Thus hysteria in this altogether unusual case is not associated with the private sphere (the familiar Freudian bedroom). Rather it is set in the public sphere (the workplace, courts of law), which in the nineteenth century was the confirmed province of men. Furthermore its unexpected scenario underscores the unequal power relations of men—in this situation, of employer and employee. Freud doesn't address the issue of power. He doesn't politicize the emotion of anger. But if in general men have the cultural "right" to express their anger, this particular man—an employee—clearly did not. He didn't experience "satisfaction" in his anger. Instead his hysterical anger feminizes him.[6]

Today we would likely consider this case in terms of harassment, which turns precisely on the analyzing pivot of unequal power relations with a "superior" taking advantage of a "subordinate." *Acting* on the emotion would be part of the therapy. We would look to the courts for "satisfaction," for the redress that was not forthcoming in the nineteenth century. Freud's then innovative answer was not legal action but rather therapy to exorcise the anger. Psychic repression was the mechanism that Freud theorized had concealed this anger in the first place. As we read in "The Unconscious," "to suppress the development of affect is the true aim of repression and . . . its work is incomplete if this aim is not achieved" (178). At this point in his practice Freud believed that therapy in the form of hypnosis would release it. The patient would be purged of the hysterical rage that was in effect *attacking him*. Here anger is understood as a debilitating emotion. In *Studies on Hysteria* both the psychic mechanism of repression and the corresponding treatment of hypnosis have as their goal the effacement or catharsis of the self-destructive emotion of anger. But

Freud was soon to reject hypnosis as ineffective, and another mechanism for containing anger would have to be found.

In *The Interpretation of Dreams* Freud explores the dream-work, a psychic mechanism he believed inhibited the emotions. For Freud the work of dreaming serves to *suppress* and *dilute* the emotions, thereby allowing them to be staged in the dream. If in the case of the hysterical employee the diagnostic complement of repression is hypnosis, here the diagnostic complement of the dream-work is the dissection of the dream-mass into its dream-thoughts, although *dream-passions* would seem to be a more appropriate term. Freud's conviction is that analysis will ultimately allow the strong emotions to present themselves and as a result they will be resolved into a calming order and disappear.

One dream in particular resonates here. In his important section entitled "Affects in Dreams" Freud considers at length the emotional storm released by what we have come to call the "Non Vixit" dream, one of his own dreams of professional ambition. Here is the complete passage:

> *I had gone to Brücke's laboratory at night, and, in response to a gentle knock on the door, I opened it to (the late) Professor Fleischl, who came in with a number of strangers and, after exchanging a few words, sat down at his table. . . . My friend Fl. [Fliess] had come to Vienna unobtrusively in July. I met him in the street in conversation with my (deceased) friend P., and went with them to some place where they sat opposite each other as though they were at a small table. I sat in front at its narrow end. Fl. spoke about his sister and said that in three quarters of an hour she was dead, and added some such words as "that was the threshold." As P. failed to understand him, Fl. turned to me and asked me how much I had told P. about his affairs. Whereupon, overcome by strange emotions, I tried to explain to Fl. that P. (could not understand anything at all, of course, because he) was not alive. But what I actually said—and I myself noticed the mistake—was, "NON VIXIT." I then gave P. a piercing look. Under my gaze he turned pale; his form grew indistinct and his eyes a sickly blue—and finally he melted away. I was highly delighted at this and I now realized that Ernst Fleischl, too, had been no more than an apparition, a "revenant"; and it seemed to me quite possible that people of that kind only existed as long as one liked and could be got rid of if someone else wished it. (SE 5: 421).*

About this angry dream I want to make three points. First, Freud's fantasy in the "Non Vixit" dream—a fantasy that is surely grandiose—is that his anger is itself a lethal weapon. Related is the implication that the dream-work, which serves to suppress (not repress) affect in the first place, may ultimately work to magnify it. To me the most memorable aspect of the "Non Vixit" dream is the "scene of annihilation" where Freud acts on his anger, terminating his friend with a wounding glance, causing him as if in some bizarre science fiction film to liquefy and finally evaporate into nothing, leaving no bodily trace (520). This scene, Freud concludes, is a reversal of the very same treatment he had once received from his employer and teacher Brücke, who had chastised him for his renowned tardiness as an assistant in his lab.[7] Thus the anger of the professor provokes the anger of the student.

Elsewhere in *The Interpretation of Dreams* Freud vividly describes this event, which so clearly had a mortifying effect on his self-esteem: "One morning he turned up punctually at the hour of opening and awaited my arrival. His words were brief and to the point. But it was not they that mattered. What overwhelmed me were the terrible blue eyes with which he looked at me and by which I was reduced to nothing. . . . No one who can remember the great man's eyes, which retained their striking beauty even in his old age, and who has ever seen him in anger, will find it difficult to picture the young sinner's emotions" (422). In the case of the hysterical employee, the anger of the employer provoked the employee's anger. The employee took his grievance to the courts where he found no satisfaction. The result is that the employee turned the anger against himself, making himself physically sick. In the case of the "Non Vixit" dream, anger also calls forth anger. But here the comparison ends. The anger is wildly out of proportion. Freud *was* late. Moreover, anger is vented in fantasy that *does* result in satisfaction and delight. What an amazing phenomenon is the dream!

Indeed the grandiose fantasy of the dream is that anger is a firearm, that Freud's anger is so powerful the mere expression of it constitutes murderous aggression. An emotion is converted into a physical force in fantasy. Freud succeeds in destroying his friend with a laserlike look of piercing anger. To his shame. And to his anxiety. For might he not expect retaliation in an endless escalation of anger and action?

In Freud's discussion of the "Non Vixit" dream he repeatedly refers to the "raging" of the emotions that accompany it. The high degree of its emotional intensity is its most striking feature, especially given Freud's argument in this section of *The Interpretation of Dreams* that the dream-work serves to weaken or dilute the emotions—to bring "about a suppression of affects" (467). As he puts it elsewhere in *The Interpretation of Dreams*, "The purpose for which the censorship exercises its office and brings about the distortion of dreams" is "*in order to prevent the generation of anxieties and other forms of distressing affect*" (267). Thus the dream-work itself possesses great power, as we see in Freud's vivid description of it: "The whole mass of these dream-thoughts is brought under the pressure of the dream-work, and its elements are turned about, broken into fragments and jammed together—almost like pack-ice" (312). Freud pictures the resulting dream as a dense and cold mass of different elements that have been fused together. I think of the dream-work in terms of my high school physics, of fission and fusion, the particles of the dream-thoughts being smashed together with a force inconceivable in terms of the weights and measures, the pulleys and levers of everyday life. Imagine, then, the force required to separate these elements, a force equivalent to that of an atom smasher. More, imagine the emotional storm that would be released.

My second point about this angry dream: given that the emotional world of the "Non Vixit" dream is far more complicated than that of the case of the hysterical employee (which revolves around the single emotion of anger), how does Freud explain his anger which was, he tells us, "strange"? What accounts for his overwhelming sense of emotional strangeness? In part it may be due to the eerie feeling arising from the altogether peculiar situation of addressing a person who is in fact dead. But more fundamentally, I think, what struck Freud as "strange" was the complex of *contradictory* strong emotions released by the dream.

In his analysis of the dream-mass, Freud focuses on the different categories of emotions—what he calls the "various qualities" of affect—that accompanied the "Non Vixit" dream at two nodal points: the "hostile and distressing" feelings when he "annihilated" his friend (who was also his enemy) with two words and a piercing look, and the feelings of "delight" and "satisfaction" at the end of the dream when he realized not only that such people could be eliminated whenever one (he) wanted but even more pleasurably, that such aggressivity was justified (480). Thus what may have been particularly troubling to Freud was the presence of contradictory emotions with regard to the same person. As we know, this emotional knot would come to be one of Freud's decisive contributions to a theory of strong attachments—that they are characterized by binary emotions, with love and hate being the primary pair.

So we should not be surprised to learn that later in his analysis of the "Non Vixit" dream, Freud traces the roots of the pattern of his present-day intense emotional relationships (to his colleagues and friends) back to the emotional world of his early childhood—to his relationship with his nephew John who was a year older than Freud and thus his "senior" and "superior" (483). As is well known and as Freud observes earlier in *The Interpretation of Dreams*, "Until the end of my third year we had been inseparable. We had loved and fought with each other; and this childhood relationship . . . had a determining influence on all my subsequent relations with contemporaries" (424). In relation to the "Non Vixit" dream, one childhood memory (or fantasy) of his nephew in particular returns to Freud. It was when Freud was not yet two and was questioned by his father as to why he hit his nephew. What was Freud's defense? "I hit him 'cos he hit me" (484). Notice that retaliation against a "superior" is at issue, one of Freud's dominant fantasies. In his discussion of the "Non Vixit" dream Freud concludes, "My emotional life has always insisted that I should have an intimate friend and a hated enemy" (483). Thus personal drama dating from childhood intersects (or infects) the professional, upping the ante of emotional engagement. We should note that the site of the first part of the dream is Brücke's laboratory where Freud had worked. We should also note that all of the major figures in the dream are men. Here again anger is gendered male.

My final point is that given Freud's emphasis on the intensity of the emotions (in particular his annihilating anger), I find it curious that nowhere does he name the emotion of guilt, which will become central to his thought later on. Instead he repeatedly uses the word "reproach" (both the reproach of others and self-reproach). With reproach we seem to find ourselves in a novel of manners rather than in a tragedy or a romance of passion. Reproach is one of the chafing emotions, not one of the strong or quiet emotions. Reproach implies disapproval, rebuke, reproval. It is primarily a social emotion. And as a social emotion it is altogether in keeping with Freud's emphasis on shame in his analysis of the "Non Vixit" dream.[8] Shame implies an external, observing other. (Although Freud does mention self-reproach he doesn't identify it as guilt—which, as we will see, he will ultimately come to associate with an action that is *not* taken, only fantasized.) Thus in the short history of the emotions I am sketching here, guilt emerges later than shame in the development of Freud's thought. Or, we might speculate that at this point in his life the emotion of guilt was too distressing for Freud and could only escape the censorship of the dream-work under the guise of shame. Or, we might say that Freud was still too young to be preoccupied with guilt.

In *Studies on Hysteria* a hysterical man, whose frenzied attacks of rage physically mimic his anger, is reduced to a feminized position. His rage and his body are out of control. Repression is ultimately an ineffective mechanism for containing anger. In Freud's "Non Vixit" dream, the dream-work (which, like repression, is an unconscious process) serves to both suppress and stage that anger. If the anger is out of proportion to the event that prompted the dream, nonetheless the dream allows the safe and satisfying expression of aggressive fantasies entailed by anger. Furthermore, the process of analysis puts those emotions into perspective. In "The Moses of Michelangelo" Freud considers a third mechanism for the control of anger, one that is conscious—indeed self-conscious.

The relay between the affect of anger and destructive action is Freud's subject in "The Moses of Michelangelo." As his analytic point of departure he takes his own powerful reaction of "intellectual bewilderment" (also a preferred Freudian emotion) on his repeated viewings of Michelangelo's sculpture of Moses. Freud comes to the conclusion that Michelangelo brilliantly rewrote the scriptural history of anger embodied by Moses. Similarly we may read Freud's essay as a rewriting of his own evolving thought on the emotion of anger and in particular on the problematic of its containment.

It is a question of reading for the plot, of the timing of action and emotion. The seated figure of Moses is traditionally understood as being in a state of anger incipient to ruinous behavior. He is understood as on the verge of bounding up and hurling down the Tablets of the Law, demolishing them in a single furious gesture. Freud, however, reads the plot differently. He advances Moses and his audience in time. He concludes that Moses has already half-risen in his rage, only to interrupt his angry action and return to a state of wrathful immobility or "frozen wrath" (*SE* 13: 229). The heat of passion is chilled to the sculptural bone. In Freud's approving interpretation, Moses resists the temptation to act on "rage and indignation," which would have been "an indulgence of his feelings" and would have entailed the annihilation of the Law. He "controlled his anger"; "he kept his passion in check" (229–30).

For Freud the statue expresses "the passage of a violent gust of passion visible in the signs left behind it in the ensuing calm" (236). It is precisely this tension between the quietude of Moses's exterior aspect and the interior storm of his rage that arrested Freud's eye. How does Freud explain the ability of Moses to contain his anger? For Freud it is a matter of character, of the attachment of Moses to a higher cause, one to which he has conspicuously pledged himself. It is, in other words, a matter of will and self-discipline, of granite control. Thus for Freud, Moses is a figure of heroic restraint, all the more noble for his wrath and the powerful self-control that countervails it. The implication is that Moses's control of his anger, rather than his indulgence of it, allows him to fulfill his responsibilities as a leader of his religious community. At this point I hardly need draw attention to the fact that the nobility of frozen wrath is gendered male.

In his dedication to a higher cause and in his prodigious self-control, Freud's Moses is larger than human, an incarnation of a mental and moral ideal, a heroic figure who upholds the law of the land. Few could be expected to follow his example. I turn, then, to *Civilization and Its Discontents*, my fourth and final example of Freud theorizing a different mechanism to counter aggressivity. Here Freud doesn't directly address anger as an emotion. Instead he deals with the drive of aggressivity to which he believed all human beings are subject and which he regarded as the greatest impediment to civilization.

That there is a clear connection between anger and aggressivity is suggested by the infamous prehistorical fable of the primal origin of guilt that Freud offers in *Totem and Taboo* (1913), and to which he returns in *Civilization and Its Discontents*. It is a scenario of power, sexual desire, and the strong—indeed primal—emotions. Freud, we recall, hypothesizes that civilization began when the sons of the despotic father (who had denied them sexual access to women) banded together in hatred, killed him, and ate his body.

What can restrain the destructive drive to aggressivity, particularly when it is inflamed by the strong and divisive emotions? In *Civilization and Its Discontents* Freud argues that the drive to aggressivity is so powerful that the sense of guilt emerges to counter its force. Indeed the drive to aggressivity, when introjected, becomes guilt. There is a kind of mathematical principle of conversion between drives and emotions at work. Guilt is thus for Freud arguably the most important achievement of civilization.

Much of *Civilization and Its Discontents* is devoted to a consideration of the etiology and origin of guilt on the levels of the individual and of the group. I won't rehearse here the complex trajectory of Freud's argument, which is in any case well known. Instead I'll confine myself to three points, hoping to gain in clarity what I may lose in simplification. First, in Freud's world the emotion of guilt is not understood as a technology of control or a disciplinary technique in the Foucauldian sense, imposed by a historically specific set of discourses and institutions. Rather for Freud the regulating emotion of guilt emerges inevitably from a primal psychology of the emotions, from the tension or ambivalence between hate and love, the emotional representatives of the two basic drives: the drive to aggressivity (power) and the libidinal drive (sexual desire). In Freud's view guilt is both genetic and structural to the human psyche from the moment of the constitution of civilization (that is, the founding moment of the sons revolting against the father). If love and hate are the two primary emotions, guilt is a secondary emotion, entailing self-consciousness. Guilt is the third term, unsettling and oppressive yet paradoxically also stabilizing. Like a point on a nuclear thermostat, guilt works homeostatically to maintain a fluctuating equilibrium between love and hate, to regulate the temperature, to keep things cool.

Second, we should note that the prehistorical paradigm on which Freud bases his theory of the constitution of civilization (out of hatred) and the emergence of guilt (out of love) is gendered male. The sons, who fiercely love the father as much as they hate him, internalize the father as their superego, thus turning aggressivity—and anger—against themselves.

Third, for Freud the sense of guilt is produced from hostile feelings that are *not* acted upon (Freud ultimately reserves the term "remorse" for the emotion experienced after one *has* committed an act of aggression). Concomitantly the sense of guilt is, startlingly, often unconscious. It is what I call a disabling emotion. Guilt is simultaneously an inhibition of aggressivity and an exacting, gnawing punishment for aggression in fantasy. I find this a stunning conclusion: an emotion is itself a self-punishment for what has *not* taken place. Guilt inhibits the development of anger—before it even exists.

Thus if for Freud the sense of guilt is "the most important problem in the development of civilization," in the final analysis it may also represent an enervating and ultimately crippling limit to it (*SE* 21: 134). In Freud's etiology of guilt we find implicit a catastrophe theory of the emotions—and of civilization. If the sense of guilt is at first stabilizing, at a certain limit it may become radically destabilizing. This is because Freud theorizes that the larger the group or community, the more intense the guilt and the greater its quotient.[9] We are presented with a dismaying future in which the burden of guilt (which inhibits the expression of anger) grows heavier and heavier, a future we may have come close to realizing today as transnational corporate structures and communication networks circle the globe, drawing everyone more tightly together and thus increasing our sense of overwhelming social suffering. The sense of guilt may become so onerous, Freud suggests, as to become intolerable, not only for an individual but for civilization as a whole—rendering culture neurotic and crippled. As he writes in *Civilization and Its Discontents*, "The price we pay for our advance in civilization is a loss of happiness through the heightening of the sense of guilt" (134). But if Freud theorizes the "fatal inevitability" of guilt (132), then we may conclude that, at its limit condition, guilt carries with it an inevitable fatality by manifesting itself as "a tormenting uneasiness, a kind of anxiety" on the level of the individual and a "malaise" on the level of society or civilization as a whole (135). Certainly the burden of guilt many carry in the face of global conditions today is virtually intolerable.

At its limit condition then, guilt—the emotion that makes possible the survival and development of civilization—may devolve into anxiety, which is, according to Freud, the most fundamental and primitive of all the emotions.[10] As he points out, "the sense of guilt is at bottom nothing else but a topographical variety of anxiety" (*SE* 21: 135). If Freud is ambivalent about the strong emotions, he is equally ambivalent about guilt. Thus the trajectory I've traced in Freud's thought about anger finds its endpoint in guilt, an emotion that is highly individualizing and isolating. Guilt turns us back on ourselves. Guilt separates us from one another. Guilt inhibits us from anger and aggressive action—and in the final analysis not just from action but also from pleasure.[11]

2

If Freudian guilt is isolating and individualizing, in the 1970s and 1980s American academic feminists conceived anger in precisely the opposite terms. Anger was explicitly understood as an emotion that is not only the basis for a group but can also politicize a group, as an emotion further-more that is *created* in a group, one that is enabling of action and not inhibiting of it. For Freud anger is gendered as male but Freud does not unambiguously approve of it. The weight of his work is on containing and regulating violent anger, on deauthorizing male anger. Conversely in the work to which I now turn, anger is appropriated, advocated, and used to establish the authority with which to challenge male-dominated society. Thus in this discursive circulation of anger in Freud and feminism, we find anger being redistributed in terms of gender. In what follows I con-sider a selection of essays by feminist literary critics and philosophers published in the late 1970s and 1980s (with one published in 1991). The essays by the literary critics Jane Marcus, Carolyn Heilbrun, and Brenda Silver all focus on Virginia Woolf, and those by the philosophers Naomi Scheman, Elizabeth Spelman, and Alison Jaggar all entertain the question of the relation of emotion to knowledge and make the case for the cogni-tive dimension of the emotions.[12]

Virginia Woolf's *A Room of One's Own*—the founding text of feminist literary criticism in the United States—was published in 1929 when Woolf was forty-six, just a year before *Civilization and Its Discontents*. One of its most remarkable passages is a scene that dramatizes and analyzes femi-nist anger (I also take up this scene in my chapters on shame and on bureaucratic rage). The setting is the British Museum where the narrator has gone one afternoon to do research for her upcoming lecture "Women and Fiction" (which is of course the subject of *A Room of One's Own*). While reading the hypothetical *Mental, Moral, and Physical Inferiority of the Fe-male Sex* by Professor von X, she finds herself, like a disruptive student, absentmindedly, "unconsciously," drawing a picture of him, a sketch that reveals to her both her anger *and* his:

> A very elementary exercise in psychology, not to be dignified by the name of psycho-analysis, showed me, on looking at my notebook, that the sketch of the angry professor had been made in anger. Anger had snatched my pencil while I dreamt. But what was anger doing there? Interest, confusion, amusement, boredom—all these emotions I could trace and name as they succeeded each other through the morning. Had anger, the black snake, been lurking among them? Yes, said the

sketch, anger had. It referred me unmistakably to the one book, to the one phrase, which had roused the demon; it was the professor's statement about the mental, moral and physical inferiority of women. My heart had leapt. My cheeks had burnt. I had flushed with anger. There was nothing specially remarkable, however foolish, in that. One does not like to be told that one is naturally the inferior of a little man. . . . One has certain foolish vanities. It is only human nature, I reflected, and began drawing cartwheels and circles over the angry professor's face till he looked like a burning bush or a flaming comet—anyhow, an apparition without human semblance or significance. The professor was nothing now but a faggot burning on the top of Hampstead Heath. Soon my own anger was explained and done with; but curiosity remained. How explain the anger of the professors? Why were they angry? (32)

Woolf astutely concludes that the anger of the professors is a self-offensive mechanism (the phrase is mine) adopted by those in power (men); anger is used as a weapon to fortify their position, to create others as inferior. Her anger is provoked by his: "I had been angry because he was angry" (34). Dispensing self-consciously with the complexities of psychoanalysis, she understands this situation in reciprocal terms and with immense clarity. "A very elementary exercise in psychology, not to be dignified by the name of psycho-analysis, showed me, on looking at my notebook" she writes, "that the sketch of the angry professor had been made in anger."[13]

In the "Non Vixit" dream Freud's anger at his angry professor results in his wishful dream of annihilating his friend and colleague with a lethal glance of anger. As we saw, Freud traces his aggressive impulses back to his early childhood. Similarly Woolf defaces "her" professor in daydreaming fantasy, doodling, doodling, until he goes up in flames. Her analysis of anger, however, is not psychoanalytical but political. What Freud doesn't take into account in the case of the hysterical employee—abusive, unequal relations of power—Woolf places at the center of her analysis of gender relations. At the root of the matter is the injustice at the heart of patriarchy. We can understand her anger as an instance of what Alison Jaggar calls "outlaw" emotions, or emotions experienced by those who are oppressed and thus have what Jaggar argues is an "epistemological privilege" with regard to the authority or appropriateness of their feelings. Here I will not take up the argument for "epistemological privilege," although I do turn to it in my chapter on shame. I consider instead the tone of Woolf's anger, which is in fact the subject of Brenda Silver's essay.

Woolf presents her anger as light, even disarming. She writes in ironic tones leavened with a deft touch of melodramatic self-humor. Her anger is altogether palatable. "Had anger, the black snake, been lurking among them?" she writes. "Soon my own anger was explained and done; but curiosity remained." Woolf leaves her anger behind, she tells us—although I do not completely believe her. She casts if off, she says, to pursue thought dispassionately.

But in point of fact not everyone has found congenial Woolf's anger in *A Room of One's Own*. Indeed in the late 1970s and early 1980s Jane Marcus and the late Carolyn Heilbrun strongly disapproved of what they understood as Woolf's "feminine" expression of anger. Instead they preferred the flat-out anger of Woolf's *Three Guineas*, a political tract on the economic and social position of women and war. For Marcus the Woolf of *Three Guineas* is, wonderfully, in "a towering rage"; she relishes the image of Woolf as "an angry old woman" (123), a "witch, making war, not love, untying the knots of social convention, encouraging the open expression of hostilities" (135). (An old woman? Woolf was only fifty-six at the time, but that is another subject—one I take up in the next chapter.) For Heilbrun her own earlier preference for *A Room of One's Own* over *Three Guineas* is a cause for shame. She revels in Woolf's "unladylike" tone in *Three Guineas*, the text where finally Woolf was, she writes, "able to indulge the glorious release of letting her anger rip" (241). Heilbrun sees this as an achievement all the more impressive because "like all women," she says, Woolf "had to fight a deep fear of anger in herself" (241). For both Heilbrun and Marcus, the Woolf of *Three Guineas* finally allows anger to drive her art, to impel her writing. Marcus especially is impassioned on this point. Although she acknowledges that thought must accompany anger in the making of art, her own rhetoric belies her preference for anger. She insists that "we must finally acknowledge that it was anger that impelled her art, and intellect that combed out the snarls, dissolved the blood clots, and unclogged the drains of that great sewer of the imagination, anger" (138).

Brenda Silver brilliantly shows how the issue of the authority of feminist anger has driven the reception of *Three Guineas* ever since it was published, for many years impeding the serious consideration of its ideas because many readers concluded that Woolf is *too* angry. As Silver argues, with the publication of the influential essays by Marcus, Heilbrun, and others, anger, *expressed angrily*, was recuperated. Flat-out anger was established as "righteous" and "prophetic"—in short, as unambiguously and purely political. Woolf's anger in *Three Guineas* is no longer heard as "neurotic, morbid, or shrill" (need I add "hysterical"?), but as the expression of "an ethical or moral stance" (361). Silver accepts Naomi Scheman's argument in "Anger and the Politics of Naming" that in such a case the expression of anger is itself a political act. For Scheman anger, viewed from this feminist perspective, is "moved away from guilt, neurosis, or depression, and into the purview of cognition, external behavior, social relations, and politics. To become angry, to recognize that one has been angry, to change what counts as being angry becomes a political act" (362).

It would be inaccurate to say that Freud regarded the strong emotions as "irrational," although as we have seen, he did view anger and aggressivity as disruptive to the fragile ties binding civilization together. He firmly believed, as he wrote in *Civilization and Its Discontents*, that "instinctual passions are stronger than reasonable interests" (112). But feminist philosophers reject the view of feminist anger as "irrational." They have argued, as do I, for the cognitive dimension of the emotions in general, using anger as their prime example and the relation between oppressor and oppressed as their paradigm. As Elizabeth Spelman observes in her essay "Anger and Insubordination," "To be angry at him is to make myself, at least on this occasion, his judge—to have, and to express, a standard against which I assess his conduct" (266). This is precisely what Virginia Woolf so astutely dramatizes in *A Room of One's Own*. Anger in this touchstone scene is a moral judgment. As Spelman correctly puts it, "There is a politics of emotion: the systematic denial of anger can be seen in a mechanism of subordination, and the existence and expression of anger as an act of insubordination" (270). For Spelman anger in and for women—as opposed to rage, which is anger in excess—has "clarity of vision" (271).

In contradistinction to Freud's emphasis on anger and aggressivity as disruptive to social bonds, anger for these feminists is the basis for a politicized group, however vaguely defined. On this point Scheman's reflections in "Anger and the Politics of Naming" are especially challenging, indeed persuasively so, to the Freudian theory of the emotions. She argues that in the social context of a consciousness-raising group, the "discovery of anger can often occur not from focusing on one's feelings but from a political redescription of one's situation" (177). Thus from a feminist perspective it need not be the Freudian case that emotions are located inside us, repressed, as if they were highly idiosyncratic personal property waiting to be discovered. Rather, they are created in the group.[14] Moreover, and crucially, *they can be created retrospectively.* A woman may, for example, retroactively identify anger as her emotional state in the past even though she didn't feel anger then. It is not the Freudian case that she *repressed* her anger and it is only now coming to the surface. Instead the emotion is being projected from the present into the past. Anger from a feminist perspective can thus be a conscious social emotion, one that *becomes* "personal." A dialectical dynamic is at work, which creates personal facts. (If I may be permitted an asymmetrical analogy from my own life: when I married my first husband I took his last name, and when we divorced I didn't feel I had to give it back—it was now *my* name. Interestingly enough, just recently— some thirty years later—I learned that this is an issue for him because he thinks of my last name as *his* and not mine. Similarly, in the retrospective feminist creation of emotions, such anger would be *my* emotion; I wouldn't want to disavow it.) "Emotions become feminist when they incorporate feminist perceptions and values," Jaggar writes. "For example," she continues, "anger becomes feminist anger when it involves the perception that the persistent importuning endured by one woman is a single instance of a widespread pattern of sexual harassment" (160). If for Freud guilt is ultimately theorized as self-punishment for what has not taken place, here anger, which was not felt in the past, is retrospectively projected into it so as to generate the needed catalyst not only for understanding the present and the past but to create new possibilities in the future.

One of the most thought-provoking questions posed by Freud about the emotions is that of transmission. How are emotions imparted? In *Totem and Taboo* Freud asserts that guilt is a heavy emotional inheritance, one experienced long after the primal act of parricide has been committed and transmitted through the family from one generation to the next. How are feminist emotions transmitted? One of the answers I would give to this question is that emotions are transmitted through rhetorical means. The essays to which I've referred constitute a significant case in point. They are intended to create a politicized community out of their readers. They are the scholarly equivalent of the consciousness-raising group. Anger is generated, sustained, and strengthened through discourse—or at least that is the goal.

But on further thought, the goal is not the sustaining of anger. Rather it is the commitment to feminist values and principles of analysis. After all, can emotion be located *in* discourse? Nothing would seem more impossible. Thus it is the word "anger" and not necessarily the emotion of anger to which it refers that in fact constellates the group. Scholarly feminist "anger" constitutes a rhetorical site around which people cluster who have similar if not the same objections and objectives. Thus feminist literary criticism shapes its own discursive tradition: a literature of anger. Marcus is explicit on this point. In her own essay she moves from the old to the young: from the anger of Virginia Woolf when she was older, to the anger of the middle-aged Adrienne Rich in her poem "The Phenomenology of Anger," to the anger of the young. This is the challenge Marcus offers: "Why wait until old age, as they did, waiting long to let out their full quota of anger? Out with it. No more burying our wrath, turning it against ourselves. No more ethical suicides, no more literary pacifism. We must make the literary profession safe for women as well as ladies" (153). What is the relation of writing to feminist "anger"? Often writing is itself the action. This is in fact the strategy I adopt in advocating anger in my next chapter. Focusing on ageism and the incompatibility of wisdom and anger, I sketch an American tradition of protest literature against the marginalization of the elderly in the United States, with angry women as my guides.

3

In *Civilization and Its Discontents* Freud perceptively observes that "a feeling can only be a source of energy if it is itself the expression of a strong need" (72). Women have so long been identified with the emotions, albeit *not* with anger, that I find it fascinating that an emotion should be the basis for a rallying cry for solidarity, even if—or more accurately precisely because—that emotion has long been identified as the forbidden fruit, or snake in Woolf's word. In the case of women it is undeniable that there's a strong need to resist patriarchal injustice. To do so we need to assert our cultural right to anger.[15] But when is anger productive? When should anger be contained? What are the consequences of flat-out anger? And in what contexts? These are the questions to which Freud in great part devoted himself and which he answered—temperately—in *Civilization and*

Its Discontents. For in advocating anger we need to be mindful both of a theoretical reservation in doing so as well as of the constraints and commands of the social contexts in which we find ourselves.

I've been known to say that "confusion" is one of the emotional states with which I have been all too familiar. At several key points in my life I've found myself confused, by which I mean that I couldn't see my situation with the "clarity of vision" that Spelman in "Anger and Insubordination" understands feminist anger to entail. In my chapter on shame I consider Sandra Bartky's important analysis of confusion, so I won't take it up here. But I do want to say that the narrative of resolving confusion into the clarity of anger is one that holds great appeal for me—even if the anger is not literally felt but is shorthand for a judgment call. There is an autobiographical dimension to my interest in this narrative of the emotions. Although I participated in several feminist consciousness-raising sessions in the late 1960s I wasn't able to judge clearly then what at this distance was so patently and obviously wrong in my marriage, which was soon to be dissolved by divorce. Of course the situation was complex, harrowingly so. But what was not complex was my husband making a unilateral decision as to where we would move—across the country. I knew there was something not right about this, but I wasn't able to label it *wrong*. (Imagine!) I should have been angry. I should have been able to make a judgment call. Instead I was confused.

"If we are confused about our emotions," Scheman writes in "Anger and the Politics of Naming," "those emotions themselves are confused" (179). Her argument is that confusion is a sign of a prepolitical state, and that we must identify these emotions, *name* them, as a way of understanding our position. With this I agree. Her implication, if not explicitly drawn conclusion, however, is that in resolving the confusion one emotion—anger—will ultimately emerge with the precision of clearly drawn lines. The scenario she offers is that of a nonfeminist becoming politicized in a consciousness-raising group. Out of confusion the emotion of guilt appears first. Guilt is then interpreted as a "cover for those other feelings, notably feelings of anger" (177). In her scenario, prepoliticized guilt must disappear to allow a politicized anger to appear. I value the pragmatic worth of this strategy (we should also note that the narrative of guilt emerging first from confusion may be specific to this period of academic feminism in the United States). Indeed I adopt it myself in my chapter on anger from the perspectives of aging and gender. And I wish that this had been my own experience in the late 1960s. But I also don't want to be naive here. For a righteous politicized anger will no doubt be accompanied by other emotions as well (revenge might be one of them as we see in Woolf's scene of defacement)—precisely because the emotion of anger will no doubt be an "action." My fundamental point here is that anger as a "political" emotion does not exist in a pure form. Emotions come in clusters.[16]

That we should interrogate our wishes for their unconscious components is so fundamental to Freud—and I hope to all of us—as to be unnecessary to relearn it here. That Freud insists that emotions are bound indissolubly together is, however, worth stressing. Let's return for a moment to the "Non Vixit" dream elaborated by Freud. There he dissects the complex of "strange emotions" that accompanied his dream—separating out the different emotions from one another, isolating them, and identifying them as if they were precipitants in a chemical experiment. (This recalls Raymond Williams's analogous notion of structures of feeling as "social experiences in solution," as opposed to social experiences that have been struck into their "precipitants.")[17] What Freud discovers is not only the diverse emotions of anger and shame, triumph and anxiety, but also that in life, as opposed to analysis, the emotions exist in compound form. Ultimately for Freud there is no such thing as pure anger or pure shame. In his homeostatic view of the strong emotions, a strong hostile emotion will be accompanied by its antidote. The converse also holds. A strong positive emotion, like love, will be accompanied by its opposite. For Freud our strong emotions are ambivalent and our motives are mixed.

Let's return to the scene in *A Room of One's Own*: "But what was anger doing there? Interest, confusion, amusement, boredom—all these emotions I could trace and name as they succeeded each other through the morning. Had anger, the black snake, been lurking among them? Yes, said the sketch, anger had" (32). In this condensed narrative Woolf resolves in a morning what has taken many of us a much, much longer time. And although it is underlined that many emotions are involved, the narrative is one that admits no ambiguity. There can be no mistaking that Professor von X is unworthy of any attempt to understand him in any way other than she does. Here is her portrait of him: "He was heavily built; he had a great jowl; to balance that he had very small eyes; he was very red in the face. His expression suggested that he was laboring under some emotion that made him jab his pen on the paper as if he were killing some noxious insect as he wrote, but even when he had killed it that did not satisfy him; he must go on killing it; and even so, some cause for anger and irritation remained" (31). The portrait is a brilliant caricature, but it is a caricature nonetheless. The result for me as a reader is that not only anger but triumph is involved in the spectacle of the narrator defacing this ugly little man. The emotions come in compound forms and we isolate them for predominately heuristic purposes—personal, political, strategic, analytical, and theoretical. In the case of the contemptible Professor von X, it is wonderfully easy to write him off with an angry flourish of the pen. Thus while I love this scenario in *A Room of One's Own* it does not, for all its virtuosity, provide us with a complex situation. We should also note that in the passages from both Freud and Woolf about their angry professors what is narrated is a fantasy. Woolf is clearly aware of this. Later in *A Room of One's Own* she discusses the emotional shape and structure that exceptional novels assume, insisting that the structure of such novels "is one of infinite complexity, because it is thus made up of so many judgments, of so many different kinds of emotion" (75). And she is explicit that one must not write out of an overwhelming anger—or fear, bitterness, hate, and rancor.

This brings me to my second point. In the essays to which I've been referring the paradigm of oppressor-oppressed is key. It is argued that oppression can be identified by anger, and that it should be responded to by anger. But what happens then? We need to advance the scenario in time and interrogate the consequences of letting one's anger "rip," in Heilbrun's word. We must focus on the longer view, on the "plot" of anger, looking ahead as did Freud in "The Moses of Michelangelo." Additionally in the essays to which I've been referring, patriarchal culture is understood as the condition of women's oppression. But what happens when the paradigm of oppressor-oppressed moves inside academic feminism itself?

Anger as an "outlaw" emotion is appropriate when it is associated with the position of the oppressed. But as we grow older—and here I am referring to feminists in the academy—relations of authority shift decisively. In general, power relations for feminists in the academic humanities have undergone a sea change in the last thirty years. Many women who entered the academy under the banner of the politics of anger find themselves today in positions of authority responsible to many others—to women. The title of a talk by Naomi Scheman in the mid-1990s—"On Waking Up One Morning and Discovering We Are Them"—gestures toward this phenomenon. Anger may be appropriate as a tool of politicization but after this inaugural point flat-out anger can be a blunt instrument, especially when it is used against other women.

More importantly, the expression of anger in public discourse—in essays, in debate—can have very different consequences from the expression of anger in, for example, the close quarters of the classroom, where the flat-out anger of an older feminist professor at a younger student can produce a flashpoint that escalates personal and professional conflict.[18] Consider, for example, an essay published in the mid-1980s on feminist pedagogy, one that takes up anger as its emotion of choice. In "Anger and Authority in the Introductory Women's Studies Classroom," Margo Culley asserts that "anger is a challenging and necessary part of life in the feminist classroom" (216). In the introduction to *Gendered Subjects: The Dynamics of Feminist Teaching*, edited by Culley and Catherine Portuges, we encounter a fundamentally psychoanalytic view of the strong emotions. Culley and Portuges note that the model of the psychoanalytic family helps them to understand why in the feminist classroom there are "outbreaks of temper, tears, denunciation and divisiveness, notions that courses must offer total salvation or else fail, strong feelings of vulnerability, awareness that students/teachers love or hate students/teachers, that students/teachers see or reject themselves/their sisters/mothers/fathers in the course of content or interactions in the classroom" (15). But if the model helps to clarify a certain aspect of this pedagogical situation, it also works to produce a volatile, adversarial pedagogical world. Perhaps most seriously, it constricts us to a hothouse vision of a two-generational family when in fact the academy houses many generations, which is to say that it itself embodies or is witness to a multilayered historicity.[19] Moreover in its emphasis on the strong emotions, the psychoanalytic model implicitly restricts us to certain forms of feeling—ambivalent and ultimately oppositional emotions. Taken to its extreme, the psychoanalytic model produces "pedagogic violence" with anger as the privileged emotion: emotion is linked to the domain of the personal, to woman, and through feminism to the political, with the classroom serving as the space for the drama.[20]

As we moved into the 1990s the rhetoric of anger in white academic feminism largely subsided. But in the opening years of the twenty-first century it has returned in several guises.[21] Linda Grasso, in her book on white and black women's literature in nineteenth-century America, insists that we must make anger at injustice central again. Anger is also circulating between the generations of academic women who identify themselves as second- and third-wave feminists, and between white academic feminists, women of color, and transnational feminists. Organizing a conference on third-wave feminism and women's studies, held at the University of Exeter in 2002, Stacy Gillis and Rebecca Mumford found themselves at first "mystified" by the "raw and—at times—overwhelming anger" directed at them by second-wave feminists (2). Anger here appears to be a symptom of a lack of understanding rather than a touchstone that, upon reflection, might provide understanding. And in a strong essay on the moral and emotional regulation of feminism and antiracism, Sarita Srivastava, observing that many white feminists respond with anger, confusion, and tears to charges of racism, argues persuasively that this emotional response is often rooted in national and racial discourses of benevolence and innocence that underwrite a white feminist's moral identity. As she reports, "One of the most common angry and indignant reactions described in my interviews was 'How can you call me racist?'" (42). Srivastava has no use for the view that emotions may have a cognitive edge. She finds anger to be inappropriately defensive, serving only to shore up that identity. Thus she understands a focus on such emotions as complicit with what she sees as the discredited liberal project of seeking change at the level of the individual, as a kind of narcissistic self-regard that blocks a commitment to structural transformation. For her feminist practices of emotional disclosure distract us from the real work at hand. "My analysis finds," Srivastrava writes, "that as some white feminists move toward new ideals of antiracist feminism, they often move toward deeper self-examination rather than toward organizational change. These findings suggest that some of the deadlocks of antiracist efforts are linked to these preoccupations with morality and self" (31).[22] As should be preeminently clear by now, I don't see a necessary contradiction between these two notions, and I certainly don't think that we should give up any "tools" at our disposal. In fact I like to think of these white women—I could be one of them—as having taken Alison Jaggar's essay (and others mentioned here) to heart and head. We will have learned to interrogate our anger, not to use it as a defensive weapon of self-absorption.

I end with a question that has been recurring in my mind. We speak approvingly of self-reflexive thought, of thought that turns back on itself, interrogating its foundation, its principles, its implications, its consequences. Is there an analogy to self-reflexive thought in the domain of the strong emotions? For Freud anger is inhibited, or regulated, by guilt. In *Civilization and Its Discontents* he offers a homeostatic view of the strong emotions. In Freud's view passions often lead to sorrows. But this system operates unconsciously; it is not consciously self-reflexive. One of the important contributions of feminist thought is the theorization of the cognitive dimension of the emotions. Here we come close, I think, to considering the emotions in a self-reflexive way. And here I return to Virginia Woolf who offers us a durable paradigm. In *A Room of One's Own* the narrator reflects on her anger, analyzing it and placing it in historical and social perspective.[23] She also draws on its energy. She writes, which is an action in itself. In my next chapter on age and anger, we'll find this scenario repeated by the long-time activist Barbara Macdonald. And in the chapter after that, "Racial Shame, Mass-Mediated Shame, Mutual Shame," we'll return to this scene in *A Room of One's Own*. There my concern will be to draw out the sequencing of the emotions by tracing the shift from shame to anger, where anger is itself a reflection on the shame that preceded it. Thus if in *Jacob's Room* Virginia Woolf remarked that our "passions remain uncharted," this is belied by her own work as well as by the rich analysis offered to us by feminists through their work on the emotions over the past three decades.

two

AGAINST WISDOM: ANGER AND AGING

> Anger, then, is only for the engaged; for those with projects that matter (not the indifferent, the insouciant, the depressed). That is to say, those for whom something has gone wrong but who "know," in their rage, that it could be otherwise.
>
> —Adam Phillips, "Just Rage"

> I certainly do not want to read more words on how to build character and develop the wisdom of old age.
>
> —James Hillman, *The Force of Character and the Lasting Life*

"It's time to get angry again." These are the mobilizing words with which Germaine Greer concludes the preface to *The Whole Woman*, published in the late 1990s. It is the very book she had vowed thirty years earlier in *The Female Eunuch* never to write. Then she had insisted it was the responsibility of each generation of women to articulate their own experiences and their own priorities. She could speak with authority only about women of her own class, background, education, and age. But three decades after the publication of *The Female Eunuch* the dismaying lack of progress around the globe in women's issues across the life course moved Greer to assume a position of authority to speak for women in general. In *The Whole Woman* she takes on a multitude of feminist issues ranging from beauty, sexuality, and work to reproductive technology, hormone replacement therapy, and the global feminization of poverty.

If in *The Change: Women, Aging, and the Menopause* Greer celebrated aging as a welcome retirement from the "career" of sexuality, I am happy to report that in *The Whole Woman* she rejects her peculiar notion of aging as a self-imposed cloister and assumes the mantle of leadership at age sixty.[1] In *The Whole Woman* Greer adopts a rhetoric of anger as a strategy, calling up the cultural memory of militant women in the 1960s and evoking anger as a powerful binding force: "It's time to get angry again." In writing as an older woman, and including older women in her inspiring view of a broad coalition of women, Greer addresses women of all ages. Thus I draw on the example of Greer to introduce the subject of this chapter: the possible galvanizing effects of anger for stimulating personal and social change and, conversely, the damaging effects of the cultural prohibition of anger in older people in the United States. The larger context of this chapter is the social politics of the emotions as they relate to life stages—in particular to aging or old age in the United States where age is associated with wisdom, an ideal that, I suggest, serves as a sugar-coated screen for ageism.[2]

The *Oxford English Dictionary* defines wisdom as the "capacity of judging rightly in matters relating to life and conduct; soundness of judgment in the choice of means and ends." In the West the time-honored association of wisdom has been with aging, where wisdom is defined in various ways but almost always understood as a capacity for balanced reflection and judgment that can accrue only with long experience. In Cicero's *De Senectute* a good old age is associated with authority, serenity, and honor—in short, with wisdom.[3] For Aristotle wisdom is a virtue associated with thought and with the mastering of feeling. And indeed wisdom has also almost always been understood as predicated on a lack of certain kinds of feelings—the passions, in particular, including anger. From this perspective, anger would seem to be the virtual opposite of wisdom. Yet for Greer the authority of her anger is based on experience across the years of her life as a feminist. And it is experience that is commonly understood to be a necessary if not sufficient ground for wisdom. Thus we can understand Greer's anger as the foundation of the articulation of a political viewpoint that is itself a kind of wisdom, one that might seem a contradiction in terms—a wisdom that is feminist, or perhaps better put, a wise anger.

In this chapter the questions I address are as follows: How does a politics of aging, one that is inclusive (not limited, say, to gender or to class), rely on a rhetoric of emotion? How has this rhetoric changed over time in the twentieth century? These questions are related to another one. How is aging theorized in relation to other life stages and the emotions? I can't be definitive or exhaustive in reflecting on these issues. But I hope to open them up to further inquiry by focusing on two major books key to the cultural history of aging in the United States. The first book is drawn from the early twentieth century: the psychologist G. Stanley Hall's *Senescence: The Last Half of Life*, which was published in 1922. The second book is drawn from the last part of the twentieth century—the feminist activist Betty Friedan's *The Fountain of Age*, which appeared in 1993. Why examine these books by Hall and by Friedan? Both writers were prominent figures well known for their contributions to their fields—for Hall it was the arena of adolescent psychology and for Friedan it was feminist activism. Further, both came to consider aging in America only when they were older, and both wrote ambitious books on aging that have been destined to be forgotten.[4]

Although their books were published some seventy years apart, both Hall and Friedan argue that we are witnessing the emergence of a "new" elderly made possible by increases in life expectancy. Both insist that the new elderly have a unique and even evolutionary role to play in our society. But Friedan doesn't build on the early cultural history of aging in the United States. We find no reference to Hall's vision of aging in her work. I mention this not to indict *The Fountain of Age* on this score. Rather, my point is that, as with the history of feminism, it would seem that in the United States the social consciousness of aging has needed to be reinvented time and again throughout the twentieth century.[5]

According to the Administration on Aging's "Profile of Older Americans: 2006," since 1900 the percentage of Americans age sixty-five and older has tripled, and the absolute number of Americans sixty-five and older has increased nearly twelve-fold. Our population as a whole is aging, and with the increase in longevity over the twentieth century our older population is itself growing older. By 2030 it is estimated that there will be twice as many older persons living in the United States as in 2005, and those age sixty-five and older will account for a full twenty percent of our population. I want to stress that aging can be said to be a women's issue. In 2005, for example, for every 100 men there were 139 women. Older women have a significantly higher poverty rate than men. Women also outlive men on average by five and a half years. We are in the midst of a demographic revolution, one made possible by stunning increases in life expectancy. But it is a quiet revolution—in great part because the elderly are dispossessed in our society.

These statistics are reflected, I would suggest, in our anxiety—as individuals and as a nation—over the financial future. It is seen in the multitude of advertisements for financial services (the investment of retirement funds is a big business) and in news stories that warn us of the strict necessity of planning for retirement. As a nation we have an acute political consciousness of some of the fiscal consequences of aging, as witnessed in the acrimonious public debates over Social Security during the 1990s and in the presidential campaigns of 2000 and 2004. Should we "save" Social Security in a public lockbox? Should we privatize Social Security?[6] Whether this effort can be sustained in the political arena in the wake of the attacks of September 11, 2001, and the wars in Iraq and Afghanistan is altogether another question. I am nonetheless hopeful that at this point in time we are developing a widespread social consciousness of the aging of our population. What can we learn from the reception of the work on aging by Hall and Friedan?

In attempting to generate a social consciousness of aging, both Hall and Friedan draw on the notion of wisdom as well as deploy a rhetoric of anger ranging from belligerence to rage. The extent to which they think of their projects as political is important here, since political energy and engagement are often understood in terms of fervor, and thus, as I mentioned above in regard to Greer, as antithetical to wisdom. In this chapter, then, I sketch a micro-rhetorical history of anger in the twentieth century in terms of the cultural politics of aging. As we will see, the category of depression is central to this story. The first section of this chapter is devoted to the broad subject of age-related emotion. I then turn to the books on aging by Hall and Friedan. I conclude with some thoughts—and an important story of an angry woman—about the moral authority of anger as voiced by those who are older.

1

Over the past twenty years in the United States the emotions have gained increasing prominence as a subject of research by historians who, along with scholars in other fields, have convincingly demonstrated that, like any other human experience, the emotions have a history and thus change in fascinating ways over time. I am not a historian. But as a scholar educated in literary studies I have found extremely suggestive the precept of the historicity of the emotions, along with histories of specific emotions. Central to this work is the distinction between emotional experience (what an individual feels) and emotional standards or ideals (what a culture demands in terms of emotional behavior or etiquette). Also central to this work, given a theoretical emphasis on the social construction of the emotions, is sensitivity to differences in emotional experience and emotional standards in terms of gender, race, ethnicity, and other social categories. But virtually no attention has been given to a history of the emotions in terms of age—and in particular, old age.

There are a few significant exceptions to this general rule. In *New and Improved: The Transformation of American Women's Emotional Culture*, John Spurlock and Cynthia Magistro investigate the emotional lives of adolescents and women from the 1910s to the early 1930s in the United States, focusing in great part on the expression of personal feelings in their diaries and letters and thus on the tension between felt or lived experience and the culture's emotional standards. But they do not devote a section to older age. In *An Emotional History of the United States*, editors Jan Lewis and Peter Stearns include an essay on age and the emotions by the historian of aging Andrew Achenbaum, who refers to his subject as the psychohistory of late-life emotionality. Spurlock, Magistro, and Achenbaum are concerned primarily with felt or individual emotional experience, not with emotional standards, and in the field of history this is indicative of much of the work in emotion studies. As Lewis and Stearns write in their introduction to *An Emotional History of the United States*, "The history of the emotions is . . . first of all, an attempt to recover that living presence, to recapture the way history felt. It is to ask what it felt like to be a Puritan immigrant to America, or an Irish one two hundred years later" (1). While both Hall and Friedan do write out of their own experience, some of it emotional, I am equally concerned with the ways in which the rhetoric of anger and the conceptualization of wisdom appear in their work. I am also especially interested in the tension between their experience of anger and their notion of wisdom as a standard they hope to foster.

Just as the capacity for wisdom has been linked with old age, specific emotions have been linked with certain stages of life in the twentieth century in disciplines ranging from psychoanalysis and psychology to cultural studies. If the emphasis in psychoanalysis and psychology is on the transhistorical nature of the emotions, in cultural studies it is on the cultural construction of the emotions. Melanie Klein, for example, theorizes an infant's psychic life as based not on primary drives, as does Freud, but rather on intense primary affects—rage, among them. Anna Freud links the stormy oedipal emotions of hate and love with adolescence. And

James Hillman theorizes certain emotions as being appropriate to certain stages of life (he remarks, for instance, that pity is not an emotion we would associate with childhood).[7] In this vein I cannot resist quoting the character Myrtle in John Cassavetes's remarkable film *Opening Night* about a middle-aged actress who is uncertain as to how to play an aging actress. As she remarks, "When I was seventeen, I could do everything. It was so easy. My emotions were so close to the surface. I find it harder and harder to stay in touch."[8]

In cultural studies, scholars of the emotions have explored the various incarnations that a particular emotion might take at different points in our lives. This is, for example, an approach that William Ian Miller takes in *The Anatomy of Disgust*, where he sketches what I would call a psycho-ontogenesis of disgust, tracing the anatomy of disgust from its emergence between the ages of four and eight through adolescence and then into late middle and old age. This later stage of life he associates with a loss of affect—with what he sees as a general self-disgust or listless resignation to a failing body and to a life now virtually over (Miller is clearly no champion of gifts that may come with old age).[9] I have myself written in *Aging and Its Discontents* about the emotion of anxiety that is fostered in our culture in relation to age. Margaret Gullette in "Midlife Discourses in the Twentieth-Century United States" terms this "age anxiety" and has called on scholars to study age-related emotions, offering a provocative account of how our culture has fostered the emotion of nostalgia as a way of socializing relatively young people into the ideology of middle age as decline (22). We see the stratification of the emotions in terms of age in popular parlance as well, with people speaking of teenage emotions, for example, or adolescent emotions. The emotions, then, are one of the important building blocks our society draws upon to construct meaning and value, and to attempt to proscribe or valorize behavior in relation to one's age.

2

Senescence is a big book—a study of what Hall calls the last half of life. An indefatigable psychologist renowned for his work on adolescence, the first president of the American Psychological Association, and the founding editor of four important journals in psychology, Hall undertook the writing of *Senescence* after his retirement from Clark University where he had served as president for over thirty years. Published when Hall was seventy-eight, *Senescence* is a sprawling compendium of research ranging from intellectual history to the results of surveys, from the biology of aging to the psychology of death.

Senescence is original in its cross-disciplinary focus on old age and impressive in its amplitude, and indeed Hall has been given the honor of being called the first American psychogerontologist.[10] It is the reader's misfortune, however, that Hall's method of surveying the research in various fields and of summarizing a multitude of opinions and findings inevitably has a dulling effect. But there are two important exceptions to this general rule. The first is the opening of the book where he speaks personally about his own retirement. He finds it a shocking change. The second is the chapter entitled "Some Conclusions." There he rises to the challenge that he has set for himself in the course of the book—to imagine a new old age. It is as if in the process of writing *Senescence* Hall found himself inspired to adopt in the conclusion a messianic tone, one that is a radical departure from his firm resolve in the beginning to leave behind the world of public affairs.

In the introduction Hall formulaically asserts that youth is "exhilarating, age a depressing theme" (viii). But on the whole the tenor of the introduction is one of amazing resoluteness and industriousness.[11] If in the introduction to *Senescence* he conceives of life expectancy in terms of the biblical number of seventy, by the conclusion we find him urging people to think in terms of living to one hundred.[12] What is his vision? That the demographic fact of so many old people is an index of the evolution of the human race, and that this evolutionary strength can only be fulfilled if older people who exemplify wisdom take on the important public role of counselor to younger generations and to the nation as a whole.

Throughout *Senescence* Hall observes that enforced isolation in old age results in stagnation—in moroseness and depression. He comes close to a political analysis of the reasons for the emotional torpor of the old who find themselves "a class more or less apart" (viii-ix) and "a caste apart" (ix), literally cast aside by the institution of retirement. If older people are morose, it "is largely due to the inconsiderate treatment" that they receive (172). Yet if Hall sees that there is "a rapport between us oldsters," this seems to be an unspoken understanding, not one that prefigures an embryonic political consciousness, in part because of what he understands as "the enhanced individuation characteristic of age" (ix).[13] Nor does he call for an end to the practice of retirement. Although he does contest the physician William Osler's infamous conviction that people do their best work before the age of forty, Hall finds himself in the contradictory position of both having determined to make a complete break with the work world of his past and ultimately concluding that the old—that is, those who have achieved a vigorous senectitude—should assume positions of leadership on the national and international stage.

This contradiction is both mirrored in his conflicting views of the emotional lives of the old and explained by them. On the one hand, Hall accepts the time-honored notion that there is a "lessening of emotional intensity" in old age, in addition to a progressive abating of sexual passion that begins with senescence (26), and that this is one of the conditions of wisdom. Throughout the history of western thought, wisdom has been associated with coolness of reason and evenness of judgment, with detachment and balance. To Hall this proves a congenial formulation. What can these people—intelligent, educated, healthy, and old—offer? They can offer "strength of reason, cool judgment, and breadth of view" (208). In a familiar metaphor associated with wisdom, Hall writes that these elite older people have the potential to reach a "summit" never before attained from which to view the world "in a clearer light" (382) and with "poise and philosophic calm" (405). Such a heightened perspective we may understand as the antithesis of the slough of despond associated with depression.

In *Senescence* Hall writes of the old in the third person. But in "Some Conclusions" he shifts to the first person. The result is electrifying. Instead of a philosophic calm, we encounter the fervor of debate. It is as though Hall is arguing a case in front of a judge and jury. Here he asserts that the old—*we*—have intense emotional lives. But we have been forced to inhibit the expression of our feelings. As a psychologist he speaks in terms of repression. If he had been a sociologist, however, he would have cast this phenomenon in terms of oppression. Furthermore Hall employs the language of social justice, referring to the "rights" of the old and to the old as a distinct "minority":

> They say our emotional life is damped. True, we are more immune from certain great passions and our affectivity is very differently distributed. But what lessons of repression we have to learn! If the fires of youth are banked and smoldering they are in no wise extinguished and

perhaps burn only the more fiercely because they cannot vent them-selves. . . . We get scant credit for the self-control that restrains us from so much we feel impelled to say and do and if we break out, it is ascribed not to its true cause in outer circumstance but to the irritability thought characteristic of our years. Age has the same right to emotional pertur-bations as youth and is no whit less exposed and disposed to them. Here, as everywhere, we are misunderstood and are in such a feeble minority that we have to incessantly renounce our impulsions. (383)

Hall insists that people who are old have the same right to anger as the young. He astutely understands that the anger of the old is willingly (if unconsciously or uncritically) misinterpreted by those younger as an un-becoming "irritability" common to old age and thus as something that can be disregarded with impunity. Given this double frustration on the part of the old, it is not surprising Hall concludes that in fact emotional life probably increases as we grow older.[14]

Hall wants to retain the capacity of wisdom conventionally reserved for the old, but given his declaration of the right to emotional intensity, he must also revise his view of wisdom—or at least add something to the emotional mix. I imagine Hall winding himself up in the writing of this chapter, bringing himself to the point where he can proclaim that what is required today is not an old age that is "merely contemplative" (407). Old age, he declares, is "not passive and peace-loving but brings a new bellig-erency" (410). Belligerency. Hall was angry and was ready for combat—impatient to fight from a position of moral authority. In his adoption of a rhetoric of defiance, he has come far from the depressed lassitude of old age that he sees as largely enforced by cultural constraints.

In addition to his own personal experience of being cast aside by soci-ety, where did Hall find the energy—the *theoretical* energy—to imagine the future of old age? What model helped him conceptualize a powerful old age? It is the analogy of adolescence to old age, I suggest, that enabled Hall to think about old age differently. The association of senility with infancy, of a second childhood with childhood proper, is altogether familiar—and demeaning to the old. But the association of old age with adolescence is original. Adolescence was Hall's area of expertise as a professional psy-chologist. He was the author of the book *Adolescence*, which was published in 1904 in two huge volumes and was well received. Adolescence he conceived as a time of new development and new beginnings—biologically, psychologically, and socially. By linking old age with adolescence, a time of life known for its emotional volatility and idealism, he borrows the energy of adolescence and transfers it to old age. "Adolescence is a new birth, for the higher and more completely human traits are now born," he wrote in 1904 (xiii). In *Senescence* he insists: "The call to us is to construct a new self just as we had to do at adolescence," (403) and "Age has the same right to emotional perturbations as youth" (383). Adolescence and old age: Hall believes that each stage has feelings distinct to it. Yet paradoxically in this regard they are also similar—and indeed some of those feelings are the same. He also envisages a kind of alliance between adolescents and the old.

"Senescence, like adolescence, has its own feelings, thought, and wills, as well as its own physiology, and their regimen is important, as well as that of the body," Hall writes in his book on old age (100). Recent research has shown that many cognitive functions do not inevitably decline with age as has previously been thought and that mental exercise is key to maintaining and strengthening those abilities. The same is true, I would suggest, of the emotions: the emotions, or passions, need not inevitably diminish with age, and exercise—*emotional exercise*—is as fundamental to their vitality as is their cultural authorization. As Hall presciently wrote in *Senescence*, "Memory fails in age only if not exercised, and this is true of all abilities" (68). The capacity to feel—including reacting to injustice with anger—is one of those critical abilities.

Hall's belligerent attitude on behalf of what we would call the marginal-ization of the elderly—or more strongly, ageism—was ignored in the con-temporary reviews of *Senescence*.[15] I suspect that Hall's anger—even if expressed in only a few places—was either considered a scandal or a tem-porary aberration or both. Perhaps it was dismissed as the unpleasant irritability so stereotypically associated with the elderly, a social prejudice that Hall himself had diagnosed. Perhaps it was not detected by his readers because an anger that is righteous is not associated with the old, but rather only the anger of peevishness and cantankerousness. Even in recent schol-arly assessments of *Senescence* Hall's anger, although recognized, isn't given its appropriate due. Instead *Senescence* is characterized as a rambling jeremiad, with the implication that Hall's statements are the ill-considered and oddly inappropriate outbursts that come from a temperament given to depression and to lament.[16]

My reading of Hall's anger is altogether different. I respect it. I understand his anger as the call to denounce the injustice of what today we call ageism. I also think even a temporary alliance of wisdom with anger is remarkable. Hall wanted to harness the energy of anger, and he called on older people who possessed what he understood as wisdom to take on an active role and to remind others of "the world of sin, righteousness, and judgment" (411). He could not, however, sustain the uneasy conjunction of righteous anger, wisdom, and leadership, and so the instances of rhetorical anger are few. But even though his language is different, Hall nonetheless reminds me of Germaine Greer. If in the beginning of *Senescence* he sees aging as a time when one retires from work, in the end he protests the cultural injunction of the withdrawal of the elderly from the active world. "It's time to get angry again," insists Greer. Thus in *Senescence* we find an incipient protest literature on behalf of the elderly who are sentenced to the margins and condemned to retirement when their greatest need, Hall believed, was to be of service to society.

Betty Friedan's *Fountain of Age* appeared in 1993 when she was seventy-one—exactly seventy-one years after the publication of *Senescence*. Like Hall's book, *The Fountain of Age* is long and ambitious, covering a multitude of topics. Although it has been disregarded by academic feminists (in part because Friedan was a liberal feminist and in part because of the ageism implicit within feminism itself), it is an important and complex book that came from years of research and of hard thinking about aging.[17] Unlike Hall, Friedan isn't interested in surveying past attitudes toward aging and the elderly. Much of her book focuses the specific issues of work, housing, menopause, long-term care, and the right-to-die controversy. But like Hall, Friedan argues that we must understand the special purpose of the additional years that the longevity revolution has given to people in western and other so-called developed countries.[18] If Hall drew theoretical energy for his analysis of old age from his view of adolescence, Friedan reflects on issues of aging largely through the lens of gender, in particular from the vantage point of the second wave of the women's movement—one that she helped decisively to shape through the publication of *The Feminine Mystique* in the mid-1960s.[19] In *The Fountain of Age* Friedan provocatively insists that the underlying cause of the women's movement was in fact the increase in life expectancy for women. As she writes, "What had really caused the women's movement was the *additional years of human life*. At the turn of the century, women's life expectancy was forty-six; now it was nearly eighty" (16).[20]

I find it fascinating that in the time between the publication of *The Feminine Mystique*, widely regarded as an angry book, and *The Fountain of Age*—a period of thirty years that saw protest movements of so many different kinds as well as a growing cultural acceptance of the appropriateness of expressing feelings—the expression of anger, or the rhetoric of anger, itself underwent inflation. For the key emotional term from the rhetorical arsenal of anger that Friedan deploys in *The Fountain of Age* is that of rage. Although she often uses rage and anger interchangeably, rage is her preferred term. It appears over and over in *The Fountain of Age*. The rhetoric has escalated, and yet the message of *The Fountain of Age* is superficially optimistic.[21]

What does rage signify? Is it intense protest, as in the black rage movement of the 1960s? Or does it carry the debilitating connotation of emotional pathology, as rage in women often does? Or is it something else? For even more than the association of anger and the elderly, the conjoining of rage and the elderly would seem to be a virtual cultural impossibility, an oxymoron.

For Friedan rage is an energy that is created by the thwarting of possibilities. When rage is turned in on oneself rather than outward it is transformed into depression—that is, into an equal and opposite force that paralyzes innate energy or healthy aggression. As Friedan writes, "In age as in youth," depression "is the outcome of rage turned inward" (61). She understands rage as a response to powerlessness. If women under the influence of the feminine mystique in the 1950s internalized their rage, which worked its will on the body, manifesting itself in headaches, depression, inchoate confusion, and the like, similarly Friedan concludes—and it is a provocative deduction—that the high rate of depression among the elderly is due precisely to the *cultural* vicissitudes of aging. "Knowing all the reasons we have to be angry, lonesome, or afraid, one can only suspect that an awful lot of older people are suppressing an awful lot of rage," she writes. "And if, indeed, depression in old and young alike is defined as unbearable rage turned against oneself, small wonder that depression is endemic in older people" (450). Thus anger—or indeed an unbearable rage—is not available as energy. Rather it is invisible and immobilized; it is masked and manifested only in depression that is, she implies, wrongly treated as a physiological disease and not correctly understood as a symptom of social suffering.[22] Rage is unconscious. It is silent.

Can we imagine the Betty Friedan of *The Fountain of Age*, like the sixty-year-old Germaine Greer, getting angry? Can we imagine her using the rhetoric of anger to politicize prejudicial cultural practices against the old? The answer is no—and some of the reasons for this answer are similar to those we find in *Senescence*. Like Hall, Friedan believes that as people grow older they become more themselves, more individual. Imagine the difficulties of forming a political interest group on the basis of age alone, a huge and heterogeneous group of people not only characterized by many social differences (class, religion, and ethnicity, among others) but also by hyperindividuality. Yet just as the empowerment of women was a rallying cry in the 1960s, Friedan insists on the empowerment of age. The second wave of feminism drew both spontaneously and strategically on anger. However Friedan doesn't think that the empowerment of age can be based on the model of the women's movement. Why not? In great part because her conceptualization of the special strengths that can come with age are in conflict with such a rhetoric of the emotions.

Friedan wants to put the accent on the positive, to substitute a model of growth for the disabling model of decline. A model of growth implies the development of something new. And in fact the word "new" rings like a bell throughout the book. For her, age means the potential of inventing new ways of living in the crucial domains of work and love. Just as the doors to the work world needed to be opened for women, so too do they need to be reopened to the old. Friedan believes—correctly in my judgment—that the institution of retirement on the basis of chronological age is the critical factor today in the ideology of age as decline (obviously many people want or need to retire because their jobs are unsatisfying or debilitating—she is not referring to such situations).[23] Thus there are contradictions here of which she is fully aware.

Friedan argues, like Hall, that the human race has been given these extra years by evolution (she cites the sociobiologist E. O. Wilson), and she concludes that these very years must have some special evolutionary significance. It is our responsibility, she insists, to fulfill that task. What special capacities will be developed with age in order to allow one to perform this task well? One of the answers is—we may not be surprised to learn—wisdom. Wisdom is, she writes, "the ability to see the picture whole, and its meaning deep, and to tell it true" (216).[24]

If Hall found a way to put wisdom to work, Friedan finds a way to put it in the workplace. "Could the growing need for such wisdom transcending narrow expertise in every field provide the pragmatic, social basis for the fountain of age?" she asks rhetorically (244). Thus Friedan's notion of wisdom is in part wisdom of a practical nature, echoing a meaning attributed to wisdom in the *Oxford English Dictionary* as "sound sense, esp. in practical affairs." She also suggests that along with wisdom in age, which implies wholeness, may come a host of qualities—"freedom from youthful competitive compulsion, cooperation, empathy" (326). Wisdom, lack of competition, cooperation, empathy: these are all qualities virtually antithetical to anger.

Where, then, does the rage go? It is not transformed into outrage, into anger at injustice. Like Hall, Friedan opens *The Fountain of Age* on a note of depression. She confides that she was depressed for weeks after her friends threw her a surprise party on her sixtieth birthday, forcing her to acknowledge publicly that she had indeed arrived at that culturally constricting number. Like Hall, in the course of writing her book (and of living her life), her depression lifts. In *The Fountain of Age* Friedan presents herself as not only reflecting in creative ways on the possibilities of age but also as embodying them—taking risks, imagining new ways of loving, and inventing a new style of being an activist.[25]

What accounts for this transformation from depression to vital aging? For Friedan one of the important strategies of the women's movement was *emotion talk* (this is my phrase). As she writes in *The Fountain of Age*, talking about one's feelings and claiming them is crucial—"the rages and angers and humiliations, the passivities and dependencies, that had been encouraged in us so long and still held us back" (156). In *The Fountain of Age* she claims her own feelings—of depression and exhilaration. But she doesn't extend the model of consciousness-raising in the women's movement to age. She doesn't imagine the sharing of feelings of anger, never mind unbearable rage. Was rage buried behind her own depression? In *The Fountain of Age* the rhetoric of rage, so prevalent and so surprising, ultimately serves merely as an empty sign of social suffering. In a sense it isn't given a body. Friedan doesn't seem to write out of anger or rage. Nor does she quote people who voice their rage.

For Friedan rage in the old is repressed, a symptom of cultural pathology. Wisdom is a sign of the achievement of one's possibilities in age, with rage expelled. Wisdom and rage: like magnets pointed toward each other, they repel one another. In the 1960s black rage as a rallying cry performed important cultural work. Rage meant outrage at racial injustice. But a wise rage? For Friedan it is a cultural contradiction in terms when it comes to aging.

But there is one curious passage in *The Fountain of Age* where a manic rage surfaces. Friedan opens her chapter "Intimacy: Beyond the Dreams of Youth" with a frightening dream:

> I had a dream: In my house, propped up against a wall, pushed out of the way, was something quite large, all wrapped up in a rug. Like a mummy. And I said, "What is wrapped up in that rug?" No one was paying any attention to it, it didn't really get in the way. But I didn't want something wrapped up, hidden like that in my house. I insisted on slitting it open.
>
> There was a woman wrapped up in the rug, and she was still alive! She was not young but she had longish light hair and a glint in her eye, and she was brandishing a knife in her hand. I woke up in horror and sat up in my bed. There was a live woman I had wrapped up in that rug, and she was going to kill me if I didn't let her out. So I went to see my old shrink, and I said, Given the realities, the numbers, my age, how could I live with the woman I had wrapped up in that rug? She was alive, but how could I let her out without her exploding with rage—that knife in her hand? And I felt the pain of my own yearning. (254)

Friedan doesn't comment on this dream. Instead she lets it stand as testimony to the banal insight that we all need love and that older women are much more likely to suffer from a lack of sexual intimacy than are men. The striking incongruity between the wild energy represented in the dream and the calm therapeutic tone of her authoritative exposition— "Without love, the human self never develops at all" (254)—belies the still-buried rage, the rage she could not conjoin with wisdom. Elsewhere in *The Fountain of Age*, in a passage that goes against the grain of the argument in her book, she remarks, "Research has shown an actual strong relationship between 'irascibility' and longevity. Could that very rage, long buried in women, which we have now managed to express, breaking down the barriers and the false images that once made us turn it against ourselves, be part of the fountain of age?" (156). She allows her own important rhetorical question to hang unanswered in the air.

3

Hall understood himself to be part of an emerging vanguard of older people. He allowed his anger at being marginalized with retirement and old age to surface, and, fortified with this energy and the paradigm of adolescence, he imagined himself at the forefront of a new generation of older people at a critical juncture in history. Wise men would be stern counselors to future generations. The aged would embody the future. With the exception of the scholarly history of gerontology, history has forgotten Hall's vision of aging.

Friedan, like the French feminist Simone de Beauvoir before her, uses her long experience as a feminist activist and writer to address old age as the next political battle to be fought. Although *The Fountain of Age* is a protest against the ideology of old age in the United States, and although, in comparison with Hall, Friedan seems to up the ante with a rhetoric of rage, that rhetoric of rage turns out to be curiously empty—it is devoid of energy, concealed as depression. Ultimately Friedan also turns to wisdom as a way of conceiving the special strengths of the old. On the one hand, her notion of wisdom is more pragmatic than that of Hall. On the other hand it is also a more romantic version of wisdom—one that relies on the twentieth-century psychological tradition of the reconciliation of gender opposites explored by Jung and others. But notwithstanding their somewhat different understandings of wisdom, both Hall and Friedan assign the social role of wisdom to the elderly. This is a clear example of what Paul Griffiths, a philosopher of the emotions, has called the social construction of emotions, where certain emotions—here the psychological stance of wisdom, a philosophic calm—are invoked to reinforce certain social roles.[26] As an ideal attribute or emotional standard long associated with the old, wisdom in effect has suppressed the emotional experience of anger.

Both Hall and Friedan advocate what thirty years ago the cultural historian Gerald Gruman called *re-engagement*. In a brilliant analysis of the forces that have worked to construct the modernist life course, one in which the elderly are relegated to the margins, Gruman argues that it is precisely the old who have a future: "In the furthering of a genuinely modern culture, it is the aging who actually have pride of place; they are where the action is, for they are something historically *new* as a large population sector" (380). Significantly, unlike Hall and Friedan, Gruman doesn't find it necessary to invoke wisdom as a way to graciously bestow a social role on the elderly, a role that over the course of the twentieth century has been extolled as crucial to society as a whole but in reality has been ignored or dismissed as useless.[27] Nor does Gruman feel obliged to rationalize the years given to us by the longevity revolution by arguing that they serve an evolutionary purpose.

It is time to declare a moratorium on wisdom. I don't mean that we would not be correct to describe certain people as wise or certain actions or judgments as wise. Indeed I'm taken with Margaret Gullette's way of approaching the question of wisdom. She is not so much interested in wisdom as an asset or an attribute that takes the linguistic concrete shape of a predicate adjective (she is "wise") or a noun ("wisdom"). Rather she is interested in the comparative quality of making judgments as one passes through time and life because one has "had more time . . . to meditate about life's risky accidents."[28] What I mean is that we should not resort to wisdom in theorizing or imagining a social role for older people in general. Wisdom should not be advocated as an emotional (or unemotional) standard or ideal.[29] Lest it be thought that this is not a widespread practice, consider the statement in 1999 by Mary Robinson, then head of the Office of the High Commissioner for Human Rights, on human rights and older persons. "The wisdom and experience which come with age are vital assets for society and should be acknowledged as such," she insists (iii).[30]

I believe that the cultural reflex of associating wisdom and age reproduces a stereotype that doesn't carry real meaning in contemporary western societies. Moreover, there is absolutely no need to have to justify—through the lens of the development of wisdom—the extraordinary extension of life expectancy that has been gained over the twentieth century. The notion of wisdom as a developmental capacity that ideally characterizes old age interferes with the crucial work that needs to be done to reclaim these years as meaningful in the broadest sense. Wisdom carries the connotation of detachment, hence, as we see in Hall and Friedan, the extreme difficulty of putting it together with engagement, or reengagement. With its emphasis on detachment, wisdom justifies the disengagement theory of aging; that is, the theory that older people "naturally" withdraw from their social roles so as to make their ultimate disappearance—death—less difficult for the smooth functioning of society. Wisdom carries the connotation of dignified behavior, hence the further difficulty of its association with a rhetoric of protest. It implies a kind of transcendence of the social world, a certain timelessness, a knowledge that is—there is of course a contradiction here—not characterized by one's placement in the world, or by what Donna Haraway long ago called situated knowledge.[31]

In terms of a cultural politics of the emotions, angry women have long been labeled by men (or male-identifying women) as irrational or hysterical. The strategy is to demean such women. Analogously, anger in the old is outlawed. Here anger is what Jaggar has called an "outlaw emotion," one that is "conventionally unacceptable" (160). On the social stage in the United States there has been one notable exception to the rule of outlawing angry old women, and that is the late Maggie Kuhn of the Gray Panthers (Kuhn founded the Gray Panthers in the 1970s in the wake of her forced retirement at the age of sixty-five). Why was her behavior acceptable? I would venture that it was tolerated in part because of her petite stature (as a diminutive woman she wasn't seen as a threat) and in part because the project of the Gray Panthers was always intergenerational and not limited to aging. Ultimately Kuhn wasn't taken seriously but rather patronized as cute, while the Gray Panthers were seen as a nonthreatening knockoff of the Black Panthers.

Angry challenges to ageism should not be dismissed. Anger can be a sign of moral outrage at social injustice and at being denied the right to participate fully in society. Anger in this sense is a judgment, or more strongly, an indictment. As the late philosopher Robert Solomon argues in *The Passions*, "An emotion is a *judgment* (or a set of judgments), something we do. An emotion is a (set of) judgments(s) which constitute our world, our surreality, and its intentional objects" (185). I find compelling Germaine Greer's declaration that it is time to get angry again. I am reminded of Gloria Steinem's very first words in her essay "Doing Sixty," published in 1994, in which she acknowledges the contradiction between the cultural ideal of detachment expected of her and her own intense reactions to injustice. "Age is supposed to create more serenity, calm, and detachment from the world, right? Well," she concludes, "I'm finding just the reverse" (249).[32]

We need to change the affect script for older people in our culture.[33] How do we do this? In great part by telling stories. Stories relay forms of feeling, and one of the stories of aging and anger that has remained long in my mind is that told by the feminist activist Barbara Macdonald. Fittingly enough the incident she recounts occurred while she was on a protest march in Boston in the late 1970s—a March to Take Back the Night, from men. Macdonald, a sixty-five-year-old lesbian, had a premonition that the march wouldn't achieve its objective. But she didn't suspect just who her antagonist would be. She wasn't sure she wanted to go, she told her partner, Cynthia. She "had a vague feeling of dragging" her feet. Wasn't this kind of march pointless because men had the power and wouldn't take it seriously? Cynthia, twenty years younger than Macdonald, persuades her to go. If it doesn't convince the men, Cynthia assures her, never mind, it will be good for us. Cynthia was wrong.

It is a dark and rainy night, and the people helping to assemble the women give them instructions. Six abreast. Walk closely together. Don't let men break your ranks. Barbara's uneasiness is gone, and she is eager to move forward. She feels strong. "I felt," she writes, "the exhilaration, the oneness with the women around me, the sense of at last doing something instead of passively grinding my teeth with anger, as I do every morning when I pick up the *Globe* to see what woman was murdered the night before" (28). Then, waiting to begin, she notices Cynthia talking quietly with one of the young women monitoring the march. Barbara joins them, and the monitor says to her, " 'If you think you can't keep up, you should go to the head of the march' " (28).

What did that mean? Understanding hits Barbara like a series of hammer blows. It's because she's perceived by a younger woman as old and therefore as weak—and, more ominously, as lacking in judgment. That the younger woman is well meaning and contrite doesn't change the fundamental situation. Barbara feels exiled by this younger woman and by the women's movement itself. She feels infantilized. And she snaps back at her. She begins and finishes the march in a rage. As she writes, "All my life in a man's world, I was a problem because I was a woman; now I'm a problem in a woman's world because I'm a sixty-five-year-old woman" (30).

Where does her rage go? Unlike Friedan's rage it doesn't remain buried in her dreamlife. Reflecting hard on this incident later, given a kind of strength from her rage, Macdonald resolves neither to direct it toward the younger woman—that doesn't seem quite fair—nor to turn it against herself and her own aging body, a body which, by her account, reads as sixty-five.[34] The intensity of her rage is wisely proportionate to the offense. It is symmetrical to the structure of power in which she finds herself unfairly meshed.[35] Her rage is dispelled when she decides to fight back with what force she has. Her rage is dispelled as she analyzes the incident, placing it in historical context, comparing the first wave of feminism with the second, and puzzling over the fact that in the first wave of feminism older women were the leaders, whereas in the second wave it is younger women —women in their twenties and thirties—who were and still are predominant. Why is that? She concludes that this can't be explained by a simple emphasis on youth culture in the United States. Today, she writes, "youth is bonded with patriarchy in the enslavement of the older woman. There would, in fact, be no youth culture without the powerless older woman" (39).[36]

If Macdonald puts aside her rage, she safeguards her anger. Her anger is the precious residue of her rage.[37] "Although much of what happened to me in the march is resolved for me," she writes, "I am still angry at the ageism in the women's movement" (35–36). I take it that her anger in part motivated the important small book she wrote with Cynthia Rich, a book that gives us this notable story. It is an instance of what Margaret Gullette has called, in *Declining to Decline*, "age autobiography." Echoing the critical race theorist Patricia Williams, I would say that Macdonald's story is "a gift of intelligent rage" (216). Would I call Macdonald a wise old woman? No, because this would call up another image altogether, of a woman who is calmly dispassionate, who has a benign and detached sense of perspective, and who can dispense a measured and balanced knowledge of the world. Macdonald's story, however, is one of an anger that, upon reflection, turns out to have been wise. It was time for her to get angry again.

Both Hall and Friedan envisage aging as a time when there is important work to be done in service to society and to the self. We might understand Macdonald's anger, then, as the impetus for a certain kind of work—as protest against injustice and as the intellectual work of the historical understanding of the roots of ageism against women. From this perspective anger provides not only the energy for work—it *is* work. When one is

three

RACIAL SHAME, MASS-MEDIATED SHAME, MUTUAL SHAME

She taught me that confusion and chaos themselves could be
a defense against clarity because of fear of pain or rage.
—Jane Lazarre, *Wet Earth and Dreams*

Fully faced, shame may become not primarily something to be
covered, but a positive experience of revelation.
—Helen Merrell Lynd,
On Shame and the Search for Identity

Shame tells a story—that we hold certain ideals, that these
represent things we value enough to strive for, that we respect
our own ability to choose them as worth striving for and our
own capacities to achieve these goals.
—Berenice Fisher, "Guilt and Shame in the
Women's Movement"

In the previous chapter I considered the relation between emotions and stages of life, focusing on older age and concluding with a story that has long been important to me about an angry older woman. How did Barbara Macdonald come to understand herself as old and exiled from the front lines? In an uncanny flash she sees herself through the eyes of a younger woman whose gaze brands Macdonald as an old woman. What I call the youthful structure of the look fixes her in its sights. In our profoundly ageist society, gender and age structure each other in a complex set of reverberating feedback loops conspiring to render the older female body paradoxically both hypervisible and invisible. For the truth is that women are deemed old in our society—are aged by culture—far earlier than are men.

But for Barbara Macdonald anger provides the necessary impetus to question the humiliation she experiences at the hands of a younger woman. The pain of her shame prompts her to reflect on the context of her experience, leading her to the searing insight that older women are devalued by both men and younger women alike. Older women, she concludes, are ejected from the social body as abject. Older women are the third term that threatens to destabilize the value placed on youth, with younger women understood as a commodity enjoyed by many older men. The anger she experiences at her humiliation serves her as an outlaw emotion.

In telling her story (and it is one that has circulated widely), Macdonald offers us the opportunity to share her important analysis and to understand our own experience in the present—or in the time to come. As Alison Jaggar writes in "Love and Knowledge: Emotion in Feminist Epistemology," "When certain emotions are shared or validated by others . . . the basis exists for forming a subculture defined by perceptions, norms, and values" (160). Thus outlaw emotions, because of their epistemological potential, may be politically constructive, leading to the building of communities. What examples does Jaggar offer? Among them are pride and anger, along with its family member, outrage. Crucial to Jaggar is the idea that we must be able to *name* our experience. As I have been insisting, we must be able to *narrate* our experience.

If in the previous chapter I support Jaggar's conviction that anger can possess a cognitive edge as an outlaw emotion, with older people as my case in point, I also call attention to the devolution of unconscious rage into depression, a situation in which anger is unavailable as a catalyst for analysis. In this chapter I explore the emotion of shame by posing the question of its cognitive potential. As with the visual economy of old age, shame in its tragic dimension is often underwritten by a brutal visual economy. If shame is most often paired with guilt, here I am primarily interested in its potential relation to anger as an outlaw emotion.

Shame, we should also remember, is associated predominantly with the young. For Freud shame is the more "primitive" or "infantile" emotion, one that in the normal course of things should be eclipsed by the more complex emotion of guilt. For Freud guilt is based on the internalization of values, whereas shame is experienced earlier and is based on external disapproval by others (here we see a visual economy at work). For Freud shame should yield to guilt in the course of moral development not only on the level of the individual but also on the level of the history of a civilization. But shame, I will argue in the course of this chapter, persists long after childhood and in given situations has the potential to be redescribed as a morally salutary and mature emotion.[1]

I open this chapter with a discussion of three influential models of shame that underscore its potentially transformative force. I then turn to two vastly dissimilar cultural worlds, from different decades in the United States, that challenge these models. The first is the poetic world of the novel. I consider Toni Morrison's *The Bluest Eye*, which was published in 1970 and set in the early-1940s in rural Ohio where the action takes place in the intimate locus of intersecting families and across generations. I argue that the racial shame Morrison portrays follows a logic that departs decisively from these models of shame. The second world is the mass-mediated one of the mid-1990s where the visual structure of shame, saturating everyday life in the United States, is beginning to go aggressively televisual. If for three centuries the press has been understood as one of the crucial components of a civil society if not the public sphere, by the mid-1990s consumer culture is indistinguishable from the mass media that sells shame as sensational news. If the psychological emotions of Morrison's characters are foregrounded in her eloquent novel, in mass-mediated scenarios of shame from the 1990s we witness the emergence of a structure of feeling where shame is, on the one hand, sold on the market as pride and where, on the other, individuals are crushed by shame in the crosshairs of the media. Shame has become a lucrative commodity, and in the process it would seem that interiority is itself evacuated, sucked up and out by the media itself. My point is that shame, generally understood as a psychological emotion, now circulates widely in mass-mediated culture as life-denying sensation. My further point is that shame persists beyond childhood and that there are many models of it, including that of mutual shame—shame as a salutary social emotion—which I consider in the final section of this chapter.

1

Consider the important accounts of shame offered over the course of the twentieth century by the existentialist Jean-Paul Sartre, the feminist writer Virginia Woolf, and the queer theorist Eve Kosofsky Sedgwick. My central concern is how these three figures envision the relationship between emotion and knowledge, or what I call the cognitive edge of the emotions. In effect I trace a genealogy of models of shame. But I don't mean to imply that the second two accounts I discuss supersede the first, although it is the case that both Woolf's model and that of Sedgwick serve to critique that of Sartre. So I begin with Sartre, whose *Being and Nothingness* was published in the mid-1940s—long after *A Room of One's Own* and long before Sedgwick's "Queer Performativity." My point is that the relationship between shame and knowledge varies radically according to context, with age being an exceedingly important factor along with race, gender, and sexual orientation. Thus as we will see, none of these three models obtains in the world of *The Bluest Eye* or in the world of mass-mediated shame from the mid-1990s.

In *Being and Nothingness* Sartre elaborates a model of how we're made conscious of ourselves and in particular of our acts, so that ultimately we can judge them and ourselves in the eyes of the world. It is through the mental act of assuming the position of an other who is contemplating us, Sartre theorizes, that we're struck into consciousness of ourselves in time and space. Central to Sartre's hypothetical scenario is the emotion of shame. "Let us imagine," Sartre writes, "that moved by jealousy, curiosity, or vice I have just glued my ear to the door and looked through a keyhole" (259). It is only when this person, surreptitiously watching someone through a keyhole, realizes *he* is also being watched that he is struck into consciousness —that is, into shame. "Somebody was there and has seen me. Suddenly I realize the vulgarity of my gesture, and I am ashamed" (221).

I want to underscore three points. First, the "I" in Sartre's account is implicitly gendered male and is understood to be a moral agent—indeed the subject of the discourse of moral philosophy itself. As an existentialist Sartre places a great stress on freedom of choice and the responsibility of the individual for his actions, or on what today we would call moral agency, if not autonomy. Second, Sartre's model is dramaturgical. There is a clearly defined structure and plot to the etiology of shame. It arises suddenly, theatrically, as if it were a flammable material, a flash point inherent in the implicit doubled-over structure of the unseen spectator. It is as if at the moment when the secretive spectator, who is watching someone else, realizes he is being watched by yet a third person that shame bursts spontaneously into combustion. Third, Sartre stresses that the "I" has indeed done wrong and is right to feel shame—that is, that shame in this case is an appropriate emotion, a self-evaluating and ethical emotion. Notice that Sartre is careful to say that this "I" is motivated to peek through the keyhole by "jealousy, curiosity, or vice," which are scarcely noble intentions (259).

In the long chapter in *Being and Nothingness* in which this thought experiment takes place Sartre is primarily concerned with what it means to be struck into being philosophically, to achieve what he refers to as a "transcendental" point of view, one to which he can "refer his acts so as to qualify them"—that is, judge them (259). His model also contains a theory of shame as a highly dramatized emotion that grants an intensely embodied sense of being. The "I" feels "vulnerable"; the "I" "has a body which can be hurt" (259). This sense of embodiment, Sartre suggests, is the ground for gaining the transcendental perspective necessary for judging one's actions. Ultimately, however, for Sartre the emotion of shame is not of essential interest here at all. Indeed emotion itself is not of essential interest. His mode is that of philosophical reason, one that in the end reinforces the divide between the abstract and the emotional in western philosophy, a divide that is deplored by Barbara Christian in her influential essay "The Race for Theory."

A strikingly different model of shame and its relation to knowledge is presented in Woolf's *A Room of One's Own*. As in my discussion of this piece in an earlier chapter, I focus on the brilliant passage in which we find the writer doing research for her upcoming lecture on women and fiction in the large reading room of the British Museum. Daunted by the sheer amount written on women by men and confused by the contradictory nature of their contents—"It was distressing, it was bewildering, it was humiliating" (30)—she responds, unconsciously at first, to one particular book entitled *The Mental, Moral, and Physical Inferiority of Women* by Professor von X. While waiting idly for other books to be brought to her desk, she doodles absently in her notebook, drawing in anger. And what is she drawing? She realizes with a start that she's drawing *his* angry face, which she then proceeds to deface with pleasure:

> Anger had snatched my pencil while I dreamt. But what was anger doing there? Interest, confusion, amusement, boredom—all these emotions I could trace and name as they succeeded each other throughout the morning. Had anger, the black snake, been lurking among them? Yes, said the sketch, anger had. It referred me unmistakably to the one book, to the one phrase, which had roused the demon; it was the professor's statement about the mental, moral and physical inferiority of women. My heart had leapt. My cheeks had burnt. I had flushed with

anger. There was nothing specially remarkable, however foolish, in that. One does not like to be told that one is naturally the inferior of a little man. (32)

This fictional scene explicitly identifies the emotion of anger as central to its hypothetical drama. But critical to it as well is the unnamed emotion of shame. The words of the pompous professor are insulting. They serve to blatantly pronounce the reader's exorbitant inferiority in every conceivable respect. They shame her as a woman, a shame that is keenly felt. "My heart had leapt. My cheeks had burnt." Shame is first. It is rapidly succeeded by anger.

In Woolf's drama the etiology of anger is shame. Anger is the boiling point of shame. Her analysis of anger, and by implication her analysis of shame, leads to knowledge. In her scenario it is crucial that both shame and anger be expressed and acknowledged.[2] Anger serves the function of appropriate self-defense and retaliation, which in A Room of One's Own is wonderfully imaginative, suggestive of the unruly student. Anger is burned away in the process, leaving the possibility of the power of re-flection in its wake. As Woolf marvelously describes her counterattack, she "began drawing cart-wheels and circles over the angry professor's face till he looked like a burning bush or a flaming comet—anyhow, an apparition without human semblance or significance. The professor was nothing now but a faggot burning on the top of Hampstead Heath" (32). Once these heated emotions subside, she turns to reflecting on them. She doesn't have "a surplus of anger," in Elizabeth Abel's phrase.[3] She uses these emotions as touchstones to probe their causes, and she arrives at an analysis of the unequal relations of power in terms of gender. "Soon my own anger was explained and done with; but curiosity remained. How explain the anger of the professors?" (32). Like Sartre's shame, Woolf's anger is a self-regarding emotion. Importantly it is an other-regarding emotion as well.

As opposed to Sartre's male "I" peering through a keyhole, here we have shame gendered female. This is shame ascribed to others by those in power—men—not on the basis of what one *does* but rather on the basis of what one *is*. What other evidence does she cite? Woolf refers us to the world of research as well as to mass culture. She quotes Trevelyan who in his *History of England* writes that wife beating "was a recognized right of man, and was practiced without shame by high as well as low" (54). She notes the headline in the daily paper heralding the pronouncements of a divorce court judge on the "Shamelessness of Women" (43). Woolf astutely concludes that in the emotional economy of patriarchy men simply aren't expected to feel shame when they do something for which they *should* feel ashamed while women are unfairly denounced as "shameless" for behavior that is routinely accepted in men. There is a double standard when it comes to shame.

Thus in Woolf's *A Room of One's Own* shame isn't presented as an ethical emotion as it is in Sartre's *Being and Nothingness*. There it is underscored that the male "I" had indeed done something for which he should rightly feel shame. In *A Room of One's Own*, on the other hand, it is the acknowledgment and analysis of shame and anger that lead to an evaluation of the larger system of the relations of power in which women are enmeshed. Shame is brought to consciousness through the medium of anger; the treatment of women, which results in the feeling of shame, is understood to be unjust. Woolf concludes that the attribution of inferiority to women, by imputation a condition of shame, serves to maintain male superiority. Thus Woolf wonderfully dramatizes Alison Jaggar's conviction that the emotions of those in a position of oppression should be accorded epistemological privilege.

Finally, I want to stress that in *A Room of One's Own* shame is not considered in terms of its relation to guilt but in terms of its relation to anger. At stake is a cultural politics of the emotions. Shame is infantilizing, but ultimately it is not an infantile emotion. I want to underscore here that the emotional sequencing of shame and anger is crucial: anger follows shame.

Eve Kosofsky Sedgwick radicalizes shame in her influential essay "Queer Performativity: Henry James's *The Art of the Novel*." This piece is a virtual extravaganza on behalf of the transformational power of shame, one itself written in a flamboyant mode. Because the stigma of being gay is so profound and the scene of such deep shame in childhood so traumatic, such shame, Sedgwick argues, is a potentially endless source of energy. "If queer is a politically potent term, which it is, that's because, far from being capable of being detached from the childhood scene of shame," she writes, "it cleaves to that scene as a near-inexhaustible source of transformational energy" (4). How can a term, which is both a symptom of prejudice and a chosen identity, transform shame into pride?

Sedgwick insists, of course, that different cultures legislate different regimes of shame. But the emphasis in her essay is on the liberation of shame as energy. Shame is a "free radical," she writes, one that "attaches to and permanently intensifies or alters the meaning of—of almost anything: a zone of the body, a sensory system, a prohibited or indeed a permitted behavior, another affect such as anger or arousal, a named identity, a script for interpreting other people's behavior toward oneself" (12). What is the example on which she grounds her argument? She offers the case of the older Henry James looking back, in shameful pain, at his younger self.

Unlike the models of shame offered by Sartre and by Woolf, here it is not another person who is looking at James, striking him into shame, but rather James himself. The older James was deeply distressed, Sedgwick tells us, over the commercial failure of one of his books (a compilation of his important short stories and novels); rereading his earlier work and witnessing its contemporary failure caused him the pain of self-shame. And yet somehow the still-surviving force of the stigma of shame from his youth provided him with the impetus to recover from this depression: shame is transformed into an eroticized "impudence," resulting in a tender bond between the older Henry James and his younger self. Writing of shame through the elegance of Henry James but also in ratcheting it up, Sedgwick offers an account of shame as almost precious in multiple senses of the term, something to be cherished, something ornamental, almost an *affectation*, a "betraying blazon" to be put "*in* circulation—as the sign of a tenderly strengthened and indeed now 'irresistible' bond between the writer of the present and the abashed writer of the past" (9). (I confess that it is not at all clear to me how this transformation in Henry James comes about. I am tempted to read it as a sign of maturity, of James's acceptance of his younger self, and to consider Sedgwick's reading of James anachronistic, one that projects the 1980s and 1990s potency of "queer" into the past.)

If for Woolf the key sequence of emotions is shame-anger, for Sedgwick it is shame-pride. Indeed Sedgwick seems to understand these two emotions not in terms of a sequence but as two sides of a coin. As she writes, "Shame effaces itself; shame points and projects; shame turns itself skin side outside; shame and pride, shame and self-display, shame and exhibitionism are different interlinings of the shame glove" (5). But not all shame, only "transformational shame" (5). What makes shame transformational? By putting it this way, it should be clear that to argue that the emotion of shame itself is—or can be—transformational is misleading. It isn't the affect itself—or by itself—that carries the potential for transformation. It is, rather, the very context of a politicized movement. Sedgwick wants to recuperate shame for activism, including a radical queer theory, and it is precisely the social context of a supportive community that provides the ground for the transformation of shame into pride, one that can be exhibited proudly, defiantly, even luxuriantly.[4] Here shame bears affinities to Alison Jaggar's notion of an outlaw emotion in that it is understood as providing a basis for a subculture. But Sedgwick insists that "affirmative reclamation" of shame will never be sufficient to extirpate the negative valence or stigma of gay shame. As she writes, "the main reason why the self-application of 'queer' by activists has proven so volatile is that there's *no* way that any amount of affirmative reclamation is going to succeed in detaching the word from its associations with shame and with the terrifying powerlessness of gender-dissonant or otherwise stigmatized childhood" (4). Thus ultimately shame serves less as an emotion with cognitive potential per se than as a source—in the context of the 1980s and 1990s—of consolidating identity.[5] What is interesting to me here in terms of theories of the emotions is that Sedwick emphasizes the importance of emotion as energy, as "transformational energy" (4). For her, shame, in the guise of queer shame, does not serve an ethical purpose, as it does in Sartre's account of shame. Nor does it seem at base a psychological emotion, as it is in Woolf's scenario. Rather her account of radical shame— although it has, as I mentioned above, affinities with Jaggar's notion of an outlaw emotion—seems similar to *intensities*.

Sedgwick wants, she says, to remove shame from a moralistic or evaluative framework. "In the ways I want to be thinking about shame," she writes, "the widespread moralistic valuation of this powerful affect as *good* or *bad, to be mandated* or *to be excised*, according to how one plots it along a notional axis of prohibition/permission/requirement, seems distinctly beside the point" (8). Among other things, Sedgwick is referring to what she calls "the neo-conservative framework that treasures shame along with guilt as an adjunct of repression and an enforcer of proper behavior"

(8). I do not, however, want to give up a moral or evaluative framework in the analysis of shame, especially as I turn now to Toni Morrison's *The Bluest Eye*.

2

In Morrison's *The Bluest Eye* it is precisely the question of moral agency that is at stake. For in the novel the spectatorial model of shame we find in Sartre doesn't result in a transcendental point of view from which the characters can freely judge their acts. Nor, as in the self-reflexive model of shame and anger narrated in Woolf, does the experience of shame and anger ultimately offer the characters of *The Bluest Eye* an understanding of their position in society in terms of power. Nor does the potent stigma of racial shame in youth serve as a near-inexhaustible source of transformational energy, as in Sedgwick's account of shame. Instead shame leads either to lacerating violence or to debilitating depression. In the Ohio steel mill town in which the main action of the novel takes place in 1941, shame spreads its fatal stain everywhere and suffocates its residents. Here shame takes on the intense form of racial humiliation or the numbing form of pervasive daily racism, resulting either in trauma or in chronic discrimination—neither of which can be overcome.

Morrison tells the story of a black community torn by multiple experiences of shame—volatile, deadening, sobering. Not only are the sites of potential shame seemingly everywhere but shame is also passed from one generation to the other as a debilitating emotional inheritance. Central to the novel is the story of the eleven-year-old girl named Pecola who is raped by her father. She bears his child, who dies shortly after a premature birth. Pecola sinks into madness, infected by the deluded notion that she has magically been granted her wish for blue eyes and now is exquisitely beautiful in the eyes of white America. A living reminder of the shameful failure of her community to protect her, she grows older as the years pass by. Irreparably stunted, she will never grow up. It is a tragedy.

The nine-year-old character named Claudia serves Morrison as a narrator of the story, a baffled but sensitive witness to Pecola's drama. This is a brilliant choice on Morrison's part because Claudia (along with her ten-year-old sister Frieda) is simply too young to understand why all this is happening. She is, however, acutely aware of the emotional currents into which they are all cast. As Morrison puts it, speaking through Claudia, "the edge, the curl, the thrust, of their emotions is always clear to Frieda and me. We do not, cannot, know the meanings of all their words for we are nine and ten years old" (16). The intelligent point is that the girls are attuned to the moods and emotions enveloping them but can't understand the "meanings" of shame because of their young age. The same holds true for Pecola's mother and father, both of whom, as Morrison makes clear in the course of the narrative, also experienced a defining shame as children.

At the very beginning of the novel we learn that Pecola was raped by her father—his name is Cholly—and thus as readers we're primed to hold little sympathy for him. But Morrison judiciously backs into the generational history of this family, telling us some two-thirds of the way through the novel things that are crucial to our understanding of the inherited and paralyzing shame of this black family born into racist America. We come to know Pecola's father as a youth, and as a boy he is immensely appealing. We come to understand how he could have done this to his daughter, tearing apart his family. Crucial is a searing event in Cholly's early adolescence, a scene of shame so brutal it assumes the proportions of humiliation, marking him for life. That it is linked by Morrison with an altogether everyday occurrence of shame that has nothing to do with racism serves to underscore the overwhelmingly different effects of various kinds of shame. The two events are telescoped into a single and emotionally charged day. Importantly it is the day of the funeral of his great-aunt who had raised him from birth (his mother had abandoned him). At this point Cholly couldn't have been more than thirteen years old.

The first event will be familiar to all of us. It is momentary and harmless, a passing adolescent shame. It doesn't have to do with right and wrong, rather with competence. It is shame that from the vantage point of adulthood would be described as an embarrassment, recounted when one is older with sympathetic humor for oneself. In contrast, the second scene of shame changes Cholly forever. It's an experience from whose humiliating shadow he never escapes and never fully understands. Both scenes serve as rites of passage—the first into adolescent male bonding (what today we call peer pressure), the second into sexuality and racial violence in America.

After his aunt's funeral service Cholly, whom Morrison has presented as a sensitive boy drawn to music and the protective company of adults, finds himself attracted to the exotic world of his older cousins—in particular to a boy named Jake who initiates him into the teenage world of smoking: "The fifteen-year-old Jake offered Cholly a rolled-up cigarette. Cholly took it, but when he held the cigarette at arm's length and stuck the tip of it into the match flame, instead of putting it in his mouth and drawing on it, they laughed at him. Shamefaced, he threw the cigarette down" (114). Here shame has nothing to do with the moral register of right or wrong or with one's essential inferiority in relation to a standard unfairly imposed. Instead shame has to do with a lack of ability or knowledge exposed in the presence of one's social superiors. In relation to Cholly these boys are older and more worldly than is he. This is a minor shame, a mere if momentary painful embarrassment. Cholly immediately seeks to recover his social balance, to reassert himself as an equal in their eyes. That he does so easily is significant given what happens next. When Jake asks Cholly "if he knew any girls," the inexperienced Cholly replies, "Sure" (114). But in truth he's scared when the girls respond to him.

Within a page, we find the young Cholly with a girl named Darlene in a beckoning vineyard of wild grapes on the edge of a pine forest. Night has fallen, and the moon has risen. It's Darlene who encourages their intimacy and guides his body toward hers. Cholly at first takes their roughhousing for child's play. He is portrayed as holding feelings for Darlene that are considerate and tender. Morrison, in other words, makes it absolutely clear that her character Cholly is the kind of boy who wouldn't do anything against Darlene's wishes or harm her in any way. Narrated from his point of view, the scene is sweetly awkward. Then it turns brutal: "Their bodies began to make sense to him, and it was not as difficult as he had thought it would be. . . . Just as he felt an explosion threaten, Darlene froze and cried out. He thought he had hurt her, but when he looked at her face, she was staring wildly at something over his shoulder. He jerked around. There stood two white men. One with a spirit lamp, the other with a flashlight" (116). Structurally this scene is similar to the scenario of shame theorized by Sartre. It is dramaturgical. The "I" is surprised into shame, caught in the act by another person who pronounces a verdict. The economy is visual, underscored by the flashlight pointed by the white men at their will. There is also a doubled-over scene of spectatorship: two men watch him looking at her. But here the similarities end.

For Cholly wasn't doing anything wrong. But he doesn't challenge their authority in any way, either physically or in his mind's eye, as does Woolf's retaliating writer doing research in the British Museum. As a young boy he is "helpless." As a young black boy held at gunpoint by white men he is defenseless in every respect. He can't embody the moral agent of Sartre's *Being and Nothingness*. He doesn't reassert himself as the equal of these men, as he had earlier with the older boys. Worse, he turns the obscene violence of these men against Darlene and not back against them in self-defense and retaliation. The white men sadistically force Cholly to continue—and he does. He's compelled to see Darlene through their voyeuristic eyes. In his eyes she's reduced to a sexual object, degraded to a body to be raped—even less, a body to be feared, a body no longer female and alluring but abjectly animal. Just as is he. About Darlene we learn little. She isn't central to Morrison's story. But as with Cholly at first, her instinctive reaction is to hide her eyes as a way of shielding herself from the shaming eyes of others. If she can't see anything, then perhaps she herself can't be seen:

> There was no place for Cholly's eyes to go. They slid about furtively searching for shelter, while his body remained paralyzed. The flashlight man lifted his gun down from his shoulder, and Cholly heard the clop of metal. He dropped back to his knees. Darlene had her head averted, her eyes staring out of the lamplight into the surrounding darkness and looking almost unconcerned, as though they had no part in the drama taking place around them. With a violence born of total helplessness, he pulled her dress up, lowered his trousers and underwear. . . .
>
> Cholly, moving faster, looked at Darlene. He hated her. He almost wished he could do it—hard, long, and painfully, he hated her so much. The flashlight wormed its way into his guts and turned the sweet taste of muscadine into rotten fetid bile. He stared at Darlene's hands, covering her face in the moon and lamplight. They looked like baby claws. (117)

In this brutal scene the sequencing of emotions is not shame-guilt but shame-rage or shame-hatred, sequences of emotions constitutive of violence. If for Woolf shame leads ultimately to an analysis of the reasons underlying anger, in Morrison shame spirals into a cold hatred against the woman who, as Morrison puts it, "bore witness to his failure, his impotence" (119). Cholly can't draw on his anger to help him understand the situation. Cholly thrusts his anger, which hardens into hate, into her.[6] Moreover he nurtures his hatred, deliberately causing it to grow. I imagine him replaying the event over and over in his mind even as he later avoids having *her* see him. "Never did he once consider directing his hatred toward the hunters," Morrison writes. "Such an emotion would have destroyed him. They were big, white, armed men. He was small, black, helpless" (119). Morrison takes care also to underscore that Cholly never reveals his shame to anyone. He doesn't acknowledge it, even to himself. He doesn't speak it. He doesn't confess it. He flees the town. He is changed forever by what happened that day, stunted in some horrible way, never able to piece the parts of his life together in a way that brings a measure of understanding.

Why can't he tell his story? In *On Private Madness* the psychoanalyst André Green argues that the doubling of anxiety—of separation anxiety and intrusion anxiety (a doubling that clearly characterizes the case of Cholly: as an infant he was separated from his mother and his father, as a youth he is assaulted by white men)—can take on torturing forms, blocking the formation of thought. As Green explains, "The invasion, the impotence, the distress, all give rise to an internal panic which drives the subject to exceed the limits of psychic space by various mechanisms: confusion—which is in fact a dissemination and dilution of conflicting tensions; cathartic action operative like a massive affect storm . . . or the overcathexis of external perception which monopolizes all psychic attention" (208). The intensity of this psychic confusion—an affect storm—explodes the chains of affect—the structures that lend meaning to our experience. Out of this terror cannot be generated a self-reflexive sequence of emotions. The energy available to Cholly from this brutal shaming—indeed to call it "energy" seems wrong—is not transformative in Sedgwick's terms. As he grows older, he cannot look back on his younger self with a warm measure of understanding and acceptance.

This will also be the fate of his daughter. She will not be able to tell her story.

If in *The Bluest Eye* racial shame can yield explosive violence, it is also present in the most mundane transactions of everyday life. This is nowhere clearer than in a scene early in the novel when Pecola, longing for the blue eyes of white America, goes to the store to buy some candy. With her three pennies she decides to buy nine Mary Janes, the penny candy with the picture of a blonde, blue-eyed girl on its wrapper. But the dehumanizing exchange with the store's owner, Mr. Yacobowski (who himself has blue eyes), rattles her anticipation, confusing her and the sources of her happiness: "Slowly, like Indian summer moving imperceptibly toward fall, he looks toward her. Somewhere between retina and object, between vision and view, his eyes draw back, hesitate, and hover. At some fixed point in time and space he senses that he need not waste the effort of a glance. He does not see her, because for him there is nothing to see. How can a fifty-two-year-old white immigrant storekeeper with the taste of potatoes and beer in his mouth, his mind honed on the doe-eyed Virgin Mary, his sensibilities blunted by a permanent awareness of loss, *see* a little black girl?" (41–42). Here Pecola's *not being seen*—that is, not being acknowledged as a member of a community—produces shame just as did Cholly's *being seen*. Paradoxically it comes to the same thing. Pecola and Cholly are both invisible and hypervisible at the same time. It isn't a matter of what one *does* but what one *is*: black in white America. The eleven-year-old Pecola senses the store owner's distaste for her. She grasps that he doesn't want to touch her hand because she's black. But she doesn't understand why she should feel shame. Her shame is to her "inexplicable" (43). In a few paragraphs Morrison brilliantly traces the rapid sequence of Pecola's feelings upon leaving the store:

> Outside, Pecola feels the inexplicable shame ebb.
> Dandelions. A dart of affection leaps out from her to them. But they do not look at her and do not send love back. She thinks, "They *are* ugly. They *are* weeds." Preoccupied with that revelation, she trips on the sidewalk crack. Anger stirs and wakes in her; it opens its mouth, and like a hot-mouthed puppy, laps up the dredges of her shame.
> Anger is better. There is a sense of being in anger. A reality and a presence. An awareness of worth. It is a lovely surging. Her thoughts fall back to Mr. Yacobowski's eyes, his phlegmy voice. The anger will not hold; the puppy is too easily surfeited. Its thirst too quickly quenched, it sleeps. The shame wells up again, its muddy rivulets seeping into her eyes. What to do before the tears come. She remembers the Mary Janes. (43)

Inexplicable shame ebbs, replaced by anger. But it's not anger at the store-keeper. Rather it's anger at herself for having tripped. It's anger displaced onto the dandelions, which she now brands as ugly. "Anger is better. There is a sense of being in anger. A reality and a presence." But the anger just as rapidly subsides and shame again takes its place. What will forestall her tears? Just as Cholly both internalizes the base contempt of the white men and projects it on and into a black woman, so Pecola internalizes the values of white America. She eats the Mary Janes. She swallows her shame. It is a total confusion—that is to say, identification—of happiness with shame. It is an instance of emotional pollution.[7]

Why can't Pecola sustain the anger that gives her a sense of presence—of life—even as the store owner denied it? Morrison suggests that she is too young to recognize its source. Her own anger is like a "puppy." It's too quickly satisfied and exhausted. But what of Cholly? He wasn't much older than Pecola is here when he was forced to turn his lovemaking into rape. Morrison portrays him as cultivating his hatred, clinging to it as an acrid animating force that serves to preempt his shame, effacing it from his consciousness. Anger turned to hatred thus serves him as an impenetrable screen emotion for humiliation. Unlike Pecola's anger, his hatred doesn't dissipate quickly. But that he subsists on his angry hatred over a long period of time in no way implies that he is able to comprehend the meaning of this all-determining traumatic event.

This situation opens up an entire series of fascinating questions. What does it mean that one's anger is "young"? What is the relation between one's age and one's ability to understand the social dynamics of one's emotions? At what age is one able to reflect on one's emotions so as to politicize them, as does the narrator of A Room of One's Own? To what extent does the duration of an emotion make a difference? As parents and teachers of young children remark every day, their emotional life is intense and their emotions are short-lived. On the one hand, Morrison's story suggests that it's not because Pecola's anger is too brief that she accepts her position grounded in shame, but rather because her powers of analysis aren't sufficiently developed. This is primarily a function of her age. But, it will be objected, there are any number of children this age who seem to be able to analyze with astonishing astuteness their anger, say, at a teacher or a parent for unfair treatment. Thus the question to ask is how do gender, race, and age intersect so as to blunt the cognitive power that emotions might provide?

It is the racial structure of shame—shame that is traumatic and chronic—in the world of Morrison's The Bluest Eye that makes shame virtually impossible to overcome.[8] Here the work of the feminist philosopher Sandra Bartky is enormously helpful. In her essay "Shame and Gender" she offers an alternative model to that of Sartre, one based not on the shame resulting from a discrete occurrence, as is his, but on what she calls, following Heidegger, "a pervasive affective attunement, a mode of Being-in-the-world" (97). For Bartky shame is not so much identifiable as a particular emotion as it is virtually inherent in the way one responds to the social world of everyday life as well as to dramatic events. It is an effect of one's subordination in society, a way of perceiving and being in the world that is reinforced at every turn. Bartky's understanding of the relation between shame and gender in a male-dominated society thus echoes that of Woolf. But her analysis of the phenomenology of the emotion of shame is radically different. Moreover Bartky writes as a philosopher, not as an essayist. For Woolf the emotions of shame and anger make themselves felt—they are literary emotions, narrative emotions—and thus are available to analysis. But Bartky calls attention to a pervasive practice of shaming so omnipresent that it recedes into the hum of the background and isn't recognized as something sufficiently dramatic to be considered a threat. Unlike Woolf's narrator in *A Room of One's Own*, women, Bartky concludes, cannot so easily draw on their emotions as cognitive touchstones, in very part because shame, in her account, isn't registered as an identifiable and felt emotion. Rather shame is the *condition* in which many women live, and as such it is virtually unremarked, unfelt, and unseen—as debilitating as toxic levels of carbon monoxide in the atmosphere.

"This shame is manifest in a pervasive sense of personal inadequacy that," Bartky writes, "like the shame of embodiment, is profoundly disempowering" (85). What is so discerning about Bartky's analysis is this: she insists that although what is consistently revealed is precisely one's inferiority, we generally don't understand or comprehend our situation. This is the crux of the matter. As she puts it, "Paradoxically, what is *disclosed* fails, in the typical case, to be *understood*" (97). Why is this so? Bartky stresses that in such situations there is a disjunction between what one feels and what one believes. Women may feel or sense that something about themselves is inadequate, for example, without *believing* themselves to be inadequate. The result is, Bartky concludes, "a confused and divided consciousness" (94). This is key. As Bartky points out, the moral agent of moral psychology and of moral philosophy is theorized as possessing clarity of vision, as "lucid" (95).

Although Bartky doesn't develop this point, central to an analysis of the phenomenology of shame in terms of oppression is *confusion* itself. Confusion, we recall, was explicitly named by the narrator of *A Room of One's Own* as one of the emotions she experienced while reading the words of the disdainful—and totally contemptible—Professor von X. What Bartky theorizes about the constitutive oppression of women can apply equally, if not with greater force, to racial oppression. This helps us understand how Morrison has presented the tragedy that Cholly and Pecola are destined to live out. In a sense neither Cholly nor Pecola *believe* themselves to be inadequate. Pecola, after all, believes that she has finally been granted her wish for blue eyes. But at the same time both *feel* inadequate in the eyes of white America.

Like a low-grade fever, this kind of confusion permeates everyday life in the world of *The Bluest Eye*. In Cholly's forced rape of Darlene and his bewildering rape of his daughter, the cognitive confusion that characterizes racism flares into full-blown psychic trauma. As the psychoanalyst Christopher Bollas argues in *Being a Character*, echoing André Green's important insight that trauma severs the chains of affect by exploding the possibility of a coherent narrative, "Psychic confusion is part of the full effect of trauma because, unable to narrate the event in the first place, the person now re-experiences isolation, this time brought on by the alone-ness of mental confusion" (67). As a young teen, Cholly was forced to rape a black woman. As a preteen, Pecola is raped by her father. Neither of them can narrate these events and both remain tragically isolated. As the psychoanalyst Michael Lewis has also observed, shame disrupts ongoing activity, resulting an inability to think clearly or to act clearly. In the scenes I've invoked from *The Bluest Eye* the confusion entailed in shame is thus not only emotional but cognitive as well. "Shame" and "mortification" are given as synonyms for "confusion" in *The Random House College Dictionary*. "Bewilderment" is noted as one of its meanings. Confusion is unintelligibility, a lack of clarity and lucidity. Indeed confusion itself can be a psychic defense against a clarity that is feared. As Jane Lazarre astutely observes in *Wet Earth and Dreams*, her remarkable memoir of grief and illness, her therapist taught her "that confusion and chaos themselves could be a defense against clarity because of fear of pain or rage" (18).

If we combine this understanding of shame as psychic confusion—an inability to narrate what has happened—with the altogether important fact that Morrison underscores *the young age* at which her characters are subjected to traumatic racist behavior, we can see why they are unable to surmount their shame and remain locked in it. As Jaggar underscores in her essay "Love and Knowledge," "When unconventional emotional responses are experienced by isolated individuals, those concerned may be confused, unable to name their experience" (160). One of the stunning achievements of *The Bluest Eye* is the way in which Morrison presents shame as dramaturgical and traumatic, born of brutalizing violence, *and* as chronic, dispositional, and pervasive in everyday life in this 1940s racist American town. These particularly insidious and potent varieties of shame can't be transformed by the characters into an ethical and political reflection of either a dispassionate or passionate nature. At the heightened pitch of the world of *The Bluest Eye* both the everyday shame and the traumatic shame of racism result in a paralysis of analysis on the part of the characters who are isolated, without a community of their own.

With *The Bluest Eye* in mind, to what extent can we draw on Jaggar's model of the cognitive dimension of the emotions? Rather than Jaggar's model serving to illuminate the novel, I would say that on the contrary the novel suggests the limits of her model. Jaggar offers three emotions—anger, pride, and love—as examples of how the cognitive dimension of emotions function. She does not offer shame as an example. But in *The Bluest Eye* shame doesn't operate as a cognitive touchstone in the instances to which I have referred. Jaggar underscores the epistemological privilege associated with the emotions of the oppressed. But in *The Bluest Eye* racial shame can't be transformed into knowledge. In *The Bluest Eye* racial shame—whether traumatic or chronic—casts the characters into psychic confusion, not cognition. With Pecola, shame isn't converted into knowledge but into depression figured as madness. With the young Cholly, shame is converted into blind anger that hardens into a hatred against someone who has even fewer defenses than he does.[9] In the narrative world of *The Bluest Eye* shame doesn't have a cognitive edge. The characters have no personal control. They exist as isolated individuals severed from any possibility of a community of equals.

For me the final question is one that has haunted the critical reception of Morrison's work. Does *The Bluest Eye* offer the possibility of change?[10] There are two answers to this question—no and yes. Within the action of the story shame can't be transformed into knowledge. To borrow the phrase of the psychoanalyst Helen Lewis, shame is a "feeling trap." Shame remains shame or is disguised as something else; it is covered up by another emotion or another emotion is substituted for it. Moreover shame is recursive. It loops back upon itself. Shame is inherited, passed on from one generation to another. Trauma is intergenerational. Within the world of the novel there is no way out of shame's enclosing circle. Here the answer is definitively no.

But the answer is also yes. *The Bluest Eye* is not philosophy. It does not present an argument. It dramatizes a cultural politics of the emotions, presenting a novelistic world in which shame cannot be transformed into knowledge. But the novel also functions aesthetically on the level of a cultural poetics of the emotions. Morrison's vision in *The Bluest Eye* is intensely moral. In its final pages Morrison creates a literary mood, one that mixes shame with grief in an elegiac mode. The final paragraph of the novel shifts to the present. We've already learned that Pecola's father—with tragic irony Morrison names him Cholly Breedlove—has died. We've learned that Pecola's baby has died. We've learned that Pecola's mother continues to work for white families. But we're not told what year it is or even what decade it is. And this is precisely the point. It is time immemorial. Morrison's conviction is that the black community failed its own and that nothing could have been done to avoid such tragedy in white America. As Morrison writes eloquently in the narrative voice of Claudia who is now older, "It's much, much, much too late" (160).

Yet ironically it is the very poignancy of the final pages of the novel that offers hope for the future. This elegiac sense of an ending is paradoxically generative of hope—of a vision of a more just world in a time to come. Importantly these final pages are written from the perspective of an older voice who at times assumes the burden of her shame, confessing it to us, acknowledging it, understanding the unthinkable tragedy of all these broken lives—Pecola, Cholly, Darlene. Older now, Claudia understands that she and her sister had failed Pecola—as inevitably they would have at that age. "We tried to see her without looking at her, and never, never went near," Morrison writes in Claudia's voice; "Not because she was absurd, or repulsive, or because we were frightened, but because we had failed her" (158). Claudia is convinced she was at fault, and that the flowers—they were marigolds—she had planted didn't grow because she had planted the seeds too deeply, too far from the sun and rain. And in fact everyone in the novel does fail Pecola.

But there is a generative tension between what ideally should have been done and what could never have been done. There is at work a politics of recognition that the fault was not their own. Here are the last lines of the novel: "And now . . . I talk about how I did *not* plant the seeds too deeply, how it was the fault of the earth, the land, of our town. I even think now that the land of the entire country was hostile to marigolds that year. This soil is bad for certain kinds of flowers. Certain seeds it will not nurture, certain fruit it will not bear, and when the land kills of its own volition, we acquiesce and say the victim had no right to live. We are wrong, of course, but it doesn't matter. It's too late. At least on the edge of my town, among the garbage and the sunflowers of my town, it's much, much, much too late" (160). Claudia understands that there was nothing they could have done. It is the very historical foundation of America that killed her people. Thus within the action of the story itself racial shame—traumatic and chronic—can't be transformed into knowledge. It can't be transcended. Within *The Bluest Eye* the black characters feel shame in the land of white America, a space they can't escape. And yet the narrative voice of Morrison's Claudia grants a profound measure of understanding, one that is complex and contradictory.

As readers who aren't part of the drama, we are literary witnesses to that shame. Here lies the possibility of the circulation of shame as literary experience. It is not that as readers we necessarily "identify" with the characters, although some of us might. It is not that we need to feel the specific emotion of shame, although some of us might. Instead the elegiac mood of the last pages—it is complex but not confused, and it conveys a deep sense of perspective—creates a cognitive emotional space where shame might be felt differently: as our collective failure in this country to live up to what should be our ideals.[11] Thus at the heart of *The Bluest Eye* is the hope that shame will be acknowledged and brought into a collective space. Ultimately shame is recast as a potentially reflective, mature emotion.[12]

3

Paradoxically the private experience of reading Morrison's *The Bluest Eye* can underwrite a sense of shame that is intensely moral, a shame associated with civic responsibility and thus dignity, a shame that carries the possibility of a public sphere. Sedgwick theorizes the possibility of a counterpublic created in part through the energy provided by shame. What can we say of the mass-mediation of shame that is played out on the omnipresent screens of televisual culture, often amplified beyond the bearable? As many have argued, the domains of the private (the individual, the family) and the public (the sphere of the citizen) have merged in a hypermediated space—one that is anti-poetic, one where there is no possibility of meaningful reparation or of civic deliberation. In this mainstream televisual hyperspace the feeling of shame—as sensation, as intensity—is a valuable commodity.

The sociologist Norbert Elias has argued that over the long arc of human history "the civilizing process" has been accompanied by "spurts" and "advances" in the "shame-threshold" (293). The increasing complexity of society—the progressive specialization and differentiation of social organization—has required increasing strictures on behavior that are codified as emotion rules. What was once not considered shameful behavior in Elizabethan England (for example, the making of all kinds of bodily noises at the table at court) would now be considered exceedingly embarrassing or shameful in what we would call polite company. Thus Elias offers us, much as does Freud in *Civilization and Its Discontents*, a model of the development of civilization as entailing a necessary and concomitant repression. But where Freud emphasizes the development of a preemptive psychological structure ruled by the internalized emotion of guilt, Elias privileges the role of shame, that most social of emotions.

Freud's analysis in *Civilization and Its Discontents* leads him to conclude that at some limit condition the degree of repression exacted may be so implacably oppressive that on the level of a society it will produce not civilization but "neurosis" (*SE* 21: 144). With shame we have reached that limit. The threshold of shame to which Elias refers has advanced to an intolerable point where shameful behavior is being produced rather than curtailed—it is exhibited on our cultural screens for everyone to see. Consider the selling of the spectacle of shame we see at every turn today when we glance at a tabloid, flip from one television channel to another, or surf the Internet. Many people appear to be reveling in their own shame, making as much money off it as they can in a market characterized by active, even frenzied, trading. For where there are sellers there are also buyers, the seekers of shame who in turn sell it to us. Others are brutally trapped in the media.

In this regard I point to three examples from the mid-1990s when it seems to me that the selling of shame in the mainstream media took off.[13] One is tawdry—a woman making her living getting gigs for people with shameful stories. Two are grievously tragic—the lives of individuals crushed in the glare of the media, in particular television, whose voracious appetite for content results in the continual replaying of the same images. The repetition of these images, a stultifying inversion of the renewing repetition of ritual, is itself shameful, a form of death.

First, consider the case of the "talent agent" who scouts for shame. I'm thinking of Sherri Spillane (she clearly trades on the name of her ex-husband Micky Spillane), whose work in the 1990s consisted of marketing people like Tonya Harding, Joey Buttafuoco, Heidi Fleiss, and John Wayne Bobbitt by getting them gigs on talk shows and pushing their workout videos. In her position at the Ruth Webb Talent Agency, Spillane established a scandal division. Where did Spillane do much of her sleuthing for shame? She spent hours reading publications such as the *National Enquirer*, looking for people whose shame could be sold up a notch or two. And where did I find out about Spillane? In a 1995 issue of the *International Herald Tribune*, a highbrow newspaper then jointly published by the *New York Times* and the *Washington Post*. The *Herald* devoted a full half-page to Spillane's business, featuring a large Hollywoodish photo of Spillane and Ruth Webb lounging on a brass bed, cuddling their cats and stuffed animals. The tone of the article is light and bemused, and it concludes with this absurd—and dismaying—possibility: "Spillane mentions another promising performer, Bakker." She is referring, of course, to Tammy Faye Bakker. " 'We have "Hello Dolly" in mind for her,' she said."[14] (Tammy Faye Bakker was then Tammy Faye Messner. She died of cancer in the summer of 2007, and I confess to being uncomfortable—a feeling akin to shame—mentioning her in this light after her death.)

As we see so clearly in this example, the commercialization of shame—the retailing of the emotions—has penetrated all levels of mass culture, moving from low to high, as though shame were contagious (as in fact some theorists of shame have pointed out). Here, however, the familiar dynamics of shame are reversed. The feeling of shame is not a touchstone to evaluate one's actions, as in Sartre's model. Nor, as with Morrison's Darlene, does one hide from the view of others even though having been brutally shamed is unjust. In this version of shame, those who should be ashamed don't want to avoid the eye of the public. They desire to be seen. Turned into commodities on the mass culture market, they hope to profit by it in turn, making money off their shame, creating a spin to their past, in the process transforming their shame into a peculiar form of pride by entering the visual circuit of celebrity where actions carry less weight than one's image. Here shame is not so much acknowledged or confessed, as the communication scholars Thomas Scheff and Suzanne Retzinger insist it must be in order for it to be understood and for escalating violence to be avoided. Rather it is both paraded and willfully ignored at the same time. In the process do they cast off their shame and cast it onto those who look at them? Are those who are looking at them taking shameful pleasure in the spectacle? Or can we even say that the spectators are ashamed of themselves? This shame (so unlike the queer shame and pride theorized by Sedgwick), even as it is paraded, exhibited, and ostentatiously performed as pride, seems to have altogether vanished, leaving only a crass and sordid taste in its wake. Here shame is reduced to what Jean Baudrillard has called fascination, the numbing of both reflection and emotion in inert sensation. Perhaps shame has even crumbled into boredom.

For a second example, consider the phenomenon of TV talk shows staging shame. One of the prime tactics of trash TV and hate TV is the ambush, the entrapment of people in what they consider to be shameful situations that masquerade as entertainment. In one extreme instance, what was presumably intended as a fleeting and harmless embarrassment resulted instead in humiliation, a shame so painful that it led to the murder of one man and the shattering of the life of another man, who has since been sentenced to prison. A shame so intense that it was traumatic. Here trauma resulted from the mass-mediated production of shame. That shame in turn ignited murder. A twenty-four-year-old man—Jonathan Schmitz—agreed to participate in March 1995 in a segment on secret admirers on *The Jenny Jones Show*. It was taped in front of a studio audience and slated to be aired nationally shortly afterward. On the show Schmitz was stunned to learn that the person who was secretly attracted to him was not a woman but a man, Scott Amedure, who revealed he had sexual fantasies about Schmitz involving whipped cream, strawberries, and champagne. Schmitz later confessed that he was "humiliated and angered."[15]

Schmitz's humiliation was played out in front of a live audience to entertainment TV and was scheduled to be shown later to millions of viewers. Like Sartre's "I," Schmitz was surprised into shame. The spectators to his shame were as much unseen as seen. But Schmitz hadn't done anything wrong. Three days after the taping of the show he discovered a romantic note from his no-longer secret admirer. He bought a shotgun and drove to Amedure's home. Schmitz shot Amedure twice, killing him instantly. Schmitz was, he reported to a sheriff, "embarrassed, humiliated —that he had handled it as well as he could on national television because he didn't want to make a scene," but his experience, he told one of the police moments after the shooting, had "eaten away" at him.[16] Much as Morrison's Cholly turns his humiliation at the hands of white men into the rape of Darlene, a person even more helpless than himself, Schmitz did not confront the vast system of the televisual mass media. How could he have? Instead he tragically turned his shame into aggression against a gay male. His shame and the resulting anger, no doubt rage, could not be turned into knowledge. In such a case we can surmise that shame, turning to rage, is the precipitate of trauma. In such a case, affect blocks thought. In such a case what is called an affect storm leads to violence. In such a case there was not a context for a self-reflexive sequencing of the emotions. Jonathan Schmitz was sentenced in 1996 to twenty-five to fifty years in prison for the second-degree murder of Scott Amedure. That conviction was overturned in 1998, and a new trial was ordered. On 15 September 1999, Schmitz again was sentenced to twenty-five to fifty years in prison. The tape was never aired on national television.

Predictably, those responsible for the show declared neither wrong-doing nor liability. But the family of Amedure filed a civil suit against Telepictures Productions and Warner Brothers Television Distribution, the syndicator of *The Jenny Jones Show*. It was argued that the show set the stage for the murder of their son. In 1999 the show was found negligent, and the family was awarded twenty-five million dollars.

For a third example, consider the case of Richard Jewell, the man who overnight was mistakenly turned from a hero into a suspect in the 1996 Olympic Games bombing. The July 1996 bombing in Atlanta's Centennial Olympic Park killed two people and injured over one hundred others. At first praised in the media as a hero, Jewell, a security guard at the Olympics, almost instantly became a suspect in the crime. He was dogged by FBI agents for months and only later was he revealed to be innocent. Louis Freeh, the director of the FBI, admitted in 1997 that in the eighty-eight days that Jewell was subjected to federal scrutiny his constitutional rights were violated. Jewell was also, of course, relentlessly pursued by the press. His purported shame was made public—over and over and over again. Broadcast time and again, the televisual image of his exposure froze shame into a virtually timeless aftereffect, one that produced an *afteraffect* (we speak in terms of cause and effect; we should also think in terms of cause and affect).[17] Could we not conclude that a situation such as this, the constant replaying of one's image on TV and the incessant repetition of the story on the radio and in the newspapers and news magazines, mimics the psychological mechanism of debilitating and ultimately traumatic shame? That the continual coverage produces traumatic shame by amplifying it and blowing it up in public—by creating shame where there was none? We will often endlessly rehearse a shameful scene in our imagination. Analogously, televisual culture, with its proliferating news and entertainment shows, replays over and over and over again scenes that not only present and represent feelings, but also produce them. Richard Jewell was sought out by the media. Images of Jewell, first imagined as a hero and then as a criminal, produced scenes of shame. In such an instance as this, shame, as well as guilt, is sold to the public. Thus here the emotions that are sold to us are better understood as *intensities*. The retailing of these feelings in crudely packaged and promoted form, so often at the expense of an individual—whether it is in the tabloids, in the print of highbrow culture, or on daytime, prime-time, and late-night TV, or on the Internet—is part and parcel of our market economy.

This phenomenon is shameless and shameful. What can we do? We can understand it. We can refuse to participate in it as a reader or as a spectator. We can offer our judgments publicly, as did Richard Jewell when he testified before the Crime Subcommittee of the House Judiciary Committee in Washington in July 1997.[18] And as in the tragic case of the killing of Amedure, our courts can offer judgments as well.

I return to André Green who theorizes the relation between affect and meaning, or knowledge, in terms of the binding of affect into chains. I call them narrative chains. On the one hand, Green writes, there is "affect with a semantic function as an element in the chain of signifiers"; on the other hand, there is "affect overflowing the concatenation and spreading as it breaks the links in a chain" (208). In *The Bluest Eye* Cholly and Pecola can't narrate the horrific things that happen to them, and this in itself is telling. For both Cholly and Pecola the chain of affect explodes. The breaking of the chain is itself constituent of traumatic affect that results in paralysis or in compulsive activity, or both. But if racial shame in *The Bluest Eye* is marked by the inability of the characters to narrate what has happened to them, in televisual culture it would seem that traumatic shame is characterized by the incessant and obsessive narration of stories (it hardly matters of whom) by the media itself. There is not a lack of meaningful narration but an excess of meaningless narration. In such cases shame doesn't carry the transformational charge of a "free radical," in Sedgwick's term, but rather is the sign of a devastating debasement of the social bond.

<h1 style="text-align:center">4</h1>

Basic to the models of shame I've considered in this chapter is a visual structure (explicit or implicit) in which one person who embodies the values of dominant culture (these may be salutary values, they may be prejudicial values) judges the actions or very being of another person as shameful. There is a subject who judges and there is an object who is judged. We saw this in the scenarios presented by Sartre and Woolf and in the narrative world of *The Bluest Eye*. This implicit structure is also the ground for the analysis of shame for Eve Sedgwick and Sandra Bartky. Sedgwick urges the boldly casting off of the stigma of shame in a flourish of pride. Bartky encourages us to recognize shame where it seems invisible, that is, where it does not register as feeling. But in the case of the mass-mediated shame, it is not so much one person judging another that is at stake as it is the weight of an entire apparatus shifting the ground of value. People are vulnerable to being trapped in its compulsive matrix with its twenty-four-hour "news" cycle, and spectators are placed in the shameful position of enjoying the abjection of others.

But there are also situations where shame is mutual, where the structure involves everyone in shame, where the distinction between subject and object is voided, and where shame is a deeply moral response. There are situations where shame, mutually acknowledged, forges a social bond. I conclude by briefly reflecting on two such cases.

Consider this passage from Primo Levi's *The Truce*, his account of the days following his liberation from Auschwitz where he had been interned for almost a year during the Second World War. The book, which has been described by Paul Bailey as "light" and "written in a careful, weighted and serenely beautiful prose," opens with the arrival on 27 January 1945, of four Russians at the concentration camp that has been hastily abandoned by the Germans.[19] Along with another man, Levi, a twenty-five-year-old Italian chemist, was in the process of taking the body of one of the men in their group to the common grave when he saw the Russians approach:

They did not greet us, nor did they smile; they seemed oppressed not only by compassion but by a confused restraint, which sealed their lips and bound their eyes to the funereal scene. It was that shame we knew so well, the shame that drowned us after the selections, and every time we had to watch, or submit to, some outrage: the shame the Germans did not know, that the just man experiences at another man's crime; the feeling of guilt that such a crime should exist, that it should have been introduced irrevocably into the world of things that exist, and that his will for good should have proved too weak or null, and should not have availed in defense. (188)

This "confused restraint," a confusion similar to but so unlike the confusion I discussed earlier, is the shame of being a witness to a crime so aberrant and on so enormous a scale as to be unthinkable, a shame in which one virtually dies, unable to have done anything to have prevented the unthinkable. This is a mutual shame each in front of the other that brings a knowledge unrelieved by knowledge, a paralysis that is not insensibility but its opposite—one where the sharp certainty of moral outrage is diminished for those moments to, in Levi's words, "moral fatigue" (189). As Levi writes, "The scars of the outrage would remain within us for ever, and in the memories of those who saw it." Of this abject shame, he says, "It is foolish to think that human justice can eradicate it" (188).

I want to conclude, however, on another note—one of a tempered hope. I close this chapter by referring to an important essay by the feminist Berenice Fisher. It has long inspired me. Published in the mid-1980s, it remains relevant today. In it Fisher takes up guilt and shame in the women's movement, redescribing shame as collective, as mutual, as an emotion that can be shared by a group of women.

As I discussed in chapter 1, Freud theorizes guilt as an emotion that strikes with preemptive force, thereby inhibiting us from destructive action. Within the women's movement liberal guilt—the guilty feelings of white women in relation to women of color—has also been associated with a lack of action, indeed paralysis. As the literary critic Julie Ellison wrote at the end of the 1990s, "Liberal guilt is about race, and it always was. 'White guilt' and 'liberal guilt' emerged as synonymous terms during the Civil Rights movement. The term designates a position of wishful insufficiency relative to the genuine radical" (171). In contrast to Freud, for white women it is precisely the lack of action, or paucity of action, that is the source of guilt, with any action necessarily always insufficient to its purpose. But by the 1990s the force of guilt had devolved. As Ellison makes supremely clear, in the 1990s liberal guilt was linked above all with the emotion of embarrassment (the word "embarrassment" rings throughout her chapter on liberal guilt). Indeed I would say that in academic circles what I will call liberal embarrassment in large part replaced liberal guilt. Embarrassment is a weak emotion. It is not a political emotion at all. It is not possible to forge a strong community—imagined or real—committed to social justice based on embarrassment.

This is why Fisher's essay continues to hold a critical lesson for us. Fisher puts shame into the service of creating a social bond. Fisher redefines shame by carefully separating guilt from it and by encouraging feminists to recast their goals in their image, making shame their own. She understands shame "not as a mark of our inadequacy but as a sign of our commitment to act, as a mark of the tension between the present and the future, as a touchstone for understanding what we expect to achieve and how" (118). If her essay is inspirational, it also is cast in a sober tone mindful of the affective consequences of failure.

Fisher's purpose is to help us find a way to put our feelings of inevitable failure in relation to our goals and the women's movement to good and thoughtful use rather than to allow them to divide us from each other and to disable us in terms of action. Thus in the context of her essay it is guilt, not shame, that is associated with inaction. Importantly, given Bartky's analysis of women's dispositional shame as stemming from women's subordination in the world, Fisher proposes to shift shame out of the context of male-dominated society at large and into the context of the women's movement itself. She refuses, in other words, to accept the dominant codes or standards of society at large as the measures by which one would evaluate one's actions *within the movement*. What is so important in her account is that these ideals are not imposed but are chosen by ourselves.

Fisher associates the feeling of shame with the desire to hide that has been so often remarked by theorists of shame. But she hopes that this impulse will be resisted, and she refers us to the work of the psychoanalyst Helen Merrell Lynd who over fifty years ago devoted a book to shame in which she argued that if shame is faced fully it "may become not primarily something to be covered, but a positive experience of revelation" (20). At the heart of Fisher's essay is the wish that our shame will be acknowledged and brought into public discourse, not in the mode of psychologized inferiority but in the mode of carefully assessing our ability to live up to our ideals. She introduces the notion of collective moral agency into the discussion of shame and yet, unlike Sartre's account in *Being and Nothingness*, she casts shame in relation to an *ideal* rather than to a wrongdoing. At the same time she is also attuned, sensitively so, to the limitations of what can be achieved given the many contradictions that we daily live out. She proposes that shame be worn differently—in public, with dignity, and *together*.

In returning to Fisher's essay, I know that it is virtually anachronistic to speak today of *a* woman's movement, much less *the* women's movement. But as I move to my next chapter on liberal compassion and compassionate conservatism, I do not want to shrink from the word "liberal" in the face of the brutal inequities we see in the United States today and around the globe. I want to retain a sense of shame—a liberal shame—for the failure of our country to live up to ideals of social justice, and I am not embarrassed to say so.

four

LIBERAL COMPASSION,
COMPASSIONATE CONSERVATISM

Compassion, like so many of our other complex emotions, has a
heady political life. Invoking compassion is an important means of
trying to direct social, political, and economic resources in one's
direction (indeed, compassion is one of those resources).
— Elizabeth Spelman, *Fruits of Sorrow*

My father's compassion and common sense as a lawmaker are my
inspiration each time I step on the Senate floor.
   And that's why I'm so alarmed, outraged, and saddened by the
damage the Bush administration is doing to our nation in the name
of their self-proclaimed "compassionate conservatism."
   You have to ask, is it compassionate to give massive, budget-
busting tax cuts to the wealthy while working families struggle with
low wages and rising gas prices?
— Maria Cantwell, U.S. Senator (Democrat, Washington)

Now this has always perplexed me: why isn't it a good thing, a
praiseworthy thing, to have a bleeding heart?
— Sandra Bartky, "In Defense of Guilt"

During the second presidential debate of the 1992 election the three
candidates—George Bush, Bill Clinton, and Ross Perot—were asked by
a woman in the studio audience in Richmond, Virginia, how their own
lives had been affected by the national debt. It was a moment that was to
prove decisive. President George Bush, perplexed and nonplussed, literally didn't understand the question. "I'm not sure I get it," he said. "Help
me with the question and I'll try to answer."[1] Opening his arms, Clinton moved toward the audience and responded that he personally knew
people in Arkansas who were suffering because they had lost their jobs.
The clear implication was that he acutely felt their pain and Bush did not.
What was at stake was the presidential politics of empathy. The rest is
history.[2]

   Two weeks later Bush, in criticizing Clinton's plan to establish an office
devoted to AIDS in Washington, insisted, "We need more compassion in
our hometowns, more education, more caring."[3] If in fact there was a
concerted effort on the part of the Bush campaign to establish compassion
as a strong theme in 1992, it failed. But as we all know, eight years later the

rhetoric of empathy uncannily returned, surfacing in George W. Bush's campaign against Al Gore. What the elder George Bush fumbled, the son repossessed. Under the well-calculated banner of compassionate conservatism, the Republicans successfully appropriated the rhetoric of feeling that had been so powerfully associated with the Democrats. Indeed the presidential race of 2000 at times seemed marked by a competition between Al Gore and George W. Bush in terms of who could lay claim to being the most compassionate. Feeling someone's pain. Compassionate conservatism. These presidential campaign slogans are testimony to the pivotal power of a national discourse of empathy, one on which the political fortunes of George Bush, Bill Clinton, and George W. Bush in great part turned.[4]

How do we understand the uses of compassion during the George W. Bush years? How do appeals to sentiment—specifically to compassion—work? What are the limits of compassion? How do liberal and conservative narratives of compassion differ? In this chapter I thread my way through some of the debates about the political effectiveness of compassion by focusing on the work of scholars of sentiment published between the late 1980s and the late 1990s—the legal scholar Lynne Henderson, the philosophers Martha Nussbaum and Elizabeth Spelman, and the literary and cultural studies scholar Lauren Berlant. Taken together, these writers can be said to present the liberal narrative of compassion; all of their work includes discussions of race, notably in reference to the experience of African Americans (although Nussbaum less than the others). I also consider statements about compassion made by Republicans, including George W. Bush as well as Marvin Olasky, the author of *Compassionate Conservatism*, and Joseph Jacobs, the author of *The Compassionate Conservative*. Ultimately I conclude that the politically astute appropriation of the discourse of compassion by the George W. Bush presidential campaign in 2000 was in part made possible by the convergence of two distinct—and usually contradictory—trends in the way emotions are experienced and performed in contemporary culture. On the one hand, we have witnessed a flattening of the psychological emotions to intensities. On the other hand, we are witnessing the emergence of the sensitive man, the development of the man of feeling. His emotional portfolio includes sympathy, a sentiment that is becoming a new form of emotional correctness in the political sphere.

As I suggested in the introduction, we're living in a cultural moment in which a new economy of the emotions is emerging. Once relatively stable, discourses of the emotions are now circulating at a rapid rate. If in the 1950s in the United States the emotions were distributed in the white middle class according to gender in conventional or stereotypical ways, this situation has radically changed. Generally speaking, we can say that in the 1950s the expression of grief was proscribed in men and the expression of anger in women. But today cultural scripts for the emotions are more flexible or mixed. The presidential campaigns of 1992 and 2000 are perfect cases in point. If conventional wisdom tells us that women are more empathetic than men, our cultural moment requires that our male leaders be both strong *and* sensitive, thus allowing them to play both conventional gender parts simultaneously. Or it might be more accurate to say that our cultural moment requires that they display or perform sensitivity. Bush's tearful emotions were on display, for example, well into his first term as president. When he visited Iraq in November 2003 it was observed that a tear slipped down his cheek when he was greeted enthusiastically by the troops in Baghdad. As the *New York Times* reporter Elizabeth Bumiller wrote, "The tear added drama to an already theatrical trip, but the fact is, Mr. Bush cries all the time. He may look like a manly man in his cowboy boots and pickup truck, but he wears his emotions on his oxford cloth sleeve. The president, a self-proclaimed compassionate conservative, has helped make it safe for men to cry in the open."[5] If our male leaders don't *perform* sensitivity, our media-dominated culture—compressing story into slogan—requires that they at least deploy the rhetoric of sensitivity. The slogan "compassionate conservatism" trades on the rhetoric of feeling even as it is curiously empty of it. "Compassionate conservatism" is an oxymoron.

It was widely remarked that President George W. Bush's inaugural speech of 20 January 2001, was long on the rhetoric of compassion and short on the principles of conservatism. But in terms of action, the converse has been the definite case in the Bush administration.[6] The masculinization of public sentiment by Republicans serves as a screen for the privatization of the state—for the divestiture of the federal government of responsibility for many of our nation's citizens. The phrase "compassionate conservatism" is also code for the federal turn to faith-based organizations to undertake what could be called private spiritual and social work with public dollars.[7] There is a canny historical logic to this. In the United States there is a long tradition of the association of the private sphere with the feminine, with sentiment, and with religion. I am thinking in particular of the nineteenth century when what has been called the culture of sentiment stretched roughly from 1830 to 1870.[8] That this period saw the publication of the most famous instance of the fictional sentimental narrative would seem to be no accident. Indeed Harriet Beecher Stowe's *Uncle Tom's Cabin or, Life Among the Lowly* is the narrative to which scholars of sentiment in literary and cultural studies inevitably return. In the United States it is the ur-text of the liberal narrative of compassion.

Published in 1852, Harriet Beecher Stowe's *Uncle Tom's Cabin* was the first book in the United States to sell over a million copies. Praised by the literary critic Jane Tompkins in her own influential *Sensational Designs* as a potent cultural force in the abolition of slavery, *Uncle Tom's Cabin* has been widely credited with accomplishing, in Tompkins's phrase, important cultural work.[9] In *Uncle Tom's Cabin* the way of justice—I use the term with its religious overtones advisedly—is that of compassion. The nineteenth-century reader is prompted to identify empathetically with a suffering character (generally through the medium of another character), and this response is read as an experience in moral pedagogy. A spontaneous burst of feeling leads to a change of heart; the emotions and morality are linked.

Consider this small scene from *Uncle Tom's Cabin*. In a chapter entitled "The Little Evangelist," the tender-hearted little Eva, herself soon to die, takes pity on Topsy, the unruly slave girl who doesn't believe in God and is driving everyone in the St. Clare household to distraction: " 'O, Topsy, poor child, *I* love you!' said Eva, with a sudden burst of feeling, and laying her little thin, white hand on Topsy's shoulder; 'I love you, because you haven't had any father, or mother, or friends;—because you've been a poor, abused child! I love you, and I want you to be good' " (409). The tears in Eva's eyes beget tears in Topsy. Compassion inspires conversion. As Stowe writes, "The round, keen eyes of the black child were overcast with tears;—large, bright drops rolled heavily down, one by one, and fell on the little white hand. Yes, in that moment, a ray of real belief, a ray of heavenly love, had penetrated the darkness of her heathen soul" (409–10). Salvation comes through love, here motherly love. Eva touches the abused Topsy, literally and emotionally. The drama has religious overtones; the laying on of hands has healing power. Topsy is granted faith. She also, as we would say today, acquires self-esteem. Thus key to the liberal narrative of compassion is a scene of personal suffering and pain. Also key to the liberal narrative of compassion is a witness—here the character of Eva and, further, the reader. Through the medium of Eva, the reader is called on to feel Topsy's pain, to understand her suffering, and to resolve to act like Eva, thus comprehending the injustice that is slavery.[10]

1

Lynne Henderson, Martha Nussbaum, Elizabeth Spelman, and Lauren Berlant can be seen as the heirs to this tradition of liberal compassion. Their work attests to the high degree of interest today in the emotion of compassion, which makes its appearance under different names as well—empathy, pity, sympathy. These four scholars, coming from different disciplines, interested in the cultural politics of the emotions, stress the importance of personal narratives of suffering—of stories—in eliciting compassion. The kinds of texts—primarily legal and literary—that they take up as paradigmatic are different, and their positions differ as well. For the most part they aren't in dialogue with each other, and thus one of my purposes in gathering them together is to point out their similarities and, as such, the important difference between the liberal narrative of compassion and the conservative narrative of compassion. I should also point out that, for the most part, studies of the sentimental and studies of trauma are not in dialogue with one another. Perhaps this is because, as Philip Fisher points out in his essay "Democratic Social Space," "one of the key sentimental assumptions [is] that suffering does not brutalize, nor does it silence its victims or lead them to save themselves by repressing what they have undergone" (100). Trauma, on the other hand, as we saw in the last chapter, is conceived of precisely as a brutalizing experience. As Cathy Caruth defines it, trauma exists "solely in the *structure of the experience* or reception: the event is not assimilated or experienced fully at the time, but only belatedly in its repeated *possession* of the one who experiences it" (5). As we saw in the last chapter, Cholly and Pecola were taken hostage by their traumatic experiences of shame, never to be released. Harriet Beecher Stowe's Topsy, on the other hand, a character in a nineteenth-century sentimental novel, is redeemed by the compassion of a white child.

Both Henderson and Nussbaum make the case for compassion (or empathy) with conviction in ways that a scholar of cultural studies might find pre-ideological and naive. Spelman and Berlant offer a more critical view of the uncertain relation between feeling and action, or the limits of liberal compassion. In the space of this chapter I'm not able to do justice to the arguments of these four scholars, strong and subtle as they are. Indeed my primary intention is to underscore the common ground among them, not to challenge or critique each of their positions at length. Although I do offer commentary, it seems to me that each of them is quite right in many respects. What concerns me, however, as I demonstrate below, is that the critique of the liberal narrative of compassion was appropriated by compassionate conservatives for their own use during the Bush years.

Lynne Henderson's purpose in her wide-ranging essay "Legality and Empathy" is to persuade us that empathy should be cultivated by judges as a moral capacity.[11] One of her main points is that there is an unwelcome tendency in legal circles to abstract the problems of individuals to the point of denying them altogether. Thus legal decisions frequently have nothing to do with a person's experience, which is often denied legitimacy and recognition. For Henderson empathy is precisely a mode of understanding that includes both emotion and cognition and therefore can reveal moral problems occluded by a reductionist legal rationality. "Empathy," she writes, "is the foundational phenomenon for intersubjectivity, which is *not* absorption by the other, but rather simply the relationship of self to other, individual to community" (1584). For Henderson sympathetic identification is the foundation of ethical experience. How does this identification take place in the courtroom? How is empathy fostered in judges?

Henderson's answer is that what elicits empathy in the courtroom is a narrative that conveys the texture of emotional experience. Drawing on four important U.S. Supreme Court cases—*Brown v. Board of Education I* (1954), *Shapiro v. Thompson* (1969), *Roe v. Wade* (1973), and *Bowers v. Hardwick* (1986)—Henderson argues that the decisions in these four cases turned on the presence (or absence) of empathetic narratives in oral argument and on the understanding of these narratives (or the egregious lack of it) on the part of the judges. "The argumentative steps taken to convey human situations to a judge," she explains, "might be described as creating affective understanding by use of a narrative that includes emotion and description ('thick' description, if you will) of a human situation created by, resulting from, or ignored by legal structures, and consciously placing that narrative within a legal framework" (1592).

My principal point here is that these four cases are all characterized by narratives of suffering: in *Brown v. Board of Education* by the suffering of African Americans who were legally barred from attending schools with whites, in *Shapiro v. Thompson* by the suffering of the poor who were denied welfare, in *Roe v. Wade* by the suffering of pregnant women who were denied access to abortion, and in *Bowers v. Hardwick* by the suffering of gay men who were persecuted for their sexual practices. Of these four cases I single out two.

Brown v. Board of Education I, a landmark class-action suit that deals with school segregation, was brought by African American parents in Topeka, Kansas, on behalf of their school-age children, claiming that their rights were being violated under the 14th amendment to the U.S. Constitution which states that no one can be discriminated against on the basis of race. (*Brown v. Board of Education* was in fact a series of five cases, with the other four filed in South Carolina, Virginia, Delaware, and Washington, D.C.; it was sponsored by the NAACP whose chief counsel, Thurgood Marshall, argued the case.) A half a century earlier in *Plessy v. Ferguson* (1896), the U.S. Supreme Court had upheld segregation on the basis of race when it ruled that separate facilities for black and whites, if deemed equal, were constitutional. The basic argument for the appellants in *Brown v. Board of Education* was that even if educational facilities were found to have no material differences, the policy of segregation undermined the education of black students because the very separation of races implies the inferiority of African Americans and a sense of inferiority affects the motivation of a child. Thus effects of segregation couldn't be separated from the quality of education.

Henderson argues that in *Brown v. Board of Education* it was the evocation of African American suffering that ultimately persuaded the hearts and minds of the majority on the U.S. Supreme Court to question the morality—and thus the legality—of segregation. The word "pain" rings throughout her discussion. *Brown v. Board of Education*, she writes, "was remarkable, and it remains so, in large part because it is a human opinion responding to the pain inflicted on outsiders by the law" (1594). She regards the opinion of the Court as conveying the crucial "recognition of human experience and pain—of feeling" (1594). Thurgood Marshall's arguments before the Court, she notes, relied repeatedly on "the narrative of the painful experience of being black in American society" (1596). Empathy for Henderson has three dimensions: first, feeling the emotion of another; second, understanding the experience of that person; and third, the specific feeling of sympathy or compassion for a person that "can lead to action in order to help or alleviate the pain of another" (1582). In the case of *Brown*, all three were present: "Feeling the distress of the blacks, under-standing the painful situation created by segregation, and responding to the cry of pain by action" (1607). Here the moral triumph is that "legality in its many forms clashed with empathy, and empathy ultimately trans-formed legality" (1594).

But when I turned to read Thurgood Marshall's oral arguments myself, I was at first puzzled. (I should confess my initial ignorance with the genre of oral argumentation; the format is question and answer and the time allotted is short, leaving precious little room for amplification through the telling of stories.) I didn't find what I had expected to find, given Hender-son's description. The language struck me as legalistic and emotionally barren if not completely flat. In testifying to the harm done to African Americans by the segregation of schools, the briefs were too overwhelm-ing, I thought, to ignore or dismiss. When I returned again to Marshall's oral arguments I saw more subtlety, even canniness, in his narrative tac-tics, which consisted in great part of digressions and asides.

I confine myself to a single example requiring us to imagine the drama in black and white that took place in the courtroom. All nine justices on the Supreme Court were white men while Marshall was an African Ameri-can lawyer. As a black man facing a row of white male justices, he alone could palpably make blackness *present* in the courtroom. At one point Marshall offered a shrewd hypothetical example of the suffering entailed by segregation when in digressing (that is his word) he asked the court to imagine this: if the 1950 African American Nobel laureate Ralph Bunche were to move to South Carolina, he wouldn't be able to send his children to a white school. (A political scientist with a doctorate from Harvard and a distinguished diplomat, Ralph Bunche was the first person of color in the world to be awarded the Nobel Prize for Peace.) Thus in addition to race, evoked here are class and parenthood. The potential suffering of a *parent* who has himself contributed so much to the world would be at stake. So too would be the suffering of his child who would receive an inferior education. Is this not the sort of suffering that the white justices could be expected to understand and wish to remedy?

If Henderson argues that scenes of personal pain are key to eliciting compassion, she doesn't assume that a narrative of suffering will neces-sarily prompt the understanding of those on the bench. She acknowledges that people are more likely to sympathize with those who are like them-selves. She understands the difficulty imposed by different cultural contexts. She is altogether aware of the power of racism, sexism, and other forms of prejudice. Indeed her examples also bear out the failure of narratives of suffering as tools of persuasion because the divide or difference between those judging and those being judged was too great to be bridged imaginatively.

Bowers v. Hardwick provides an instance of such narrative failure, a case in which there was a complete absence of sympathetic understanding. Indeed the dominant emotion seems to have been hate, a "perversion of empathy" (1638). Here is the situation. Through a series of coincidences a police officer happens upon a man named Michael Hardwick engaging in consensual oral sex in his own home with another man. He arrests Hardwick under the Georgia law against sodomy (it covered both anal and oral sex). Hardwick is charged with a felony. Incredibly the U.S. Supreme Court voted to uphold the sodomy law. Henderson suggests that the very absence of vivid sympathetic narratives about the prejudice suffered by gay men may have contributed to the unfeeling verdict. (Importantly *Bowers v. Hardwick* was overruled in *Lawrence v. Texas* in 2003.)

Although Henderson questions a necessary connection between a compassionate judgment and narratives of compassion, she is nevertheless optimistic about the possibility that they might prompt action, which for her would mean good judgments.[12] I can imagine, however, a narrative of suffering—or a rhetoric of suffering—that elicits sympathy of the wrong kind. Consider the two cases, consolidated into one, brought by parents before the U.S. Supreme Court in 2007 that involved the assignment of students to schools in Seattle and Louisville on the basis of race. Ruling that race can't be a factor in assigning students to public schools, the decision is the most far-reaching on the question of racial integration since *Brown v. Board of Education*. Take the oral argument in one of the cases—*Parents Involved in Community Schools v. Seattle School District*. At no point is suffering invoked. But ironically suffering is mentioned in the opinion of Clarence Thomas, the only African American justice on the court, who concluded: "Every time the government uses racial criteria to 'bring the races together' . . . someone gets excluded, and the person excluded suffers an injury solely because of his or her race. . . . This type of exclusion, solely on the basis of race, is precisely the sort of government action that pits the races against one another, exacerbates racial tension, and 'provoke[s] resentment among those who believe that they have been wronged by the government's use of race.' "[13] Here, however, the school children being excluded are white, not black. This is a clear case of compassionate conservatism, not liberal compassion.

Like Henderson, the philosopher Martha Nussbaum argues that compassion is the basic social emotion. Like Henderson, she believes that emotion in general and compassion in particular can possess a cognitive edge; indeed for her compassion is a moral sentiment characterized by a mode of reason or judgment. Like Henderson, she sees compassion as an emotional bridge between the individual and the community, as "a bridge to justice"—a metaphor I think Henderson would admire (37).

For Nussbaum compassion is an instance of what she has elsewhere called the "narrative emotions," emotions called up by literature that teaches us about the suffering of others (and our own suffering as well, I would add). As literary examples she offers Sophocles's Philoctetes, the work of Dickens, E. M. Forster's *Maurice*, and Richard Wright's *Native Son*. She calls for a multicultural education in our schools that would include the study of literature of suffering. As she insists, "Public education at every level should cultivate the ability to imagine the experiences of others and to participate in their sufferings" (50).

Nussbaum's primary purpose is to recuperate under the rubric of *compassion* the Aristotelian meaning of *pity*: pity, for Aristotle, entails the spectator's sense that he or she could suffer similar misfortune—an understanding that is crucial, she argues, to a vision of social justice. Over time, however, as she notes, pity has acquired the injurious sense of the superiority of the spectator and thus the negative connotation of condescension, an attitude that works against a vision of social justice. Nussbaum is concerned predominantly with the possibility of a "sense of commonness" (35), not with the dangers of the appropriation of feeling. This is a liberal position. But she is clearly sensitive to questions of difference. This is also a liberal position. I quote her at some length:

> Pity does indeed involve empathetic identification as one component: for in estimating the seriousness of the suffering, it seems important, if not sufficient, to attempt to take its measure as the person herself measures it. But even then, in the temporary act of identification, one is always aware of one's own *separateness* from the sufferer—it is for *another*, and not oneself, that one feels; and one is aware both of the bad

lot of the sufferer and of the fact that it is, right now, not one's own. . . .
One must also be aware of one's own *qualitative difference* from the
sufferer: aware, for example, that Philoctetes has no children and no
friends, as one does oneself. For these recognitions are crucial in getting the right estimation of the meaning of the suffering. (35)

With Henderson, then, Nussbaum cautions that in responding to suffering we must take care to take our own difference into account, to understand it. But there is a significant difference between them. As is attested
in the cases that Henderson discusses, she identifies, if you will, predominately with people who are suffering at the hands of social injustice,
namely those suffering from the cruelties of a prejudiced society. Nussbaum, on the other hand, writes primarily from the point of view of the
person who witnesses suffering—from the point of view of the reader or
spectator—and her focus in the passage above is telling.[14] Philoctetes is a
tragic hero, a subject of tragedy. He is an exemplary person, not an ordinary one. We should not be surprised by her point of view. Nussbaum is a
classicist and one of her impulses is to show how this work remains
important to this day. At the same time, however, she understands that the
tragic drama is highly abstracted from the trials of everyday life today. Thus
she singles out the realist novel as more appropriate for our cultural moment. As she writes, "The novel goes further, by connecting the reader to
highly concrete circumstances other than her own, and by making her
imagine what it would be like to be a member of both privileged and
oppressed groups in these circumstances" (51). And although she names
Richard Wright's *Native Son* as an example, I can equally imagine her
referring to Morrison's *The Bluest Eye*.

Finally, Nussbaum argues convincingly that one may understand a
situation with compassion even though one does not have the *feeling* itself.
This is an exceedingly important point. Just as emotions can in effect be
created retrospectively, as we saw in the chapter on Freud and feminism,
so too one may respond to a situation feelingly in the absence of the
emotion itself. At base Nussbaum understands compassion as "a certain
sort of thought about the well-being of others," as "a certain sort of reasoning" (28). How is this possible? If one has had the experience of the feeling
of compassion, if one has learned to be sensitive to suffering and if one
feels passionately about social justice, and if this has become part and
parcel of how one evaluates situations and is moved to action, then, Nuss-

baum concludes, one "has pity whether he experiences this or that tug in his stomach or not." "No such particular bodily feeling is necessary," she continues (38). This is a crucial theoretical distinction, one that has significant aesthetic consequences: it allows Nussbaum to distance herself from the aesthetic of the sentimental. One need not be, in Nussbaum's world, moved to tears in order to be moved to compassion (or to pity, her preferred term). In fact given her taste in narrative (she is drawn to Beckett, not Stowe), she would no doubt agree with the poet Wallace Stevens that the sentimental "is a failure of feeling" (162).

In *Fruits of Sorrow: Framing Our Attention to Suffering* Elizabeth Spelman, unlike Henderson and Nussbaum, does not so much make the case for compassion as she explores some of the complex contradictions that can be involved in the various ways our attention is focused on suffering. She draws on a wide spectrum of work—from Plato and Aristotle to Jean Fagin Yellin and Bill T. Jones. But in the context of my chapter, most relevant is her discussion of the former slave Harriet Jacobs's *Incidents in the Life of a Slave Girl*, which was written as a first-person narrative and published under the pseudonym of Linda Brent in 1861. For as Spelman shows, Jacobs was herself exquisitely attuned to the dangers as well as the promises posed by using compassion as a political tool in calling attention to the evils of slavery. Specifically Spelman suggests that Jacobs rewrote *Uncle Tom's Cabin* by adding outrage to the emotional score of sentimentality, thereby emphasizing not just the importance of an individual's compassionate response to another's pain but also the importance of judging the institution of slavery. In such an instance compassion includes the element of recognizing suffering as not only existential but also structural—that is, as a result of political and social conditions that are unjust.

Spelman quotes this passage from the book written by the former slave: " 'Could you have seen that mother clinging to her child, when they fastened the irons upon his wrists; could you have heard her heart-rending groans, and seen her blood-shot eyes wander wildly from face to face, vainly pleading for mercy, could you have witnessed that scene as I saw it, you would exclaim, *Slavery is damnable*' " (78–79). Jacobs draws on the conventions of the sentimental but then stops short, surprising us by withholding the rhetoric of tears that is the stock in trade of nineteenth-century sentimental literature and inserting instead the rhetoric of outrage. A narrative scene of suffering is key. But the emotional response demanded of the reader is more complex than that in the scene I quoted earlier from *Uncle Tom's Cabin* where Eva sympathizes with Topsy as a motherless child. The tender feeling of compassion, Spelman suggests, can be seductive, serving to seal a short circuit of feeling and confining it to the individual. Outrage, on the other hand, is "informed passion" (85). Outrage is here directed at the slave owners, which is just as it should be. Deserving of compassion, the slave isn't reduced to a mere victim but retains moral standing by issuing a judgment call.[15]

Not surprisingly, Spelman shrinks from the social structure of hierarchy and condescension implied by the contemporary understanding of pity. Although she understands that compassion and pity are often used interchangeably, unlike Nussbaum she doesn't want to recuperate pity as a useful political emotion—and I agree that there is no reason to fight what would be a vain rhetorical battle. Yet for Spelman, as with Nussbaum, a person who experiences compassion for another person is one who in fact imagines that they too could be the subject of suffering. All in all Spelman strikes a wise balance between the illicit appropriation of the pain of others and the possibilities of understanding that pain. As she writes, "despite the ever-present possibility of such exploitative sentimentality— and here again is the tension, the paradox, in appropriation—it would be absurd to deny that in some important sense people can and should try to put on the experiences of others" (119). I appreciate her common sense. At the same time, one of the continuing concerns throughout the pages of her book is the following question, and in her hands it is both a philosophical question and a political one: When does the feeling of feeling compassion become an end in itself and thwart responsible action? Ultimately for Spelman a cultural politics of compassion is understood as one that can have valuable effects and must be judged case by case.

The most trenchant indictment of the contradictions implicit in the sentimental narrative in relation to the politics of the American nation has been offered by Lauren Berlant.[16] In a brilliant essay entitled "Poor Eliza," she examines a rich archive of texts that draw on the strategies and tropes of *Uncle Tom's Cabin*, the literary touchstone for the American liberal narrative of compassion. Indeed her title refers to *Uncle Tom's Cabin* through the textual relay—what Berlant wonderfully calls "emotional quotation or affective citation" (647)—of Rogers and Hammerstein's 1949 musical *The King and I*. This production contains a memorable scene in which a female slave in the king's court in Siam herself stages the scene from *Uncle Tom's Cabin* where the slave Eliza runs for her life. In a complex reading of the musical, Berlant acknowledges the salutary effects associated with the musical's affective citation of Stowe's novel, among them the will of the people to be socially progressive at a critical historical juncture. But ultimately the scaffold of the sentimental, Berlant insists, collapses under the untenable weight of its contradictions: "When sentimentality meets politics, it uses personal stories to tell of structural effects, but in so doing it risks thwarting its very attempt to perform rhetorically a scene of pain that must be soothed politically. Because the ideology of true feeling cannot admit the nonuniversality of pain, its cases become all jumbled together and the ethical imperative toward social transformation is replaced by a civic-minded but passive ideal of empathy. The political as a place of acts oriented toward publicness becomes replaced by a world of private thoughts, leanings, and gestures" (641).

The sentimental framing of suffering, Berlant insists, is corrupt for many reasons, not least of which is that the sentimental narrative relies on scenes of pain that wrongly presume such suffering is universal. For the pain of slavery can't be understood fully by a white middle-class reader; the politics of personal feeling can't address the structural reasons for injustice. The narrative, Berlant insists, affords the pleasure of consuming the feeling of vicarious suffering—and its putative moral precipitate, the feeling of self-satisfaction that we wish to do the right thing and thus are virtuous. But the experience of being moved by these sentimental scenes of suffering, whose ostensible purpose is to awaken us to redress injustice, works instead to return us to a private world far removed from the public sphere. Thus in a crippling contradiction, Berlant concludes, the result of such empathetic identification is not the impulse to action but rather a "passive" posture. Fundamentally, therefore, the sentimental narrative is deliciously consumable and cruelly ineffective. Berlant's critique of the sentimental narrative, or sentimental liberalism, is unforgiving. The genre of the sentimental narrative itself is, she believes, morally bankrupt.

But in "Poor Eliza" Berlant identifies as well what she calls the postsentimental text, and she offers as examples James Baldwin's essay on *Uncle Tom's Cabin* entitled "Everyone's Protest Novel," Robert Waller's *The*

Bridges of Madison County, and Toni Morrison's *Beloved*. What differentiates these texts from sentimental texts? Among other things, Berlant argues, they possess a clear-eyed if nonetheless ambivalent refusal of the fantastical optimism central to the sentimental narrative. More specifically, "Everyone's Protest Novel" possesses, in Berlant's words, the "powerful language of rageful truth-telling" (656). There is at work, Berlant implies, both a cultural politics and a cultural poetics of the emotions. Like Harriet Jacobs, Baldwin adds outrage to the sentimental score, in effect understanding such a complex response to suffering as necessarily having a cognitive component. In "Poor Eliza" Berlant's purpose is not only to critique the sentimental liberalism she abhors but also to explore the possibilities of an affecting radicalism. Her own essay, concluding with an eloquent discussion of *Beloved*, itself rises to the condition of possibility beyond both cynical reason and an empty commodified optimism based on falsely shared suffering.[17]

Although these four scholars differ in their understanding of the efficacy of narratives of compassion, they all invest a response to suffering—whether it is called empathy, sympathy, pity, or compassion—with the possibility of a cognitive component. All four emphasize scenes of suffering and of pain as basic to what I am calling the liberal narrative of compassion, and all are concerned (although not exclusively) with injustice that is structural, in particular injustice at the hands of prejudice. Further, all four are concerned, albeit to different degrees, with the potential corrupting relation of unequal power between the one who suffers and the one who witnesses that suffering, as well as with the related question of the ineffectiveness of compassion in achieving social justice.[18] All four stress the cultural politics of narrative emotions in relation to the injustice suffered by black Americans. This is crucial given the signal injustice of slavery on which this country was built. As we read in the last paragraph of Morrison's *The Bluest Eye*, "It was the fault of the earth, the land, of our town. . . . This soil is bad for certain kinds of flowers. Certain fruit it will not bear."

I have two final comments before I turn to compassionate conservatism. First, in the work of Henderson, Nussbaum, Spelman, and Berlant compassion is figured in terms of unequal relations of power. As we saw in the last chapter, mutual shame—an example of which is drawn from Primo Levi's *The Truce*—calls attention to the structural situation of shame in which everyone is embedded. Could we not envision a situation of *mutual compassion?* I could imagine that in the very same scene from the Russian prison camp in which Primo Levi was horrifically interred, mutual compassion might in fact succeed mutual shame.

Second, although my primary purpose is not to evaluate each of the arguments of these four scholars, I do want to say a word about the emphasis on the issue of "action." The question of the relation of an emotion (here compassion) to moral redress (here action) is complicated, and I think many cultural critics, in offering critique, are demanding too much of literature and the practice of reading. Consider Berlant's incisive but in great part merciless analysis. Yes, I agree, the aesthetic of *Uncle Tom's Cabin* (or *The King and I*) doesn't adequately address the reading public of today. But as Glenn Hendler reminds us in *Public Sentiments*, reading practices in the mid-nineteenth century were different; we shouldn't judge them by our aesthetic standards today. Yes, I agree an individual may find simple self-satisfaction in an easily consumed sentiment of sympathy. Yes, reading may be useless in terms of moral redress, or it may be worse than useless by sealing shut the moral soul with self-congratulatory feelings. But equally, in the texts Berlant admires, even if no "action" is immediately forthcoming upon reading them, if one's moral imagination is enlarged, one may respond in a future situation in moral terms. I believe in what I call the *reading unconscious*: we may safeguard these texts in our memory so that they may be called upon when we can hear them or when they are needed. Understanding that there is no necessary connection between the literary emotion of compassion and a newfound sense of structural injustice (how could there be?), I nonetheless agree with Spelman that invoking sympathy is an important way of trying to redirect social, political, and economic resources. Indeed, as she writes in *Fruits of Sorrow*, "compassion is one of those resources" (88). Yes, structural change is required. But the first and crucial step is to understand that it is necessary, and that is no small step. Yes, there is a danger, but I prefer to put the emphasis on the positive. My sympathies, if you will, lie with the potential promise of learning through literature or of being inspired by literature, where the poetics of narrative and of language may make us feel more alive in the present to the suffering of others and committed to the best we might be able to offer. I do not wish to cede compassion to the conservatives who have appropriated with gusto the rhetoric of compassion and to whom I now turn.

2

If in the academy today attention is being given to the cultural politics of compassion, along with serious concerns about its effectiveness, the rhetoric of compassion as appropriated by George W. Bush had a resounding success in the presidential election of 2000. What calculus is involved in a conservatism that is labeled compassionate? What characterizes a conservative narrative of compassion?

In the liberal narrative of compassion, the word "compassion" is used primarily as a noun or a predicate adjective in relation to people. A person feels compassion or is compassionate. Compassion is a feeling, and it is embodied. In the conservative narrative, in contrast, compassion is deployed predominantly as an adjective, one that characterizes an ideological stance, policy, or program. Bush not only ran on a platform of compassionate conservatism, he has described his budget as compassionate. Detached from people, compassion is attached to policies and practices. Oddly, in the mouths of conservatives, the adjective "compassionate" seems to have no referent to a feeling at all—or at least not to the feeling of sympathy that is associated with compassion. It is merely a word that refers, through a relay of rhetoric, to *economic conservatism*. Here is another instance of the waning of emotion that pervades postmodern culture.

Furthermore even if sentiment, or sensitivity, is performed, it doesn't seem linked to sympathy for others. Consider, for example, the way in which during the delivery of his inaugural speech in 2000 Bush seemed moved by the rhetoric of his vision for America. At the same time a politics of gender is also at work. If compassion doesn't entail sympathy, it clearly does refer to a strict and stern paternalism—to the demand for discipline and responsibility. Under the screen of the feminine, compassion is masculinized in conventional tones. In Indianapolis on 22 July 1999, in what is regarded as his first major policy address as a presidential candidate, for instance, George W. Bush pledged to "rally the armies of compassion in our communities to fight a very different war against poverty," and he praised programs that practice "severe mercy."[19] How far we are from the teary sentimental rhetoric of *Uncle Tom's Cabin*, from Thurgood Marshall's presence in the U.S. Supreme Court arguing on behalf of racial integration for *Brown v. Board of Education*, from Harriet Jacobs's outrage, from Richard Wright's harrowing *Native Son*, and from Toni Morrison's eloquent *Beloved*.

What kinds of stories do compassionate conservatives tell? In our televisual political culture, a narrative of compassion is condensed into a visual sound bite. Bill Clinton, in his 20 January 1999 State of the Union address, introduced Rosa Parks, calling up decades of struggle over civil rights and evoking her suffering as a profile in courage. To whom did George W. Bush gesture in his speech to Congress outlining his budget proposal on 27 February 2001? Bush first pointed to the mayor of Philadelphia who supported faith-based organizations in that city, and second, to Steven and Josefina Ramos: "With us tonight, representing many American families, are Steven and Josefina Ramos. They are from Pennsylvania, but they could be from any one of your districts. Steven is a network administrator for a school district, Josefina is a Spanish teacher at a charter school, and they have a 2-year-old daughter. Steven and Josefina tell me they pay almost $8,000 a year in federal income taxes; my plan will save them more than $2,000. Let me tell you what Steven says: 'Two thousand dollars a year means a lot to my family. If we had this money it would help us reach our goal of paying off our personal debt in two years time.'"[20]

Compassion is here referred to through the implied relay to economic conservatism, which is in fact what compassionate conservatism is. Here the calculus of compassionate conservatism is laid bare. The financialization of daily life is extolled in a presidential address. Note also that none of the members of this small nuclear family are suffering in the ways underlined in the cases brought before the U.S. Supreme Court that Henderson discusses. The *feeling* of compassion is not evoked. We are not told a story, which implies a past. Indeed there is no real *story* here; instead we have an *information-story* in which we are presented with the possibility of a bright economic future and the principle that people are to be rewarded for identifying financial goals and working hard to achieve them. Bush appeals to their economic interests only. Note also that there is only a gesture to difference—Steven and Josefina Ramos are presumably Hispanic—but the possible harsh realities of prejudice based on difference are not invoked. Instead these three people represent "many American families." Here we have a condensed version of the American dream. As Berlant incisively puts it in *The Queen of America Goes to Washington City*, the American dream "fuses private fortune with that of the nation: it promises that if you invest your energies in work and in family-making, the nation will secure the broader social and economic conditions in which your labor can gain value and your life can be lived with dignity" (94).

What is the model for this condensed narrative of conservative compassion? Marvin Olasky's *Compassionate Conservatism: What It Is, What It Does, and How It Can Transform America*, published in 2000 and graced with a foreword by the then-governor George W. Bush, provides a template for this model. A professor of journalism at the University of Texas at Austin and a born-again Christian, Marvin Olasky has been credited with the formulation of "compassionate conservatism," although ironically, as he himself points out, it appears that the phrase itself was first used by none other than Bill Clinton's good friend Vernon Jordan in 1981 (9). *Compassionate Conservatism* is the triumphant sequel to Olasky's *The Tragedy of American Compassion*, which traces the policies of compassionate conservatism to their roots in colonial America. If *Uncle Tom's Cabin* provides the reader with a sentimental education by enacting a moral pedagogy of the emotions, *Compassionate Conservatism* is a narrative of the political education of the younger generation, rehearsing the political—and spiritual—pedagogy of entrepreneurship, faith, and tough love. If *Uncle Tom's Cabin* and *Incidents in the Life of a Slave Girl* foreground scenes of feeling that are coded as feminine, Olasky's narrative is gendered male.

The father of four sons, Olasky recounts the journey he took in 1999 with his fourteen-year-old son Daniel to visit programs around the United States that embody the tenets of compassionate conservatism. As a political travelogue of discovery and a field trip about government for a high school student, the narrative is, like *Uncle Tom's Cabin*, one of transformation. The transformation here, however, is not a matter of enlightenment about the suffering of other people—rather it is about what works. "The travel changed Daniel in several vital ways," Olasky writes, "but had also changed me. I became convinced that the best way to understand compassionate conservatism is not to go through a list of theoretical statements but to walk the streets of our large cities and talk with those whose faith is so strong that they refuse to give in" (22).

In the course of the narrative, father and son (they are from Austin) visit

Houston and Dallas, Indianapolis and Camden, Philadelphia and Minneapolis, St. Louis and Washington, D.C. Consider Olasky's account of their visit to Indianapolis, the city where in 1999 George W. Bush delivered his first major speech as a presidential candidate. Olasky begins his chapter on Indianapolis by briefly sketching its business history and then taking us to the twenty-fifth-floor office of Mayor Steve Goldsmith. As mayor, Goldsmith had established the Front Porch Alliance, which throughout the 1990s brought together "faith-based and other civic organizations to develop eight hundred partnerships for neighborhood action" (62). From the height of government, we descend into the streets of Indianapolis and are introduced to one person after another, all of whom have successfully developed a program or a center with support from city government, and virtually all of whom have a strong belief in Christianity. They are described. They are given names. Reverend Jay Height, the executive director of the Shepherd Community Center. Olgen Williams, a part-time pastor and long-married father of ten children who was forced to quit his job as an oil refinery foreman when he fell and broke both wrists; now he manages Christamore House, which provides food to the poor in exchange for work. Ermil Thompson, a sixty-eight-year-old believer in Christ "who worked her fingers to the bone for several years cooking and selling lunches to raise thousands of dollars to buy and convert a dilapidated house" into what became the Lifeline Community Center (76). And the list goes on.

Who are the people for whom these programs are designed? They are identified only as drug dealers, killers, prostitutes, and gang members. Olasky tells about the people who have established these programs. But we don't hear the stories of people who have been helped by them. Not one such person is individualized or given the dignity of a name. It is clear that the reader's admiration is to be directed toward the organizers of these faith-based programs. They are the ones who have triumphed over the odds. If we are indeed to have sympathy for anyone it is elicited primarily for them, and it is a sympathy that is meant to be rapidly converted into respect for their achievement. Take Tim Streett, a minister who when he was fifteen years old witnessed his father's murder in a mugging by two inner-city young men. Now thirty-six and married with a child of his own, he has established an after-school sports program for inner-city youth. Even the evocation of abused children does not work so much to solicit our compassion for them as it does to engender our dismay at their parents. As we saw with *Uncle Tom's Cabin*, the suffering child is the stock in trade of sentimental literature. But here the focus is not so much on the suffering child as it is on the parent as victimizer. Olasky quotes Judge James Payne, who has allowed faith-based organizations to work with the juvenile court system in Indianapolis: "We see fetal alcohol abuse, mothers on drugs physically and emotionally aggressive with children" (81).

Overall the emphasis is on *action*: on getting things done and on what has been called *effective* compassion, with the stress on results and not on sentiment. The narrative is entrepreneurial, with tough love one of its major lessons. For example, as one of the administrators of Teen Challenge (a national program for drug treatment) puts it, "We have a rule: If you don't work, you don't eat" (219). As George W. Bush commented approvingly in his July 1999 speech, "This is demanding love—at times, a severe mercy" (219).

This pragmatic stress on what works is also clearly seen in Joseph Jacobs's *The Compassionate Conservative: Assuming Responsibility and Respecting Human Dignity*, the second edition of which was published in 2000 and was endorsed enthusiastically by the then-governor George W. Bush on its red-white-and-blue cover: "Great Phrase! Great ideas!" In *The Compassionate Conservative* Jacobs, a former businessman and now a philanthropist, adopts the American form of the jeremiad and lays out what he sees as the principles of compassionate conservatism. At its core is economic conservatism. As he writes, "Compassion is an overarching moral value fundamental to all of us, no matter what our stand on specific moral issues. Wresting exclusive ownership of it from the liberal left will be easy if we say what conservative compassion will do. Elevating the debate to differences in how we make compassion work will attract the economic conservatives to our cause" (xxiii).

Pointing to some of the very problems identified by the scholars of sentiment that I discuss in the previous section, Jacobs asserts that liberal compassion has failed but that conservative compassion will *work*. His attention is not focused on the suffering body. Rather his concern is that liberalism creates dependency—emotional and economic dependency (I take up the question of dependency in my chapter "Bureaucratic Rage"). Jacobs perceptively observes that the pleasures of compassion, identified by Spelman and Berlant, can create a "double dependency": those who find themselves uplifted by the feeling of compassion must maintain a constituency of people who require their compassion, a phenomenon he vividly calls "moral greed" (44). Compassion is corrupting. It is an "emotional narcotic," a by-product of which is the toxic "feeling of superior moral strength" (84).

In the texts I've discussed that deal with liberal compassion—from Stowe to Berlant—there has been in particular a sustained interest in the suffering of African Americans in the United States. In *The Compassionate Conservative* we find instead the rhetorical transformation of the fact of this history of slavery and suffering into a brutal metaphor for dependency across the entire population of America that Jacobs believes is the responsibility of liberals. "The welfare state created by liberals in pursuit of their compassion has assumed the role of the benevolent slave owner of the twentieth century," he proclaims, crudely drawing on America's history of slavery to delegitimate Democratic policies (xxiv). What does Jacobs propose? His interest is not in faith-based charities—even if animated by tough love—but in the creation of jobs.

For Jacobs the creation of jobs is itself an act of compassion. What kinds of stories does he tell about compassion? Business stories. Early in his book he tells us about the difficult times he himself endured in 1984 when, as the head of his company, he was forced to restructure his workforce, including "reducing permanent staff by almost half" (28). "The emotional toll on those of us who had to do this restructuring was debilitating," he writes. "We spent many sleepless nights as our compassion for those people who were being fired (I refuse to use softer words) was constantly being challenged by our compassion for the rest of the people who would lose their jobs if the company were allowed to fail. This is one more illustration that compassion is not an unalloyed virtue. Even with that noble virtue one needs to make choices—tough choices" (28). I need hardly note that the focus is directed first to his wretched feelings, not those of the soon to be unemployed. But how, given the importance of the creation of jobs, does this narrative that begins with unemployment come to an end? On a note of enterprising optimism. In the business world, which Jacobs regards as a microcosm of America, his firing of people proved successful: some fifteen years later the company is four times larger—the result of tough love, among other factors. Thus calculation of compassion is at base quantitative, economic. As Jacobs recounts later in *The Compassionate Conservative*, in telling another business story of compassionate conservatism and writing of the successful measures he put in place to reduce the number of injuries in his company, there was also an economic benefit, a brightening of the bottom line. The conclusion of this narrative? "Our insurance premiums are reduced," he notes. "Therefore, self-interest is served" (154).

The liberal narrative of compassion asks us to have sympathy for those who are suffering unjustly. Such suffering is understood as social suffering, an apt term used by the medical anthropologist Arthur Kleinman and others in their important book *Social Suffering*. George W. Bush, in appropriating the rhetoric of compassion and drawing on the above two models of compassionate conservatism, has shrewdly excised the suffering body— one characterized by difference—from his national narrative of the future of the United States. Foregrounded are not the suffering bodies of African Americans and the poor, but ministers and businessmen. With Bush's plan for faith-based charities and calling on ministers who provide spiritual healing, we find ourselves in an uncanny return to the nineteenth century. Compassion is not only given a religious dimension, it is masculinized. With Bush's belief in economic conservatism, we return to the Reagan years under the banner of compassion.

Yet Bush doesn't ask us to focus on people in pain. He doesn't concern himself with the problem of the appropriation of feeling or of an unequal balance of power. If Nussbaum asks us to resurrect the emotion of pity in social and political life today by placing pity in a historical narrative and contending that we must recuperate its former sense of "fellow-feeling, sympathy," then Marvin Olasky does not go to so much trouble. He simply insists on the obsolete definition of compassion given in the *Oxford English Dictionary*: "Suffering together with another, participation in suffering; fellow-feeling, sympathy." Compassion is, he declares in *Compassionate Conservatism*, "suffering with" (2). In a politically brilliant move, by the sleight of hand of definition, the problem of an imbalance of power is eliminated. Thus in the conservative narrative of compassion—indeed in a sense *there is no narrative*, merely citations, and thus virtually no emotion can be enkindled—the very critique of the liberal narrative of compassion (epitomized by Berlant's argument) is converted into a strength for conservatives. If the liberal focus is on the uncertain connection between feeling and action, the calculated response of conservatives has been to incisively sever the link between feelings of compassion for people and action, thus eliminating the feeling of compassion altogether and stressing the action that is *work*. One of their prime messages is that work *works*.

But I would be remiss if I concluded on the above note. As I did research for this chapter, I was surprised by the ways in which I felt drawn to several of the pragmatic arguments advanced by conservatives and by the unexpected directions in which my reading took me. Jacobs ends his book not with his own words but with a confession on the part of two self-identified compassionate liberals—Jennifer Vanica and Ron Cummings. They have worked for ten years as directors of the Jacobs Family Foundation and the Jacobs Center for Neighborhood Innovation (formerly the Jacobs Center for Nonprofit Innovation) and refer to themselves as having been converted by the experience. Having spent twenty years in the nonprofit world, they were more than skeptical of Jacobs's free-market strategies, including the tenet of accountability. But after some five years with the Family Foundation they realized that grants that do not lead to self-sustainability simply do not work, and they pursued the bolder strategy of what they call venture philanthropy with the Jacobs Center for Neighborhood Innovation. And they have seen successes. They thus refer to his story of the 1984 restructuring of his company with respect, not cynicism. "Dr. Jacobs tells the story of coming out of retirement when Jacobs Engineering was floundering and having to fire middle management and restructure the company," they write. "He says it was the most painful experience of his professional life. But it saved the company and resurrected it to employ many more people" (263).

I found their testimony sobering and I also found immensely hopeful the possibility that some action might *work* after all. What was stirred in me was not compassion but hope, the feeling that something could be done. Perhaps I was only responding to being hailed as a caring citizen, seduced by an empty promise. Certainly the workings of the Bush administration have not given me reason to increase my expectations. But I did find myself open to entertaining new possibilities. I was attracted to the meditations on compassion by the philosopher Simone Weil in great part because she asks us—in an unsentimental way—to take on the responsibility of doing good works. For her—although I simplify here—justice is a form of compassion, and justice is a social act, as we see in her books *The Need for Roots* and *First and Last Notebooks*. For her compassion is not so much a sentiment as it is a belief.

I also turned to the challenging work of the German philosopher Agnes

Heller, who argues that conscience is an emotion—an idea that is intriguing because she reverses the conventional understanding that feelings of caring are ethical by suggesting instead that an ethical sense is itself a feeling. Heller prefers to use the word "concern" to describe this moral orientation to the world. For Heller concern includes helping those in need. Here she recalls Lynne Henderson's inclusion of the desire to alleviate the suffering of others in the meanings of empathy. But Heller's emphasis falls less on feeling and more on involvement. "Decent persons indeed feel empathy," she writes; "however their predominant emotional state of mind is one of concern rather than one of compassion (though it does not exclude the feeling of compassion). . . . Being concerned includes the readiness 'to do something about it' " (130).

The legal scholar Martha Minow has written about the blurring of boundaries between the public and the private, the secular and the religious, and the nonprofit and the profit worlds. In the essay "Partners, Not Rivals?" she closes with an invitation to join her in a "search for ways to turn rivals into partners in the service of fairness, skill, and compassion" (1094). Minow suggests that we need new metaphors to help us build this world together—not the language of boundaries and lines but of commitments and values. I would further suggest that the boundaries are blurring, appropriately so, between the emotions and judgment or reason, and that we need to find a way to avoid accenting one term over the other.

The philosopher Annette Baier offers us one such way. She theorizes trust as a value that mediates between what she sees in contemporary philosophical debates as a feminist emphasis on caring and compassion and a male emphasis on law, obligation, and contract, where both are ultimately inadequate positions for many reasons—for what we might without blushing or wincing call humane reasons. I like her singling out trust as a value. Trust does not belong to what Berlant would call a passive world of feeling, one that can be satisfied with the narcotic of feeling itself. Trust is a declaration of respect, an appraisal of the world—in the form of another person or an institution, for example—and is thus a judgment. Trust therefore has a cognitive dimension. It also has an affective dimension.[21] It belongs not just to a world of solipsistic self-regarding feeling, which is, as we have learned, one of the dangers of compassion. Trust assumes a world of interdependency. Trust confers agency on others. Trust can itself be a gift, in the hope that it is offered wisely.

STRUCTURES OF FEELING, "NEW" FEELINGS

New and emerging social structures generate new forms or sites of feeling. These feelings in turn provide us with what can be an elusive yet palpable register of these changes, a register theorized by Raymond Williams as a structure of feeling conveyed in the creative work of literature and other arts.[1] As I hope I have been able to show in the chapters in part 1, a related approach is a self-reflexive phenomenology. This is a form of what Stephen Muecke has called the archeology of feeling, or what I would call a critical phenomenology, one goal of which is to comprehend the ways in which the spheres of subjectivity—here feelings—and sociality mutually constitute each other. Writing the history of social formations and cultural forms thus entails a history of the emotions.

In part 2 of this book I turn to what I call "new" feelings—sympathy for nonhuman cyborgs, bureaucratic rage, and statistical panic. Or perhaps it would be best to think of them as familiar feelings in new sites. It is my hope that I am not promising far more than I can offer. But it should be clear that I am not so much making an argument as I am offering these elastic rubrics in the spirit of speculation, as cultural hypotheses, suggesting that they might help us understand some of our experience in everyday life today.

Here I engage the cultural politics and poetics of the emotions in terms larger than the politics of identity. To do so I touch on broad-based and interrelated changes in our thoroughly mediated postmodern society as witnessed in literature and film—the emergence of robot culture, the accelerating bureaucratization of everyday life, and the omnipresent penetration of statistics into every aspect of our lives. A major preoccupation in American culture is health and illness, and thus it is no accident that illness narratives are taken up in each of the chapters in part 2, albeit not exclusively.

The final chapter in part 1 focused on compassion by drawing attention both to the liberal narrative of compassion, with the suffering body as its subject, and to the rhetoric of compassionate conservatism invoked by the George W. Bush administration—a rhetoric, drained of sympathy, that serves as a screen for economic conservatism. Sympathy is also the subject of the first chapter in part 2. But it is sympathy found in a surprising place. As I mentioned in the introduction, the psychoanalyst Christopher Bollas and the historian Peter Stearns have argued that consumer culture promotes the cultivation of a self devoid of subjectivity, a self that conceives of itself as an object and functions without friction in the world. If the philosopher Charles Taylor has brilliantly traced what he calls the growth of forms of inwardness as the process of the making of modern self, we have been witnessing the atrophy of those forms. But sympathy is in fact circulating in another site, one in which we are sutured to nonhuman cyborgs in an emotional economy that links us to emerging imaginative, virtual, and material worlds.

The emergence of the science of cybernetics since the Second World War, in addition to the recent developments in robotics, neurology, and artificial life, has generated "new" feelings, or familiar feelings, for the new beings (fictional, virtual, and material) that are nonhuman cyborgs. Robots have been present for years in the cultural imagination but suddenly they are everywhere—in short stories and books and films. Virtual beings are appearing on cinematic screens and in video screens in art galleries. I predict these virtual as well as material beings—robots in various guises and shapes—are on the cusp of populating our everyday life. I call these feelings of attachment to this emerging life-form "prosthetic emotions," and I am interested in particular in the emotion of sympathy, hence the title of the chapter—"Sympathy for Nonhuman Cyborgs." Sympathy is a social emotion and as such tends to promote reciprocity, mutual interdependence, and thus intersubjectivity. Suffering engenders sympathy, as it should, and illness is a ubiquitous form of suffering, one that in our technological imagination extends to the nonhuman world where even nonhuman cyborgs fall sick. In this chapter I consider works of science fiction mainly from the late 1960s to the 1980s (among them Arthur C. Clarke's trilogy *A Space Odyssey* and the film *Blade Runner*); the everyday practice of treating media as well as robots as if they were people (My Real Baby, Cog, and Kismet); and theories of techno-artifacts and the emotions.

In the chapter "Bureaucratic Rage" I speculate about a class of feelings I call the bureaucratic. Bureaucracies of all kinds both require our participation in their machinations and thwart it. Randy Martin in *Financialization of Daily Life* calls this "bureaucratic suffering" (4), and the sociologist Ruth Gilmore, in her research on the prison industry in California, has brilliantly referred to the "infrastructure of feeling" that is produced by such totalitarian systems. My focus is on the feelings engendered by the experience of taking care of people and having to negotiate our health-care system. I draw on three memoirs from the mid-1980s to the early 1990s that deal with AIDS, Alzheimer's disease, and schizophrenia in the context of brazen bureaucracies. I consider them prescient works, calling our attention in that period to the emerging health care crisis in this country while focusing on diseases that were then both harrowing and baffling (what was AIDS, Alzheimer's, schizophrenia?). Raised to a new pitch in today's consumer culture, illness is an existential reality, a national scandal, and a consumer good, with the preservation of our health sold to us as our individual lifework and as shortcomings to be surmounted and bodily improvements to be undertaken. Illness has spawned virtually impenetrable and bloated bureaucracies in the United States that are, using Hendrik Hertzberg's term, "sadistic" in complexity, thereby generating what I call bureaucratic feelings, with rage a prime example. As is preeminently clear, the state of health care in the United States is a national disaster, with the revelations in February 2007 of the disastrous state of care of wounded soldiers in the so-called outpatient facilities at the Walter Reed Army Medical Center in Washington, D.C. a shameful case in point.

Finally, in the last chapter of part 2 my focus is on the deployment of statistics that address our health. If a diagnosis of illness, along with the requisite sheaf of statistics, can result in panic, today the very possibility of the *loss* of health insurance—in addition of course to the lack of it in the first place—is itself a source of intense anxiety for millions of people, thus disclosing the painfully iatrogenic nature of what is euphemistically referred to as our health care system.

In the introduction I referred to the distinction that Fredric Jameson makes between the culture of modernism, characterized by a psychology of depth, and the culture of postmodernism, characterized by a waning of the psychological emotions. This distinction underwrites the chapter on statistical panic where I contrast the technological culture of modernity, condensed in the figure of the train, with that of postmodern media culture. In *The Origins of Postmodernity* Perry Anderson calls the televisions and computers of our media culture "perpetual emotion machines" pouring "out a torrent of images" and "transmitting discourses that are wall-to-wall ideology" (89). For Anderson, the technological transition to postmodernity is marked by the introduction in the early 1970s of color television, a media machine whose tsunami of images virtually silences art. In my chapter "Statistical Panic" I open with a media story from television, an episode from a prime-time TV medical drama whose message is the supposedly supreme clarity of truth provided by statistics (this is one of the omnipresent discourses of which Anderson speaks). But I hold on to the interrogating

five

SYMPATHY FOR NONHUMAN CYBORGS

I always used to wonder, do machines ever feel lonely? You and I talked about machines once, and I never really said everything I had to say. I remember I used to get so *mad* when I read about car factories in Japan where they turned out the lights to allow the robots to work in darkness.

—Douglas Coupland, *Microserfs*

Turing, who demonstrated that a self-reproducing machine was theoretically possible, was a logician, and understandably limited the problem of self-reproduction to asexual techniques; but if we are interested in the problem of human simulation, the race of automata must be perpetuated not only by knowledge but by passion. . . .

The creation of a human automaton would require an affect system.

—Silvan Tomkins, *Shame and Its Sisters*

Signification, technology, and subjectivity coevolve.

—N. Katherine Hayles, *My Mother Was a Computer*

In Donna Haraway's lively little book *The Companion Species Manifesto* she turns to the marvelous species that is comprised by all manner of dogs. She calls our attention to the process of the coevolution of species as well as to the serious pleasures offered by the cohabitation of humans and dogs. "Love, commitment, and yearning for skill with another are not zero sum games," she insists. Haraway singles out the happiness that arises in the discipline of dogs and humans developing expertise together. She underscores the generative nature of working together with mutual respect, a process that fosters "acts of love like caring about and for other concatenated, emergent worlds" (61). What is involved is no less than the forging of new kinship structures, which are characterized ideally by trust and respect. In such a case I understand love as a "prosthetic emotion," one that connects us to beings in the nonhuman world—both the world of nature and the technological world (I understand that these are problematic terms but I use them here for the sake of simplicity). What is at stake is the creation of a continuum or interpenetration between these worlds, one suggested by the conviction that we are living in a posthuman age. Thus I understand prosthetic emotions as a subset of social emotions.

With regard to our emerging digital culture, the dominant discourse of the emotions is not that of the social emotions or dispositions—love, care, and respect—but rather that of intensities. Mark Hansen in his excellent book *New Philosophy for New Media*, for example, theorizes the coevolution of the human body and the digital technosphere through the radical aesthetic interface provided by new media artworks themselves. Hansen offers a strong and subtle argument that our bodies, brought into contact with the digital in these new ways, *experience* the virtual. He also vividly testifies to the new experiences of time and space, of perception and embodiment, that emerge in the process—the affects of bewilderment, vertigo, strangeness, disorientation, and irrelevance. I consider these to be nonsubjective affects in the Deleuzian sense and they are not my concern here.[1] Rather my story will take the form of a more sentimental tale, one that might be called a science fiction itself—except that I have come on some fundamental level to believe it.

Why have I chosen the phrase "prosthetic emotions"? One widely held view of technological development is that of an increasingly elaborated regime of tools and machines—prostheses—that extend and amplify the capabilities of the human body. Thus the various strengths of the body are understood to be augmented by prostheses in the broadest sense: the muscle power of the arm is heightened through the lever, the sensory function of the eye through the telescope, and the computational-solving skill of the brain through the computer. To a great extent this narrative is based on an ideology of progress defined in terms of increases in efficiency and in productivity—in short, a kind of economic rationality. But if we turn our attention to the emotions, we find another narrative of technological development, one that does not privilege cool rationality but rather empathetic understanding. Over the long history of western culture, rationality has generally been contrasted with emotion—where reason is accorded positive value and emotion is considered a potential pathogen. But in the complementary narrative of technological development that I sketch below, the emotions themselves are considered a strength, not a weakness. More precisely, specific emotions are sanctioned in the narratives I single out in this chapter—the complex of emotions we designate by such words as sympathy and love and trust.

The history of the reception of technology in America itself has an affective history, one marked by the oscillation between the opposite emotional poles of technophilia (the ecstatic embrace of technology) and technophobia (the fear of technology).[2] I want to underscore a *third* tradition of the reception of technology in American culture—and more broadly, western culture. This tradition is captured in the words of the computer geek I invoke in my epigraph from Douglas Coupland's *Microserfs*, a novel about employees from Microsoft who leave the company to form their own business. "I used to wonder," he says sympathetically, "do machines ever feel lonely?" He feels neither in awe of nor threatened by technology as embodied in robots. Neither the technological sublime nor technological determinism are at stake for him; neither technophilia nor technophobia characterizes his response. Rather the emotions of everyday life are entailed. He feels sorry for the machines. He feels a warm and knowing sympathy for them. He feels distressed—indeed angry—that these robots have been forced to work in a car factory in the dark, thus sentenced to a space from which sociability has been struck.

He has, in other words, "a feeling" for these working robots. I am evoking here *A Feeling for the Organism*, the title of Evelyn Fox Keller's influential biography of the geneticist Barbara McClintock. Keller's book has been taken up by feminists—including Alison Jaggar in her essay "Love and Knowledge"—as offering an alternative model for scientific research, one based not on detachment but rather on a feeling of closeness to the subject of one's research, a feeling described by Keller in terms of affection, empathy, kinship, and a love that respects difference.[3] That feeling here might best be called sympathy. Hence I have given this chapter the title "Sympathy for Nonhuman Cyborgs," by which I mean to honor the work of both Evelyn Fox Keller and Donna Haraway, whose seminal essay "Manifesto for Cyborgs" appeared almost twenty-five years ago. Indeed my own chapter can be understood as a low-keyed manifesto in favor of respect for the material lifeworld for which we are collectively responsible. I thus depart from much of the criticism in technoscience studies that diagnoses our cultural response to innovation in terms of unrelieved anxiety. In this chapter I reserve the capacious term "cyborg" for nonhuman technoartifacts.

In the first and longest section of this chapter I discuss three texts in American science fiction and film from the late 1960s to the 1980s—Arthur C. Clarke's trilogy *A Space Odyssey* (1968, 1982, and 1987), Philip K. Dick's novel *Do Androids Dream of Electric Sheep?* and the subsequent film

Blade Runner (1968, 1982), and the film *Silent Running* (1972). In these works emotions are attributed to machines in the form of computers, replicants, and robots.[4] I then jump to the twenty-first century, turning to Michael Cunningham's novella *Like Beauty* where new kinship structures are forged not between a human and a nonhuman cyborg, but rather between a nonhuman cyborg and a serpentine-like alien from another planet. In this quartet of texts, artificial entities are endowed with life through the attribution of an emotional nature to them, in particular through *their* capacity for sympathy and for self-sacrificial behavior. The nonhuman cyborg is for the most part figured as a hybrid organism endowed with feeling—that is, as an artificial entity that becomes an organism precisely because of its capacity for feeling. One of my primary interests in this chapter is thus to suggest a trajectory of technological evolution by touching on these terms—artificial intelligence, emotional intelligence, artificial emotions, and artificial life. Crucial to this development is precisely the sympathy of humans for nonhuman cyborgs, with bodily suffering (including illness) calling this feeling forth. Thus subjectivity is figured as being mutually constituted, in Donna Haraway's words, in "acts of love like training in Vicki Hearne's sense breeds acts of love like caring about and for other concatenated, emergent worlds" (61).

In the second section of this chapter I turn from the representation of the intersubjectivity of these species to touch on the sociology of human-technology interaction in the age of media and the robot. My stress is on the ordinariness of these interactions, where our experience of our technological habitat is what we would call sociable—that is, created by the binding emotion of sympathy, an attitude of respect, and a comic view of everyday life. In the final section I consider theoretical work on the emotions and technology, and I conclude on the note of a feeling for the cyborg (both human and nonhuman) as I perform it myself—namely sympathy for literary nonhuman cyborgs.

My method is in great part the accumulation of texts from different domains—fiction, sociology, artificial life, anthropology, neurology, theory, and studies of the emotions—that point to this phenomenon of an emergent feeling for the nonhuman cyborg. This strategy is intended to simulate the process of our accommodation to our evolving technological habitat. But accommodation is too weak a word because it suggests a dimension of capitulation. For me the accumulation of these texts—and I could refer to many more—has had a cascading effect, one that proves persuasive about what our future holds for us. And indeed the beginning of that future is now. If over the course of decades popular literature and film have been attuning us to cohabitation with nonhuman cyborgs, today robots are *everywhere* in the visual media where they are rapidly populating our cultural imagination. Given the advances in computer animation techniques and other digital technologies, today these figures are more convincing, more compelling, and more *lifelike*. Consider Steven Spielberg's *AI* (2001). Consider the independent film *Robot Stories* (2002), a quartet of love stories about robots, the first of which is about a baby robot (or a robot baby) and the last of which is about a widower whose late wife appears to him as a virtual being. Consider the film *I, Robot* (2004) starring Will Smith, which is based on Isaac Asimov's 1950 collection of short stories under the same title. Consider the summer 2007 blockbuster film *The Transformers*, a goofy sentimental action film that is a cross between *E.T.* and *Star Wars*. It features two strains of robots characterized by Kleinian emotional splitting—hatred and rage on the one hand, and sympathy and caring on the other. The good autobots ("auto" is for autonomous) are sensitive to humans, and in turn the two teen-aged heroes—a boy and a girl—come to respect and trust and have sympathy for them (tears are shed when one of these autobots is gravely injured). At the end the two adolescents form a nuclear family of sorts along with their newfound guardian, the autobot action figure that can morph into a car. Diminutively named Bumblebee, he inspires affection and is portrayed as a much better parental figure than is the boy's bumbling biological father. This familiar narrative has historical precedents, to which I now turn.

1

In western culture there is a long history of the blurring of boundaries between the animate and the inanimate—a history that in the past three centuries has in particular involved humans and nonhuman cyborgs.[5] An important strand in this history is precisely the attribution of the emotions of sympathy and love to the inventions made in our bodily image. Prominent examples include Mary Shelley's famous Frankenstein-created creature whose nineteenth-century heart appropriately swells with sentiment and pounds with fear, and Frank Baum's Tin Woodman in *The Wizard of Oz* who yearns for a heart and whose wish is granted even if only in Dorothy's dream. We could cite as well the whimsical characters created by

Stanislaw Lem in *The Cyberiad*, notably the two appealing idiosyncratic robots named Klapaucius and Trurl who write love poems out of the bits and pieces of mathematics and science. We could refer to Robbie in *I, Robot*, the companion robot to a little girl who comes to see him as a feeling friend and whom he melodramatically saves from a sure death. That our inventions will possess a good heart would seem, in other words, to be a deep dream (if not the only dream) of what I would call our technological unconscious.

But what might have been a wish some three hundred years ago now seems much nearer to reality today.[6] That our inventions will be capable of artificial emotions—emotions that can't be distinguished from genuine emotions, thus eliminating the distinction altogether—seems within possible reach. As an important speculative case in point I turn first to Arthur C. Clarke's *A Space Odyssey*, a classic science fiction narrative that exemplifies the cultural logic of emotional growth across the spectrum of scientists and nonhuman cyborgs, one made possible by the very projection of the emotions as prostheses that create relationships of attachment in the psychoanalytic sense. Strict boundaries are definitively erased in the process, thereby creating new kinship structures.

Spanning sixty fictional years, the first three novels of *A Space Odyssey* trace the emotional evolution of three of its characters—the young and dispassionate astronaut David Bowman, the central computer intelligence known as HAL, and Dr. Chandra, the computer scientist devoted to HAL. In the first and best known of the volumes (no doubt because of the celebrated film *2001: A Space Odyssey* directed by Stanley Kubrick), HAL is presented as a computer possessing artificial intelligence as it is commonly defined. With his English-speaking male voice, he exhibits extraordinary computing ability. But when his skill goes tragically awry the resulting malevolent behavior toward humans leads them to completely disable him.

Most readers of *A Space Odyssey* stop after the first volume. This is a mistake. We learn in the second volume that HAL's behavior was all the result of an unfortunate glitch in his program. He was sick, we could say, and he has returned to health. Over the course of the next sixty years (and the next two volumes in the series), HAL evolves into a disembodied entity possessing an emotional intelligence so deeply altruistic and wise that it is characterized as spiritual.[7] Thus in the first three books of *A Space Odyssey* the capacity to respond to a situation with sustained feeling, not just logic or reason, is ultimately figured as an *evolutionary strength* and as a critical component of life, whether biological, electronic, or spiritual. How does this transformation come about? Critical to the evolution of HAL are his relationships with humans—Dr. Chandra, the scientist who invents him and loves him, and the wary astronaut David Bowman who comes to trust him again.

In *Understanding Media* Marshall McLuhan writes about the relationship between the human body and technological invention in terms of "autoamputation," observing that a given technology serves to decrease stress on the part of the body at stake. In *A Space Odyssey* the emotional feedback loops that are created serve precisely to redress the initial "numbness" that McLuhan noted. But here it is *emotional numbness* that is repaired. For it is also the case that both the cool Bowman and the efficient Chandra are transformed in their long contact with HAL over time. We learn in the second volume of *A Space Odyssey* that Bowman had repressed an intense emotional past characterized by strong emotions of attachment (his grief at the death of his brother is compounded by guilt for having been intimately involved with his girlfriend). Indeed it was this profound emotional reservoir that was crucial in his honored selection as a cosmic probe. Ultimately Bowman is released from the emotional emptiness of professional technoculture through his encounter with beings superior in both scientific and emotional respects.

Similarly Dr. Chandra, depicted as unemotional in the extreme, himself awakens into an emotional existence as HAL comes back to life (he also dies of a broken heart when later separated from HAL). It is Chandra who is given the role of insisting that computers can possess emotions. Indeed the ontological status of computer emotions is for him not even a matter of debate. As we read in *2010*, Chandra "had long since broken off communications with the dwindling body of philosophers who argued that computers could not really feel emotions, but only pretended to do so" (22–23). When HAL is reactivated he returns to what I am tempted to call his natural emotional state: HAL is friendly, not hostile. Co-emotional evolution is one of the emotional logics of *A Space Odyssey*.

"Our machines are disturbingly lively," Donna Haraway has remarked, "and we ourselves frighteningly inert."[8] How are capacities for emotional connections created and revived? What is represented in *A Space Odyssey* is the process of technocultural feedback loops generating emotional growth—namely the development of human-artificial entity intersubjectivity that is itself a deeply benevolent form of intelligence. It is Bowman who becomes a tool. HAL is figured as a self-conscious cyborg. In the end they are virtually indistinguishable from each other. As Gary Downey and others rightly insist in "Cyborg Anthropology," "Human subjects and subjectivity are crucially as much a function of machines, machine relations, and information transfers as they are machine producers and operators" (343). The vision is one of the co-evolution of both species as companion species, one in which the emotions—they are prosthetic emotions, emotions of attachment—figure prominently. This process might best be understood as "a causality of *coupling*," to refer to the philosopher of science Isabelle Stengers, and not a causality that is linear or circular.[9]

Even more vividly than the first three volumes of Clarke's *Space Odyssey*, Philip K. Dick's touchstone novel *Do Androids Dream of Electric Sheep?* exemplifies the redemptive emotional logic of the intersubjectivity of humans and cyborgs. Published in 1968, *Electric Sheep* was in 1982 made into the now-classic film *Blade Runner* starring Harrison Ford as Rick Deckard. Just as *Uncle Tom's Cabin* serves as the ur-text of the liberal narrative of compassion in American literary studies, so Philip K. Dick's narrative is one to which people in technoscience studies repeatedly return.[10] Significantly, both narratives turn fundamentally on the capacity for empathy.

The premise at the opening of Dick's story (in both the novel and the film) is that the distinction between humans and nonhuman cyborgs (made in our image) is precisely the (human) ability to feel sympathy for other humans. (In the novel the nonhuman cyborgs are referred to as "androids" but in the film they are referred to as "replicants"; I will use the term "replicant" when referring to either the novel or the film.) By the end of the story, however, that distinction is called thoroughly into question. In the novel in particular, it is precisely the undecidability of whether or not the emotions circulating in the distrustful culture of the future are artificial that results in the breakdown of the distinction between humans and replicants. And in the film it is the capacity of the replicants to form bonds of love and trust with one another and across the human-replicant divide that represents their evolution into genuinely artificial life. As Vivian Sobchak observes in *Screening Space* with regard to the science fiction films of the late 1980s, "Alien Others have become less other—be they extraterrestrial teddy bears, starmen, brothers from another planet, robots, androids, or replicants. They have become familiars" (293). As I am suggesting, one of the representational strategies deployed to accomplish this shift is the attribution of emotions to machines that have been invented in the image of the human. *Blade Runner* thus illustrates the shift from understanding intelligence as rooted in logic, problem solving, information processing, and computational skills to understanding intelligence as a mode of knowing that includes an emotional component as well, or what the science writer Daniel Goleman has influentially called "emotional intelligence."

In 1950 the British mathematician Alan Turing described the now famous Turing Test in an essay on machine intelligence. What is the Turing Test? A computer is said to pass the test and thus possess artificial intelligence if a human being, not knowing whether it is communicating with a machine or a person, doesn't guess that they are. (If a human passes the test—that is, doesn't identify the interaction as one with a computer—could we say they possess trust? What would that mean?) It is altogether appropriate then that in the fictional world of 2021 (one in which replicants are threatening to pass undetected in human society), the test for distinguishing replicants from humans is designed to measure not logic but emotional responses—in particular empathy in the face of another's pain.[11] "Empathy," we read early on in the novel, "evidently existed only within the human community, whereas intelligence to some degree could be found throughout every phylum and order including the arachnida" (26).

The replicant Roy Batty (Rutger Hauer) was designed for optimum self-sufficiency and combat. But by the close of the film he cares deeply for fellow replicant Pris (Daryl Hannah). He also saves Deckard, the human forced to hunt him down, from a certain death. That he spares Deckard is the unequivocal sign of his transformation from a preprogrammed being to a charismatic martyr who speaks eloquently about the pain of loss—his grief over the death of Pris and his acutely elegiac sense that the memories that bind him to her will vanish with his own imminent death. Here are the last words his character is given in *Blade Runner*: "All those moments will be lost in time like tears in rain. Time to die." This statement is followed by Deckard's voice-over: "I don't know why he saved my life. Maybe in those last moments he loved life more than ever before. Not just his life. My life." In the end Batty is shown as possessing heroic emotional stature. The unambivalent message is that superiority in physical strength and in computational skill—artificial intelligence—must be complemented by emotional intelligence.

Deckard ultimately finds himself gazing at Batty in sympathetic understanding, and he watches him die in a silence that speaks of compassionate respect, even admiration. Similarly Deckard comes to find himself not only attracted to the replicant Rachael Rosen (Sean Young) but also to feel sympathy for her, which is the ground for his capacity for empathy for replicants in general. The cultural critic Mark Dery has described Deckard as a "deadpan, monotoned flatfoot," a prime example of the "flattened affect that characterizes Homo Cyber" (252). This characterization is altogether apt for Deckard at the beginning of the narrative. But as with *A Space Odyssey*, one of the fundamental points of this technological narrative is precisely the development of the emotional world of the human characters through their very interaction with the replicants themselves.

How do the emotions of the replicants come into being? In *Blade Runner* artificial emotions are generated by the implantation of memories that grow, as it were, into emotional memories, thereby giving depth to being. The head of the Tyrell Corporation explains that the implantation of emotions is designed to render the replicants easier to control: "If we give them a past, we can create a cushion, a pillow, for their emotions, and consequently we can control them better." At the same time the Tyrell engineers acknowledge that in a matter of a few years the replicants "might develop their own emotional responses. Hate, love, fear, anger, envy." The epigraph from J.-B. Pontalis with which I opened this book is resonant here: "It's rare nowadays to hear words which, belonging to no one in particular, can be the property of anyone, words that are solid and inexhaustible like 'grief' or 'hatred'" (103). In *Blade Runner* these emotions can belong to *anyone*—even replicants. Paradoxically emotional growth, which is characterized by the development of ties to others, results in *independence* as well. Subjectivity is itself stimulated by the interdependence of beings, which also entails independence. We thus can read *Blade Runner* as a fictional forerunner of android epistemology—that is, a new interdisciplinary domain of research that explores "the space of possible machines and their capacities for knowledge, beliefs, attitudes, desires, and action in accordance with their mental states."[12]

What is particularly fascinating to me is that unlike HAL in *A Space Odyssey*, the replicants are figured not as boxlike computers but as biological organisms "designed," we are told in the film, "to copy human beings in every way except their emotions." *Blade Runner* thus also offers a model of emotional life arising out of complex organic embodiment, with emotional intelligence coming to complement artificial intelligence. Emotions arise in these nonhuman cyborgs not only by virtue of the development of intersubjective ties but also spontaneously, as it were, by the very virtue of their embodiment. Embodiment would seem, therefore, to be a necessary if not sufficient condition. Modeled here is Francisco Varela's theory of "enaction," a science of cognition based on concrete situatedness and embodiment, although here the lever is the prosthetic emotions.

In addition, as spectators, we are explicitly encouraged from the very beginning of *Blade Runner* to identify with the replicants and to feel sympathy for them. The prologue scrolls down before us, introducing us to the dark cityscape of the Los Angeles of the future, home to the Tyrell Corporation. How are the replicants used? As slave labor on worlds beyond the earth. Like the computer geek in Coupland's *Microserfs* who sympathizes with robots, worrying about their working conditions, we are primed to feel sympathy for the replicants who are unjustly sentenced to serve as slaves.[13]

There is a further twist. In the 1982 release of *Blade Runner* we are led to believe that Deckard is human. As we learn definitively in *Blade Runner: The Final Cut*, which was released in 2007, Deckard is himself a replicant. As Ridley Scott has said, "He was always a replicant."[14]

The intersubjectivity of nonhuman cyborgs and human beings, along with the more specific thematic of sympathy for nonhuman cyborgs, is a staple of science fiction films. We're encouraged to adopt the perspectives of cyborgs and of human beings, perspectives that ultimately converge into one, with both human beings and cyborgs portrayed as sharing similar emotional values. A wonderful case in point is *Silent Running*, the 1972 cult science fiction film directed by Douglas Trumbull and starring Bruce Dern. In *Silent Running* the botanist Freeman Lowell (Dern) takes it upon himself to save from destruction the last living species of earthly flora and fauna. Under his care trees have been preserved in giant geodesic domes adorning a spaceship. For him they are companion species.

Scott Bukatman has written about this film in terms of the artificial sublime, a visual aesthetic that engenders awe, fear, and wonder.[15] I am interested in another discourse of the emotions in the film, one of a much more mundane variety that is captured in the developing bonds between the botanist and the "drones" on the ship cast in the guise of little robots. After killing the other members of the crew on the ship (because they were under orders to explode the domes), Lowell invents a social world for himself, one in which he educates the drones to care for the last living specimens of earthly nature. Consider these three scenes. First is the charming, leisurely scene in which Lowell gives the drones whimsical names (Huey, Dewey, and Louie, an allusion to the nephews of Donald Duck), thereby identifying them as individuals and inaugurating his relation to them as a teacher of the emotions. In this scene we are presented cinematically with the perspective of the robots themselves through classic shot/reverse shot sequences. We see Lowell through their eyes, as if he were himself a televisual image with his very being and body mediated by technology, as is theirs. If this is how we look to them, so different from our image of ourselves as bodily present, we are led to wonder how they look to themselves. We find ourselves speculating, in other words, about their point of view.

Second, as if in a prophetic rebuttal of the 1997 chess match between Garry Kasparov and IBM's newly enhanced supercomputer Deep Blue (it was hyped in the media as a showdown between humans and machines), shortly afterward Lowell, Huey, and Dewey (Louie has by now been tragically lost to space) are shown playing a game of poker—not with angst but with pleasure. Lowell displays a heretofore unseen conviviality, laughing in delight at the skill of the robots. Because he is not threatened by their intelligence he takes pleasure in it (no technophobia here). Moreover he explicitly hails them as human, at one point exclaiming, "The man had a full house and he knew it!" Third, a later sequence adds the emotions of remorse and sympathy to their small circle of three. Having accidentally injured Huey, Lowell must operate on him—an operation that causes Dewey to feel Huey's pain as if it were his own. In *Silent Running*, then, a computer—one that is given a body in the form of a robot who can move in the world and communicate—is represented as indeed able to feel someone else's pain. As in *Blade Runner*, what is represented in this fictional world is the growth of subjectivity and independence generated in the context of the interdependence of humans and nonhuman cyborgs. At the end of the film Lowell destroys himself (and the injured Huey) in an act of conscience, but not before he releases the last remaining dome, with its precious forest, into space under the stewardship of Dewey. The habitat of the film is thus affectionately mundane as well as supremely sublime.

From outer space we shift back to earth. The time is postnuclear meltdown in Michael Cunningham's strange and lovely novella *Like Beauty*, the third and final section of his book of linked stories entitled *Specimen Days* (2005). Here we move into a different future. The two main characters are not a human and a nonhuman cyborg but rather a nonhuman cyborg (the simulo Simon) and an alien (Catareen). At his core Simon is mechanical, with flesh as his outer surround, cognition his base (there are no false memories as in *Blade Runner*), and a survival implant that urges him on. The narrative, which reads like an anthropological science fiction fable, is set in motion when Simon is saved from brutal extermination by Catareen (she works as a domestic, taking care of the children of a wealthy couple). If the landscape of *Like Beauty* seems to resemble that of *Blade Runner* in the beginning (it opens in a large city where both simulos and aliens are under strict surveillance), this quickly shifts as Simon and Catareen flee New York to New Jersey, then cross the polluted country (although some of the flora are coming back to life) to get to Denver, which is the point of Simon's origin (he has been programmed to return to his maker by a certain date). Thus in *Like Beauty* Cunningham eschews a high-tech vision of the future. The derelict houses of New Jersey yield to a rural landscape populated with a ragtag bundle of gruesome characters. On the outskirts of Denver is a ramshackle spaceship that can barely take off, one that is cobbled together by a black seventy-year-old inventor named Lowell (he is married to a Nadian, the species to which Catareen belongs).

The narrative focuses on the relationship between Cunningham's two central characters, male and female. Theirs is a love story, with Simon's growing appreciation across the boundaries of species for the singularity that is Catareen rising to the level of the aesthetic. Here are the opening words of *Like Beauty*. "She might have been beautiful. 'Beautiful' was of course an approximation. An earthly term. The nearest word in her language was 'keeram,' which more or less meant 'better than useful' " (217). Thus the very first adjective in the novella points to the aesthetic heart of the narrative, with Simon represented as not so much ruing his lack of feelings of the sentimental sort as longing for an understanding that is aesthetic. "I want *something*. I feel a lack," Simon explains to Catareen early in the narrative; "I don't know what to call it. I'm not really all that interested in feelings, frankly. Not of the boo-hoo-hoo variety. But there's something biologicals feel that I don't. For instance, I understand about beauty, I get the concept, I know what qualifies, but I don't feel it. I almost feel it, sometimes. But never for sure, never for real" (253).

Later in the novella, in a key scene of transformative insight, Simon comes to comprehend—phenomenologically, aesthetically, morally—Catareen's singular way of being in the world, and he can call her being beautiful. While traveling across the country (in, of all things, a Winnebago—no high-speed action here—*and* with a deformed twelve-year-old human named Luke, thus fashioning an interspecies family of three), they come upon a pond at the close of day. And they swim.

> In the water she looked wilder than she ordinarily did. She looked wilder and more true. She had a creaturely inevitability. Simon understood; he thought he understood. She would be feeling the layer of warm water floating on the cold, the sensation of skimming across a shallow bowl of purple light surrounded by a darkening world as the first of the stars came out. She would be disappearing into this just as she disappeared into her dream states, her lizard song.
>
> Simon was the first to get out of the water. He stood naked on the bank, letting the air dry him, and watched as Catareen and the boy emerged. Catareen naked was all sinew, with thin, strong arms and legs, tiny breast-buds, and a small, compact rise of boy, squarish pelvis. Who was the sculptor? Giacometti. She looked like a sculpture by Giacometti. . . .
>
> "Beautiful," he said. He was not entirely sure what he meant by the word at that particular moment. It seemed almost like a new greeting he and Catareen had agreed to exchange—a variation of common language, newly encoded.
>
> She turned at the sound of his voice. She was startled and shy. There was something about her at that moment. He could not describe it. There was perhaps no term for it in human language. He could not give it a name.
>
> He said instead, "How beautiful and perfect are the animals! How perfect is my soul! How perfect the earth, and the minutest thing upon it! (287)

Simon speaks involuntarily these words of Walt Whitman articulating a vision of the possibility of America, a dream of a common language across multitudes. For Simon has been supplied with a chip of poetry, one that Lowell had hoped would give him a moral sense. It is a moral sense underwritten by the aesthetic imagination that grasps the singularity of a life. His is a hybrid body, one that *contains* poetry. Hers is a lizard-like body, with emerald skin, prominent orange-yellow eyes, and a voice like a flute. As Simon learns more about Catareen's past (she was a member of the resistance on the planet of Nourthea, she had five children, all of whom were murdered) and about her character (she is defiant and stern, deeply reticent and resilient), he can imagine her as she was in her life, "a life that was hers and no one else's." And he takes deep pleasure in so doing. "Here was the bittersweet savor of it, the piercing somethingness of it— the pure sensation of being Catareen Callatura, at that moment, on an afternoon of no consequence, just before the rain" (323).

When we are first introduced to Simon, he is working as a thug for Dangerous Encounters, Ltd., a firm that sells tourists simulations of menacing urban encounters—muggings, sexual assaults, whatever. At the story's end he gently cares for Catareen. The two have become fictive kin, bound together by an attunement to each other—by respect, trust, gratitude, and the appreciation of the distinction that is beauty in other worlds and in other words. At work is a cultural poetics of the binding emotions across concatenated, emerging worlds. As Catareen lays dying, Simon can't bring himself to abandon her to save himself, and the spaceship on which he has a place pulls away without him. He understands that although he can do nothing to save her, what he *can* do—and this is of the utmost importance —is be with her while she dies. He takes his place on the bed with her, cradling her, falling asleep, waking to find that she has died. Earlier Catareen had a dream that Simon's future would contain beautiful mountains and that he would be a changed . . . man. Both of them thought this meant he should leave the planet earth on the spaceship with the others. But after her death he remains on earth and his future will indeed contain mountains—the Rocky Mountains—as he heads out to the Californian sea.

Emotions are learned; this is a point stressed by the philosopher Ronald De Sousa and the cultural critic Megan Boler, among others. But to understand Simon's decision not to escape earth with the others, to understand

Dewey's decision in *Silent Running* to disobey a preprogrammed command, to understand Roy Batty's decision to sacrifice himself for another, we may also refer to the principle of emergence. Emergent behavior is one of the key principles of the field and the theory of artificial life, which is a descendant of the field of artificial intelligence but based on organic science, not cybernetics. As Claus Emmeche writes in *The Garden in the Machine: The Emerging Science of Artificial Life*, "The essential feature of artificial life is that it is not predesigned. . . . The most interesting examples of artificial life exhibit 'emergent behavior.' The word 'emergence,'" he continues, "is used to designate the fascinating whole that is created when many semisimple units interact with each other in a complex, nonlinear fashion," producing a self-organizing system (20). From the perspective of the theory of emergence, the behavior and experience of these characters—HAL, Roy Batty, Simon, and Dewey, but also Bowman, Chandra, Deckard, Lowell, and Catareen—can be read as based on emergent emotional experience, on developing subjectivity. It is in interaction with key figures in their environment—indeed they *are* the environment—that they are *all* presented as developing sympathy as a capacity and as a substrate of knowledge. Sympathy is represented as emergent as subjective experience in intersubjective contexts.

Thus in all four of these science fiction texts—*A Space Odyssey, Blade Runner, Silent Running,* and *Like Beauty*—it is through the mutual interaction between humans and nonhuman cyborgs (or nonhuman cyborgs and aliens), with its complex feedback loops, that emotions emerge, and thus in turn permit the development of companion species. What is thematized is second-order emergence, one based on the prosthetic emotions distributed across species. As Katherine Hayles explains in her brilliantly titled book *My Mother Was a Computer*, "Second-order emergence arises when a system develops a behavior that enhances its ability to develop adaptive behaviors—that is, when it *evolves the capacity to evolve*" (198). For Hayles our own capacity to evolve rests in great part on respecting digital difference (this is my phrase) in terms of alternate ways of knowing and engaging with it. As she writes, "I think, therefore I connect with all the other cognizers in my environment, human and non-human" (213). Her emphasis is on the mutual interaction between distributed cognitive environments. As I have been suggesting, we must add to this the intelligence of the emotions.

In terms of the cultural politics of the emotions, what is at stake in these science fiction texts? As we have seen, the figure of the scientist empty of feeling is transformed into one full of feeling—one connected morally to others—by virtue of his interdependence with the inventions made in his own image. These science fiction tales speak to a cultural desire (it is perhaps a utopian wish) that new and imagined technologies will help repair our own insufficiencies—here impoverished emotional resources in relation to others. Hence the emotions of sympathy and love are prosthetic emotions. Moreover we can read these stories as underscoring the importance of respect for material culture, for the world of our own making. It is a complex interdependent system for which we must have "a feeling" (to allude once again to Evelyn Fox Keller's biography of Barbara McClintock). Thus this work calls for what my colleague Thomas Foster has termed "cyborg democracy," which I understand as equality and fairness for everyone before a democratic rule of law. In addition, I'm sure it will not have escaped notice that these science fiction stories are gendered predominantly male and trace the emergence of men of sympathetic feeling (a phenomenon I discussed in the previous chapter on compassion), relinquishing, as in the examples of Deckard and Simon, their programmed mandate to do harm to others and turning instead to the work of care. Whether human or nonhuman cyborgs (the distinction is rendered undecidable in these stories), ultimately they are figured as deeply moral beings and as stewards of the earth. Finally, our growing sense that these nonhuman cyborgs are part of our everyday life creates another kind of feedback loop, one that renders human cyborgs more familiar and acceptable to us. I am thinking in particular of the advances in prosthetic technologies. Consider, for example, the case of Claudia Mitchell, who lost her arm in a motorcycle accident. In 2005 she was the first woman (and fourth person) to be fitted with a bionic arm that can be controlled by thinking. She is a human cyborg, although the media prefers to describe her as a "bionic" woman. What once might have been perceived as a phobic disabled body—from war, from accident—is now being received with admiration as a common feature of everyday life.

2

As I move from the domain of representation to the sociology of human behavior with computers, media, and robots populating our technological habitat, I turn first to a text from science fiction. It is intended to serve as a bridge between this section and the previous one by demonstrating that representation and behavior are really two faces of the same coin. I am referring to three interconnected novels by Orson Scott Card—the novels *Ender's Game* (1977), *Speaker for the Dead* (1986), and *Xenocide* (1991). One of the major themes of these three novels is the cosmic conflict among four intelligent species and their ultimate reconciliation. A computer consciousness named Jane represents one of these species. What interests me is not just that Jane is presented as having deep emotional ties to two human beings in particular; instead, I am especially intrigued by the way Card explains how she took shape as a character—perhaps because in the context of this chapter I take it literally, or fantastically. In his introduction to *Speaker for the Dead*, Card writes: "The character of Jane wasn't in any of the outlines I made. Oh, yes, I gave him [the main character, Ender], a computer connection through the jewel in his ear, but I didn't know it was a *person*. Jane just grew because it was so fun to write her relationship with Ender. She helped bring *him* to life (he could so easily have been a stodgy, dull adult), and in the process came to life herself. By the time I was done with *Speaker for the Dead*, Jane was one of the most important characters in it, and much of the third book, *Xenocide*, centers around her" (xx).[16] My point is that in the process of writing, Card found himself treating the computer as a fictional character—as, in his word, a person, one that brought another character to life. He didn't make a consciously deliberate decision to do so. It just happened in what I am tempted to say was the natural course of mutual interaction.

This may strike us as commonplace. But that is precisely my point. In the world of daily life we also behave as if computers, for example, had personality traits. "Equating mediated and real life is neither rare nor unreasonable," Byron Reeves and Clifford Nass point out in *The Media Equation*. "It is very common, it is easy to foster, it does not depend on fancy media equipment, and thinking will not make it go away. The media equation—*media equals real life*—applies to everyone, it applies often, and it is highly consequential" (5). I find the results of their research fascinating, perhaps because their conclusions seem so sensible and almost charmingly ingenuous at the same time. They have found that we tend to perceive media as real places and people. As opposed to other technological artifacts (dishwashers, for example), we are inclined to treat media in accordance with the rules for social interaction in everyday life. My favorite chapters in their book are entitled "Politeness" and "Flattery." Here we learn that we're likely to respond with good manners to certain behaviors by a computer. Similarly we learn that people "will like the computer more and think the computer is better when it praises them than when it criticizes them" (55). We perceive computers as being part of our social world, not our purely artifactual world. Overall, Reeves and Nass conclude, "The most important implication of the research is that media experiences are *emotional* experiences" (136).[17]

Here is an example from *Being Digital*, a book by Nicholas Negroponte that addresses social interaction in the age of the Internet. In the chapter entitled "Digital Persona" Negroponte writes, "In general, our opinion of a computer's personality is derived from all the things it does badly. On occasion, the reverse may happen. One time I doubled over laughing when my spelling-check program looked at my dyslexic-style typo aslo and proudly suggested that *asshole* was the correct spelling" (217–18). In terms of the reception of technology, here we find ourselves in the comic world of everyday life that is far from the melodramatic world of technophobia or technophilia. This ease of adaptation to digital life is further underscored by Negroponte's predictions for the future. As he envisions it, the future will be populated by "systems with humor, systems that nudge and prod, even ones that are as stern and disciplinarian as a Bavarian nanny" (218).

In *Life on the Screen: Identity in the Age of the Internet* the sociologist Sherry Turkle observes that there has been an important shift in cultural mood regarding how people feel about interacting with computer programs, including diverse forms ranging from therapy programs and computer judges to bots in online chatrooms. During the late 1970s and early 1980s, our anxiety about computers lessened considerably, she argues. Today there is no question that people view computers with a nonchalant pragmatism. For me what is essential here is that these new programs must project or exhibit subjectivity so that there can be the simulation of an intersubjective exchange. What is the key to believing that a digital life-form possesses subjectivity? To treating a digital life-form as if she or he were a person? Indeed as a person? Joseph Bates, a researcher associated with "alternative" artificial intelligence, is convinced that it is the simulation of emotion that is central. I am suggesting that this alternative artificial intelligence is characterized by what I have been calling emotional intelligence, or artificial life itself at its fullest.

Finally, in *Flesh and Machines* Rodney Brooks, the former director of the Computer Science Artificial Intelligence Laboratory at MIT and a pioneer in the building of robots based on principles of situatedness and embeddedness in the world rather than on pure computational power, predicts that the robots of the future will have complex emotion-based systems. "We have built emotional machines that are situated in the world," he writes, "but not a single unemotional robot that is able to operate with the same level of purpose or understanding in the world" (201). In the future Brooks expects that emotion-based intelligent systems will eventuate in robots that "will have empathetic reactions to us" (202). He also forecasts that the converse will be the case. And in fact this is happening all around us. Consider the following small story about Jim Lynch, a member of the lab responsible for designing the internal emotional electronics for a robot doll named My Real Baby, which was launched during the 2002 holiday season. My Real Baby has moods (she is alternately distressed and happy) and a lively bodily life (she gets virtually hungry and actually damp).

> One day Jim had just received a doll back from a baby-sitter. As it lay on the desk in his office, it started to ask for its bottle: "I want baba." It got more and more insistent as its hunger level went up, and soon started to cry. Jim looked for the bottle in his office but could not see one. He went out to the common areas of the Toy Division and asked if anyone had a bottle. His doll needed one. As he found a bottle and rushed back to his office to feed the baby, a realization came over him. This toy, that he had been working on for months, was different from all previous toys he had worked on. He could have ignored the doll when it started crying, or just switched it off. Instead, he found himself *responding* to its emotions, and he changed his behavior as though the doll had real emotions. (158)

As with my examples from fictional worlds, with Jim and the robot baby doll (which is it? a baby? a doll? both?), we see the attachment of a human to a human-like invention where the process of technocultural feedback loops generate emotional connections.[18] Also presented is the principle and process of emergence.[19]

Robots are already present in record numbers in the workplace and on the battlefield. I predict that they will soon be omnipresent in domestic space and in hospital space—that is, in domains where we expect, or at least hope, to find sympathy. For example, the South Korean government, in focusing on service robots rather than on military or industrial robots, is planning to have them in place in every home between 2015 and 2025.

One of the robots in development is Jupiter, who stands two feet tall, has a rotating head, and can recognize voices and faces. His big eyes change shape to simulate emotions.[20] Closer to home, one of my friends who just had back surgery told me that there was a roving robot—named Dr. Delillo —on her hospital floor. The robot served as a material avatar for her doctor in absentia, who spoke to her through a video screen embedded in the robot. How does she describe Dr. Delillo? As charming, fetching, friendly.

3

Bruno Latour in his wonderfully quirky book *Aramis, or the Love of Technology* (about the proposed subway spur for Paris dubbed Aramis) also extends subjectivity to a technological artifact—and a hypothetical one at that. As a sociologist of science and technology, Latour surprises us by giving Aramis speech. He writes from the point of view of the subway system, which is a humorously poignant strategy since the system was destined never to be built. Latour posits the interdependent subjectivity of the human and the artifactual in asking this remarkable rhetorical question: "Could the unconscious be full of machines as well as affects?" While his view of the world in general is profoundly comic, we should nonetheless take this question seriously—and we should do so by turning it partly around. If machines are inhabiting our unconscious, could not affects inhabit machines in an intersubjective exchange?

Intersubjective systems can be self-correcting systems (they can also, of course, be profoundly dysfunctional). The question of the integration or coupling of self-correcting systems was posed by the brilliant anthropologist Gregory Bateson in *Steps to an Ecology of Mind*, one of the great books of the American 1970s. "The problem of coupling self-corrective systems together," he writes, "is central in the adaptation of man to the societies and ecosystems in which he lives" (443). To ecological systems and social systems we must add *technocultural systems* as well. What I have been suggesting is that the representation, rhetoric, and performance of the attribution of emotions to computers, replicants, cyborgs, bots, and robots, a lifeworld that extends to ours—indeed *is* ours—serves as just such a coupling device. The emotion of choice is sympathy—or empathy, its generalized form. Thus the emotions as they are thematized in the science fiction I have been discussing and the emotions as they are experienced in our technological habitat populated by the computer, the Internet, and the robot together serve as a kind of bridge—as an intangible but very real prosthesis that helps us connect ourselves to the world we have been inventing.

In short, the emotions are themselves an important dimension of phenomenological accounts of human-technology relations. Indeed what I have been describing is precisely a phenomenology of technology, both as it is represented and as it is experienced. For the most part, phenomenological accounts of technology have been given in terms of experiential categories such as time and space—of speed and slowness, of immensity and contraction, and of distance and closeness, for example. But we need to consider the emotions as well.

Our technological habitat is changing profoundly in terms of the distribution of the emotions. In the past we've routinely ascribed anthropomorphic qualities to our fictional technological creations as well as to our inventions, as I noted earlier. But the attribution of emotions to the new forms of our technological lifeworld represents a quantum leap, one that is accelerating. We are behaving as if the emotions of these new forms are real, as our science fiction insists they are. As an attachment or prosthetic device to new technological lifeforms (one that is reciprocal), the emotions, intangible yet embodied, differ radically from the conceptualization of tools as a prosthetic extension of the body that connects us to the world—as the cane, for example, puts the person who is blind in touch with the world around them, or the telescope amplifies our power to see into the distance.[21]

The body is central to phenomenological accounts of experience, which returns us to the subject of embodiment and the emotions. The psychologist Silvan Tomkins has insisted that "the creation of a human automaton would require an affect system" (41). The philosopher Hubert Dreyfus argued in the early 1970s that in order to be truly intelligent, computers would require embodiment. In 1985 the artificial intelligence researcher Marvin Minsky wrote in *The Society of Mind* that "the question is not whether machines can have any emotions, but whether machines can be intelligent without any emotions" (163). As Turkle reports, by the late 1980s students at MIT "were suggesting that computers would need bodies in order to be empathetic . . . and to feel pain" (111). And in the mid-1990s Rosalind Picard's *Affective Computing* appeared. As the founder and director of the Affective Computing Research Group at MIT's Media

Laboratory, Picard argues that "if we want computers to be genuinely intelligent, to adapt to us, and to interact naturally with us, then they will need the ability to recognize and express emotions, to have emotions, and to have what has come to be called 'emotions intelligence' " (x).

How could affects inhabit machines? As we have seen, Rodney Brooks has given one answer. He believes that in the future machines will be built that have both consciousness and emotions. Recent research by neurologists, who underscore the materiality of the emotions, has also sounded the theme of the importance of the emotions in our definition of intelligence. In *The Emotional Brain* Joseph LeDoux seeks to redress the imbalance that has been the legacy of cognitive science (and more specifically the field of artificial intelligence). Indeed LeDoux concludes in effect that the emotional "wiring" in our brains is stronger than the rational wiring. In a somewhat similar vein in *Descartes' Error*, the neurologist Antonio Damasio argues that the neural systems of reason and emotion are intertwined, thus giving rise to mind, and that emotions are critical to health of all kinds, including making appropriate decisions in everyday life. Importantly for my purposes, Damasio concludes "that there is a particular region in the human brain where the systems concerned with emotion/feeling, attention, and working memory interact so intimately that they constitute the source for the energy of both external action (movement) and internal action," including reasoning (71). That a certain spot in the brain has been identified as crucial to emotional intelligence underscores the radical materiality of Damasio's theory of the emotions.

Finally, perhaps in part because of all the science fiction I've been reading and watching, along with work from such widely disparate fields as media theory, artificial intelligence, neurology, and science and technology studies, I find that even such analytically dispassionate books as LeDoux's *Emotional Brain* and Damasio's *Descartes' Error* have the effect of encouraging me to think that one day artificial life—embodied in nonhuman cyborgs of all shapes—will indeed possess emotions. LeDoux explicitly states that a computer "could not be programmed to have an emotion" because it is an assemblage of machine parts, not the slow and unpredictable result of biological evolution (41). But I am nonetheless inspired to think otherwise, in great part because of his use of the metaphor of "wiring," which implies a technical feat we can surely accomplish, and also in part, paradoxically, because of the biological basis of his theory of the emotions—that they are grounded in the body, that they are biological functions of the nervous system and not mere intangible psychic states.

In the process of doing research for this chapter, then, I have become singularly well socialized to the prospect of what I have been calling nonhuman cyborgs possessing emotions.[22] The postmodern nonhuman cyborg will have a body and will be able to feel pain. The postmodern nonhuman cyborg will be complete and endowed with true artificial life because it will be capable of making decisions based in part on emotional intelligence. Embodiment is key. Researchers in artificial intelligence at MIT are not following the lead of IBM with Deep Blue, a computer contained in twin black monolithic boxes. Instead they are experimenting with embodiment by building robots that interact bodily with the environment. The name of one of the projects is Cog, a reference to the intent to make a robot that can think self-reflexively. Even more to the point, Cynthia Breazeal, who was central to the Cog project in the 1990s, has designed a robot named Kismet who has received well-deserved attention. As Peter Menzel and Faith D'Aluisio write in *Robo Sapiens: Evolution of a New Species*, "The pink-eared, rubbery-lipped Kismet alternatively pouts, frowns, and displays anger, along with a host of other expressions that outwardly display human emotion" (66). As the director of the Personal Robots group at the MIT Media Lab, Breazeal subscribes to an interactive simulation theory of the emotions, in which she understands emotions to be shared and exchanged, with communication fundamentally dialogic in nature. Her model for the interaction between human and nonhuman cyborgs is based on infant learning. Her robots possess what she describes as a "rich cognitive affective architecture," with feedback learning loops critical to development. Her aim is to create socially intelligent nonhuman cyborgs.[23] What is Breazeal's relationship to Kismet? Kismet "is my baby," she remarks.[24]

Along with My Real Baby, Breazeal's robots are a beginning, one that recalls the whimsical robots of *Silent Running*. Another beginning is to be found in the marvelously creative work of the multimedia artist Lynn Hershman Leeson, who recently invented a "character" she calls Agent Ruby.[25] As an artificially intelligent Web agent who exists on a multitude of platforms, Agent Ruby will respond to your questions (although as I discovered when I tried to interact with her in December 2005 at the Henry Art Gallery at the University of Washington, she can also fall silent if a glitch troubles her program). She has been joined by Leeson's new creation, a presence on a flat-screen monitor named DINA who, like Agent Ruby, has the face of the beautiful Tilda Swinton but is much smarter and draws you to her.

If the time-honored trajectory of liberal thought as well as of critical theory is dispassionate reflection enabled by perspective (especially historical perspective) then I depart from that tradition here. I conclude this chapter in the world of science fiction that has for me taken on the form of future fact. I end not with the reflex of critique but with an openness to the future provided by a feeling for the cyborg—a cyborg that is simultaneously human and nonhuman, and one that is a condensation of the result of mutual intersubjectivity over an evolutionary period of time. This is my feeling for the cyborg: I consider it a structure of feeling in Raymond Williams's sense, one that is supported by important imaginative, scientific, theoretical, and critical work in many disciplines.

I close by referring to Sarah Zettel's *Fool's War*. Set centuries into the future, *Fool's War* introduces us to a character named Dobbs, a short, funny, resourceful, courageous troubleshooter and stress reliever who has accepted the position as a fool on the spaceship *Pasadena*. It is only when we are halfway through the novel that Zettel discloses that Dobbs was born as a sentient artificial intelligence. It is only after Dobbs matured that she learned how to assume the shape of a human being. Now she can both navigate information pathways bodilessly and pass, embodied, as a human being.

Imagine my sense of confirmation when I read in *Fool's War* that many centuries before in our not-too-distant future, maps of human neural pathways were applied to silicon chips, thereby producing the first sentient artificial intelligence (named Hal Clarke in an allusion to *2001*). I will not rehearse the plot here but rather only remark that in the course of the novel the main human character—the woman who is captain of the spaceship—comes to have both respect and sympathy for Dobbs and her travails, just as I do as a reader. The theme of the embodiment of artificial intelligence is crucial to the story. It is in the state of embodiment that emotions are learned—in particular the emotion of sympathy. And it is through the cross-species communication of the caring emotions that the peaceful cohabitation of humans and cyborgs is imagined as possible, thus producing in the reader—*I am, of course, referring to myself*—a feeling of sympathy for the cyborg.

But this may not be a mere literary dream of mine about reading. In early 2006 the far-reaching implications of mirror neurons for learning and understanding social emotions, first discovered in monkeys ten years earlier, were reported in the *New York Times*, thus circulating this knowledge widely. As the neuroscientist Giacomo Rizzolatti puts it, "Mirror neurons allow us to grasp the minds of others not through conceptual reasoning but through direct simulation. By feeling, not by thinking."[26] V. S. Ramachandran, a neurologist at the University of California, San Diego, has been influential in popularizing the implications of this discovery, and he refers to mirror neurons as "empathy neurons."[27] The development of empathy, it has been shown, has a distinct neurobiological basis. This research is based predominantly on visual mirroring in face-to-face situations. But I have not a shred of a doubt that literary and cinematic emotions contribute to it as well.

six

BUREAUCRATIC RAGE

There is latent ressentiment against all forms of bureaucracy—not
only against that of the state. It is a type of ressentiment which
grows stronger as the bureaucratic forces become more anonymous and impregnable, as they are increasingly removed from the
realm of give and take.

—Henry Jacoby, *The Bureaucratization of the World*

Something huge and impersonal runs through things, but it's also
mysteriously intimate and close at hand. At once abstract and
concrete, it's both a distant, untouchable order of things and a
claustrophobically close presence, like the experience of getting
stuck in a customer service information loop every time you try to
get to the bottom of things.

—Kathleen Stewart, *Ordinary Affects*

A commitment to the equality of *all* requires an equality that is connection-based, an equality that acknowledges a common fate and
shared humanity which lies as much in our need to care for others
and be attended to in caring relationships as in properties we possess as individuals.

—Eva Feder Kittay, *Love's Labor:
Essays on Women, Equality, and Dependency*

One fall day while I was working in my office at the University of Wisconsin I got a phone call from a Milwaukee County sheriff. "Are you Kathleen
Woodward?" he asked. "Yes," I answered, guardedly tentative. I, or more
precisely my credit, had been mixed up with another Kathleen Woodward
from Wisconsin. She had ripped off my AAA number (using up all my
towing privileges) and hadn't paid her bills at a local pharmacy where I also
had an account. I had heard from my teller at the credit union where we
both banked that she was a druggie who was always overdrawn. Recently it
had been confided to me that she had died some months before—to my
considerable bureaucratic relief.

So I wasn't altogether surprised when the sheriff said he wanted to
serve me with a subpoena. I protested. "But I'm not *that* Kathleen Woodward." What was my middle initial? "M" I responded confidently, almost
triumphantly. After all there are twenty-six letters in the alphabet and I was
sure the odds were with me. He brusquely announced, however, that he

was coming right over because Kathleen M. was the very woman he was seeking. When he arrived, a gun on each hip, he told me—what else?—that he was just doing his job. Even as I took the papers summoning me to an upstate Wisconsin court for delinquent medical bills, I continued to try to disentangle myself from his bureaucratic grip. All the while I knew how preposterous my explanations sounded. Imagine. I concluded by declaring in a low conspiratorial voice edged with hysteria that I had a tip for him. "The Kathleen M. you're looking for is dead!"

"Sure, Lady."

He handed me the subpoena.

Two years later I found myself still ensnarled in an ugly credit dispute. "My" credit history was housed in the self-importantly entitled Trans-Union Company (it still is), which was located a thousand miles away from Wisconsin in the state of Delaware. I had spoken with their computers. I had sent them by registered mail my version of financial events along with copies of supporting documents, on which the substantiating sections were scrupulously highlighted with a light-green marker.

In return I received countless form letters, all curiously printed in capital letters as if to signal the urgency of the now-defunct telegram. They informed me that TransUnion was investigating my case carefully. I was not so easily assured. In every letter my middle name (Middlekauff) was misspelled—in different ways. And I had thought it was to be my saving grace. I called and was told—this time by a real person—that information could not be released over the phone. Period.

One of their form letters had piously promised that TransUnion would send me within ten working days a printout of their summary of my credit rating (mortgage/credit card/loan numbers and payments). I had not received it. I was frustrated. I called again. And this is what happened when for the second time I got a real person on the line. I pushed the clipped voice, my tone assertive. It was bureaucratic tennis, back and forth, voices hardening. Then the flash point. She said, "If you get smart with me, I'll hang up." That did it. Normally polite to a fault (or at least I think so), I virtually screamed into the phone at a person I had never met, calling her something rude, knowing all the while that she had my name and number and I didn't have hers and that I wasn't doing my case any good (what was she writing in my file?!). I ended by slamming down the phone —but not unfortunately before she did. No bureaucratic satisfaction there. All this took approximately a minute and a half.

The escalating anger incited by my encounter with an impersonal, unsympathetic, unyielding bureaucratic structure is an illustration of what I call a bureaucratic feeling. In fact my coining of the phrase "bureaucratic feelings" came about when I found myself entangled in this case of partial identity theft and became frustrated and finally enraged at the impenetrability of the large credit report company that refused to understand the unfairness of my situation and correct it. As an "emotional" response, anger—not to mention rage—is considered by those "in" the structure to be wildly out of line with appropriate behavior. The "proper" mode is calm patience. One should display, to draw on Peter Stearns's history of the emotions in the United States, "American cool." Indeed one must be armed not only with steely stamina but also with a sophisticated technical knowledge in order to win a dispute. For displaying "hysterical" anger or rage only deepens your trouble.

Today the three mammoth credit report companies constantly encourage us to request copies of our reports (they want us to pay for them, of course), and I should note that in my little home office, in a file folder labeled "Credit Reports," I have recent printouts from all three of them. It is a wry source of bureaucratic satisfaction to me that at this point in time my ratings from all three companies are in the highest range.

I intend this little story to serve as an introduction to the subject of the bureaucratic emotions. But it took place almost twenty years ago. Today extricating yourself from identity theft, which is rampant, is agonizingly difficult and time consuming. Although I called my little story a case of identity theft, my use of the term is in fact anachronistic. The term "identity theft" didn't actually enter into common use until the 1990s. It was not until 1998 that the Identity Theft and Assumption Deterrence Act was passed, thereby making identity theft a federal offense. And if in the early 1990s identity theft was associated with dumpster diving and mailbox theft, it is now associated with the exponential increase of information technology in general and Internet spamming and data mining in particular. My point is that opportunities for identity theft are escalating rapidly, as is the retailing of anxiety to sell services to protect people against identity theft. In general it would be safe to say that bureaucratic feelings are increasing. Certainly surveillance through bureaucratic systems of administrative power is escalating at an astronomical rate.

In the first section of this chapter I elaborate on my understanding of bureaucratic emotions in general, speculating that they constitute a strand of a postmodern structure of feeling key to our highly mediated society. In the second section I consider three illness narratives published from the mid-1980s to the early 1990s in the context of autobiographical theory and criticism and the explosion of illness narratives in recent decades—Paul Monette's *Borrowed Time: An AIDS Memoir* (1988), Marion Roach's *Another Name for Madness: The Dramatic Story of a Family's Struggle with Alzheimer's Disease* (1985), and Elizabeth Swados's *The Four of Us: The Story of a Family* (1991). Before today's widespread recognition of the health care crisis in the United States, these narratives bear witness in particular to the potential emotional violence of everyday life at the hand of the medical bureaucracy with its countless rules and regulations, its impersonal and methodical techniques of "rationality," and its forms and filing deadlines, as well as the violence that can be entailed precisely by the very lack of a medical system, bureaucratic or not. As Kathy Ferguson writes in *The Feminist Case Against Bureaucracy*, "The requirements of depersonalization in bureaucratic relations mean that individuals are isolated from one another and meaningful social interaction is replaced by formal association" (13). In this section the point of view I take is that of people who are "outside" a bureaucratic system and must deal with it as clients (or consumers), who occupy, in Ferguson's words, "the lowest rung of the organization's internal class structure" (123).[1] I conclude in the third section with some thoughts on imagined empathy, dependency, and caring.

1

I understand bureaucratic institutions—the Internal Revenue Service (IRS), for instance, the Federal Emergency Management Agency (FEMA), the U.S. Citizenship and Immigration Services (USCIS), and the various governmental programs associated with entitlement plans—as being part of what the rhetorical critic C. Thomas Goodnight has referred to as the technical sphere as distinct from the public sphere and the private or domestic sphere.[2] But I also want to expand the notion of the "bureaucratic" beyond the technical sphere for it has so obviously penetrated many aspects of our lives. My small personal example is taken from the vast and interconnecting credit "service" bureaucracy. But there are countless others. All of us have our own stories of our interactions with bureaucracy, many of them linked to feelings. Consider what I call bureaucratic panic. It is produced by deadlines and other inflexible requirements of a bureaucracy. Remember, for example, the panic on the faces of people careening in their cars down to the local post office, tax forms in hand, rushing to make the April 15 midnight deadline of the IRS. Or imagine the panic of a senior at a large state university in late March who has just discovered that he is lacking a requirement to graduate in May. Or conversely, think of what I call bureaucratic relief. It is occasioned when something hoped for unexpectedly actually happens. Imagine the relief of a person who "passes" an IRS audit of income tax returns for three years. Or of a deathly ill person who finally receives "permission" to use an experimental drug from the powerful Federal Drug Administration. Or a person who at long last receives support from the Federal Emergency Management Agency after a natural disaster has left them homeless for months. Consider bureaucratic rage. Imagine the fury of highly skilled immigrants in the United States being encouraged to apply for green cards by an imminent deadline, with mountains of paperwork to prepare, only to learn *after* the deadline has passed that there were in fact no green cards available to begin with.[3] Is there such a feeling as bureaucratic embarrassment? That must be in part what I felt when I opened the form letter telling me I had been turned down for a VISA credit card last year.

I wonder, too, if the counterpart of these intense, short-lived feelings is the long-term numbing or bureaucratic depression that can occur when one's life is consumed by a problem with a bureaucracy. As a case in point, consider the experience of a forty-eight-year-old woman reported in 1992 in the *New York Times* under the headline "Finding Meager Help in a Sex-Complaint System."[4] According to psychiatrists, the woman suffers from long-term depression that is directly attributable to sexual harassment at work—a depression perpetuated if not exacerbated by her lack of success in gaining retribution from the system in which she has been trapped for years—formally since 1985 when she filed her first complaint with her employer, the U.S. Postal Service. Since then she has filed a complaint with the Equal Employment Opportunity Commission and both a suit and an appeal with a Federal District Court (complaints have been dismissed on the grounds that they were untimely). Accompanying the article is a photo of her standing in front of an institutional structure that is adorned with columns and a flag. It could be either a post office or a courthouse. That you cannot tell which one is precisely the point. And the woman? She is gazing blankly, numbly, off into the distance. If Freud's hysterical employee is furious at his employer who has physically beaten him, here a woman appears to have descended into bureaucratic depression, with the two cases reinforcing a familiar gendered politics of the emotions.

I offer the term "bureaucratic feelings" as a rubric for what might be called a class of feelings in the spirit of supposition. Does it help to make sense of our experience in even a small way to give it such a name? The smile of recognition I've seen when I mention the bureaucratic emotions suggests that it does. Indeed without being prompted, people respond by inventing on the spot new categories that encapsulate their experience—bureaucratic triumph, for example, and bureaucratic guilt. I cannot begin to pretend to historicize this in any meaningful way; to do so would require a cross-cultural history of bureaucracy in order to map its different forms, varying scales, and changing obsessions. It would require engaging the work of Max Weber, Anthony Giddens, and Michel Foucault. But I do want to note that if a rational bureaucracy is one of the fundamental features of modernity, many agree that postmodern bureaucracy is coincident with the rise of information culture.[5] Many agree that postmodern society is characterized by what Nicholas Luhmann has called the performativity of procedures—an all-pervasive cultural practice that has replaced the normativity of law.[6] Indeed you will note that I have put the stress on the adjective ("bureaucratic") rather than on the noun ("bureaucracy"). An adjective attaches itself to a noun; it is not a person, place, or thing. As for "bureaucracy" itself, I am drawing on the term in the more general sense, not a specific one. Thus of the three definitions of "bureaucracy" offered by the *Merriam-Webster Online Dictionary*, the third meaning is most relevant to my purposes: a bureaucracy is defined as "a system of administration marked by officialism, red tape, and proliferation" (I bypass the more specific first meaning: "a body of nonelective government officials" and "an administrative policy-making group," as well as the second: "government characterized by specialization of functions, adherence to fixed rules, and a hierarchy of authority"). Certainly we commonly refer to as bureaucratic various types of large organizations—not just governmental groups but also corporate and nongovernmental organizations and large public universities. Thus perhaps simply naming a class of feelings is a promising beginning because it offers an avenue into such research. It may allow us to "re-describe" our situation, as Naomi Scheman puts it in "Anger and the Politics of Naming."

Bureaucratic feelings are site specific, although the site within the site may be exceedingly difficult to identify. These feelings have much in common with the "intensities" that characterize the postmodern condition in general, and thus we can understand them as constituting a significant strand in the structure of feeling of postmodernism.[7] I would go further and speculate that there has been a sizable increase in bureaucratic emotion. In January 2006, for instance, a Customer Rage Study conducted by Arizona State University with the Customer Care Alliance found that " '70 percent of us experienced rage' while dealing with a service representative recently and 33 percent yelled at the person who was supposed to be helping."[8] That rising tide of rage is one index of the failure of our civic life and public culture.

It's important to recognize that bureaucratic emotions are not what I would call personal, although by this I do not mean that we do not feel them personally. On the contrary. We feel them intensely, personally, thus confirming Michelle Rosaldo's theoretical observation that emotions "are embodied thoughts, thoughts steeped with the apprehension that 'I am involved' " (143). But in another sense they are relentlessly *impersonal*. In almost all cases we don't know the people with whom we come into contact. Our connection is highly mediated. Many people won't tell us their names if we ask them point-blank on the phone (indeed they've been instructed not to). Dialing an 800 number, we may well find ourselves outsourced to India where the names Peter, Bob, and Jack are surely labels for the workplace only, where they are meant to simulate people located in a call center in the United States. As callers, we may have absolutely no regard for them "personally," understanding them only as representatives of the bureaucracy (that is *their* position—they represent the bureaucracy). Similarly they may have no regard for us: "Don't take it personally" is a telling phrase.[9]

Indeed there may not be a person there at all. For the past twenty years we have been witnessing the emergence of what the social theorist Scott Lash, in an interview entitled "Information Is Alive," calls "the mediated society where classical social relations have been commuted into much more communicational relations" (97). Today we find ourselves in a period of ever-expanding channels of mass-mediated information and exploding networks of digital communication. We make phone calls to credit companies and insurance companies and find ourselves connected to the voices of computers (they are certainly not, in my experience, sympathetic nonhuman cyborgs). We answer the phone and find a recording at the other end of the line. We turn to the Web site of a company or our local government and search in vain for information and a number to call. We are deluged at virtually every moment with e-mail from people we don't know —and actually it is very likely not a person but a program spamming us. If as Lash has brilliantly noted, we live in a time in which we have outsourced our own subjectivity to experts (to therapists, personal trainers, plastic surgeons, whatever), then subjectivity itself has been largely drained from our mediated society.

Thus bureaucratic feelings are not binding emotions. They are not emotions that attach us to other persons, as do the strong emotions of love and hate, grief and jealousy. I do not think of them so much as psychological emotions as intensities. For the most part bureaucratic feelings separate people by alienating them from one another. Such feelings are oddly impersonal. The flaring anger I felt when speaking with the woman from TransUnion was not personal, but incredibly impersonal. In terms of the emotions, then, I am interested here in the relay between the personal, the impersonal, and the positional played out in three memoirs I consider later in this chapter. Could the bureaucratic feelings invoked in these memoirs be said to disclose the world in a meaningful way? Are they outlaw emotions, in Alison Jaggar's sense? Why consider book-length memoirs when stories of illness—indeed stories of all kinds of catastrophe —circulate endlessly in the media?

Walter Benjamin offers us an answer to this question that is just as relevant today as it was when his essay "The Storyteller" was first published in 1936. As he astutely observes, when we remove events from their complex and capacious contexts and place them in news stories, we no longer have *stories* but rather a new form of communication—information itself. "The value of information does not survive the moment in which it was new," Benjamin insists. "It lives only at that moment; it has to surrender to it completely and explain itself to it without losing any time" (90). Thus notwithstanding Lash's view that information is alive, if it is alive it has an exceedingly short and unsympathetic life.

Today it would be an absurd understatement to remark that we are deluged by information in our mediated society. Information-language, as I call it, is the solvent of distinctiveness. We live in a world permeated by the homogeneous voices of CNN at home and in airports, the uniform language of *USA Today*, the wallpaper of Web sites. In promiscuously crossing mediums, information-stories, like statistics, circulate endlessly on television and radio, in newspapers and news magazines, on the Internet and cell phones. The people we routinely encounter in them do not so much speak for themselves as they are pressed into service to represent norms and tendencies in society at large. Often reduced to a name and a chronological age, they are subordinated to the point of the information-story they inhabit. Seemingly anchored by the facticity of name and age, quotations are in fact virtually interchangeable and could be attributed to almost anyone.

Consider a front-page piece on Alzheimer's disease that appeared in the *New York Times* in 2002.[10] "If I knew it was coming on for sure, I might not want to stay alive," seventy-three-year-old Stanford Smilow is quoted as saying. "I wouldn't want to be a drag on my wife." For several years Smilow's older brother has been suffering from Alzheimer's disease. "I look at him," says Smilow, "and it's like I'm looking in a mirror." I hope I will not be understood as ungenerously holding the language of Stanford Smilow against him. His words, plucked as they are to fit the compact and condensed frame of a news piece, necessarily lack the sense of a vital connection to a unique life, to a voice that articulates the tone and tenor of a particular experience. In these stories the depth of form given shape by an individual voice has been flattened; experience has been downgraded to a dulling sameness. For the logic of the genre of the information-story is additive, not the intensification of complexity. Easily absorbed, information-language is just as easily forgotten. I find myself longing for the contours of individual voices reflecting on their own experience and speaking, so it seems, directly to me and not in words mediated by the Web site content provider or the news writer. I find myself longing for the unpredictability and color of adjectives and adverbs, for sentences that stretch beyond the boundaries of sound bites, for entire paragraphs and chapters that meditate on time and meaning, for something I could never imagine. I would like to listen to the story of the forty-eight-year-old woman who was trapped in the sex-complaint system. For as Nancy Mairs writes in *A Troubled Guest*, "Unlike information, emotional knowledge comes only from experience" (96).

2

My little story about identity theft and the bloated bureaucracy that is the TransUnion Company is also intended to illustrate one of the limits of the view that the "self" is nothing more substantial than a sequence of masquerades and performances, of language as unstable and unattached, unsound and unsteady.[11] I want instead to hold fast to the sober notion of the referentiality of language, to assert that *Kathleen M. Woodward* refers to me and my particular history. (Middlekauff was my father's last name. I took the name Woodward when I married my first husband.) In the 1980s autobiographical theory and criticism was marked in great part by the poststructuralist view of the ultimate fictionality of autobiography, taking its direction from Paul de Man who had insisted in 1979 that the distinction between autobiography and fiction was "undecidable."[12] Twenty years later Ross Chambers, writing about AIDS diaries that appeared in the late 1980s and early 1990s, invokes not the poststructuralist "death" of the author but the "sadly literal" deaths of these writers (I). I welcome this shift wholeheartedly. For me the force of autobiography lies in its implicit ontology and not its dubious epistemology. For me the very power and ultimately the authority and politics of autobiography lie in its connection to materiality—and to mortality. "As opposed to all forms of fiction, biography and autobiography are referential texts," Philippe Lejeune wrote some thirty years ago in his seminal essay "The Autobiographical Pact."[13] Lejeune is absolutely right. The vector of referentiality is key to autobiographical writing. And in the past twenty years there has been a veritable explosion of critical writing on autobiography, which takes its impetus precisely from the belief in referentiality and largely from a politics of gender, race, class, nation, ethnicity, sexual preference, and, most recently, disability. With the surge of trauma studies, the interest in autobiographical work has both taken on new life in the domains of identity politics and publics as well as moved beyond identity politics to claim a common ground.

Of the innumerable subjects engaged by memoirs, it is the topic of illness that strikes me as especially prominent. Why illness? In part because we are continually exhorted by our doctors and in the media to preoccupy ourselves with our health and our fitness, thus avoiding illness, with both the preservation of health and the loss of health being multibillion dollar businesses.[14] If we live in the information age, we also live in the risk society, as I point out in the next chapter on statistical panic. Understanding ourselves to be at all times "potential" patients, we are pressed to minimize our risk of illness. Both horrified and fascinated by disease, although it is the most normal of things, we are encouraged to believe we should be able to eradicate it in the body of society and in our own bodies. We are avid consumers of health care, which is a global market of ever-expanding proportions. Is it any surprise, then, that illness memoirs are so widespread? I would observe as well that illness memoirs serve the important cultural function of transcending the divisive identity politics of the past twenty-five years that have fragmented the body politic. For if there is one thing that is certain it is that the experience of illness crosses differences.

Nancy K. Miller in her essay "Autobiography as Cultural Criticism" puzzles over what she calls "personal" criticism. Is there a difference between the "personal" and the "positional," she asks, trying to get at the distinction by understanding feminist theory itself as concerned with thinking through the relation between the two terms. At times the personal and positional would seem to be identical; more often the personal would seem to exceed the positional. Can the positional, I wonder, ever exceed the personal? Miller doesn't offer a clear-cut distinction between the personal and the positional, and I don't see how she—or anyone—could. The relation between the two terms will depend, at the very least, on the situation at hand and on the context. What I find intriguing for my purposes is that in her essay the emotions emerge first and foremost as an important dimension of the personal (Miller singles out anger and embarrassment in particular).

But as I have been insisting throughout, the emotions should also be construed as political (and Miller would not disagree). Anger, as we have seen, has long been understood in Anglo-American literary feminism as a political emotion, although as one with a varying degree of effectiveness. Recall Virginia Woolf's brilliant analysis of anger in *A Room of One's Own*. There the anger of the silenced narrator who is working on a paper about women and the novel is directed at an arrogantly voluble male author, a German professor of unbelievable pretension. The emotion of anger itself is taken as a sign of injustice; it has a cognitive force, identifying those very relations of inequality. There is thus no question that an emotion can be associated with a position, in this case the position of women in male-dominated society. This subject I have already taken up in other chapters. Here I want to return to my opening anecdote. For in my autobiographical account of mistaken credit identity it is clear that a feeling itself—namely anger that escalates to rage—is the nodal point of my narrative. But in this situation anger is a manifestation of what I call a bureaucratic feeling, rage that surfaces in the memoirs to which I now turn.

The three books I discuss in the pages that follow all revolve around illness and loss. In them the antagonists are the medical establishment and disease itself—AIDS, schizophrenia, and Alzheimer's disease. All three books deal with the glaring inadequacies and injustices of the health care system in the United States. Importantly, all three are biographical as much as they are autobiographical, poised on the wavering divide between the two.[15] They recount the events in the life of the person who is suffering from illness as much as they do the experience of the writer in "managing" care for someone fiercely loved. Paul Monette writes of his partner Roger's suffering and death from AIDS; Marion Roach, of her mother who has Alzheimer's disease; Elizabeth Swados, of her brother who had schizophrenia and her mother who suffered from depression. At the center of these narratives we find two people (or three), not one.

Thus these memoirs are not primarily self-concerned or confessional in the way we tend to assume autobiographical narratives will be (although it would be wrong to infer that they are not in any measure confessional—they are). The primary politics of location inheres not in gender, class, or race but rather is to be found in the disease itself (although this is of course more complex). Biography, the narration of a life (here virtually the end of a life), coincides horribly with the story of a disease inhabiting a body. The impersonal or bureaucratic feelings are pivotal, and they form one of the critical impetuses for writing these books. Rage at the unresponsiveness of the health care system (or lack of it) is a motivating force—one not to be underestimated. The word "force" in fact I use advisedly, alluding to the anthropologist Renato Rosaldo who has underscored what he calls "the cultural force of the emotions" in an effort to capture their importance in structuring a culture by writing out of his own devastating experience of loss.[16]

Finally, what I find most remarkable about these narratives is their elaboration of the binding emotions. Grief out of love is perhaps the strongest and constitutes the other key impetus from which these books were written. The alienating effect of bureaucratic feelings is countered by the deeply personal and social emotions that hold us together by attaching us to one another. Taken together, these books provide us with a courageous parable of caring for others. This is important not the very least because the emotions can not only be learned and acquired, but also taught to us throughout our lives. As readers of these books, then, we are students of the binding emotions. These narratives are bounded, circumscribed by time, person, and place. The grief is for a lover, a brother, a mother. As a reader I feel bound to these stories and to life by the autobiographical pact; I am moved by these deaths. "For what matters," as Nancy Miller writes in her measured and moving book about the death of parents, *Bequest and Betrayal*, a book both autobiographical and interpretive, "is this bond between writer and reader" (18). As she writes elsewhere, "It takes two to perform an autobiographical act—in reading as in writing."[17] Here it takes at least three.

But also at work in these memoirs is a pedagogical imperative, an ethics of instruction. The books offer a geography of feeling that helps us map what may be the unknown territory of illness. Thus my aim in writing about these memoirs, however briefly, is not to "analyze" them but to live with them for the space of these pages.

Paul Monette was urged by the physician who treated Roger Horwitz, his partner for twelve years, to write *Borrowed Time*—both for himself and for the rest of us. For readers who have not been close to those with AIDS, Monette's impassioned chronicle of the nearly two years he fought to contain the plague of the disease before his partner died is harrowingly enlightening. We follow the course of Roger's illness. Weeks in the hospital with pneumocystis carinii pneumonia, then home again; the cycle repeated and then agonizingly halted when Roger returns to the hospital, never to leave it alive. The sudden terrifying attack of aphasia. The blindness. The fevers and sweats. Cryptococcal meningitis at the end. We follow, too, the medications—the arms against the invading and spreading virus. Bactrim, pentamidine, and HPA-23. Suramin, foscarnet, isoprinosine, and AL-721. Ribavirin, azidothymidine (AZT), Florinef, Xanax, acyclovir, amphotericin, and Benadryl. Less than two years after his diagnosis Roger is dead at the age of forty-four. The year is 1986, just a few years after AIDS, at first a confusing rumor, emerged on the American scene.

We learn what this lacerating ordeal in hell felt like to Monette.[18] The intensity of *Borrowed Time* inheres in its mapping of the geometry of the emotions for us—in particular, the chaos of their Brownian movement, the strength of their often contradictory force. It is as if *Borrowed Time* presents us with a catastrophe theory of the emotions, as when dread turns instantaneously and thrillingly into relief, when fear turns to exaltation at the moment an operation is pronounced successful, when despair turns into hope. Monette's emotional experience is structured by the extremities of opposites, by the "strange double nature of it all." "The obverse of this optimism was the hair ball of fear at the pit of my stomach," he tells us (316). The emotional trajectory is a never-ending roller coaster. Up, often manically so. Down, plunging into desolation. At the same time these emotions are also "tangled" (43). But they always seem outsized and over-scale—the grief and terror, the panic and hysteria, the love and full joy, the horror and woe, the tenderness that is opulent, the fear that is as pure as oxygen on a line. There is not in Monette a shred of American cool. Statistical panic is in abundance, along with the caustic sense that what was needed were "management skills" (30).

Roger's emotional palette has an altogether different hue. He could be said to possess emotional willpower, his terror in the face of AIDS is for-lorn. In comparison, Monette's anger is volatile and raw. At times his anger is directed everywhere at once—and then it explodes in rage. As Roger's condition deteriorates, Monette's anger increases. As Monette writes in retrospect, he continues to rage savagely. If only the wonder drug AZT had been available a year sooner, perhaps. . . . He savagely indicts the indifference of the drug companies/federal government/medical establishment/the press. The frustrating glitches of everyday life drive him berserk. He runs to the drugstore to fill a prescription: "It was not the last time I wanted to open up with an Uzi in the long line at a drugstore" (97). He leaves the hospital to do an errand, and this is what happens: "One afternoon in the underground garage beneath the city of pain, the Jaguar locked in gear again. I came racing up to use the phone in Roger's room, ranting as I dialed and then screaming at the dealer in a sort of free-fall rage. It was a reaction that would soon become a reflex, at every little thing that went wrong in the world of errands and customer service. Pure displacement: I was angry at Roger for being sick" (185–86). Later he corrects himself. He is angry at the disease. Anger, in truth, is aimed everywhere—at the FDA which had refused to authorize a drug that had been used safely in France for a decade, at the death sentence that then was AIDS, at the man he loved with such a passion and tenderness.

In *Borrowed Time* anger is a bureaucratic feeling that is ravagingly im-personal. At times it is explicitly politicized. As Monette knows only too well, "Unless you have a private doctor with privileges, which is another way of saying you'd better have money, you are lost like Hansel and Gretel in the system's beige-flecked corridors. The peaks of insurance pale beside this Everest of a condition" (38). For the two of them the system is not just characterized by red tape, it *is* red tape. At one point Monette resorts to bringing in "illegal" drugs, which have been "driven underground by the FDA," over the Mexican border (175). The hospital is an alien place, and as Monette is quick to point out, they pulled what strings they could and had access to virtually the best that was available.[19] The government continued to do nothing. Anger is positional, leveled at the disease. Anger is also personal. Monette is particularly angry at Roger's brother, who is also gay and whom he portrays as strangely disconnected from it all. Monette is enraged as well at his own doctor who frets about his Ferrari. But terribly, anger is also free-floating. It escalates to rage. Indeed *Borrowed Time* presents us with a kind of anatomy of rage, a passion that can both set you against people and connect you to them. It can be both deadly impersonal and personal. These three years, Monette tells us, "have taught me that fear—terror, that is, with a taste like you are sucking on a penny—is equal parts rage and despair" (48). That rage erupts. Early on, he tells us, he'd "begun screaming at bureaucrats on the phone and erupting in major outbursts while standing in line at the post office" (48). At times rage can reach a limit when it alienates you from yourself, annihilating your better self. At his moral worst Monette finds himself "almost wishing the horror" of AIDS on others (47). Even then he knows that "it was wrongheaded" (47). In the philosopher Noel Carroll's terms, Monette recognizes in this situation "a moral fact."

But the force of devotion and the devastation of grief are as strong as the rage.[20] Here are Roger and Paul in the hospital just before Roger's death:[21]

> I'd been there a few minutes, setting up command, when Roger began to moan. It was the saddest, hollowest sound I've ever heard, and loud, like the trumpet note of a wounded animal. It had no shape to it, nothing like a word, and he repeated it over and over, every few seconds. "Why is he doing that?" I asked the nurse, but she didn't know. I assumed he must be roaring with misery and anxiety, and he hadn't had any Xanax since the previous day. I ordered him a tranquilizer and told him everything I was doing. It wasn't till ten weeks later, on New Year's Day, that I understood the trumpet sound. I was crying up at the grave, and started to mimic his moaning, and suddenly understood that what

he was doing was calling my name. Nothing in my life or the death to come hurts as much as that, him calling me without a voice through a wall he could not pierce. (338–39)

This I can understand through the lens of my own experience as well as through the force of Monette's prose. As my partner of years ago was dying in the American Hospital in Paris, unable to speak, hardly able to move, I found myself at night unconsciously imitating his curtailed movements as if to inhabit his suffering, which had in some uncanny way become my own. To label *Borrowed Time* an illness narrative seems itself unfeeling, the professional application of a generic category. It is a death story, it is a love story. It is also activist in tone and ethos. As Monette was to write later in *Becoming a Man: Half a Life Story*, "Every memoir now is a kind of manifesto, as we piece together the tale of the tribe" (2). Monette died of AIDS in 1995.

Of AIDS Monette writes in *Borrowed Time*, "It turns out all the certainties of health insurance and the job that waits are just a social contract, flimsy as the disappearing ink it's written in. Has anything else so tested the medical system and blown all its weakest links? I have oceans of unresolved rage at those who ran from us, but I also see that plague and panic are inseparable" (83). Today, I would suggest, the "plague" that haunts our cultural imagination is not that of an infectious disease—although we hear much about a possible pandemic of avian flu from the media and we should fear it and take preventive action—but rather that of a disease whose cause is unidentified and threatens everyone as they grow older. Indeed the body under the spell of Alzheimer's disease is the figure of what Christopher Gilleard and Paul Higgs have termed the de-civilized body, an aging body, a body that in a very real sense has lost its mind.

It is at this point difficult to imagine a time when Alzheimer's disease was little known. In 2007 it was reported that over five million Americans suffer from Alzheimer's disease, with this number projected to triple by 2050.[22] Like AIDS it emerged in our cultural consciousness in the 1980s. Like Monette's *Borrowed Time*, the journalist Marion Roach's *Another Name for Madness* chronicles the confusion and uncertainty surrounding an eventual diagnosis of a disease for which there was—and still is—no cure. Imagine. The diagnosis of the disease afflicting Marion

Roach's mother, who had just turned fifty-one, doesn't come until after her family had been seeking help from doctors for two years. As readers we don't learn the diagnosis until halfway through the book. During those two years Marion Roach's own confusion was virtually unrelenting. Was her mother's repeated losing of her keys a symptom of menopause? Was her brutal killing of the cats a side effect of her hysterectomy? Were her mood swings a response to the recent death of her husband? Today these potential explanations seem like folk beliefs from another era. In her mid-twenties and working for the *New York Times*, Roach was, as she elaborates without sparing herself, acting out in all kinds of ways. Losing it. The deputy editor of the *Times* suggested she write a proposal for a feature story on her mother and the disease for the *New York Times Sunday Magazine*. Imagine. He didn't know what Alzheimer's disease was. There was no entry on Alzheimer's in the encyclopedia that Marion Roach consults.[23]

He accepted Roach's proposal and her piece appeared in January 1983. I vividly remember reading her article on a Sunday morning twenty-five years ago and finding it unsatisfyingly impersonal. It was, I realize in retrospect, an information-story, albeit one of greater length than the piece on Alzheimer's disease in the *New York Times* to which I referred earlier. Indeed that's the point; the piece focused on the disease. But *Another Name for Madness* is first and foremost about Marion Roach's mother and her father (we learn how they met), her own life as a child (her first memory), her sister (so unlike herself), *and* it is about their experience with this disease, which she notes, following Lewis Thomas, is the disease of the century. She tells us in *Another Name for Madness* that her twin motivation for the piece in the *New York Times Sunday Magazine* was first to inform people about this relentless disease and to expose the cruel vagaries of health care in the United States, and second to come to terms with her grief. Its publication did not mark, however, "the beginning of the end" of her grief, as she had hoped it would (161). Hence the book *Another Name for Madness*.

Still, an impulse to inform her readers remains. In *Another Name for Madness* the autobiographical pact has taken on the explicit shape of what I would call a pedagogical pact. One of the virtues of *Another Name for Madness* is that Roach tells us in a calm tone about Alzheimer's disease— its discovery and etiology, its symptoms and its course. But the disease is always placed in the context of the experience of illness that it brings with it. Ironically enough, given that my book takes the emotions as its subject, Alzheimer's disease was first described in 1907 as "progressive jealousy." If short-term memory loss (accompanied by confusion and loss of identity) and ultimate impairment of physical function are signs of Alzheimer's disease, so too are the emotions that swing turbulently out of character, affecting everyone. The disease itself is, Marion Roach writes, an anguishing and "angering disability" for everyone close to it (112).

As Monette does in *Borrowed Time*, in *Another Name for Madness* Roach tries to map what is a constantly shifting geography of anger—one that is a dangerous minefield. Early on, before her mother's condition has been diagnosed, Marion learns that her mother—whom she tells us admiringly was a strikingly beautiful woman—had not been to work for a week. Alarmed and irritated, Marion calls home. "Someone answered. A groan, and then the phone was slammed down, but not in its cradle" (71). Racing back home from New York to New Jersey, she finds her mother in bed. "As I approached the bed, she shifted her head, but showed no recognition. She didn't speak. She smelled. Her hair was dirty and oily and matted and there was an empty vodka bottle in the trash basket and one in an open underwear drawer" (73). Ten minutes later her mother's mood—first anger, then insensibility, then anger—shifts again. It is now the mother who is concerned about the daughter. As Roach writes, "I hoped I was losing my mind. In the course of the past hour she had seemed comatose and then just angry and stubborn, and now she was up, talking, making sense, recognizing me" (74). The perplexing swings in her mother's behavior are matched only by the hideously incommensurate diagnosis by a neurologist at that time. He concluded that it was only a slight memory problem.

If the opening of the book is devoted to allowing us into the lives of the members of this family, later the narrative follows the course of the disease, first unnamed and then finally identified. *Another Name for Madness* is a thick inventory not only of anger (to which I will return) but other stormy emotions as well—fear and pitched embarrassment, guilt and resentment, shame and self-disgust. Toward the end of the book, it is as if the emotions accelerate, becoming dizzying hyperstates of being. The emotions are so strong they are almost reified. It is all Marion Roach can do to name them. Their very names take up entire sentences as if they were hard objects. Here is her account of a particularly unnerving encounter with her mother when the disease was fairly advanced. "So what did you do today?" Marion asked her mother one day when she came to pick her up for one of their difficult and infrequent outings (her mother was still living at home, with help). "She flipped her head to my side and I saw that the look of vengeance had passed. 'I had sex!'" (204). After this Roach doesn't see her mother for a week. "I was afraid to. Guilt. Grief. Sadness. Despair. Now fear. Now I was afraid of her. I thought I had learned to manage the other ones. But fear? Things just seemed to go wrong when we were together. Now I thought I was going to die if I saw her" (206). Twenty years later Elinor Fuchs published a memoir of her mother who suffered from Alzheimer's disease for years. Unlike treatment for AIDS, treatment for Alzheimer's has not progressed. "The entire decade," Fuchs writes, "felt like one long shriek" (94). Her mother, Fuchs adds mordantly, lived out the end of her life in a "filing cabinet for the ambulatory dead" (131). It was a horrific "bureaucratic" death in life. But as Fuchs can also write, "The last ten years: they were our best" (187).

At one horrible point Roach's admirable older sister Margaret has a terrible asthma attack (she has taken on the primary responsibility of caring for their mother and is exhausted). She is rushed to the hospital. In a hideous coincidence it is the fifth anniversary of their father's death *and* she is put in a room with an Alzheimer's patient, a woman who is asking over and over again what day it is. Roach tries to get her sister moved to another room. But people at the hospital don't seem to know what Alzheimer's disease is. Roach, whose temperament may remind us of Paul Monette, responds frantically with fury of the bureaucratic kind:

> I went berserk. I collared the doctor and I threatened insanity, in front of him immediately. Of course I was being unsympathetic and selfish. But I thought it was about time. I had had it. The woman wasn't moved.
>
> I never explained the problem. I didn't tell him about my mother and Margaret's stress. I just waved my arms around and yelled about having her moved. The staff must have thought I was crazy or selfish or both. I was not able, calmly, to start from the beginning and explain the causal factor. I didn't want to blame my mother. I didn't want to talk to strangers. I didn't seem to be getting anywhere. I don't think that the staff was familiar with Alzheimer's disease, which I did name as my mother's illness. I got a blank look from one nurse and a dull smile from another. I thought they should just understand. I was too frantic to be articulate. (174)

In time this frantic fury is transformed into an articulate anger, one that is informed by social judgment. Like Barbara MacDonald in *Look Me in the Eye*, she dispenses with her fury but safeguards her anger. For later Roach's anger is directed beyond the hospital and at the larger bureaucracy of the federal health insurance system. She testifies before the House Subcommittee on Aging. She is not cool but angry. "I was damn mad. And I had vented my anger in the best possible arena. . . . I had been on six talk shows, and I had reached the point where I could look Representative Pepper in the eye and tell him that my mother was losing her mind in handfuls, because she was, and that the federal insurance stank, because it did" (210). What did this daughter want? "I wanted them to change their laws and help us" (210). Here, as the cultural critic Douglas Crimp would put it, mourning is coupled with a form of militancy.

Of these three memoirs, Elizabeth Swados's *The Four of Us* has less to do with bureaucratic anger (although it does address this issue) and more with confusion, if not depression. *Borrowed Time* recounts Monette's searing experience of his partner Roger's diagnosis and death by AIDS in the 1980s; it was published in 1988, two years after Roger died when Monette was forty-one. *Another Name for Madness* focuses on Roach's mother's baffling entrance and relentless decline into Alzheimer's disease; Roach was twenty-three years old when the first dramatic signs that something was desperately wrong surfaced in 1979 and her book appeared six years later. Both Monette and Roach were adults, and the diseases that invaded their lives, if at first horribly confusing, ultimately acquired names and plots. But confusion takes on an entirely different scale in *The Four of Us*. It expands to fill two entire decades, indeed more, in the life of Elizabeth Swados who begins her memoir of her family and its consuming illnesses when she was only four. Like the children in Toni Morrison's *The Bluest Eye*, she was too young to understand what was happening in the chaotic household that was her home. But she absorbed its dark and manic moods—feelings she couldn't articulate. It was only in her twenties that she came to learn that her brother—he was eight years older—had been suffering from schizophrenia for literally years. She hadn't been told he was sick. When he had to be hospitalized his freshman year in college and was in and out of hospitals for the next five years, she was informed that he had dropped out of school. When in a gruesome effort to commit suicide in his mid-twenties he threw himself in front of a New York subway and lost an arm and a leg, she was told instead that he had been hit by a bus.

Her mother fell into a deep and debilitating depression for a multitude of reasons, not the least of which was the suffering of her son. When Elizabeth was in the sixth grade, her mother collapsed in front of her. Here is how she tells the story years later:

> One evening in the early winter, around 6 p.m., I was sitting on my mother's bed watching her try on a new outfit in front of the mirror. She was walking unsteadily and her conversation didn't make much sense. "Here I am on the runway," she said. "And Bess Myerson is right behind me." My mother attempted a dramatic turn and lost her balance. "Jewish girls are breaking barriers. They're marching in the parade." Suddenly my mother toppled over and fell on the floor. Her body was dead still. I sat for a minute thinking maybe she was acting out a scene or doing a joke. My mind went strangely quiet inside. I could hear the lights hum. I called the maid, who took one look at my mother and called 911. Then she called my aunt and rushed me into my bedroom and slammed the door. I heard sirens and voices. Hours passed. The darkness was cold and damp. I sat unmoving on my bed. I felt very calm. My father knocked on my door and let himself in. He looked pale. His eyes were red. His mouth was pursed as if he was thinking very hard. "Your mother had herself a little fainting spell," he said lightly as if I hadn't been there. "It seems she's got an infection of the inner ear." (191)

Her mother didn't have an inner ear infection, of course. She had been admitted to the psychiatric wing of the local hospital. (Her mother commits suicide by overdose years later when she is fifty-one.)

Empathy is generally understood to be a sensitive awareness to the experience of someone else, one that is thus conscious. But for a child it can take on the form of unconscious imaginative identification as one is possessed by waves of negative (or positive) emotions that are transmitted to us from others. As Swados tells us, "As her daughter, I was given to silently watching her moods, with constant anxious attention. I could tell what my mother was feeling by her eyes and the way she held her hands— by the speed of the exhale of her cigarette smoke, by her posture and the pitch of her voice. I learned empathy and I hated it, because often I fell into strange dark moods without knowing why" (87). Later her unconscious identification with her mother's mood took on mortal proportions. This is how Elizabeth Swados tells us she felt at twenty-two. "I believed my hippie life and bad temper kept me safe, but it didn't. I struggled along with my mother inside myself, and as she became more distant and introverted, I began to think hungrily about dying" (109). From the perspective of adulthood she understands this now as a form of what I would call self-destructive magical thinking.

Elizabeth Swados takes us back to the decade of the 1950s when mental illness in the aspiring middle class was unspeakable, "the shame of shames" (25). This stigma was exacerbated by the fact that her family was Jewish; her father was a brilliant lawyer driven to succeed at work and in the community (the family settled in Buffalo after he had not been hired by law firms in New York City). Moreover it was in her father's unyielding temperament to refuse to recognize mental illness as a disease and instead relentlessly and vociferously interpret its symptoms as a lack of discipline, energy, and will. Thus so many things conspired to render these overwhelming illnesses invisible—as secrets that could not be spoken. The entire household denied the existence of what bound them together and drove them apart day after day.

In addition Elizabeth's youth brought with it her own woefully misinformed interpretations of their suffering. As she confesses ruefully of herself when she was in high school, "I chose to interpret my mother and brother's behavior as political and spiritual rebellion against the ambitious, materialistic world. In my mind, mental illness was a good thing. It was a form of protest or artistic integrity" (194). When her mother commits suicide her daughter romanticizes it. "I was still at the age when suicide is interpreted as a fascinating artistic act unrelated to death," she confides unflinchingly. "I had not one notion about its misery or selfishness" (76).

For Elizabeth it is the extremity of what is unknown—compounded by the fact that as a child and then a teenager she has only a shadowy awareness that knowledge was being kept from her—that produces such incalculable shame and guilt. She constantly fantasizes that she is being brought to court for crimes she has committed. There are four sections in *The Four of Us*, one for each member of her small nuclear family. It is as if as an adult she needed to focus on each of them separately (herself included), so as to be able to understand them—their gifts, their needs, their temperaments—as best she could. It is also as if years later she had to keep telling these stories over and over—four times over—from their refracting and reflecting points of view in order to work them through.

The first section she devotes to her brother Lincoln. She remembers the seductions of his manic imagination when he was young, his mercurial affection, and his protective arrogance. She also remembers his vicious rages, his icy injustices, and his callous physical (not to say sexual) abuse. Desperately ill, severely handicapped, alienated from his family and they from him, Lincoln ultimately comes to live alone in a shabby storefront apartment in lower New York, where he plays music on the street to make a living of miserable sorts. When he is evicted from his apartment, he refuses to leave and is found dead at the age of forty-six in unbearably squalid conditions. It is a testament to his remarkable courage and tenacity that he managed to live so long.

In this section of the book Swados writes not so much to understand her own life and her own past (although she does that too), as to understand her brother and to communicate the suffering spread by the disease of schizophrenia—a pain everyone was forced to endure. If she is guilt- and grief-ridden, she is also angry at the system—"angry at the medical profession for their lack of solution for his state of being" (53). But this anger arrives predominantly retrospectively, when she is older. It is an anger made possible by the perspective the years had brought. One of Swados's strong points is that schizophrenia is more than a "mental" illness; it entails strictly physiological conditions as well. As she tells us, her brother's body was found with a "blockage in his bowels and intestines, a tumor on his lung, emphysema, and arteriosclerosis, which was very advanced for his age" (53).

Here is Swados's description of one of the final encounters she had with her brother. It is a scene that I have not been able to forget:

Several months before my brother's housing crisis reached its peak, I was walking down Broadway on my way to a Korean deli. I saw two derelicts seated in the middle of the sidewalk. They were dressed in layers of rags and having a heated argument about Jesus Christ. One of them had paraphernalia spread around him in a semicircle, as if to sell his wares. But none of his rags or rusty pieces of metal or torn papers was a recognizable item. He wore a jaunty cap pulled to one side and there was tinsel in his filthy hair. His face was smeared black. A few steps farther along, I realized the "derelict" was my brother. I leaned down next to him, softly said his name, and waited. He stared at me for several moments and didn't recognize me at first. When he finally saw that it was me, he let out a cry like a man who'd had a stroke and couldn't express his joyous thoughts. We embraced for a long time. His smell meant nothing to me.

"We're just sitting here today," Lincoln said. "Oh, what a perfect day."

"I'm so glad to see you," I said.

"Yes," my brother replied. "You look beautiful. We get a big audience from Tower [a record store], but of course you know that, you know all that, and besides, my music requires a different audience."

I didn't want him to go off in an angry direction.

"I like your hat," I said.

He grinned. The rotten brown condition of his teeth made me wince.

"You like it? It was a gift from my friend Ann."

"I love it," I said.

"We'll be doing a lot of playing today," said my brother. "The band decided to try a new location. It's very important."

"I'd like to hear it," I said.

He frowned.

"It won't be for a while," he said.

I hugged him again and he rocked me back and forth.

"Now this is good and enough," he said.

I let go of him, turned around, and went home. I lay down on my bed and slept for fourteen hours. (57–58)

Sleeping for fourteen hours. When we can't do something, anything to help, we may find ourselves taking refuge in sleep, sick with ourselves, depressed. Elizabeth Swados interrogates herself—indicts herself—for her lack of action: "I've asked myself many hundreds of times why I didn't find an apartment for my brother, and I have no real answer" (56). What are the limits at which we withdraw our sympathy and support for a person? For a cause? At a certain point with regard to her brother, Swados reached that limit, with agonizing results. Her experience is ordinary moral experience and from it she draws a moral about the homeless: "Generalizations are worthless. Each person on the street has his or her own story. He or she was brought low by a specific, personal demon—be it economic, social, or otherwise. When you think in this way the conditions become unbearable. You are in touch with the humanity of each individual and can't block his or her suffering out by blaming a 'global' condition" (57).

But we can understand this in another way as well. The very personal impasse for Swados is that she *can't* withdraw sympathy from her brother and she *can't* do anything more for him.

4

What can we say is the cultural work being done by books such as these? I suspect that the real emotional and bodily pain to which these books bear witness draws people, many of whom face similar experiences, into transitory reading communities, imaginary and actual self-help groups that are constituted by the autobiographical act.[24] I think of these transitory reading communities as publics in the sense given to the term by the political philosopher Nancy Fraser, as groups of people who are concerned with a problem that is here delimited by the personal and is also politicized. All three of these memoirs testify to the potential cultural force of the emotions.

Their aesthetic is not that of the sentimental. Their world is charged and enervating, complex and rich, characterized by both bureaucratic feelings and binding emotions. As I have been suggesting, in terms of bureaucratic feelings, anger—if not fury or rage—is predominant. But present also is bureaucratic numbing. When anger is explicitly politicized it takes on the quality of an outlaw emotion by registering the vast inequities of our health care system. When these three books were published was our health care system in the state of crisis that it is today? Nothing would seem less possible as the United States, the only country among the major postindustrial nations without a national health care system, moves further in the direction of privatization. Thus we must take care not to sentimentalize the notion of transitory reading communities—especially those formed around the ethic of self-help. Zygmunt Bauman is both trenchant and persuasive on this point, arguing that postmodernity is characterized by the shift of as much risk as possible from the state to the individual, thereby reminding us of Tocqueville's insight that the idea of the individual is the worst enemy of the citizen, one who believes in and contributes to the public good. Indeed the sharing of intimacies, Bauman writes in *Liquid Modernity*, "can only spawn 'communities' as fragile and short-lived as scattered and wandering emotions, shifting erratically from one target to another and drifting in the forever inconclusive search for a secure haven: communities of shared worries, shared anxieties or shared hatred —but in each case 'peg' communities, a momentary gathering around a nail on which many solitary individuals hang their solitary individual fears" (37).

These books were written, I suspect, in ignorance of each other some fifteen to twenty-five years ago. Today there is a growing collective outrage at the abysmal state of health care in this country. The singular experience of the intensity of an enraged anger is, hopefully, yielding to the productive emotion of outrage. Individuals are coming to understand the structural injustices that are in place. If subgroups have formed around particular diseases (AIDS, breast cancer, Huntington's), the new media are being used in creative ways not only to provide support but to bring research to people stricken by disease—and to the families—much more rapidly. Consider, for example, the communities that have sprung up around the innovative Web site *Patients Like Me*.

At the same time, an index of the abject low to which we have sunk in this country in relation to providing health care can be found on night-time TV. Consider the popular night-time TV show *Extreme Makeover* that debuted in the 2003–2004 season. This program focuses on "elective" surgery by foregrounding what the medical philosopher Carl Elliott has called enhancement technologies; it is not a matter of life or death but of self-transformation, where the popular American practice of contrasting "before" and "after" appearances is highlighted. Even more to the point, consider the medical reality TV show that debuted midseason on ABC in 2006. Five episodes were aired. Entitled *Miracle Workers*, the show follows seriously sick people whose surgeries are provided free of charge in exchange for the rights to televise their experience, thus giving new meaning to the notion of selling of one's body. As the Web site devoted to *Miracle Workers* states, each week it "features two stories of ordinary people who do not have the network, access to the necessary medical community or in some cases the resources to these procedures."[25] The spectacle of surgery has long been a staple of television, and many such surgeries are actually performed, not just simulated. But on daytime TV (I am thinking of soap operas where an aesthetic of realism is assuredly not at work) finding one's way through the medical system has never been posed as a dilemma. Indeed physicians and nurses appear as if by magic, and everyone has seemingly boundless medical insurance. *Miracle Workers* acknowledges outright that ordinary people don't have access to high-stakes health care (they don't have access to long-term care for chronic illness either, but that's not televisual) and that the best we can hope for is a chance at a kind of lottery provided by the media-entertainment complex. Thus the series itself is a manifestation of magical thinking, a form of wish fulfillment. "We live in a country that does not believe in preventive medicine; in a country where someone suffering from a condition without a cure is without medical reimbursement," wrote Marion Roach over twenty years ago (195). In 2005, the number of people who did not have health insurance in the United States increased to 46.6 million;[26] a full one-sixth of our national economy is devoted to health care.[27]

In January 2006 the new Medicare prescription drug benefit went into effect. By all accounts it has proliferated new forms and files of overwhelming and frustrating proportions. As the journalist Jonathan Cohn reports in his book *Sick*, for example, "In Maine, a hotline for confused seniors logged 18,000 calls in one day" (112). My wonder is that there has not been more outrage from older people. Why? One reason may be because anger in older people is both proscribed and belittled. But it may also be that bureaucratic confusion is the first and foremost reaction and that it is difficult to convert it into an outlaw emotion. As my Seattle pharmacist Steve Cone told me when I asked him this question, "They're confused, not angry. I'm the one who's angry." I agree with Germaine Greer. "It's time to get angry again."

5

Why did I choose these three memoirs? I turned to memoirs as a medium promising (although not always delivering) intimate voices that allow us entrance into their lives—that is, into the emotional and self-reflective knowledge that can be occasioned by writing. These memoirs draw us into the nuanced sphere of subjectivity, where experience is not diminished to a sentence or two but elaborated and embedded in the uninflected language of information-prose. The books invite us to respond to it with our own experience, to live ourselves into the subject of the lives recounted therein.

In *Borrowed Time* and *Another Name for Madness* we are privileged to possess a palpable record of the harrowing emergence in our culture's consciousness of two lethal diseases, both of them stigmatized. With *The Four of Us* we are reminded that not so long ago mental illness was a secret to be hidden at all costs. Today mood disorders are routinely diagnosed and prescriptions are dispensed with alacrity; and with the mapping of the human genome, markers of greater genetic risk are being investigated at breakneck speed. But then, as Elizabeth Swados writes, "If there was any evidence that mental illness might have genetic causes, the information wasn't available at the time" (90). It is thus my hope that the historical perspective provided by these three books will encourage us to be receptive to the suffering of people today with sicknesses that go unnamed or are largely unfamiliar to us.

The feminist philosopher Lorraine Code would call this "responsible imagining," an openness to the experience of others that requires epistemic humility. "Imaginative efforts to understand something of how it *is* to be so differently positioned from the imaginer" demands, she writes, "that nothing can be assumed before the fact" (206). While Code's paradigm is listening and not reading (she cautions against what may be the epistemic blindness of elite literature), I think she would admire these books, finding that they inspire what she, along with the historian Lynn Hunt, calls "imaginative empathy." "This imaginative empathy," Code explains, "is less about knowing than about *believing*, in a reconfigured sense of belief where the standard definition of knowledge as justified true belief undergoes a reversal" (234). For her such listening is "neither disembodied nor closed to affect, and neither purely objective nor perfectly rational" (234).

But my primary reason for gathering these memoirs together in this chapter is that they are doubled-over narratives of illness. They remind us of the fierce determination we must have to care for another person who is sick unto death in our society—and they remind us of our own limitations. As Marion Roach writes of one of the doctors her mother saw, "He was a kind and observant professional and a good and honest friend. He understood completely—unlike so many other doctors I have met—that this disease takes more than one victim; that it takes the family as well and creates a new and wholly unstable environment around all concerned" (143–44).

This bears repeating: these diseases create new and volatile environments for everyone involved. Thus I'm also grateful to these books because in a very real sense they led me to the feminist philosopher Eva Kittay's important work on dependency. In *Labor's Love: Essays on Women, Equality, and Dependency* she argues that dependency—embodied in infancy and childhood, frail old age, and severe disability and sickness—is an elemental condition of all of our lives (albeit one that is unevenly distributed). As such it is foundational. Dependency, she argues, should be the ground for theorizing equality and for shaping the institutions of our society, and not the autonomous and rational self-interested individual on which the liberal theory of the state, as articulated by the political philosopher John Rawls, is now based. "If we begin our thinking . . . with persons as they are in connections of care and concern, we consider commonalities that characterize this relatedness," Kittay explains. "These would form the basis of a *connection-based* equality rather than the *individual-based* equality more familiar to us" (27–28). Within the context of this chapter, Kittay calls attention precisely to the appalling lack of social justice in our health care system—a system that puts us all at risk, with many families as well as individuals in extreme jeopardy. She would argue that equality is more important than liberty, and justice more important than freedom. It is our interdependency, not our autonomy, that fully characterizes our experience across our lives.

Roger Horwitz was dependent upon Paul Monette. Allene Roach was dependent on her two daughters, Margaret, first and foremost, and Marion. Lincoln was dependent financially on his father, who denied his disease from the start. Eva Kittay would call Monette, Margaret, and Marion (although not Lincoln's father) dependency workers, thus underscoring the exhausting, difficult, and psychically painful work of caring for those they loved who were seriously sick, as well as underlining the fact that this labor is largely invisible to us—unless of course we ourselves are involved—and thus shamefully unacknowledged by our society. But love's labor also creates something precious. As Kittay writes, "The labor either sustains ties among intimates or itself creates intimacy and trust—*connection*. And affectional ties—*concern*—generally sustain the connection, even when the work involves an economic exchange" (31).

The significance of my little story of bureaucratic rage at the Trans-Union Company shrinks in the darkening shadow of the testimony of these three memoirs. My own heart sinks that I need go no further than my own family to add to them. When I mentioned the title of this chapter to my brave sister-in-law a few weeks ago, she understood instantly. There are three of them—my sister-in-law, my brother, and their twenty-six-year-old daughter who has suffered from a brutal form of anorexia for more than ten years. A beautiful young woman who has the gift of an enlivening curiosity, she has been in and out of hospitals and treatment centers throughout this long and alarming stretch of time. My sister-in-law has devoted herself to her daughter's care and has occasionally been unjustly

seven

STATISTICAL PANIC

Probability and statistics crowd in upon us. . . . There are more explicit statements of probabilities presented on American prime time television than explicit acts of violence. . . . There is nothing to fear (it may seem) but the probabilities themselves.

—Ian Hacking, *The Taming of Chance*

I was never able to remember more than smatterings of what the surgeon said just after Alice's operation in June of 1976. He told me the tumor had been malignant but that he'd taken it out, along with a lobe of Alice's lung. I don't remember whether he mentioned then that there'd been some lymph-node involvement; I'm not sure I would have known what that meant anyway. After he summed up the operation in a couple of sentences, I asked him about Alice's prognosis, and he said something about "ten-per-cent chance." I didn't quite understand what he was talking about. I thought I had missed something. I asked, "Ten-per-cent chance of what?" And he said, "Ten-per-cent chance that she'll survive."

—Calvin Trillin, "Alice, Off the Page"

Defined by floating attacks of terror that occur without any apparent cause, panic disorder is estimated to afflict millions of people in the United States. In 1982 a drug called Xanax, manufactured by the Upjohn Company, appears on the market, quickly becoming a best-selling treatment for panic attacks and anxiety.

—Jackie Orr, *Panic Diaries*

Consider the statistical body. It is found everywhere in contemporary culture, where bodies are composed of—and harrowingly decomposed by—statistics. As a collective and intangible body, the statistical body has nonetheless a compelling force. Statistics tell us how many African Americans hold management positions in the financial district in New York. How many Asians make up the student body at the University of California. How many people over sixty-five are employed full time. Statistics such as these are based on what I call "difference demographics." Statistics also stream from the worlds of sports and beauty. We learn about baseball batting averages and yards rushed in football. About how many men and women are having cosmetic surgery. About the reduction in the appearance of face wrinkles if a certain cream is used.[1]

But of all the statistics that call up figures of the body, an extremely large proportion has to do with the vulnerable body—with disease and ill-being, accidents and violence, and ultimately death. "Every year, congestive heart failure contributes to about 300,000 deaths in the United States," we learn in an article entitled "Next Frontiers" in the 25 June 2001 issue of *Newsweek*, "which is nearly twice as many as stroke and seven times as many as breast cancer" (44). "The more women a man has sex with, the higher his risk of developing prostate cancer in middle age," reported the *New York Times* on 17 July 2001. "By far the most powerful risk factor for osteoarthritis," John L. Zenk announced in *Total Health* in 2001, "is age. It is estimated that 68 percent of individuals older than age 55 and over 80 percent of people older than 75 have osteoarthritis" (64). Karen Olsson reported in the *Boston Globe* on 1 January 2006 that since 1973 the number of exonerated people formerly on death row in America's prisons has climbed to 122, a statistic that has led many to call for an end to the death penalty. "One out of three women over 40 experience it," declares an advertisement for Serenity Thin Pads in the August 2001 issue of *Good Housekeeping*, "The issue of bladder control" (17). On 1 August 2001, CNN Headline News reported that eighteen high school and college football players have died of heat-stroke deaths in the United States since 1995. *Time* magazine, reporting on a study published in the *New England Journal of Medicine*, warned us on 25 July 2007 that, like the common cold, obesity may be contagious among friends. Our bodies are figured as being in a perpetual state of risk. The statistics profiling the body are for the most part melancholy and grim.

When our own individual future is at stake (the future of members of our family, our financial future, our own health), what I call statistical panic can strike with compelling and sustained force. As Calvin Trillin recounts in the epigraph above, after his wife's operation to remove a tumor from her lung the physician tells him that the prognosis is 10 percent. Trillin was bewildered. What was the doctor talking about? "I thought I had missed something. I asked, 'Ten-per-cent chance of what?' And he said, 'Ten-per-cent chance that she'll survive'" (56). It was a figure that Trillin never forgot but also repressed. Statistical panic: fatally we feel that a certain statistic, which is in fact based on an aggregate and is only a measure of probability, represents our very future—or the future of someone we love.[2] We may deny such a number. But it is clear that a specific body statistic can drastically color our very lives. Thus here I am particularly interested in statistics as a discourse of *probability* rather than as a discourse used to make sense of the past or of the present. I am interested in *the statistic as a figure, one that looms on the horizon.*

In the first section of this chapter I consider how contemporary illness narratives of different kinds—prime-time TV, experimental film, the memoir—contribute to, disclose and dissect, confront, and question the omnipresent discourse of medical statistics. I turn in the second section to what I call the society of the statistic, of which medical statistics are but a subset, suggesting that it is coincident with what has been termed the risk society.[3] This is followed by a discussion of structures of feeling, both modern and postmodern—a discussion that opens out to a larger historical frame in the fourth section of this chapter.

1

Statistical panic. It isn't an unusual occurrence. It's the stuff out of which prime-time television is made, as illustrated by the 13 April 1997 episode of the medical drama *Chicago Hope*. In one of the narrative lines in this episode, a middle-aged woman—she is a wife and the mother of two children—insists to a young male surgeon that she wants a double mastectomy. He isn't merely reluctant to do the operation. Instead he's horrified because she doesn't in fact have breast cancer. But as she explains, she has an 86 percent chance of getting breast cancer (this statistic is based solely on family history—her mother and her two sisters have died of breast cancer). For her the statistic is like an oncoming train she must avoid at all costs. Although the statistic is an abstraction and isn't linked to a certain outcome, it has for her a galvanizing force.[4]

Here we so clearly see the difference between the scientific use of the language of risk and its experiential dimension: this fictional woman's experience of the feeling of being at risk—statistical panic—discloses a terrifying future: the certainty that her life will be cut short by disease.[5] The doctor's initial reaction is that she's suffering from paranoia and hysteria, two emotions assuredly not associated with rational decision making. But in the end the doctor is persuaded to perform the operation by the woman's unwavering determination and the gravity of her statistical prognosis. (Along the way the woman with whom he is romantically involved teaches him the lesson that a woman's sexual attractiveness shouldn't be irrevocably linked with her breasts and that love should triumph over such dramatic bodily change!) What to the surgeon at first seems an insane course of action is revealed in the course of the narrative as preeminently rational in an unequivocally calculating sense. If we generally regard statistics as a depersonalizing force, here we see that when we apply them to ourselves, creating our own emotional dramas out of them, they can have an overwhelming power that orients us to the world in a particular way and focuses our attention on eliminating risk. In order to avoid being reduced to a statistic, which in this case seems to entail a certain death sentence, this fictional character from *Chicago Hope* uses her panic as energy to guide the surgeon's knife to her breasts and thus to obliterate altogether—she thinks—her risk of such cancer.[6]

The narrative is designed to persuade us, along with the surgeon, that her decision is "rational." Her clearly defined role as a wife and mother is represented as the maintenance of her health at all costs. The all-powerful protagonist of the story is the figure of risk: an 86 percent chance. That her panic carries with it a financial price as well as an emotional price is never mentioned. The surgeon is carefully represented as never lobbying for the operation, for which he would presumably charge a big fee. Instead he's represented as firmly opposed to it and must be convinced to perform it. The mutual entailment of the society of risk, which requires the production of statistics, and of consumer culture is never suggested. The high figure of 86 percent represents the high cost of maximizing the woman's health. In our health care system this carries a price tag, and it results in what I call the pricing of panic. And indeed sustaining health is, as we know, a major preoccupation in contemporary consumer culture, one that relies upon statistical reports to increase demand for its products.[7] This episode from *Chicago Hope* is thus a clear instance of the medical melodrama, where public and private space intersect in the operating room, where fraught decisions are reduced to no-brainers, and where good motherhood is represented as taking a knife to the body and spending a lot of money in the process. In short the feminine (albeit in a new guise) and the work of consumption are yet again aligned in the representational space of television.[8]

In this unambiguous melodramatic world, the woman is presented from the beginning as unambivalent and thus having no questions or qualms about her decision. But the very experiential quality of statistical panic, or risk, is that it carries uncertainty with it—an uncertainty that is intrinsic to it. The *Chicago Hope* narrative is cast in black-and-white terms as a debate between two competing and supremely confident positions. But what panics us is that we can't be certain of our own future, however much epidemiologists have quantified it in aggregate numbers. What is peculiarly reductive about this television narrative is that the woman is never represented as hesitating over what she thinks she should do. This accounts for my uneasiness with the narrative, my sense that the story is truly bizarre. How could we possibly allow a single number to have such decisive and unambiguous power over us?

But the cultural injunction to avoid such risk is all-pervasive. Phyllis Rose, a writer in her middle years, comments on this from the perspective of her own experience with breast cancer testing in *A Year of Reading Proust: A Memoir in Real Time*. When she is told by her doctor to have a breast biopsy to test some small spots of calcification, she puts it off—judging that the odds of one in five were not overwhelming. Her friends are aghast and censorious. They think her frivolous and self-destructive. "To cling to any personal preference, to value personal convenience in the face of a threat of cancer," Rose concludes, "is to defy a cultural style so widely approved that it has the force of wisdom and responsible practice. . . . Committed to having the biopsy, nevertheless I talked about it with a studied levity which to me signaled equanimity and mastery of my fate, but which to many of my friends bespoke shallowness, until, one day, talking to a good friend, I was reduced to tears and bewildered questions" (131). Rose was judged as being deficient—*morally* deficient—because she wasn't suffering or displaying statistical panic, much less acting on it. As Solomon Katz and others have argued, we live in a culture where for many people moral concerns aren't associated with religious tenets and values but with rather illness and health; in an instance such as this, morality—what is referred to as "secular morality"—is based on calculations of risk emerging from the field of epidemiology.

How do we survive into the future in the postmodern society of risk? By eliminating as much risk as possible. By understanding every day as one in which our ability is tested to survive not only actual threats (a holdup at gunpoint in the city, a car accident, a fall), but also the invisible atmosphere that everywhere radiates risk and projects it far into the future. As Zygmunt Bauman has so aptly suggested in his essay "Survival as a Social Construct," the "postmodern strategy of survival" is to slice "time (all of it, exhaustively, without residue) into short-lived, evanescent episodes. It rehearses mortality, so to speak, by practicing it day by day" (29). Our daily work—our career, in the sociologist Erving Goffman's sense—is to manage our futures in terms of avoiding risk.

But more importantly we survive by dissecting the deployment of statistical discourse and its effects upon us and by reflecting on our affective response to the language of risk. In what follows I consider statistical panic in two striking works that serve as counterpoints to the breast cancer narrative from *Chicago Hope*: Yvonne Rainer's feature-length film *MURDER and murder* (1996), which explores the disturbing discrepancy between the scientific language of statistics and their experiential dimension in relation to breast cancer, and the historian Alice Wexler's *Mapping Fate* (1995), a memoir that engages the experience of being at risk for Huntington's disease. In both *MURDER and murder* and *Mapping Fate*, statistical death is the underwriter of alternative futures. If *MURDER and murder* entertains the question of what statistical panic feels like and how it can get you in its grip, Wexler shows us how she finally resolved not to concede control to it.

Rainer's bold film *MURDER and murder* takes up the subjects of breast cancer, aging, and love between two older women. For Rainer murder in capital letters (*MURDER*), as opposed to murder in the lower case (*murder*), is death from clearly defined social causes that could be prevented—that is, deaths caused by nuclear testing and DDT, or deaths from homophobia and other forms of stigma. In what Rainer has herself termed the most psychologically realistic of her films, *MURDER and murder* contains a running commentary on statistics—thematically, literally, figuratively, and perhaps most courageously, autobiographically. It also thematizes the possibility of seeing into the future by having the younger ghosts of the characters haunt the action that takes place in the present—on which they comment wistfully, wryly, and even statistically on possible futures. As the young ghost of one of the two main characters says dreamily, "Just think of it: if in one year only one girl from every graduating class in every high school in the country becomes a lesbian, that means 33,000 lesbians! In a decade that would add up to 330,000. And in thirty years it would be a million!" (101).

In the course of the narrative the sixty-three-year-old Mildred is diagnosed with breast cancer and undergoes a mastectomy. While the credits roll at the end of the film, she says in voice-over, referring to statistics specifically about lesbians and breast cancer, "these statistics make me tired" (117). To which Doris, her younger partner, replies, "So many ways to get messed up. Your numbers are even more terrifying than mine." Mildred: "They're just numbers. Everyone has a different set of numbers. You can't live your life by numbers." But as I've been suggesting, we're virtually required to do so by what I call the society of the statistic. And often for what we would term good reasons—acting in a manner in accordance with avoiding mortal disease, maximizing our health. Doris takes this position. Doris: "But you can use the numbers as cautionary. Like, when did you last get a pap smear and mammogram?" If the tone is for a moment ironically light (fun is occasionally poked at statistics in the film), the implications of Mildred's answer are horrifying. "Oh don't start on me now. I don't know, two or three years ago." Two or three years ago! My first reaction is to wish that she had had a mammogram! I react like Phyllis Rose's friends who castigate her for delaying the biopsy her physician had advised. (This is also complicated: having a mammogram provides no guarantee.) Then we remember: Mildred is a fictional character. But the final frame of the film returns us to the sobering light of the real world before it fades out. It reads:

IN MEMORIAM
NANCY GRAVES
SHIRLEY TRIEST.

Within the context of the film the deaths of these two real women seem to be statistical fatalities. Death by statistic. And in a horrible irony the deaths of these women will in fact be reduced to statistics—to data going into the aggregate to generate a new mix and new probabilities for the future of other women. Yet at the same time Rainer's film is dedicated to the memory of these women, to the meaning that their lives held for other people. It is a refusal to allow them to be reduced to statistics.

It has been said of some fictional narratives (of Thomas Hardy's late nineteenth-century novels, for example) that the landscape assumes the status of a character. In MURDER and murder statistics are both the environment in which these women live and an uncompromising force that is mercurial in nature. Even if you follow all the rules (you eat the "right" food, you exercise, you don't live next to a toxic waste dump), you may be hit. Sobering if not menacing, statistics appear as crawling titles across the bottom of the screen, accompanying much of the film. Here are some examples. *"There are 1.8 million women in the U.S. who've been diagnosed with breast cancer. One million others have the disease and do not yet know it"* (88). *"One out of four women who are diagnosed with breast cancer die within the first five years. Forty percent will be dead within ten years"* (89). In one scene, fragments of a statistic are stenciled on the wall, and in another scene we see a statistic being carefully inscribed on another wall, as if it were graffiti. It reads: *"In 1992 thirty-seven and a half million people in the U.S. had no health insurance"* (112). In one of the most important sequences in MURDER and murder statistics about breast cancer are stenciled on the canvas of a boxing ring, literally covering the floor on which the two women both fight and make love. One of the signal achievements of MURDER and murder is to show how statistics constitute the very stage upon which we act out our lives. In MURDER and murder statistics are literally made visible. There is a striking visual poetics at work.

Yvonne Rainer, a lesbian who was in her early sixties when she made this film, appears as herself in MURDER and murder. In the film she interrupts the fictional narrative with her own autobiographical commentary. In the boxing ring scene mentioned above, she sits in the audience right in front of the ring. She is wearing a fighter's robe, and at one point she addresses the camera, slightly offside. She speaks in an even, almost toneless voice, one verging on the deadpan:

> All right, I've been putting this off. . . . Five biopsies in eight years following up on that first diagnosis of lobular carcinoma in situ. . . . "A marker of higher risk," that first breast surgeon kept repeating, and I in turn repeated it like a mantra. "Not breast cancer, but a marker of higher risk." He wanted to take 'em both off. No breasts, no breast cancer. I did my research, found a more conservative surgeon, and weighed the odds. Twenty to thirty percent higher risk than the general population. At that time one woman out of every ten or eleven got breast cancer. Now it's one out of eight or nine. "You're more likely to die in a car accident," Dr. Love had said. Since I didn't own a car, I didn't know quite what to make of that. (102–3)

Rainer understands the deadly looniness of being lumped into a statistical aggregate that doesn't represent your own life but that you are told represents your statistical future. As she dryly puts it, " 'You're more likely to die in a car accident,' Dr. Love had said. Since I didn't own a car, I didn't know quite what to make of that." Rainer also knows that self-deception is one of her preferred strategies for survival. She reports having practiced an ironic form of statistical thrift, shopping for lower odds, which would presumably result in a lower medical bill and a longer life. If the fictional woman from *Chicago Hope* reacts to her familial history of statistics with determined certitude (in that reductive narrative she has only one conclusive figure to deal with—86 percent), Rainer shops for other numbers. She acts like a postmodern version of the urban sociologist Georg Simmel, calculating and enumerating. She weighs her chances, worrying, shopping, worrying, shopping. If in our consumer society skill as a shopper is required, here we see, as Bauman incisively puts it in *Liquid Modernity*, that we learn "to treat any life-decision as a consumer choice" (89).

While Rainer delivers these words she opens the left side of her robe to reveal her mastectomy scar. At a chance moment, we so visibly learn, her risk had climbed to 100 percent. She is one of those women. But other statistics are still out there, radiating risk. In fact the odds seem to be increasing at a crazy-making rate. It is as if Rainer is living to the terrifying tempo of a statistical countdown. One out of every eight women will get breast cancer. One out of every seven. Six. In a situation such as hers statistical panic may be never ending—until it is fatal. Five. Four. "Thirty women die from breast cancer every hour," she reports later in the film in voice-over, "That's one every two minutes. By the year 2000 cancer will be the leading killer of everyone" (109). Rainer's caustic irony exposes the crazy cultural logic of the risk society. It is the panic produced by the statistics that has reached epidemic proportions as well.[9]

In a brilliant sequence of jump-cuts Rainer, still facing the camera, tells us about the ever-present strange feeling of tightness in her skin after the mastectomy, and she intones the death rates from cancer, revealing how the phenomenology of the body and statistical panic intersect in harrowing ways:

> I'm a sucker for statistics. They make your head spin with the dizzying prospect that the body is a quantitative entity, and death can be determined with easy calculation. In the United States cancer is the leading killer of women between the ages of thirty-five and forty-five. . . . At first you feel a tremendous tautness across this area . . . That means 2.8 million women have breast cancer . . . and you have very limited mobil-

ity in your arm. Of 182,000 women newly diagnosed with breast cancer in 1993, 46,000 will be dead in five years . . . They give you exercises (*she demonstrates*) . . . more than 75,000 will be dead in ten years . . . and after a few months you regain almost a full range of motion. One out of nine women will develop breast cancer sometime in her life. That rate has more than doubled in the last thirty years. That taut feeling, however, never quite disappears. One out of three Americans will face some form of cancer. Of these, two out of three will die from the disease. That taut feeling . . . The death rate . . . however, never quite disappears . . . from breast cancer has not been reduced in more than fifty years . . . Yet there are some of us who escape . . . and some of us survive. (*She crosses her arms and takes the "macho" pose.*) (108)

The staccato recitation of statistics strikes home—at her singular body and the collective body of women. It is as if this stutter-like sequence could go on forever, oscillating between the palpable feeling of her body where once her breast had been and the probable prospect of death, which is the ultimate implication of these disembodied statistics. The figures themselves constantly change at what seems to be a dizzying speed. Yet paradoxically the rate also seems ominously—or boringly—slow. In *MURDER and murder* statistics, both fully formed and fragmented, metastasize in every direction, materializing everywhere. They appear on the walls. They are written on the floor. They crawl across the bottom of the screen like the stock market figures on CNBC, the financial cable television channel. They virtually constitute our everyday life.

How do we understand the experience of medical statistical panic? It is a stressful ambiguous state that is new to the postmodern culture of medical risk—a state that Sandra Gifford in "The Meaning of Lumps: A Case Study of the Ambiguities of Risk" has so astutely identified as being "somewhere between health and disease" (215). Thus the affect of statistical panic is fundamentally related to the experience of uncertainty. Freud in *Inhibitions, Symptoms and Anxiety* provides a distinction between anxiety and fear that is useful here. Anxiety, he insists, "has an unmistakable relation to *expectation*"; unlike fear, which is attached to a specific object, anxiety "has a quality of *indefiniteness and lack of object*" (165). Statistical panic falls somewhere in between the two states. Like anxiety, it's related to the expectation that something may happen in the future, but unlike anxiety it's not so vague or indefinite. Yet unlike fear—the fear, say, of being in the path of an oncoming train—statistical panic isn't related to a known object that exists for us in the present. Rather it is related to a probability, to varying scenarios, to futures that are statistical in nature. When we're angry, our anger is directed at a specific object, most often a person; our anger binds us to that person. Jean-Paul Sartre in his book on the emotions, for example, draws on anger as a model for the way emotions bind us to the world. As he puts it, "The affected subject and the affective object are bound in an indissoluble synthesis. Emotion is a certain way of apprehending the world" (52). But how can we be bound to something indefinite? To a statistic? To a figure that represents a possible future and thus contains in and of itself a narrative, but is at the same time a fragment of a series of possibilities? This ambiguity accounts in part for the peculiar quality of statistical panic, a structure of postmodern feeling that oscillates between urgency and boredom.

I hope I won't be stretching a point if I suggest a parallel here with Freud's analysis of obsessional neuroses. In *Inhibitions, Symptoms and Anxiety*, Freud also writes that in an "obsessional neurosis the technique of undoing what has been done is first met with in the 'diphasic' symptoms, in which one action is cancelled out by a second, so that it is as though neither action had taken place, whereas, in reality, both have" (119). It is as though the sensation of panic is canceled out by reassurance, only to be succeeded by panic, as though neither had taken place, whereas in reality both have. In analogy with after-images, could we not say that we are left with *after-affects*—after-affects that are associated not with the past but with the future, which is one of risk.

How do you live when you are at such risk? Alice Wexler provides a different answer to this question in her remarkable *Mapping Fate: A Memoir of Family, Risk, and Genetic Research*. Her sensitive account contains two narratives that are as intertwined as is the double helix: Wexler's personal story as the daughter of a mother who suffered from Huntington's disease, and the scientific story of the search for the gene that causes Huntington's (it was discovered in 1993). As Wexler writes in her introduction to *Mapping Fate*, she wants to illuminate the "emotional meanings of being at risk" for a devastating and terminal disease such as Huntington's that has no known cure (xvii). She is interested in conveying what it's like to live in its "toxic shadow" (xix-xx). For the body inhabited by Huntington's disease is at the end a depressed body, a body that can't communicate, a spastic body suffering from the ravages of chorea (an involuntary movement disorder).

Unlike Rainer's MURDER and murder, Mapping Fate doesn't deluge us with statistics. But one figure haunts the entire narrative: fifty-fifty. When Alice Wexler learned in 1968 (she was then in her mid-twenties) that her mother had been diagnosed with Huntington's, she simultaneously learned that she had a 50 percent chance of inheriting the disease. Although her father later told her that her immediate response to the even odds was, "That's not so bad" (43), in fact she was overpowered by this uncertain knowledge, which was transformed into denial and translated into uncertainty about her own talents for living. As her sister Nancy Wexler, a psychologist and activist for Huntington's, was to write, "The ambiguous condition of 50 percent risk is extremely difficult to maintain in one's mind, if not impossible. In practice a 50–50 risk translates to a 100 percent certainty that one will or will not develop the disease" (223).

We are routinely urged to weigh the odds as a way of deciding what course of action to take. But Wexler couldn't do this because the odds weighed exactly the same. Instead her mother became a kind of mirror for her of her future body, one she would often deny by turning away from her mother as if she were turning a mirror to the wall. "As a feminist," she writes in the introduction to Mapping Fate, "I particularly wanted to examine the relations between genetics and gender in our family, since I knew it somehow mattered to my own experience of growing up female that my mother—my same-sexed parent—was the parent at risk and that she was the one who had developed the disease" (xvii). "What map of the body is taken in by the daughter who sees chorea memories written on her mother's face?" she asks (xvii). But by the book's end she comes to feel an appreciation for her mother's grace under the pressure of the disease and thus forms a positive identification with her, one that allows her to dedicate Mapping Fate, itself a memoir of great clarity and honesty, to the memory of her mother.

Wexler's anxiety—her statistical panic—is palpable throughout the pages of her book as she apprehensively inspects herself for the signs of the disease, witnesses her mother's long and harrowing descent into Huntington's, offers her own help in the search for the dreaded gene, and tries to get pregnant (understanding all the while the tragic future that could be in store for her child and the all-too-predictable guilt she would suffer as a consequence). With a horrifying irony, the discovery of the gene and the development of a test for it, she writes, "opened an abyss in all our lives, a vast space between prediction and prevention" (221).

Now her anxiety about whether or not she carries the gene for Huntington's is compounded by her anguish over what might be the emotional effects of the results of the test itself. As she discovers in talking with people at risk for Huntington's, virtually "everyone mentioned the need to escape the oppressive uncertainty" of genetic inheritance (236). They also report that as they grew older their anxiety increased even though the odds of having the disease decrease with age. She is helped by the knowledge that people in different cultures treat being a member of a family with Huntington's differently. That frees her from her own culture. As Wexler tells us, the people who live in San Luis, a small community in Venezuela racked with Huntington's, have a different way of apprehending their future and of acknowledging what they are in fact *certain* is their inheritance. "The people here believe that everyone who has a parent with the disease always inherits it from that parent, but only some people actually develop the symptoms," she explains. Wexler herself then assimilates their way of handling disease to our scientific category of risk and to our discourse of statistical probability. "Perhaps it is a way," she reflects, "of acknowledging the emotional burdens of being at risk, and the worry of constantly wondering when and if you'll get the disease. Being at risk means being different, from those who are not at risk and from those with Huntington's. It's a state all its own." Her generous conclusion is that these people "seem, to understand this—better, perhaps, than North Americans, who do not tolerate ambiguity well" (198–99). This is another instance of the new medicalization of the body—of living in a state between health and disease.

Having lived so long with this statistical condition, Wexler ultimately makes a kind of peace with being at risk. She rejects the test for which she had longed (the test, it is important to remember, doesn't provide absolute prediction but rather narrows the probabilities). She makes a conscious decision to choose to live in risk, refusing the cognitive map of her body that is held out to her in the form of genetic testing and statistical probabilities. She elects to face a future that holds two possibilities rather than a virtual certainty; it is a future she can now name a destiny, one that for her remains open. In Wexler's *Mapping Fate* we not only see a nuanced and strong portrayal of what it feels like to be caught in the tension between the scientific language of risk and its experiential dimension. We also see how her analysis of her statistical panic, understood as uncertainty about the future, allowed her to put the paralyzing implications of the fifty-fifty odds behind her and to live into a future that is not ruled by a statistical roll of the dice. Thus fundamentally, she tells us, her story is "less about an illness than about the possibility of an illness, less about the medical dilemma of living with disease than about the existential dilemma of living at risk" (xxii). In effect Wexler redefines risk. Instead of risk ominously waiting for her in the future in the form of a statistical probability, Wexler chooses to risk fate. She decides to live in a "third space," one that is neither certainty nor complete uncertainty (xv). She refuses to take the test for the gene that causes Huntington's. She takes a risk. She risks an untimely death, choosing to live, in the words of the British writer Gillian Rose, "before her time."[10]

In the episode from *Chicago Hope* described above, the TV feelings are clichés and banalities, emotions flattened to stereotypes, feelings so easily consumed they could be said to be fast-food feelings or junk feelings. In the hybrid texts that are MURDER *and murder* and *Mapping Fate*, as well as in the account by Phyllis Rose, we're offered both a sense of the imperiling intensity that is the sensation of statistical panic and complex emotional reflections on that experience—thought that is felt and feeling that is thought. We're offered multifaceted narratives that I take to be antidotes to narratives reduced to melodramatic fragments. At the same time these texts attune us to the saturation of statistics beyond the medical sphere or the consumer culture of health, calling our attention to the postmodern society of the statistic, a subject to which I now turn.

2

If we turn our attention to contemporary culture in general, to the culture we breathe in and out everyday, we find everywhere deployed the altogether banal and reductive language of the statistic, a language that continuously offers itself up as a way of understanding our lives and the world. It is the quantitative language of our global capitalist public culture, one that we have all internalized. It is the logic and preeminent expression of late capitalism.

Statistics are routinely used today to make sense of an event or moment in time, and in the process they often create the contours of history—a history of economics or of politics. Consider the endless statistical reports of consumption figures (a high percentage of a market share may itself stimulate demand). Consider the announcements of the political ratings of presidents, prime ministers, candidates, and would-be candidates (a low rating in the polls may precipitate a politician's rating even further). Desires and preferences are quantified and then reduced to mathematical expression. Statistics have also become a form of entertainment and exhibition, invoked whimsically in virtually any issue of a newspaper, thus performing the postmodern numerological analogue to the sixteenth-century curiosity cabinet that housed all kinds of peculiar and exotic objects.

Statistics is the science that, according to the definition given in the *Random House College Dictionary of the English Language*, "deals with the collection, classification, analysis, and interpretation of numerical facts or data, and that, by use of mathematical theories of probability, imposes order and regularity on aggregates of more or less disparate elements." In this chapter my focus is on statistics as a discourse of *probability* rather than as one used to make sense of the past or of the present. It is especially in this guise that the discourse of statistics can be understood as the expression of late capitalism: for however a statistical probability may appear to be related to the material world, in particular to the world of our bodies, as the product of a science of probability a statistic is in fact completely detached from the world, much as today's global financial markets are detached from actual production in a local economy. In this sense, statistics are probabilities cast into possible and alternative futures that for the most part take on a dark dimension. These statistical probabilities seem to implicate us as individuals in scenarios of financial ruin and of disaster by disease and weather; that is, abstractions expressed by the ultimate abstraction, one that is infinite—numbers. As I argued in the section above, a statistic often seems to contain a complete narrative in and of itself: I have an 80 percent chance . . . you have a 10 percent risk. . . .

Risk is the critical concept. Economics is known as the dismal science, but that title should instead go to statistics. For it is a "science" that now circulates interminably in everyday life as a discourse of risk. We are at risk, it seems, of anything and everything. Of death by mad cow disease. Of high cholesterol. Of unemployment. Of crossing the street. Of rape. Of toxic waste. Of hormone replacement therapy. Of earthquakes. Of crushing a finger with a hammer.[11] Even when the citation of statistics is meant to provide reassurance, it may more often than not produce its opposite: a sense of foreboding and insecurity. In the immediate aftermath of the September 11, 2001, destruction of the twin towers of the World Trade Center in New York, the discourse of risk at the hands of terrorist attacks was omnipresent in the United States, with the emphasis falling on bioterrorism (anthrax, small pox, typhus)—that is, threats targeted specifically to the body and not to property or symbolic structures. How to allay the public's panic? It should come as no surprise that one of the chief ways was to counter the (hopefully) statistically minimal threat of bodily harm from terrorism with the deployment of statistics of risk from everyday life. Consider this excerpt from the article "Don't Lose Sight of Real, Everyday Risks" by Jane Brody that appeared in the *New York Times* on 9 October 2001: "The current focus on potential acts of terrorism is diverting people from responding to real and immediate risks to their well-being, and in some cases prompting them to take real risks because they are so busy avoiding hypothetical ones." The real risks, she implies, are those encountered every day—eating a lot of beef, smoking cigarettes—with the risks from terrorism reduced to the "hypothetical." What does Brody single out as her first example? "A case in point: driving long distances instead of flying. On a per-mile basis, flying is much safer, even in these uncertain times. Each year, tens of thousands of people are killed on the roads, whereas the annual number of airplane deaths almost never exceeds a few hundred, as was the case even on Sept. 11" (D6).

But narratives are spun out of just such numbers, even when the number is only one. Indeed as the cultural anthropologist Arjun Appadurai has stressed, the number one, "the numerical sign of the individual, is the key number for liberal social theory" (59). In the wake of terrorism, he argues, we have succumbed to a fear of small numbers. Consider this banal example before September 11, 2001. In late 1997 it was widely reported in the media that an older woman had died from injuries caused by air turbulence on a flight from Japan to Honolulu. The airline industry quickly released the following statistic, which was announced in turn by the media, in an effort to reassure us so that we'd forget any newly engendered fear of flying: only two people, we were told, have died of air turbulence over the last fifteen years.[12] My informal and highly unscientific survey of friends and colleagues revealed instead that many found themselves wondering about the circumstances of the death of that other person. How did he or she die? What happened? Where? When? They created the outlines of a narrative based on this single statistic and even vaguely fantasized about their own possible future death from air turbulence, in the end resolving to always keep their seat belts fastened to diminish their risk. In this case a statistic about the past is extrapolated into a scenario of possible mortality in the future. Ultimately, as the philosopher Ian Hacking has suggested, in the end what we may have come to fear is not a specific thing—any *thing*—but rather probability itself, the future. As the sociologist Ulrich Beck has persuasively argued, industrial society has been succeeded by the risk society. What we fear is risk itself.[13]

Thus if we live in a visual culture where society is distinguished by the spectacle, we also live in a society of the statistic. Rather than anchoring us to a stable lifeworld, statistics that forecast the future engender insecurity in the form of low-grade intensities that, like low-grade fevers, permit us to go about our everyday lives albeit in a state of statistical stress. Statistics are the very atmosphere we breathe, the strange weather in which we live, the continuous emission of postmodern media life. In the United States we adopt, for example, the stance of medical self-surveillance, monitoring our own vital statistics even as we listen to the nation's medical statistics routinely announced by the Centers for Disease Control. We subject ourselves to financial self-scrutiny, worrying that we will not have enough resources for college, a house, medical bills, retirement (I know about that, as I explained in the introduction).

Statistics are transmitted at every moment of the day and night—on the Internet, in the newspaper and magazines, and on TV and the radio. Statistics hail us in the Althusserian sense. The statistic and the anecdote are the pervasive conventions of media culture. Statistics often open what is called a "story" in print, broadcast, or Internet news, to be followed by an anecdote—or vice versa. Often statistics in and of themselves are the story and our imaginations supply a corresponding anecdote or scenario. In the United States, for instance, we learned in 2005 from the director of the Department of Justice's Office on Violence Against Women that "one third of female homicide victims are murdered by their intimate partners."[14] Here statistics are themselves the deep structure and manifest content of the story; they are numerological protagonists that stalk their potential victims. Here a narrative has been compacted into the most minimal and impersonal of fragments—a statistic. Death and destruction is the story, with the round number of deaths and their location by nation constituting its critical elements. Consider this headline in the 20 December 2005 issue of the *New York Times*: "Atlanta Homicide Rate Drops as Nation's

Murder Level Rises." This is a statistical variant on what Freud termed the declaration of desire by negation, although here it is not desire but the state of risk that is announced. That the number of murders has declined is supposed to be good news for people who live in Atlanta. But there is no doubt that the situation of fewer murders remains a forecast of violent death. Moreover, that the very subject of the sentence fragment is the homicide rate itself suggests that statistics, although an impersonal and implacable force, possess a peculiar fateful agency akin to that of the ancient Greek gods. Being reduced to a statistic, as we say, is definitely not a fate to be desired. And there is a further dark complexity. In linking the decrease in murders in Atlanta to the increase in murders elsewhere the ignoble emotion of schadenfreude is invoked.

3

I have been associating the society of the statistic with a particular form of feeling—what I call statistical stress or, in its extreme form, statistical panic. The flip side of panic is boredom. I suggest that statistical stress and statistical boredom, which is related to it, can be understood as constituting a particular structure of feeling, one that discloses the society of the statistic in which we live today—a mediatized, marketized, and medicalized culture in which the notion of being at risk has assumed dominant proportions.[15] I offer this in the spirit of speculation, as a cultural hypothesis, and I do so by returning us briefly to the turn of the twentieth century, drawing on the history of the structure of feeling of modernity in order to suggest a comparison with what I have been calling the postmodern society of the statistic and its concomitant structure of feeling.

Earlier in this chapter I referred to the train when I remarked that for the character in the episode of *Chicago Hope* the statistic of having an 86 percent chance of contracting fatal breast cancer has for her the force of a train heading straight for her. I chose this as an analogy because the train in fact recalls the much earlier cultural form of the "cinema of attraction," as Tom Gunning has named it. The cinema of attraction was a nonnarrative cinema that flourished at the turn of the twentieth century; indeed it dominated the very idea of the cinema until 1906–1907 when it took a narrative turn. In the cinema of attraction, space and time were envisioned as a forum in which to elaborate a series of shocks, in particular the shock of the new theorized by Walter Benjamin as associated with turn-of-the-century urban culture and the technology so characteristic of it. The aesthetic was preeminently one of assault. The Lumière brothers' famous film *Arrival of a Train at the Station* (1895) serves as the quintessential example. The title encapsulates the action of the film: a train arrives at the station, with the spectators positioned in front of it as it advances. The technological protagonist of the film—the train—is an invention that changed our very sense of time and space and thus the nature of perception itself, an alteration in perception that is indexed in certain affects, requiring what I call a phenomenology of technology expressed in terms of feelings.[16]

By all accounts the spectators reacted with terror and panic to the Lumière brothers' film of an onrushing train. The invention represented what was unknown—that is, new—in addition to unimaginable speed and force. It represented the penetration of the urban in the countryside, or the machine in the garden, as the Americanist Leo Marx has so aptly phrased it, and thus represented a fundamental change in social structures. As a film, *Arrival of a Train at the Station* not only represented the shock of the new, it also elicited the response of the shock of the new that, as a structure of feeling, distinguished this period of technological change. But this experience was a simulation of an experience, one that took place in a space devoted to entertainment. Thus the bodily and psychic sensation of panic felt by the spectators was leavened by the sense of expectation and excitement, one that Gunning associates with a conscious enjoyment of visual shocks and thrills. "The onrushing train," Gunning explains in "An Aesthetic of Astonishment," "did not simply produce the negative experience of fear but the particularly modern entertainment form of the *thrill*, embodied elsewhere in the recently appearing attractions of the amusement parks (such as the roller coaster), which combined sensations of acceleration and falling with a security guaranteed by modern industrial technology" (37).

I would add that the cinema of attraction functioned as a virtual space, a space of safety in which the spectator could become accommodated to the new technology—and thus to the new urban culture—in the guise of entertainment (one that has its analogues in today's video games). As we know, accommodation—both in real space and time as well as in representational space—leads to adaptation, and adaptation can yield to boredom. It's thus crucial to understand boredom as the inevitable counterpart of the shock of the new associated with the modern metropolis. As the film theorist Patrice Petro has so persuasively argued, modernity had another affective side—that of boredom. Boredom was not a sensation but the lack of sensation, less an emotion than a mood. Boredom set in, she writes, "when the 'shock of the new' ceased to be shocking, when change itself had become routinized, commodified, banalized, and when the extraordinary, the unusual, and the fantastic became inextricably linked to the boring, the prosaic, and the everyday" (265).

If the shock of the new was theorized by Walter Benjamin, boredom was for him also a critical affect for understanding modern subjectivity.[17] The same is true for Georg Simmel. In his well-known essay "The Metropolis and Mental Life," Simmel argues that the extreme stimulation experienced in the modern city was intertwined with the money economy that underwrote it, one that demanded a mind that was necessarily consumed with "weighing, calculating, enumerating and [with] the reduction of qualitative values to quantitative terms" (328).[18] For Simmel, the counterpart of urban stimulation is what he called "the blasé attitude" (329). Together, then, shock and boredom, linked to technological innovation and urban culture, constitute what we could call a dominant structure of feeling of modernity.

With the affect of boredom twinned to shock I return to the postmodern society of the statistic. The train is exemplary of the technology of urban modernity, a technology characterized by concreteness and materiality. The all-pervasive discourse of statistics is exemplary of the postmodern. It is a social technology that, like finance capitalism, is preeminently abstract.[19] And it is altogether clear that we respond to the litany of statistics with which we are daily bombarded with boredom as surely as we do with panic. More so. Consider the all-pervasive recitation and quotation of statistics we encounter in enormous quantities every day—the number of housing starts in any given month, the percentage rise or fall of the closing of Dow and other stock exchanges, the amount of precipitation in a particular period, the numbers of wins and losses of a sporting team, the percentage of various groups that voted for a certain candidate, and so on. The list is endless. "Let's do the numbers," intones National Public Radio at night, the voice in an upbeat mood no matter what, trying to beat the boredom or head off the panic, maintaining an equable tone of entertainment. We live in a climate of numbers virtually vying for our attention. We talk statistics as much as we talk about the weather. We take note, we end by turning off, numbed, perhaps enervated, only to begin again the next day. (In retrospect it is a matter of some irony to me that as an economics major in college I was thrilled to have a summer internship in Washington at the Bureau of Labor Statistics. My project was disemployment at the plant level. And it was boring! But the reason itself is also ironic. In the three months I was there, the figures it was my responsibility to assess literally never arrived. So I asked if I could go to the library, where I read economic history. That, it turned out, was the place for me.)

The matter is further complicated because we must find ways to creatively use statistical language to effect change. We can't "say no" to statistics any more than we could "say no" to trains—nor should we want to do so in an unreflective way. In part the challenge for those who are activists is to convince others to understand the urgency implied in the tedious quantitative language of the statistic. Boredom must be converted into concern. Much public policy depends upon mobilizing statistical panic—for gathering support for curtailing teenage smoking, for increasing funds for AIDS in Africa and research on autism in the United States, for fighting the spread of avian flu, and for decreasing the rate of growth of the population in certain countries, for instance. Statistical language itself is one of our tools to argue for human goods, such as the alleviation of human suffering.

Some twenty-five years ago Jacques Derrida commented on what he identified as the apocalyptic strain in postmodern thought, suggesting that the tone of apocalypse represents a continuity between modernism and postmodernism. I have been suggesting that there is a continuity between the shock of the new, or the affect of modernity, and the panic generated by the postmodern society of the statistic, although their constituting technologies are different. The tone of apocalypse is deployed in much statistical discourse: 86 percent! Market slides 3.5 percent! The population is falling! The population is skyrocketing! But at the same time there is something altogether banal, if not altogether boring, about a future cast in numerological terms or calculated in quantitative bundles.

To figure the modern, Walter Benjamin imagined a visionary "angel of history" who, although turned toward the future, faces in fact the past and the "wreckage" wrought by catastrophe (259). Today we face a future figured as statistical risk, with wreckage everywhere dispersed into the years that lie ahead. There is something both strangely unnerving and numbing in the phenomenon of statistical panic, a structure of feeling associated with the postmodern society of risk, one that produces risk as a commodity and then offers goods and services to assuage that same sense of panic. Although it bears similarities to the emerging structure of feeling at the turn of the twentieth century (we no longer experience the shock of the urban technological new in the same way, we are thoroughly habituated to it), this postmodern structure of feeling is decidedly different.

4

The global language of statistics that characterizes our society is a discourse in the Foucauldian sense that, like capitalism, also has a history of development. Importantly this history is in the process of being written, three moments of which might include the late sixteenth century, the beginning of the nineteenth century, and the end of the twentieth century.

The feminist literary historian Mary Poovey has studied the emergence of techniques in the sixteenth century—double-entry bookkeeping, among them—that helped codify commercial transactions in the early modern period.[20] What especially fascinates me in Poovey's account is that the category of risk initially contained everything that could *not* be represented by numbers, with shipwrecks and instabilities in world demand being leading examples. It was only later with the development of techniques (such as bills of exchange) that risk was to a certain extent institutionalized. But the notion of the statistic is central to her history of the emergence of the modern fact.

The philosopher Ian Hacking in his brilliant book *The Taming of Chance* shows how probability is, as he puts it, "*the* philosophical success story of the first half of the twentieth century," a development he traces to the consolidation of statistical thinking in the nineteenth century, one made possible by the systematic collection of data starting around 1820, the beginning of an "avalanche of printed numbers" that continues to deluge us today (18). In addition Hacking explores the development of statistical fatalism in the 1830s, strains of which I see everywhere today.[21] By the late nineteenth century the statistical concept of the "normal" was, according to Hacking, "the premier statistical idea" (145), a concept that continues to have force today yet has also taken a paradoxical turn. In the nineteenth century the normal was associated with the state of health. But if we are today everywhere and always at risk, the normal seems virtually sure to turn catastrophically into its opposite at any moment: *to be normal is to be in a state of risk*, a state that at some inevitable future time will be fulfilled as a state of disease or death. Today statistical thinking and its concomitant affective tone, a sense of being at risk, have been internalized by virtually everyone in our consumer culture. Statistics are endlessly produced. They are broadcast day and night by the media. They are prime determinants in how we feel and what we do.

Today, as opposed to the sixteenth century, we think of risk as precisely what *can* be represented by numbers, by figures that represent the future. Today, as opposed to the nineteenth century when the collection, maintenance, and deployment of statistics was predominately the province of the state, statistics circulate in virtually every domain of culture on all levels— from the personal to the global. Indeed statistics inextricably intertwine the two. As Theodore Porter has pointed out in *The Rise of Statistical Thinking: 1820–1900*, it is difficult for us to imagine that before the 1820s societies in the West didn't make decisions (or what today we would call public policy) based on unemployment figures or crime rates. With the rise of mass culture in the late nineteenth and early twentieth centuries and with the continuing invention and consolidation of mass media throughout the twentieth century, it is, I suggest, even more difficult to imagine a world not saturated by statistics as a discourse of knowledge, ranging from the trivial to the life threatening.[22] If in the nineteenth century statistics were used by the state—from city governments to national governments—as a management tool, today statistics of probability, delivered as a discourse of risk, are disseminated endlessly and internalized by individuals as tools for living out their lives, a tool so forcefully exposed by Rainer and by Wexler.[23] The structure of feeling I have been calling statistical panic (and its oscillating partner, boredom or numbness) is an effect of the social technology of statistics, one that has both contributed to the creation of the omnipresent discourse of risk and produced a calculus to avoid that very risk, a prime contradiction of capitalistic culture in the twenty-first century. Like other feelings, then, panic has a history.[24]

In this chapter my primary concern has been to suggest two particular points in that history in relation to emerging technologies in the twentieth century—the shock of the new associated with urban technologies at the turn of the twentieth century and statistical panic associated with the convergence of the information revolution and the probabilistic revolution at the turn of the twenty-first century.[25] As a structure of feeling, statistical panic, sutured to statistical boredom, is the opposite of a mathematical sublime. Statistics are not a discourse of awe or wonder but rather the stuff of everyday life. They are a routine currency in which we plot our lives in terms of a calculus of risk and in which, when we are jolted into mortal attention, we find ourselves living on the razor edge of panic, beset by what Paul Monette in his memoir *Borrowed Time* has called the "thundercloud" of statistics (48).

I have focused on the medical body as it is represented in illness narratives, and I have been particularly concerned with those who reject the statistical body as all-determining of the course of their lives. Many other texts bear witness to the subjective experience of illness as something palpably distinct from the clinical understanding of disease as organic dysfunction. And many of these texts also resist the lure of conflating one's own unique body with the aggregate body of statistical risk. These stories are antidotes to the often ennervating effects of the discourse of risk. If I have concentrated on work that portrays women's bodies at risk, my intent has not been to suggest that the medical statistical body is gendered female.

In closing, then, I refer to one last text, *The Noonday Demon*, Andrew Solomon's remarkable study of clinical depression, an illness he takes care to insist is a bodily disease. In addition to tracing the history of depression and examining the cultural politics of the disease as well as its treatments, Solomon presents us with the scientific research that outlines the contours of the statistical body of clinical depression. Approximately 3 percent of all Americans suffer from chronic depression. Nearly one in ten Americans will experience a major episode of depression in their lifetimes. Women are twice as likely to suffer depression as men. Solomon doesn't ignore the statistics of depression. But neither does he submit to them. It is his conviction that, as he says, "the hard numbers are the ones that lie" (13). "Many authors derive a rather nauseous air of invincibility from statistics," he writes, "as though showing that something occurs 82.7 percent of the time is more palpable and true than showing that something occurs about three out of four times" (13). Instead, the primary goal of his book, he tells us, is empathy, and with great insight and in prose that often rises to eloquence he tells us his own alarming story and the stories of others, conveying to us the devastating experience that is depression, one that can be "described only in metaphor and allegory" (16) and definitively not in terms of the impersonal statistical body.

INEXHAUSTIBLE GRIEF

The goal of psychoanalysis is, broadly, to claim as one's own
the power of one's feelings.
> —Nancy Chodorow, *The Power of Feelings*

The dominion of the objective being in me, the sensuous out-
burst of my essential activity, is *emotion*, which thus becomes
here the *activity* of my being.
> —Karl Marx, *Economic and*
> *Philosophical Manuscripts of 1844*

Psychoanalytically speaking, any form of life will tend to generate a fantasy of what it is to get outside that life.
> —Jonathan Lear, *Happiness,*
> *Death, and the Remainder of Life*

In Marion Roach's *Another Name for Madness* a daughter cares for her
mother. In "At the End of the Line," a beautiful prose poem by the French
psychoanalyst J.-B. Pontalis, a son reflects on his relationship to his mother.
But here there is no impulse to inform readers. Here the aesthetic is not
psychological realism but that of a poetic meditative mode, one with its
roots in the routines of everyday life. "At the End of the Line" was published
in 1986 when Pontalis was sixty-two and his mother was, by my count,
ninety-two. The final essay in his book *Love of Beginnings*, "At the End of
the Line" moves effortlessly—as if by free association—from anecdote to
memory, from memory to the figure of another old woman (one lost to old
age), and from her death-in-life to a transformational fantasy involving his
mother. The mundane technology of the telephone serves as the literal
device of attachment between the two, with the narrative set in motion by a
simple phone call from his mother. It concludes with a vision of the
restoration of harmony between them, one that seems to emerge out of the
very act of remembrance and writing itself. Created is an oneiric psychic
space in which a vision of mother and son appears with the two of them

poised on a plateau at the edge of life. That Pontalis casts his piece in the third person, not the first, suggests the degree to which we are removed from the confessional world of the autobiographical. Instead we find a prose poem that is a gentle parable of intimacy.

Here is the first sentence of "At the End of the Line": "When the high-pitched ring can be heard at that time of day, he knows it's her. He doesn't have to wait, he knows, he doesn't have the slightest hesitation. It can only be her, the telephone rings every evening at the same time, almost to the second" (166). His mother is confined to her apartment—apparently by choice—and hasn't changed or rearranged the furniture of her existence for years. She subsists in a virtually lifeless homeostatic state, surrounded not by people but by family photographs taken many years before, photographs to which she's no longer attached. Here are the next two sentences of "At the End of the Line":

He imagines her staring at the small clock in her bedroom where nothing has changed for so many years, where not a single object has been moved even by a millimeter, where the photographs she no longer sees are all, in little oval frames, carefully placed on the mantelpiece: the picture of her mother with the light eyes, that of her brother in an airman's uniform, that of her two sons with the sailor-suit collars—these are the photographs taken by professionals, and there are many others that she herself took once upon a time, "snapshots," with a Kodak box camera placed upright against her chest, and then others again that he took, but those too are ancient, twenty years, thirty years, it has been a long time since, for her, life stopped.

Here it is, it's time, he picks up the telephone, at first there's a small silence and that silence confirms, if there were any need for confirmation, that it is indeed her, he hears her voice, she says a few words, that it was very cold today or that it'll rain tomorrow or else she announces an illness, a death, François is in the hospital, it's his heart, Anne Dubac will be buried at Père-Lachaise, poor thing, or else, and it's said in the same tone, which isn't one of complaint, which isn't one of calamity: your brother waited all day for the plumber. (166–67)

The ostensible content of his mother's conversation—the weather, a funeral, news about his brother—is inconsequential. Her voice is toneless. It doesn't vary as she relates these bits and pieces of meaningless information. Trying to warm her into life, he responds with news of the everyday variety of his own. But all the while he knows her call will contract to a single question, one so elemental and urgent that it has taken on the form of a demand, one posed of him every day. Will he be there tomorrow at the same time? Will he be there tomorrow at the same time? Will he be there tomorrow at the same time? (The psychoanalyst Adam Phillips told me that he's been in Pontalis's apartment when this call has come—more than once.)

> And he, on his side, tries to give her more comforting news, that he met someone really interesting today, that the children came back from the mountains very proud of their exploits, that the hyacinths she gave him for Christmas are beginning to flower on the balcony, anything that may signify to her that life goes on, it doesn't matter what so long as it's a sign of life, but the slightest signs are undoubtedly already too much for her, since she simply wants to assure herself of his presence at the end of the line and is already asking something she knows, whether he will be in tomorrow at the same time so that, like this evening, like yesterday, like the previous weeks and months, she can reach him at that hour, which is the time when he has finished work and got back home. (167)

If her life has stopped, she holds tenaciously onto life. It's as if his promise that this ritual will persist into the future, a promise she exacts day by day, assures that life—her life—will continue. It's as if there is an ontological dimension to this repetition that is teleological in nature, one forecasting a perpetual future made possible by the elementary technology of the telephone. For if the appointed time has to be changed because his routine varies, if he hesitates for a moment, her anxiety is palpable:

> Sometimes all the same he's not going to be there, he'll go directly from his office to the restaurant, to the cinema, to some friends, and then, cautiously, he must tell her: "No, tomorrow I won't be in but the day after definitely."—"At the same time?"—"Yes, at the same time." And that disturbs her, she'll call back right away to ask him: "That's right, tomorrow?"—"No, the day after."—"At the same time, quarter past eight?" "Yes, or earlier if you'd prefer, I'll be in earlier." That disturbs her too, she doesn't like the time to be changed, no modification must be introduced into the time-table, not the slightest modification must be introduced. Anywhere. Everything that can happen has for her one name only: accident.

> She must be in control of her call, in control of her time. He must be
> there at the end of the line. It must be an absolute certainty. Now *he's* the
> mother. (167–68)

Allaying overwhelming anxiety is her pressing need and thus she's insis-
tent and inflexible. It takes the form of the control of her son. Is this not an
uncanny version of the *fort-da* of early childhood, a method his mother has
invented of assuaging her awareness of vulnerability in late life and of
controlling her fear of abandonment and death?

> There's something odd. When he speaks about it to others, no one
> understands. "What, she never asks to see you, yet she telephones you
> every evening. She lives far away? Abroad?"—"No, very near. But very
> far also. And it's not that she doesn't ask to see me, she doesn't *want* me
> to come. Stubbornly refuses. If I insist, she gets angry. What she wants
> is to have me at the end of the line, at the appointed time."
> To have me at the end of the line. In her time.
> He repeats these words, he repeats them as she repeats every eve-
> ning: "Tomorrow, I shall call you at a quarter past eight. Will you be
> there?"—"Yes, tomorrow at a quarter past eight, I'll be there, don't
> worry."
> Ten years ago, she would sometimes say: "One shouldn't live so long.
> If I had the courage. . . ." Now she no longer says it. (168–69)

Freud theorized the *fort-da* as he watched his eighteen-month-old grandson play a game he had invented. He would throw a spool with a string
attached to it out of his crib and reel it back in, uttering *fort* and then *da*, in
Freud's view symbolically controlling the disappearance (*fort*) and return
(*da*) of his mother.[1] In "At the End of the Line" it's not the child but the
mother casting out the line as if it were the umbilical cord that links them
even now, controlling her son. Now it's his role to provide reassurance—a
holding environment, in the psychoanalyst's D. W. Winnicott's words.[2]
Like an infant, the mother demands "absolute certainty," as if it were
possible (168). "Now *he's* the mother" (168).

In a short meditation on the *fort-da* in his book *Windows*, Pontalis
suggests that the *fort-da* constitutes the elemental rhythm of our lives.[3]
"What if, throughout our entire lives, we do nothing but throw the bobbin,
over there, in order to make it come back *here!*" he writes. "And this thread,
as fragile as it is, is what connects us to the other, to life. Should it break—

existence is held only by a thread—then it's death. What would the child have felt if the bobbin hadn't returned to his hand?" (60). What would his mother feel if he simply didn't answer his phone call? Unthinkable anxiety.

Roland Barthes, in *A Lover's Discourse*, tells us that Freud wasn't fond of the telephone because he understood it to convey, in Barthes's phrase, the "*wrong voice*, the false communication" (114–15). By contrast the telephone serves an almost magical purpose in "At the End of the Line." It's not a question of the content of a message or the timbre of the voice but of the open line of attachment that in and of itself soothes anxiety. Barthes also understands the telephone in terms of the *fort-da* but his emphasis is on separation and distance, not connection. "No doubt," he writes, "I try to deny separation by the telephone—as the child fearing to lose its mother keeps pulling on a string; but the telephone wire is not a good transitional object, it is not an inert string; it is charged with a meaning, which is not that of junction but that of distance: the loved, exhausted voice heard over the telephone is the fade-out in all its anxiety"; "*I'm going to leave you*, the voice on the telephone says with each second" (115).

A string can serve both as a symbol of "separateness and of union through communication," as Winnicott so memorably observed in *Playing and Reality*, commenting on the remarkable way a two-and-a-half-year-old deployed a tangle of string while Winnicott talked with his mother (43).[4] If a string can function both to separate and to connect, when does one predominate over the other? Surely it's a question of one's role in relation to the other. Just as surely it's a question of temperament and disposition as much as anything else. If Barthes emphasizes separation, Pontalis gravitates to connection: "Yes, tomorrow at a quarter past eight, I'll be there, don't worry," says the son every evening to his mother, as if bestowing a kiss goodnight.

It might be objected that this daily call is only the repetition of an empty routine. But it would seem his mother's very willfulness underwrites what is in fact a ritual just as the ritual seems to sustain her will. That her son will answer her call every evening—tomorrow and tomorrow and tomorrow—seems to guarantee her attachment to life in general as well as her attachment to her son, the life to which she gave birth. It also seems to serve as protection against the disabling inertia that has seized the mother of one of his friends, an old woman whose lifelessness frightens him: "An image persists. It was another old woman, the mother of one of his child-hood friends. She stayed in bed all day. Doctors pronounced her very weak:

there comes an age when one no longer goes to the trouble of naming the illness. He had come to pay his respects. She too had been active, this bedridden woman. He had wanted to say a few words to her, to speak to her about her son's successes, about the beauty of her house in the autumn sun. She wasn't listening to him, she wasn't looking at him. In front of her, at the foot of her brass bed, a television set had been installed" (169).

One of the latent fears children have in relation to their parents is that they will disengage from the world when they are old—that they will irrevocably remove themselves from us, ceasing to listen to us or to speak to us in any meaningful way, thus revealing a deep and disturbing indifference. That they will fall prey to the numbing orbit of television is a ubiquitous figure of this fear. Horrified by her mother's precipitous decline into Alzheimer's disease, Marion Roach offers this portrait in *Another Name for Madness*. "My mother, a college graduate, a journalist and then a teacher, used to tell me that watching television 'rots the mind.' Now, it's almost all she wants to do. It's her favorite pastime," she writes. "Most of the time she doesn't have the sound on; she just stares at the screen" (122–23). Similarly, in his moving essay "The Makeup of Memory in the Winter of Our Discontent," Herbert Blau writes this about his father's final illness: "When he suffered a double stroke which left him in a wheelchair and blind in one eye, [he] took it as a sign of weakness, almost a personal fault and, in the excess of pride with which he had lived, refused any solace or therapy and virtually inflicted upon himself the lonely humiliation of death. When I flew across the country to visit him, the television would be on. He'd stare intently at the screen no matter what was there, never looking at me with his single eye, as if canceling the oedipal contract and asking, among all the hopeless desires, that we forget his crippled being, as if he'd never been at all" (17). (I am married to Herbert Blau, and this passage troubles me for the reasons that can be imagined. Indeed it occurs to me with a fateful start that I am the one who bought my husband a television when twenty-five years ago he didn't own one. As he has said more than once—indeed *weekly*—it has ruined his life.)

And here is Pontalis describing this other mother, bound to the flickering shadows of a televisual world: "Her gaze was caught by what flashed past on the screen: images of war in Afghanistan, a regatta at Newport, a building in flames in the 15th arrondissement, then a singer in sequins, and she was watching it, mute, she was letting herself be absorbed by it, deaf, as if all these ghostly shadows, rock stars and guerillas jumbled, merged, were the reality that was awaiting her and as if these shadows were coming slowly, inexorably, to seize her, to take her with them into this intermediate world which was no longer that of the living and already, not completely but almost, that of the dead" (169–70). In this threefold cluster of passages television is figured as an alien invader abducting life on earth, drawing old people up and into it where they live a shadowy, zombie-like existence mediated by images and in between life and death, reduced to grey ciphers of their former selves, captured by a machine they no doubt earlier feared could harm their own children, bound by an invisible cord to the technology that is television, staring incommunicado. It is a frightening vision of the annihilation of the social space of familial life, the sundering of the implicit contract of intergenerational continuity, the abandonment of the younger generation by the older generation in a disconnect that is total and unforgiving, the contract between parent and child canceled. That the agent of this definitive withdrawal takes the shape of the most significant mass medium and most important communication technology of the twentieth century is profoundly ironic. Found in virtually every home and in every hospital room as well as in the day rooms of nursing homes and assisted care facilities, television is distributed throughout the space devoted to domestic life, disability, and illness as if lying in predatory wait.[5]

In psychoanalytic terms we might say that here television is figured as a third term, one that divides child from parent. It's as if television itself, with its constant and unremitting flow, possesses the strength to hurl the parent out of the orbit of the child—*fort*. And there is no *da*. Is this what dying is like in our postmodern televisual culture? As Pontalis asks:

Like a child, he wondered "where does one go when one dies?" and he stole out of the big red room. He walked for a long time across hills with supple forms like the breasts of a woman, among the vines. He wanted to exorcize that vision of the bedridden old woman. He told himself that this must be what it is to die nowadays, to die gently under hypnosis: without noticing it, to pass to the other side, into the screen you are no longer watching but which is watching you, which gradually absents you from the people close to you, from yourself, from memory of the world, to rejoin the anonymous insubstantiality and endless disorder of images. (170)

If this old woman has capitulated to the televisual netherworld, his mother, anything but compliant, lives in the future tense. Even as his emotions are mixed, he admires his mother's strong will and drive, taking a certain pride in her tenacity: "She, by contrast, was vigilant, the one who telephoned him every evening to say nothing except that she would telephone him the next day. Sometimes it exasperated him: this fixed habit of an obstinate old person, this control which, without realizing it perhaps, she exercised over him. He had to be there, at his post" (170).

If Pontalis has agreed to this daily phone call from his mother, he is nonetheless as ambivalent about his mother as he is about being under her control. If she never seemed to pay attention to him in the past (a familiar complaint we have about our parents), the two of them are also alike in ways that sting him. Thus he confides his own fear of resembling her, of being bound to her by the inflections of his body reflecting hers:

> She had been, he believed, hardly present in his life. What did she know about him? So little. Nothing. Nothing about his work, nothing about his loves, nothing about his buried sadness that she had passed on to him, he was sure of it, even less about what made him happy, which he had to win despite her, she who had always been afraid of the future. (Like her, in the street, he walked with small steps and, as soon as he noticed it, he would change his pace, but through a deliberate decision which only underlines the imprint.) And he, what did he know about her? He had in him only an image that had scarcely moved with time. The distance between them had been immense. Or the excessive close-ness, to the point of identity, but a secret identity. He didn't really know. (168)

That they were never close hurts him. That they were too close, their identities secretly mirroring each other, hurts him also. But in the course of reflecting on his past, he moves from his caviling point of view to consider hers. If she knew nothing about him, he comes to the symmetri-cal conclusion that he too knows nothing about her. "And he, what did he know about her?" (168). What must she have wanted?

In "Delusions and Dreams in Jensen's *Gradiva*" Freud writes, "We remain on the surface so long as we are dealing only with memories and ideas. What is alone of value in mental life is rather the feelings. No mental forces are significant unless they possess the characteristic of arousing feelings" (*SE* 9: 48–49). What is important is not the memory but the feeling engendered by it—in this case, the mood. Remembrance, Pontalis writes in *Windows*, can be a "resuscitation" of the past (69). What does he call into life? Here is the memory to which he returns in "At the End of the Line": "He thought she had never moved him, never touched him and that for her it was exactly the same: he had never managed to move her, to touch her. Yes, once: she had come from Brittany, where she was living at the time, to have supper with him. He still remembers thirty years later where they had supper, Place Pereire, on a terrace. It was summer, they had turbot with mousseline sauce and wine from Boyzy. He was alone in Paris, held back by the oral part of an exam, and she had come specially for him. Thus in the course of fifty years they had had one lovers' rendezvous" (168). This is the single time he remembers when the long distance between them was bridged, when they were transparently close and at ease with one another, untroubled and unvexed. That his mother came from the west coast of France to meet him is crucial given the daily calls he must now return home from work to receive.

Thus thought yields to feeling. The past perfect surfaces in a memory that releases for him the mood of emotional harmony, a perfect union between them.[6] In the aftermath of this generative memory of the past, his irritation vanishes in the mood of well-being betokening reparation: "He had to admit that he was at last extraordinarily moved. At bottom they must share the same irrational conviction: that as long as they were both at the end of the line, the life-line would not be broken. Often, when younger, he had told himself when she died he wouldn't experience much grief" (170). But grief, as he writes elsewhere in *Love of Beginnings*, is "solid and inexhaustible"; "belonging to no one in particular," it "can be the property of anyone" (103). And indeed it belongs to him.

If the daily ritual of this recurring phone call is similar to the *fort-da*, it is also different. For Freud's grandson the game was a solitary one. But two people are involved in "At the End of the Line." I think of their evening tradition as a grown-up version of Winnicott's squiggle game (with his young patients Winnicott would make drawings in order to elicit their spontaneity and to delineate a space where they—analyst and patient— could make something together). Created is what Winnicott calls a potential space. In his essay on the *fort-da* Pontalis writes that "this thread, as fragile as it is, is what connects us to the other, to life." The line is not an end in itself. It is not the thread of life but a means to an end, which is the other—life. Together the son and mother play *fort* and *da* as a serious game, one that attains the status of a ritual and enriches psychic space. A potential space is instantiated where the elaboration of the self is encouraged and where communication, not the mere passing of information between people, is fostered, thereby engendering security and trust so that we may believe that *fort* will be followed by *da*. If his mother initiated this ritual, Pontalis realized the promise of this potential space in the writing of "At the End of the Line," thus creating something out of the ritual of their evening call.

In "At the End of the Line" we find a narrative of the emotions—estrangement yielding to attachment. But we also find the anticipation of overwhelming grief. This is not the dazzling grief of parting momentarily from a first love; rather, it is a wise grief. When he was younger, Pontalis imagined that when his mother died he wouldn't feel much grief. Now he fears the force of devastating grief to come. Freud was himself near sixty when he watched his grandson invent his forth-and-back game to alleviate the anxiety he felt in his mother's absence. Freud had more than once expressed the wish that he would die before his mother. Under the transformative pressure of feeling so does this son. "Now he would like to die before her" (170).

But then how could he be at the end of the line?

In "Perdre de vue," a piece published two years before "At the End of the Line," Pontalis writes about the suffering of a son—I've been told the son is Roland Barthes—in the wake of his mother's death. His pain is expressed in the anguished cry that he will never see her again. She is lost to sight. As Pontalis wisely adds, perhaps more devastating is that Barthes will never again experience his mother's gaze. In *Windows*, a collection of short meditative pieces published after the death of his mother, Pontalis asks this fundamental psychoanalytic question: "Are there mother substitutes?" (97). "As unsatisfying as she had been, she was the only one. I tell myself that the only being who has no substitute, still less is interchangeable, who is perhaps immortal, is the (if not our) Mother, and I capitalize, I attribute a capital letter, to my tiny Mother" (97). Such grief is inexhaustible.

The psychoanalyst Christopher Bollas writes eloquently about moods in "Moods and the Conservative Process," arguing that generative moods are a psychic process akin to dreaming, one in which we can experience the self in special ways. In this important essay he explains that "going into a mood is an essential condition for the creation of a being state that, like the dream state, may represent some child element in contemporary life. . . . If a person enters a mood, he approximates in this form of psychic activity another means of establishing and elaborating elements of the infant-child self: sleep creates the dream, some moods establish fragments of former self-states" (100). What is necessary for a mood to be generative? A person "must be able to emerge from a mood in such a way that he can reflect upon the mood as an object," Bollas explains, "without feeling the migratory effects of mood experience overlapping into ordinary affects" (101). This affords us one way of understanding the emotional transformation we witness in "At the End of the Line." But we could equally say that the migratory effects of a mood transform the experience of everyday life into a waking fantasy. For as Bollas writes in his wonderful essay "The Evocative Object," "To be touched by the other's unconscious is to be scattered by the winds of the primary process to faraway associations and elaborations, reached through the private links of one's own subjectivity" (45). It is as if the son has been touched by his mother's unconscious and in responding to her demand is placed in touch with his own faraway associations saturated in feeling.

If moods for Bollas often register the existential "moment of a break-down between a child and his parents" (115), the very opposite is the case in "At the End of the Line." The mood betokens union through communication. For Pontalis the mood engendered in the act of remembrance and writing is one of fluent ease in relation to his mother, not the disabling guilt we find in Freud's "Disturbance of a Memory upon the Acropolis," for example.[7] Although Pontalis seeks to understand in the deepest sense his relation to his mother, his mode is not analytical, as is Freud's. Rather it is meditative, poetic, and generative of a mood out of memory.[8] Is this mood mere nostalgia for the past? Pontalis would not, I think, accept this belittling way of understanding nostalgia. As he writes in *Windows*, "Nostalgia carries the desire, less for an unchanging eternity than for always fresh-beginning" (29). Here the mood—a compound of harmonious transparency and anticipatory grief—is generative of a literary fantasy, a fresh beginning, a prose daydream that allows the fulfillment of at least four wishes. It is as if the link between son and mother, figured in the cord of the phone, leads to the dream's navel where a prose daydream takes shape.

Disarmingly, his prose daydream involves the banal technology of the answering machine: "Now he would like to die before her. He would have taken care to plug in an answering machine on which the following message would be recorded. Yes, darling mother, you can call me tomorrow, as usual, at a quarter past eight. She would hear his voice recorded for eternity, and in her own way she, who had told him repeatedly over the years that she wasn't gifted for conversation, would be able to speak to him" (170–71). What four wishes are fulfilled?

First, the quelling of his grief to come, for he would die before her.

Second, the ability to respond to his mother's demand and stay at the end of the line, thus remaining forever a good son, relieving her anxiety and providing her eternal reassurance.

Third, the means to ensure that his mother retains the important capacity to be alone, in Winnicott's sense.[9]

Fourth, his experience of a perfect and intimate knowledge of her.

Here is the beautiful paragraph that brings "At the End of the Line" to a close:

> And so the whole secret between them and everything that had remained hidden inside both of them in the clumsiness of gestures, in abortive impulses, in the unease of bodies, everything that must indeed have been registered, like the message on the answering machine, but falling short of and beyond all speech, would unwind along the line, endlessly. And together they would go through a succession of rooms, of rooms whose double-locked doors would open one by one at the sound of their voices. They would begin the journey again several times, each time with a more supple step, and it would no longer be an interlocking of rooms but a high plateau stretching as far as the eye could see, where a slight wind would be blowing. They would stop walking once they had come to love this vast and light region of silence. (171)

Thus a fifth wish is fulfilled: the creation in fantasy of a place for them to dwell together.

If Freud theorized the *fort-da* as staging the symbolic disappearance of the mother, along with her return, Pontalis imagines only her presence. If this is the illusion of the future, it seems also to be a possible future of illusion, a rewriting of the dismal and disabling guilt of Freud's "Disturbance of a Memory upon the Acropolis" in the register of hope. This is a reparative fantasy, one in which the secrets they hadn't been able to divulge to each other would be spoken and they would greet the future together. Pontalis envisions a transparent intimacy between them in a tenderness that is a supreme fiction—one that recalls for me the eloquent words of T. S. Eliot in *Four Quartets:*

> Words move, music moves
> Only in time, but that which is only living
> Can only die. Words, after speech, reach
> Into the silence. Only by the form, the pattern,
> Can words or music reach
> The stillness, as a Chinese jar still
> Moves perpetually in its stillness,
> Not the stillness of the violin, while the note lasts,
> Nor that only, but the co-existence,
> Or say that the end precedes the beginning,
> And the end and the beginning were always there
> Before the beginning and after the end. (121)

I've quoted T. S. Eliot because "At the End of the Line" draws us into an aesthetic space that is similar to that of *Four Quartets,* one that speaks to our sense of the mystery of life, to our love of beginnings and our anguish at the loss of life—and to our belief that they are somehow intertwined. Pontalis is gently critical of Freud, suggesting he was driven to solve enigmas—enigmas have answers just as puzzles have solutions—but had no real feeling for mystery that does not yield itself to thought alone. An aesthetic experience, Bollas has written in his essay "The Spirit of the Object at the Hand of Fate," does not stimulate the self into thought. Instead it "holds the self within an experience of reverie or rapport" (34).

It may be objected that this daydream of union is just that—a dream, albeit one elaborated in writing and confined to a book. It may involve a fantasy of perfect communication between son and mother but the fantasy is the son's alone, one not communicated to his mother. But think of this. Because the book in which this piece is included was published long before his mother died (she died twelve years after it appeared), it's certainly conceivable she read these intimate words and accepted them as a gift. This is how I would wish her to have received them. As a reader who is also a mother (like Pontalis I am writing from the point of view of the adult child) this is how I take them for myself, although I understand this may be mere wish fulfillment. I read these words as a daughter who waved goodbye to her own mother not too long ago. She is in her eighties and lives in the Atlantic South. I live on the West Coast. She is a woman who is herself bereaved. As a woman not unlike, perhaps, Pontalis's mother, she doesn't have a temperament that inclines her to intimacy. I would wish the fantasy of intimacy offered by "At the End of the Line" to be a part of our future.

In the introduction I mentioned that I'm drawn to the literary emotions. When I gave a lecture on "At the End of the Line" to an audience in London a few years ago, I confided that my deep wish was to simply present the piece to them as the gift I take it to be, to offer it unelaborated so that we might have the opportunity, as Pontalis might put it, to inhabit the space of the dream feelingly and not rush to the cognitive surface of interpretation. For Pontalis the dream is an object in the psychoanalytic sense, one to which we attach ourselves.[10] "At the End of the Line" is an object to which I attached myself some fifteen years ago when I read it for the first time. I consigned it to a file folder where I like to think it waited for me. I never forgot it. And if in my talk in London I was obliged to quote only excerpts from "At the End of the Line," it is to me a source of happiness that in the pages above I have quoted the entire piece. Every single word.

I referred earlier in this coda to nostalgia, and I want to return to it here to make two further points. In *The Future of Nostalgia*, Svetlana Boym suggests that nostalgia is a historical emotion, "a longing for that shrinking 'space of experience' that no longer fits the new horizon of expectations" (10). In a peculiar and insidious way in our society, the old who are invalid —as is the mother of Pontalis—exist out of historical time as they are ejected from the social world by prejudicial virtue of their very age and illness. But they are still painfully inscribed within it, figured as holding onto the vestiges of social space by the now tenuous, now implacable ties offered by communication technologies—the telephone and also the television, as we saw in the accounts by Marion Roach and by Herbert Blau of their parents. For the oldest old, then, we may find ourselves longing for the space of the nuclear family where the family is unmediated by technology, a space offering the fantasy of perfect communication of care, intimacy, and repair on the edge of death.

But if nostalgia is an emotion born of modernity, it is as much if not more a longing for a certain temporality than a longing for a place or homeland. As Boym writes, "At first glance nostalgia is longing for a place, but actually it is a yearning for a different time—the time of our childhood, the slower rhythms of our dreams. In a broader sense, nostalgia is rebellion against the modern idea of time, the time of history and progress" (xv). I have already remarked on my strong attachment—why not call it love—to "At the End of the Line." My relation to this piece of writing could certainly be described as nostalgic in the best sense both in terms of time and space. That emotional attachment underscores and illuminates for me the immense change in my reading life over the past decade. In the introduction I mentioned that I regard myself as a reader by both profession and temperament. I first read "At the End of the Line" in a stately library in Paris. The space itself engendered a meditative rhythm of contemplation, one that rhymed with the rhythm of "At the End of the Line" itself. But my life is now full of *hundreds* of e-mails that must be answered and filed—the tempo is staccato, the affect often anxiety of the bureaucratic kind, or perhaps there is no feeling at all, just busyness—and it has been years since I have been in a library to read. I miss that—for me the library is a space for reflection and respite—and thus I hold onto "At the End of the Line" as what Bollas calls an evocative object, one that preserves and conserves the possibility of the emotional and reflective power of the literary, which is at the end of a certain line.

I opened this book by quoting these words of Pontalis in *Love of Beginnings*: "It's rare nowadays to hear words which, belonging to no one in particular, can be the property of anyone, words that are solid and inexhaustible like 'grief' or 'hatred'" (103). It might seem that with "At the End of the Line" we are far from the explicitly marked cultural politics of the emotions. But consider this. If grief has been understood to be predominantly the work of women, here a man's grief—anticipatory grief—is at stake. If our literature devotes little of its attention to the subjectivity of people in old age, here a woman in her nineties is the central figure.

Although grief—and the accompanying rituals of mourning—will assume different shapes across cultures and periods, we can't imagine it won't be experienced by everyone in some way. It is one of the strong emotions. In *Death's Door: Modern Dying and the Ways We Grieve*, a book altogether remarkable for its vitality and range and its immediacy and deeply felt intelligence, Sandra Gilbert considers the elegy through the converging prisms of literary and cultural studies as well as her own experience. If Paul de Man's words on the rhetorical figure of prosopopoeia in "Autobiography as De-facement" are to me opaque and lifeless, Gilbert captures the enigmatic force of believing, *really believing*, that the person grieved for is speaking from beyond the borders of life. In the desperation of grief there can be an undeniable impulse to follow the dead, who are still somehow so much alive. "How could I not have wanted, in those early days of grief, to follow my husband through that door, to warm him, to comfort him, to 'be dead with' him?" she writes (19). In "At the End of the Line" Pontalis magically reverses the vector of death, imagining that he forestalls his mother's death until long after his own so they can together go through death's door, "go through a succession of rooms, of rooms whose double-locked doors would open one by one at the sound of their voices" (171).

Joan Didion's husband died on December 30, 2003. Toward the end of *The Year of Magical Thinking*, she writes: "I realized that since the last morning of 2003, the morning after he died, I had been trying to reverse time, run the film backward. It was now eight months later, August 30, 2004, and I still was" (183–84). After the death of his mother Pontalis was sick, so sick that he needed to be hospitalized. As he suggests in "Taking Care of Yourself" in *Windows*, he split himself into two in the wake of his mother's death. It is important to him—and to me—that his insight comes from a novel he had been reading. "It often happens, said Thérèse," a character in the novel, "that one invents sicknesses for oneself after a death. It's a way of feeling less alone. You split in half if you will. You take care of yourself as if you were an other. You are two again: myself and the one I'm taking care of" (82). How far this is from the contemporary notion of *managing* one's grief as if one were managing money. Of just getting over it in a matter of weeks and moving forward with one's life, as we are routinely advised.

In the introduction to *Love of Beginnings* Pontalis writes that for him the importance of the primal psychoanalytic question—Where do babies come from?—has faded with time. Now for him the meaningful question is "Where do our thoughts come from?" (xvi). We can provide one answer. If feeling comes from thought, thought also comes from feelings.

NOTES

introduction
THINKING FEELING, FEELING THINKING

1   In the past twenty years there has been much important work on the emotions done by philosophers. Among those whose work I have found particularly formative to my own thought are Sandra Bartky, Alison Jaggar, Martha Nussbaum, Naomi Scheman, and Elizabeth Spelman.

2   In *Feeling Power: Emotions and Education*, Megan Boler tells a story uncannily similar to mine in terms of the inception of her book: it was the *absence* of the study of emotion in recent theories of knowledge that prompted her research, an absence that "was not a coincidence" (xv); she focuses on "pedagogies that invoke emotions in an historicized sense" (20). In the past twenty years there has been a veritable explosion of work in the academy on the emotions—not only in philosophy but in anthropology, sociology, history, literary studies, cultural studies, and media studies. I will refer to some of this work throughout my book, but here let me mention Catherine Lutz's *Unnatural Emotions: Everyday Sentiments on a Micronesian Atoll and Their Challenge to Western Theory*, a book that has circulated far beyond the discipline of anthropology and offers an extremely cogent discussion of the cultural construction of the emotions, in particular of the dominant discourses of the emotions in the West.

3   The theological historian Thomas Dixon cautions that this is too sweeping a generalization, and he argues in *From Passions to Emotions: The Creation of a Psychological Category* that the emotions as a psychological category emerged in the nineteenth century, thereby encompassing what had previously been understood as the passions, the affections, and the sentiments. My interest, however, is precisely in the politics of the emotions as represented in a dominant narrative.

4   We may feel grief not just at the loss of a person we loved but also—Freud offers this as an example—for the loss of an ideal. Grief, or the inability to mourn, may be collective as well as private. See, for example, Alexander Mitscherlich and Margarete Mitscherlich's *The Inability to Mourn: Principles of*

Collective Behavior, which deals with post–World War Two Germany where the inability to mourn is at the national level. In contemporary culture, as Saidiya Hartman has written, "grief is a central term in the political vocabulary of the diaspora" (758). If grief here is interminable, it can be understood as, in the words of David Eng and Shinhee Han, "racial melancholia," another form of the inability to mourn. In such cases grief could be said to be what I would call a "diasporic emotion." Psychoanalytic theory, largely dormant for a decade if not longer in the U.S. academy, has resurfaced in large part through the interest in mourning and melancholia in postcolonial theory. In terms of the cultural politics of mourning and melancholia in the United States, see also Anne Cheng's *The Melancholy of Race: Psychoanalysis, Assimilation, and Hidden Grief*.

5   *SE* indicates *The Standard Edition of the Complete Psychological Works of Sigmund Freud*. I use this abbreviation throughout this book.

6   See my essay "Grief-Work in Contemporary American Cultural Criticism," where I call attention to cultural criticism on grief by men (Mitchell Breitwieser, Douglas Crimp, Philip Fisher, Renato Rosaldo, and Eric Santner) that appeared in the United States between 1989 and 1991.

7   See my essay "Late Theory, Late Style: Loss and Renewal in Freud and Barthes."

8   As Joseph Smith shows in "On the Structural View of Affect," Freud's understanding of affect shifted over time. See the chapter "Affect in Freud's Work" in André Green's *The Fabric of Affect in the Psychoanalytic Discourse*, which first appeared in French in 1973. See also his chapter "Conceptions of Affect" in *On Private Madness*, which is a shorter account of the previous chapter and first appeared in 1977. For Freud the sentiments of tenderness and friendship are distinct from states of pleasure and pain, which are the prototypes of affect.

9   For Freud affect is understood as associated with a bodily drive and the psychological. Affect as a theoretical category is emerging as a keyword in cultural studies. This is not the place to offer a genealogy of affect in cultural studies, but I do want to point to a few key figures and to some recent work. In *Mixed Feelings: Feminism, Mass Culture, and Victorian Sensationalism* Ann Cvetkovich pioneered the study of affect in cultural studies with a focus on literature, understanding affect through the prism of Foucauldian, Marxist, and feminist thought, as well as psychoanalysis; she argues that affect—by which she often means emotions of the psychological kind—are constructed by mass culture. The late feminist philosopher Teresa Brennan formulated a theory of affect that is psychoanalytic in nature but powerfully associated with the social. In *Shame and Its Sisters* Eve Kosofsky Sedgwick, along with her coauthor and coeditor Adam Frank, introduces the work of the psychologist Silvan Tomkins who theorizes affect in terms of an innate bodily system, drawing on multiple theories (including cybernetics, systems theory, and ethology) and understanding shame—and affects related to it—as basic (he postulates eight other affects). The thinker who has perhaps most influenced

cultural studies of affect is the philosopher Gilles Deleuze, who draws on Spinoza's categories of "affect" and "affection" (neither of which have anything to do with the "personal") and theorizes affect in terms of ontology, that is, with becoming. For recent work influenced by Deleuze and Brian Massumi, see Clare Hemmings, "Invoking Affect: Cultural Theory and the Ontological Turn," in *The Affective Turn: Theorizing the Social*, edited by Patricia Ticineto Clough; and "The Affect of Nanoterror" by Luciana Parisi and Steve Goodman. A range of approaches to "affect" from the perspective of cultural studies may be seen in the special issue of *Angelaki* titled "Subalternity and Affect," edited by Jon Beasley-Murray and Alberto Moreiras.

10   Although I privilege the work of feminist philosophers on the emotions, I do not want to be misunderstood as suggesting that other philosophers have not contributed to theorizing the relation of the emotions to cognition. Taking a different tack, Ronald de Sousa is one of them; see *The Rationality of Emotion* in which he argues that "the cognitive may turn out to be more like the emotional than we had assumed emotion could be like cognition" (69).

11   A variant of this figure—one's net worth—has been popularly referred to as "the Number." See Lee Eisenberg's *The Number: A Completely Different Way to Think About the Rest of Your Life*, a book intended for the educated general public. See also the late Myrna Lewis's *A Proactive Approach to Women's Concerns: Women's Longevity Groups and Funds*; Lewis cites the statistic that in the United States women live 5.3 years longer than do men.

12   In "Raymond Williams: Feeling for Structures, Voicing 'History,'" David Simpson masterfully lays out the development of what he calls Williams's "famously personal concept" (19) of "structures of feeling" over the course of his career, objecting in particular to the "vitalist-empathic" element in Williams's thinking, one Simpson opposes to the "more familiar theoretical-analytical paradigms of the European tradition" (24). The very structure of Simpson's essay betrays his devaluation of the emotions as a subject in their own right. Written in the aftermath of Williams's death, the first part singles out the individuality of Williams's voice and focuses on what we might call the personal, while the bulk of the essay sets to the "real" work of tracing what Simpson sees as the woefully misguided and theoretically soft notion of "structures of feeling." Tellingly, toward the end of the essay Simpson notes that in *The City and the Country* Williams offers moving invocations of personal memories as well as of unknown agricultural workers, and he concludes on this hand-slapping note: "All too often these affirmations and identifications work to head off any reflection of the sort that is now widely held to be obligatory for a fuller historical argument conducted at the level of theory" (22). See also Paul Filmer's "Structures of Feeling and Socio-Cultural Formations: The Significance of Literature and Experience to Raymond Williams's Sociology of Culture."

13   If in 1992 Simpson could make the point that the notion of structures of feeling "has not proved to be an exportable concept" (15), this is decidedly no

longer the case. Jennifer Harding and E. Deidre Pribram make the case for the cultural studies of the emotions, drawing on the work of Raymond Williams and Larry Grossberg. Glenn Hendler employs the notion of a structure of feeling to understand the connection between a genre—sentimental sympathy in narrative form—and the politics of the emotions in nineteenth-century American culture at large. "Structures of feeling name the simultaneously cultural and discursive dimension of our experience," writes Boler in *Feeling Power*, "but do not neglect that these experiences are embodied and felt" (28). See also Heather Love's *Feeling Backward: Loss and the Politics of Queer History* and José Muñoz's "Feeling Brown: Ethnicity and Affect in Ricardo Bracho's *The Sweetest Hangover (and Other STDS)*." See Tara McPherson's *Reconstructing Dixie: Race, Gender, and Nostalgia in the Imagined South*; and Jeffrey Santa Ana's essays "Affect-Identity: The Emotions of Assimilation, Multiraciality, and Asian American Subjectivity" and "Feeling Ancestral: The Emotions of Mixed Race and Memory in Asian American Cultural Production." See as well Milette Shamir and Jennifer Travis's introduction to their edited collection *Boys Don't Cry: Rethinking Narratives of Masculinity and Emotion in the U.S.* See too the essay by Fred Pfeil where, drawing on the work of Laurie Anderson and Philip Glass, he argues that the postmodern structure of feeling is characterized by "an unstable play between a primal delight and a primal fear" (386), one far more complicated—in part by the emergence of materialist feminism, which he takes up—than this excerpt suggests. See as well Marianne DeKoven's *Utopia Limited: The Sixties and the Emergence of the Postmodern* in which she argues that "the sixties encompassed the shift in structure of feeling from dominant modernity to dominant postmodernity" (8).

14 David Simpson, "Raymond Williams: Feeling for Structures, Voicing 'History,' " 23.

15 Referring to Bourdieu's 1997 short essay entitled "Le précarité est aujourd'hui partout" (translated as "Job Insecurity Is Everywhere Now"), Zygmunt Bauman in *Liquid Modernity* enlarges on Bourdieu's theme: "Precariousness, instability, vulnerability is the most widespread (as well as the most painfully felt) feature of contemporary life conditions. . . . The phenomenon . . . is the combined experience of *insecurity* (of position, entitlements and livelihood), of *uncertainty* (as to their continuation and future stability) and of *unsafety* (of one's body, one's self and their extensions: possessions, neighbourhood, community)" (161).

16 In *The Vehement Passions* Philip Fisher astutely considers what he calls "paths among the passions," arguing that some passions are regarded as opposites (love and hate is one such pair), but that others—anger, fear, and grief are his prime examples—do "not seem inherently to be half of some imagined pair" (31). While they may not be considered to have opposites, they do often appear together in what I am calling "sequences" (thus I consider the conversion of shame into anger in my chapter on shame). Drawing on Aristotle, Fisher understands instead that a passion may "block" another passion (anger block-

ing fear, for example). "Blocking," he writes, "is the single most important feature of the dynamic of the passions" (34). There is an important difference between blocking and sequencing. In the example of shame yielding to anger, it may be said that shame vanishes, yielding to anger. In the example of fear being blocked by anger, I would suggest that the fear remains. Fisher would disagree; he would define a passion as "being in one and only one state" (47). Fisher also counts pleasure and pain as a pair of passions that are opposites. Pleasure and pain are elemental Freudian categories of affect and have much in common with Jameson's notion of intensities; this provides us with a conceptual link for understanding intensities as "structures of feeling" characterized by opposites.

17 Jameson stresses the euphoric character of these "intensities," while in my chapters on statistical panic and bureaucratic rage I stress their negative valence. A dominant "intensity" today would be the addictive euphoria associated with playing video games. I am quoting from the essay as it appeared under the title "The Cultural Logic of Late Capitalism" in *Postmodernism, or, The Cultural Logic of Late Capitalism* in 1991.

18 Damasio distinguishes between the emotions and what he calls "background feelings," which he believes preceded the development of the emotions over the long course of evolution. Background feelings originate not in emotion states but in states of the body. They are inseparable from bodily states but are not moods, although they are related to moods. A background feeling is "our image of the body landscape when it is not shaken by emotion" (150–51). It is precisely an image of their lived body landscape—an image that is coeval with a background body feeling—to which a person such as Elliot does not have access. Disassociated from their body, they can have no integrated sense of self, if they can be said to have a self at all.

19 In *On Private Madness* André Green notes that "Freud's logic is a logic of hope because it counts on wish fulfillment. Borderline cases open up the horizons of the logic of despair (negative therapeutic reaction) or that of non-commitment (splitting)" (241).

20 See the National Institutes of Mental Health, *Post-Traumatic Stress Disorder: A Real Illness.*

21 Alex Gregory, *New Yorker*, 22 January 2007.

22 In an excellent essay entitled "Obsessional Modernity: The Institutionalization of Doubt," Jennifer Fleissner explores the contemporary fascination with the figure of the obsessional in the context of modernity and offers it as an alternative dialectic of the Enlightenment.

23 My reference here is to Nancy K. Miller's *But Enough About Me: Why We Read Other People's Lives*, where she observes that she has come to understand her life "as an unwitting but irresistible collaboration between other texts and other lives" (xiii).

24 Such an antidote works only at the level of the individual and doesn't address the question of structural change. Zygmunt Bauman understands the om-

nipresent telling of first-person stories on talk shows as a symptom of our contemporary moment in which individual stories serve only as examples of how an individual copes with his or her private problems; see his chapter "Individuality" in *Liquid Modernity* (53–90). I would argue that the kinds of narratives I am privileging are much more than mere symptoms of the retailing of emotion stories. Although the lines have certainly blurred dramatically, daytime TV and nighttime TV continue to be gendered, with daytime soaps still devoted to melodramatic wounds of passion and the family romance and daytime talk shows devoted in great part to pop therapy.

25 In what I hear as an echo to Raymond Williams, Michelle Rosaldo writes, "Feeling is forever given shape through thought and that thought is laden with emotional meaning" (143). See Nancy Chodorow's *The Power of Feelings: Personal Meaning in Psychoanalysis, Gender, and Culture* for an astute commentary on the work of Rosaldo and Lutz.

26 Jane Gallop, in her wonderfully titled *Anecdotal Theory*, draws on the feminist epistemological value "of revealing the concrete conditions that produce knowledge" (52), but both the methodology and effect are quite different from what I have been suggesting here. In *Anecdotal Theory*, theory is associated predominantly with a form of thought that is not literary in an expressive sense, although it is embodied. See also Meaghan Morris's *Too Soon, Too Late: History in Popular Culture*, where she theorizes the critical and creative practice of elaborating on specific cases that have the potential to become "a parable of practice," which "converts them into *models* with a past and a potential for reuse, thus aspiring to invest them with a future" (3). Virginia Woolf's *A Room of One's Own* is a perfect example of this notion. See as well Morris's *Identity Anecdotes: Translation and Media Culture*.

27 With regard to professional affect, I cannot resist referring to Carolyn Steedman's marvelous book *Dust: The Archive and Cultural History* in which she observes that in Britain in the first part of the nineteenth century the category of occupational disease appeared, which was associated from 1820 to 1850 with the work of the scholar itself. She hilariously identifies this as a form of archive fever (alluding to Jacques Derrida's *Archive Fever*), a professional anxiety linked both with the enormity of conjuring "a social system from a nutmeg grater" and the banality of the constraints of travel schedules and closing times of the archives themselves (18). See also Marjorie Garber's characteristically brilliant and witty essay "Discipline Envy" in *Academic Instincts*, 53–96. See as well Melissa Gregg's welcome *Cultural Studies' Affective Voices* in which she calls for affective writing that expresses our political investments and herself devotes attention to the "register and cadence" of five important voices in cultural studies—Richard Hoggart, Stuart Hall, Larry Grossberg, Andrew Ross, and Meaghan Morris (14).

28 What is understood as knowledge in postindustrial society may no longer be "principally narrative," as Jean-François Lyotard points out in *The Postmodern Condition*, but I privilege it here (26). The phrase "narrative emotions" is

also used by the philosopher Martha Nussbaum whose chapter "Narrative Emotions: Beckett's Genealogy of Love" in *Love's Knowledge* takes up in sophisticated and impassioned ways many of these questions, including that of the cognitive power of the emotions: "*Narratives* are essential to the process of practical reflection: not just because they happen to represent and also evoke emotional activity, but also because their very forms are themselves the sources of emotional structure, the paradigms of what, for us, emotion *is*. . . . For the whole story of an emotion, in its connections with other emotions and forms of life, requires narrative form for its full development" (296). In a related vein Margaret Urban Walker identifies the *story* as "the basic form of representation for moral problems" (67); see her essay "Picking Up the Pieces: Lives, Stories, and Integrity."

29 See, for example, Svetlana Boym's superb book *The Future of Nostalgia* in which she argues that nostalgia as a historical emotion emerged decisively in tandem with mass culture and nineteenth-century romanticism; her method —the alternation between the telling of stories and critical reflection—is particularly attractive to me. See William Ian Miller's impressive book *Humiliation: And Other Essays on Honor, Social Discomfort, and Violence* in which he traces the devolution of the grander emotion of shame that belonged to Icelandic heroic culture to the lesser fear of experiencing humiliation in contemporary culture within the context of cultural expectations and regulations of gift giving and violence. See also Joan DeJean's wonderful chapter "A Short History of the Human Heart" in *Ancients Against Moderns: Culture Wars and the Making of a Fin de Siècle* in which she traces a large historical shift in affective culture in France, showing how in the second half of the seventeenth century the emotions were reinvented, a fertile period that was famously succeeded by the Enlightenment. In the field of history, for example, see William M. Reddy's *The Navigation of Feeling: A Framework for the History of Emotions* in which his concern is to find a way to narrate changes in what he calls the navigation of the emotions, without recourse to the notion of the construction of the emotions or categories of race, class, or gender. "We need a conceptual frame that acknowledges the importance of management (as opposed to construction) of emotion," he writes, "that allows political distinctions among different management styles on the basis of a concept of emotional liberty, and that permits the narration of significant historical shifts in such management" (118); his period is France from 1700–1850.

30 I am indebted to Joel Pfister for pointing out this passage in "Structures of Feeling." See his essay "On Conceptualizing the Cultural History of Emotional and Psychological Life in America" in *Inventing the Psychological: Toward a Cultural History of Emotional Life in America*, as well as the other essays in this welcome volume.

31 In *Multitude* Michael Hardt and Antonio Negri briefly discuss what they call "affective labor" in their account of the erosion of the hegemony of industrial labor and the emergence of immaterial labor that creates immaterial products

such as knowledge. Affective labor "is labor that produces or manipulates affects such as a feeling of ease, well-being, satisfaction, excitement, or passion. One can recognize affective labor, for example, in the work of legal assistants, flight attendants, and fast food workers (service with a smile)" (108). Hardt and Negri underscore, as does Arlie Hochschild before them, the importance of class in their analysis of affective labor, stressing that "it is still most often performed by women in subordinate positions" (111). The shift in vocabulary from "emotional labor" to "affective labor" signals an increasing use of the term "affect" in cultural studies.

32 Pinch's notion of epistemology in relation to the emotions differs significantly from that of Jaggar. For Pinch, the epistemological question inheres in asking where feelings come from "in a period generally characterized as one in which feelings were coming to be considered as characteristic of the individual" (3). For Jaggar the question of epistemology has to do with the ways in which (and under what circumstances) the emotions themselves may have a cognitive dimension. See also Philip Fisher's provocative essay "Thinking about Killing: Hamlet and the Path among the Passions" in which he suggests that *Hamlet* dramatizes the historical shift from a kingly economy of the passions characterized by grand public drama to a bourgeois economy largely devoid of the passions and characterized by the sexual and commercial interests of the nuclear family; grief in the figure of Hamlet is privatized and *Hamlet* is "a mourning for the passions themselves" (77).

33 In *Inventing Human Rights: A History*, the historian Lynn Hunt echoes Armstrong's account by arguing that new feelings—understood collectively as "imagined empathy" for ordinary people—emerged in response in particular to the reading of the epistolary novel in the eighteenth century, a genre that, like autobiography itself, adopts the first person as its point of view, thus elaborating a subjectivity of interiority (32). As Hunt writes, "New kinds of reading (and viewing and listening) created individual experiences (empathy), which in turn made possible new social and political concepts (human rights)" (34).

34 See Susan Miller's brilliant chapter "Coda: Fundamentals of Authorship" in her *Assuming the Positions: Cultural Pedagogy and the Politics of Commonplace Writing*. Miller discusses three texts, one each from 1824, 1854, and 1897; the first is a legal petition for divorce written in the third person, and the third is a memoir written by a daughter about her father, where emotions are "now cast as interior realities . . . imagined to be divorced from official discursive sites, which become the 'impersonal' political exteriority of dominant public statements" (256).

35 In "Affective Economies," Ahmed refers to such feelings as "binding" emotions, using the term in precisely the opposite way that I do.

36 While Teresa Brennan provides a strong critique of the western modern notion of the self-contained individual, she does not deny that affects also come from within. In calling attention to the "physical toxicity and stress of daily life

in the West" (22), Brennan also suggests that there has been an increase in negative affects in contemporary culture, one that leads us to "calculate more and feel less" (23). This calls to mind Damasio's diagnosis of Elliot, the man without feelings.

37 Freud was of course aware of the work of Gustave Le Bon. In *Group Psychology and the Analysis of the Ego* he takes up Le Bon's work, among others. As Mikkel Borch-Jacobsen has argued, for Freud the emotional tie that binds individuals to the group is based on "love for the leader" and not on vague suggestibility or the power of words and images (72). "Far from being a mass affective contagion," Borch-Jacobsen concludes, "the social tie indirectly expresses the affects of individuals" (72). Thus ultimately in *Group Psychology* Freud is more interested in the psychology of the individual than that of the group. See Ahmed's excellent chapter "The Organization of Hate" in *The Cultural Politics of Emotion.*

38 Hjort offers an exceedingly intelligent example of the strategic use of the emotions in the setting of the academic department, where a positive emotion emerges over time as an effect of purposive behavior that is not initially in fact *felt* (168–69).

39 At the same time I understand that in focusing on what the philosopher Sue Campbell has called the classic or traditional emotions (anger, shame, grief, and compassion or sympathy)—emotions that are, she writes, "conceptually well behaved" (6)—I am also focusing on emotions in which social norms are likely to be highly implicated; the psychological and the social are closely aligned, even when what Alison Jaggar has called outlaw emotions are at stake. What Campbell calls "idiosyncratic" feelings (10), unusual feelings specific to a particular person, are for the most part not taken up in this book.

40 I am indebted to Mary Jacobus for this reference. See *The Poetics of Psychoanalysis: In the Wake of Klein,* 136.

41 Another concern of Massumi in his brilliant *Parables for the Virtual* is to imbricate thought with feeling, but the feeling at stake has more to do with sensation than emotion. Regarding the process of a form of "thinking" itself, he writes: "Imagination is felt thought, thought only-felt, felt as only thought can be: insensibly unstill. Outside any given thing, outside any given sense, outside actuality. Outside coming in. The mutual envelopment of thought and sensation, as they arrive together, pre-what they will have become, just beginning to unfold from the unfelt and unthinkable outside: of process, transformation in itself" (134).

42 Anna Gibbs, in "Contagious Feelings: Pauline Hanson and the Epidemiology of Affect," argues that "the media act as vectors in affective epidemics in which something else is smuggled along: the attitudes and even the specific ideas which tend to accompany affect in any given situation" (1).

43 See Jameson's essay "Culture and Finance Capitalism."

44 In *Parables for the Virtual* Massumi accents the process of becoming and affirmative, inventive methods of thinking—and being. But he has long been

concerned with the cultural politics of fear. See the collection he edited under the title *The Cultural Politics of Fear*. In Massumi's more recent work his emphasis has been on what Gibbs calls "the epidemiology of affect" in relation to the management in the West—in particular on the part of the George W. Bush administration—of the affect of threat. Massumi's analysis of threat in relation to terrorist attack is similar to my analysis of statistical panic. See his essays "Fear (the Spectrum Said)" and "The Future Birth of the Affective Fact."

45 I am employing mood in a psychological and psychoanalytic sense, not in the sense of the mood of a historical period, as we find in Thomas Pfau's formidable book *Romantic Moods: Paranoia, Trauma, and Melancholy, 1790–1840*. "When approached as a latent principle bestowing enigmatic coherence on all social and discursive practice at a given moment," he writes, " 'mood' opens up a new type of historical understanding: no longer referential, thematic, or accumulatively contextual. Rather, in its rhetorical and formal-aesthetic sedimentation, mood speaks—if only circumstantially—to the deep-structural situatedness of individuals within history as something never actually intelligible to them in fully coherent, timely, and definitive form" (7). Pfau's understanding of mood thus has much in common with Raymond Williams's notion of "structures of feeling," although it does not share the latter's fundamental materialist base.

46 See Gabriele Schwab's important essay "Words and Moods: The Transference of Literary Knowledge" in which, drawing upon Bollas as well as Kristeva, she insists "that the transformational processes facilitated by literature also reflect upon and critically intervene in the ways in which cultures value certain moods over others, or, more generally, pursue a certain politics of emotions" (124).

47 I am here alluding to Elizabeth Spelman's *Repair: The Impulse to Restore in a Fragile World*.

one
CONTAINING ANGER, ADVOCATING ANGER

An earlier version of this chapter appeared as "Anger . . . and Anger: From Freud to Feminism" in *Freud and the Passions*, edited by John O'Neill (University Park: Pennsylvania State University Press, 1996), 73–95.

1 I borrow the term "expansive emotions" from Edith Wharton's *The House of Mirth* (118).

2 As Freud states in "Delusions and Dreams in Jensen's *Gradiva*," "We remain on the surface so long as we are dealing only with memories and ideas. What is alone of value in mental life is rather the feelings. No mental forces are significant unless they possess the characteristic of arousing feelings" (*SE* 9: 48–49).

3 See Michael Franz Basch, "The Concept of Affect: A Reexamination."

4   Anthropologists have also taken anger as a focal point. See the work of Michelle Rosaldo who, with Renato Rosaldo, studied the Ilongots of the Philippines. The Ilongots conceptualize anger in altogether different ways from Freud. Although anger can be hidden, it is not a disturbing energy that can be repressed or buried in the unconscious. In addition the Ilongots can be "paid" for "anger" or can simply "forget" an anger (144). The work of the Rosaldos appeared in the 1980s; the anthropologist Jean Brigg's book on anger in an Eskimo family appeared in 1970.

5   The literature on anger is extensive. I have already mentioned some of the work in anthropology that appeared in the 1970s and 1980s. Important work that historicizes anger includes *Anger: The Struggle for Emotional Control in America's History* by the historians Carol Stearns and Peter Stearns. For work by literary critics, see Gwynne Kennedy's *Just Anger: Representing Women's Anger in Early Modern England* and Andrew Stauffer's *Anger, Revolution, and Romanticism*. In terms of the psychology of anger, see Silvan Tomkins, who identifies anger-rage as one of nine innate affects, or what I call affect clusters. See also the educational psychologist Sandra Thomas's edited volume *Women and Anger*, "the first large-scale descriptive study of women's anger" in everyday life (11).

6   As Elizabeth Spelman observes in the collection published in 1989, in women "anything resembling anger is likely to be redescribed as hysteria or rage instead" (264). Lest we think that the sexist trope of the irrationally angry woman has disappeared from view, the rhetorician Barbara Tomlinson has some news for us. See her essay "Tough Babies or Anger in the Superior Position," which focuses on the textual violence delivered to academic feminists by unreconstructed men. In terms of senatorial and presidential politics in the United States, this phenomenon persists, with Hillary Clinton being branded as "an angry woman" by the chairman of the New York GOP in 2000 when she was running for the U.S. Senate (Maureen Dowd, "A Man and a Woman," *New York Times*, 20 September 2000, A31). In 2006 Clinton was labeled by the chairman of the National Republican Committee as "a Democrat brimming with anger and a representative of the far left wing of her party," when talk was swirling about her possible presidential candidacy (Adam Nagourney, "Calling Clinton 'Angry,' G.O.P. Chairman Goes on the Attack," *New York Times*, 6 February 2006, A16). The strategy here is the reification of the emotion of anger; a woman is said to have an angry temperament, thus occluding the context in which her anger has arisen.

7   I take a dream that Freud reports earlier in *The Interpretation of Dreams* as an elementary version of the "Non Vixit" dream. The text of the dream runs as follows: "*His father was scolding him for coming home so late.*" What the dream conceals through the reversal of affect is that the son is angry at the father. The dynamic of the Oedipus complex is at its familiar work: "The original wording must have been that *he* was angry with his *father*, and that in his view his father always came home too *early* (i.e. too soon). He would have preferred it if

his father had not come home *at all*, and this was the same thing as a death-wish against his father" (*SE* 4: 328).

8   Here is Freud in *Totem and Taboo* on the "social emotions": "We may describe as 'social' the emotions which are determined by showing consideration for another person without taking him as a sexual object" (*SE* 13: 72). The communications scholar Suzanne Retzinger argues in *Violent Emotions: Shame and Rage in Marital Quarrels* that shame, as the primary social emotion, is concerned above all with the survival of a relationship. In her study of the quarrels of married couples, she concludes that it is *shame* that incites anger rather than anger responding *tout court* to anger.

9   Freud notes in *Civilization and Its Discontents*: "What began in relation to the father is completed in relation to the group. If civilization is a necessary course of development from the family to humanity as a whole, then—as a result of the inborn conflict arising from ambivalence, of the eternal struggle between the trends of love and death—there is inextricably bound up with it an increase in the sense of guilt, which will perhaps reach heights that the individual finds hard to tolerate" (*SE* 21: 133).

10   As Freud argues in "The 'Uncanny,' " "Every affect belonging to an emotional impulse, whatever its kind, is transformed, if it is repressed, into anxiety" (*SE* 17: 241).

11   I am thinking here of Freud's somber autobiographical essay, "A Disturbance of Memory on the Acropolis," which he published in 1936—six years after *Civilization and Its Discontents*—when he was eighty years old (*SE* 22: 238–48). In it Freud broods on guilt as a paralyzing impediment to a past pleasure. He also presents guilt as casting a long shadow into the dubious future as a fateful emotion. Thus for Freud the emotions "belong" not just to the past but also to the future. See the chapter "Reading Freud" in my *Aging and Its Discontents* for a discussion of "Acropolis," aging, and guilt (26–51).

12   During this period the politicization of anger was not confined to feminists. See Peter Lyman's excellent essay "The Politics of Anger: On Silence, Ressentiment, and Political Speech." Lyman comes to similar conclusions, identifying two practices that are entailed in what he calls "authentic political anger": "The first is self-criticism, an interrogation of one's suffering . . . in order to understand clearly one's experience and its meaning. The second is the overcoming of the isolation of anger through the formation of political collectivities that create the possibility of political action" (68). I have been emphasizing the cognitive edge of the emotions, but I am also mindful of Sandra Bartky's important point in "Sympathy and Solidarity: On a Tightrope with Scheler" that in feminist theory there has been a consensus "around the idea that the proper means to overcome bias is cognitive in nature" (177). As she writes, and I agree, what is sought "is a knowing that transforms the self who knows, a knowing that brings into being new sympathies, new affects as well as new cognitions and new forms of intersubjectivity" (179).

13 As Boler points out in *Feeling Power*, Woolf's analysis is "an exemplary example of tracing the genealogy of an emotion" (203).

14 In Ahmed's chapter "Feminist Attachments" in *The Cultural Politics of Emotion*, there is a section devoted to "Feminism and Anger" where she takes issue with Wendy Brown's influential argument in *States of Injury: Power and Freedom in Late Modernity* that a feminist politics based on pain and anger is limited because it can only be reactive. I agree with Ahmed that "a politics which acts without reaction is impossible" (174).

15 In *Killing Rage* (1995), a collection of essays by the black feminist bell hooks, the rhetoric has shifted from anger to rage, with rage retaining a cognitive edge. As hooks writes, "Confronting my rage, witnessing the way it moved me to grow and change, I understood intimately that it had the potential not only to destroy but also to construct. Then and now I understand rage to be a necessary aspect of resistance struggle. Rage can act as a catalyst inspiring courageous action" (15–16). I find it fascinating that in *Wounds of Passion: A Writing Life*, hooks, like Freud and Woolf, also recounts a fantasy of threatening to kill (she chooses a gun) one of her professors (he is white), an experience of rage that at the time threatened *her* (132–33).

16 I borrow the term "clusters" from Carol Tavris's *Anger: The Misunderstood Emotion*.

17 Raymond Williams, "Structures of Feeling" (132).

18 In this chapter I can only refer briefly to feminist pedagogy in the context of the mid-1980s. But I do want to note that there is an extensive literature theorizing pedagogy in terms of the emotions. In addition to Boler's *Feeling Power*, see Shoshana Felman and Dori Laub's *Testimony: Crises of Witnessing in Literature, Psychoanalysis, and History* and Michalinos Zembylas's "Witnessing in the Classroom: The Ethics and Politics of Affect." All of these texts stress the potential of the classroom to become a community, and all employ the tropes of trauma and witnessing as well as stress the possibility of transformation. If Felman and Laub engage trauma through Freud, Zembylas draws on the Deleuzian theory of affect. See also David Benin and Lisa Cartwright's essay "Shame, Empathy, and Looking Practices: Lessons from a Disability Studies Classroom."

19 See my essay "Tribute to the Older Woman," in which I critique the two-generational view of psychoanalysis.

20 See Lynn Worsham's essay "Pedagogic Violence."

21 See Brenda Silver's wonderful remarks in *Virginia Woolf Icon*, where she points to the conservative media uptake on angry academic women that greeted the very public and angry retirement of Carolyn Heilbrun from Columbia University's Department of English. Kathleen Helal returns to the question of Woolf and anger in an essay that begins by quoting the "angry" scene in the British Museum. She argues in "Anger, Anxiety, Abstraction: Virginia Woolf's 'Submerged Truth'" that in *A Room of One's Own* Woolf's relation to anger is

predominantly "anxious" (78) and that, more generally, "as a feminist subject, anger has become increasingly difficult and impossible in that it has continued to produce anxiety and abstraction, even among feminists" (78).

22 I should note that the overall tone and trajectory of Srivastava's essay belies her qualifying use of "some" (as in "some white feminists" and "some of the deadlocks").

23 In *Speaking from the Heart: Gender and the Social Meaning of Emotion*, the psychologist Stephanie Shields coins the term "meta-emotion" to mean "thinking about one's own and others' emotions" (9). While in *The Transmission of Affect* Teresa Brennan focuses on the negative affects, her argument about the process of understanding is relevant; she writes that "any faculty of discernment must involve a process whereby affects pass from the state of sensory registration to a state of cognitive or intelligent reflection; this does not mean that the process of reflection is without affect, just that the affect is other than the affect that is being reflected upon" (120). This is relevant to the sequencing of the emotions, as I understand it, and to understanding how an *emotion* might serve as an antidote to an explosive or nagging *intensity*.

two
AGAINST WISDOM

An earlier version of this chapter appeared as "Against Wisdom: The Social Politics of Anger and Aging" in *Cultural Critique* no. 51 (spring 2002): 186–218.

1 In *The Change* Greer theorizes two broad periods in an adult woman's life—the reproductive period and the reflective period that succeeds menopause—as well as seven stages, of which menopause is the fifth (56).

2 There is of course also a history in the West of the periodization of the life course as well as a history of the metaphors in which the life course has been cast. See Thomas Cole's *The Journey of Life*.

3 For a brief discussion of *De Senectute*, see Helen Small's *The Long Life*, 7–12.

4 With the exception of Theodore Roszak's *America the Wise: The Longevity Revolution and the True Wealth of Nations* and his *Longevity Revolution: As Boomers Become Elders* (an updated version of *America the Wise*) I know of no other similar books written in the twentieth century in the United States by people not dedicated to a career in gerontology. If old age came for Hall on the event of his retirement in his seventies, and for Friedan on the occasion of her sixtieth birthday party, what rallies Roszak to a consciousness of aging? Roszak begins *Longevity Revolution* by citing his near-mortal illness as his initiation into aging and as providing the inspiration for his vision of the potential of the elderly to transform the United States. This surgical experience assumes such importance in his life that I understand it as an illness narrative in miniature or a micromemoir of a critical turning point in his life—namely his entrance into the territory of old age (and he was only fifty-seven).

5 We see this also in Erik Erikson's book-length essay *The Life Cycle Completed: A Review.* Erikson, who has a fine sense of historicity, writes that old age—in the sense of the massification of old age (this is my term)—was only discovered in the 1960s and 1970s.

6 An index of our heightened consciousness of aging is that Social Security has come to be associated almost exclusively with transfer payments to people sixty-two and older, when it also provides a safety net for people with disabilities and to children whose parents have died.

7 As James Hillman writes in *Emotion: A Comprehensive Phenomenology of Theories and Their Meaning for Therapy*, "There are emotions appropriate to what tradition calls the stages of life in so far as there are different symbols effective at different moments of life. . . . The child knows little of pity, of mercy, or of a father's holy rage" (255).

8 For comment on this film, along with aging in general, see Anca Cristofovici's *Touching Surfaces: Speculative Photography, Temporality, and Aging.*

9 "The scalings-back" of disgust, Miller writes in *The Anatomy of Disgust*, "that attend middle and old age are more a function of a general loss of affect; they represent a giving up in the losing battle against physical deterioration, a general sense that less is at stake, that the game, even if not nearly over, has a determined outcome" (15).

10 See Munnichs's "A Short History of Psychogerontology."

11 Henry Fuller opens his review of *Senescence* this way: "In the poignantly personal Introduction to his latest work Mr. Hall wonders if he will not be found 'depressing'" (150). Although Fuller observes that Hall in fact has a "gallant spirit" that is inspiring, it is telling that he opens the review on the note of depression. It is as if depression is a subject that both cannot be avoided and is condemned.

12 This is one of the strategies of Alan Pifer in *Our Aging Society: Promise and Paradox.* He refers to what he calls the third quarter of life, which implies a life expectancy of one hundred years. A cultural consensus is emerging that one hundred years of life is our due. Among the many examples is Gloria Steinem's statement that she plans "to reach a hundred" (283).

13 It is hardly a surprise that Hall writes of old age predominantly from a male point of view. He associates women with domesticity and motherhood, and he sees women, whose function in life depends upon their sexual attractiveness, as aging earlier than men; if senescence—the second half of life—begins for men in their early forties, it commonly comes earlier for women in Hall's account.

14 Later in *Senescence* Hall writes that the old do not form a class but rather are "hyperindividualized" (172).

15 I find it fascinating that a contemporary reviewer of *Senescence* singled out for disapproval both Hall's attitude of discontent and his remedy for it. In "The Last Half of Life," a full-page review of *Senescence* that appeared on 28 May 1922 in the *New York Times Book Review and Magazine*, Maurice-François Egan describes the book as "melancholy" and concludes that Hall's problem is one

of his own making. Hall made the mistake of devoting his entire life to work, to conducting his life at an energetic rhythm that Egan finds unnatural to old age. "An old man who can be gently idle has every chance of being a happy man," Egan writes, chastising Hall; "When one is old one needs so little" (7).

16 The most influential definition of the American jeremiad is given by the literary critic Sacvan Bercovitch, who characterizes it as "a mode of public exhortation . . . designed to join social criticism to spiritual renewal, public to private identity, the shifting 'signs of the times' to certain traditional metaphors, themes, and symbols" (xi). I am referring to the historians Thomas Cole and Andrew Achenbaum, both of whom describe *Senescence* as a jeremiad and emphasize the mood of depression in the opening pages, thus leading them to devalue his anger.

17 One of the most important contributions of *The Fountain of Age* is Friedan's insistence that many older people, under the influence of the model of old age as a long and disastrous physiological decline, mistakenly regard themselves as objects of continuing or imminent care and thus in effect give up their future; she cites research showing that seriously debilitating heath problems for the most part only occur in the short period right before death.

18 The "longevity revolution" was coined by Robert Butler, to whom Friedan gives much credit for inspiring her to write *The Fountain of Age*.

19 Friedan is a feminist and so we should not be surprised that gender is the most important analytical category in *The Fountain of Age*. In terms of sociological variables, illness would be the second most important category; race, class, and ethnicity do not enter her discussion in any major way.

20 Key to *The Fountain of Age* is this passage from *The Feminine Mystique*: "A woman today who has no goal, no purpose, no ambition patterning her days into the future, making her stretch and grow beyond that small score of years in which her body can fill its biological function, is committing a kind of suicide. For that future half-century after the child-bearing years are over is a fact that an American woman cannot deny" (293).

21 In her biography of Friedan, Judith Hennessee informs us of Friedan's legendary narcissistic temper. But for Hennessee, "The fine-tuned fury that gave *The Feminine Mystique* its compelling power was gone, replaced by optimism and uplift" (273).

22 I take the term "social suffering" from the medical anthropologist Arthur Kleinman. In *The Change* Greer analyzes menopause in similar terms. "The irrational certainty that the womb was the real cause of the ageing woman's anger or melancholy," she writes in *The Change*, "effectively obscured the inconvenient possibility that she may have had genuine grounds for protest; women on the other hand obligingly internalized their own rage and produced a bewildering array of symptoms" (2). But Greer also focuses on the expression of rage. "We are only dimly coming to a recognition that the antisocial behaviour of demented old women might be an expression of justifiable rage too long stifled and unheard," she writes (137).

23 As Friedan writes in *The Fountain of Age:* "To look at people over sixty-five in terms of work, health, and productivity would be to treat them like full people again, not just objects of compassionate or contemptuous care. It was in terms of work that the issue of the personhood of women was finally and fully joined—and the women's movement was born" (199).

24 In *The Life Cycle Completed*, Erikson reconsiders his theory of human development and associates the final and eighth stage with grand generativity, drawing on the analogy with grandparenting. In *Insight and Responsibility*, Erikson defines the task of the eighth and final stage as the achievement of wisdom, which was the outcome of the successful struggle between integrity and despair: *"Wisdom, then is detached concern with life itself, in the face of death itself*. . . . If vigor of mind combines with the gift of responsible renunciation, some old people can envisage human problems in their entirety (which is what 'integrity' means) and can represent to the coming generation a living example of the 'closure' of a style of life" (133–34).

25 Reviews of Friedan's book, for example, single out her recounting of going on an Outward Bound expedition as exemplary of her idea of adventure in old age. While the reviewer Nancy Mairs finds this exhilarating (*New York Times Book Review*, 3 October 1993, 1, 28), Mary-Lou Weisman, in a caustic piece, considers Friedan's optimistic attitude ridiculous (*New Republic*, 11 October 1993, 4949–51).

26 In "The Development of Wisdom across the Life Span," V. P. Clayton and James Birren, defining wisdom as "the integration of general cognitive, affective, and reflective qualities," find that while the older people in their study did not link their older age with wisdom, younger people did associate growing older with the development of wisdom. I would argue that notwithstanding this association of wisdom with old age on the part of younger individuals, which may in fact simply be a stereotype of old people, wisdom is not translated into a meaningful value on the level of society.

27 Ernest Burgess has called attention to what he has aptly termed the "roleless role" of the elderly.

28 See Margaret Gullette, "On Dying Young."

29 In this view I counter what not a few people in critical gerontology are advocating. See Achenbaum's essay on late-life emotionality, Harry Moody's *The Five Stages of the Soul*, and Ronald Manheimer's "Wisdom and Method: Philosophical Contributions to Gerontology." See also "Aging, Morale, and Meaning," where Bertram Cohler adopts the following skeptical definition of wisdom: "The so-called wisdom achieved in later life consists of the ability to maintain a coherent narrative of the course of life in which the presently remembered past, experienced present, and anticipated future are understood as problems to be studied rather than as outcomes to be assumed" (119–20). I should acknowledge that in *At Last, the Real Distinguished Thing: The Late Poems of Eliot, Pound, Stevens, and Williams*, I consider how wisdom is represented in the form and substance of the late poems of these great American modern

poets. My point there is not so much that these men themselves were wise, or that they advocated wisdom in general as the salient criterion of a social role for older people, but that they were able to create compelling fictions of wise old men in their poetry.

30 Here is another example of the cultural reflex of invoking wisdom to justify increasing life expectancy. In a feature story by Susan Dominus entitled "Life in the Age of Old, Old Age" that appeared in the *New York Times Sunday Magazine* on 22 February 2004, a middle-aged molecular biologist responds in this surely unpersuasive way to his teenage son's caustic query, "Do we really want all these geezers fighting for resources, destroying the environment?" "I think society benefits," he says. "People who are mature are major contributors to society—they're around longer, they have cumulative wisdom and I think progress will go faster" (26).

31 As Haraway writes in *Simians, Cyborgs and Women*, "Feminist objectivity means quite simply *situated knowledges*" (188).

32 In her wonderful essay on midlife memoirs on both sides of the Atlantic, Isabelle de Courtivron contrasts the responses of Anglo-American and French authors to that great divide in terms of emotion—activist anger versus elegant resignation.

33 The term "affect script" comes from the psychologist Silvan Tomkins. See his chapter "Anger-Management and Anger-Control Scripts" in *The Negative Affects: Anger and Fear*. Tomkins understands an affect script as a succession of affects over time, a pattern that is repeated over the lifetime of an individual. I am using the term not in the sense of an individual life but in the sense of a larger cultural pattern, a cultural affect script.

34 As Silvan Tomkins provocatively puts it in *Cognition: Duplication and Transformation of Information*: "Cognitions coassembled with affect become hot and urgent." He also posits the reverse: "Affects coassembled with cognitions become better informed and smarter" (7).

35 I take the notion of an emotional response being symmetrical (or not) to its context from the critical race theorist Patricia Williams in *The Alchemy of Race and Rights*, 46.

36 See Rosemary Hennessy's description in *Profit and Pleasure: Sexual Identities in Late Capitalism* of the process of disidentification, one that draws on affect and is similar to the experience that Barbara Macdonald narrates. As Hennessy writes, "This is the 'excess' that is often 'experienced' as an inchoate affect of not belonging, of not fitting in or not feeling at home within the terms that are offered for identity. The process of disidentification can zero in on the affective component of this misrecognition and invite consideration of the ways it is named and routed into emotions (of shame, denial, resentment, etc.) that can naturalize the existing categories. Disidentification invites the renarration of this affective excess in relation to capitalism's systemic production of unmet need" (231).

37 I am suggesting a distinction between rage as a visceral response to an event,

and an intelligent rage or anger that is informed by analysis and reflection on the context and thus calls for that response, a distinction that is echoed in Margaret Gullette's *Declining to Decline: Cultural Combat and the Politics of the Midlife* where she draws a line between anger and a "higher" anger (232).

RACIAL SHAME, MASS-MEDIATED SHAME, MUTUAL SHAME

An earlier version of this chapter appeared as "Traumatic Shame: Toni Morrison, Televisual Culture, and the Cultural Politics of the Emotions" in *Cultural Critique* no. 46 (fall 2000): 210–40.

1   As the less "mature" emotion, shame has been implicitly understood to be less worthy of study. Across a wide variety of disciplines in the past fifteen years, however, there has been an explosion of interest in the emotion of shame. In the process shame has been decoupled from guilt and put to all kinds of cultural uses, some of which I will explore in this chapter. For important work on shame, see the philosopher Bernard Williams's *Shame and Necessity*, the cultural studies critic Elspeth Probyn's *Blush: Faces of Shame*, the psychologist Silvan Tomkins's work in *Shame and Its Sisters: A Silvan Tomkins Reader*, the psychoanalyst Serge Tisseron's *La Honte: Psychanalyse d'un lien social*, the literary critic Gail Kern Paster's *The Body Embarrassed: Drama and the Disciplines of Shame in Early Modern England*, and the historian Bertram Wyatt-Brown's *Southern Honor: Ethics and Behavior in the Old South*. See also *Edith Wharton's Prisoners of Shame: A New Perspective on Her Neglected Fiction* by Lev Raphael, who argues that "shame is a touchstone for understanding Wharton herself" (2), and Andrew Gordon's "Shame and Saul Bellow's 'Something to Remember Me By.'" See *Scenes of Shame: Psychoanalysis, Shame, and Writing*, edited by Joseph Adamson and Hilary Clark, which focuses on literary scenes of shame; their excellent introduction considers the work of many important theorists of shame. For a consideration of shame and class, see Rita Felski's "Nothing to Declare: Identity, Shame, and the Lower Middle Class."

2   The emotion of anger might be said to be the "counteremotion" of shame. I draw the notion of a counteremotion from Yanhua Zhang's *Transforming Emotions with Chinese Medicine* in which he shows how "treating emotions with emotions" is a time-honored Chinese practice (72), with one emotion serving to overcome another emotion. Within this cultural system, anger is a stigmatized emotion and the emotion of sadness is understood as one that overcomes anger.

3   See Elizabeth Abel's *Virginia Woolf and the Fictions of Psychoanalysis*, 86.

4   I should add that Sedgwick herself offers a commentary on the contextualizing limits of her own essay. "Queer Performativity" appeared in 1993. In her book *Touching Feeling: Affect, Pedagogy, Performativity*, which appeared ten

years later, there is another version of her essay, and in it her claims for shame have undergone a marked shift. We are no longer in the 1990s when "queer" was such a potent term. Instead Sedgwick opens her essay with an evocation of the loss of the twin towers of the World Trade Center, and although at this point in time she still sees shame for some people as a "structuring fact of identity" (64), one that can't be excised by dint of the cultural slogans offered up by identity politics, her tone is thoughtful, not high-spirited, and the power of shame as transformative is vastly circumscribed.

5 In "Shame and White Gay Masculinity," Judith Halberstam makes the bold point with great clarity of thought that gay shame—associated predominantly with white men—has been romanticized and in large measure cannot account for the experience of today's youth. She thus historicizes the meaning of shame, arguing that the constellation of shame and pride is reductive of this experience. "Shame," she argues, is "a gendered form of sexual abjection; it belongs to the feminine, and when men find themselves 'flooded' with shame, chances are they are being feminized in some way and against their will" (226). She also makes no apologies for using shaming in an academic context as a tactic "in the struggle to make privilege (whiteness, masculinity, wealth) visible" (220).

6 In *The Transmission of Affect* Teresa Brennan writes about the "dumping" of affects, of which this is an instance: Cholly projects his negative energy out and onto Darlene. As Brennan explains, "affects have an energetic dimension. This is why they can enhance or deplete. They enhance when they are projected outward, when one is relieved of them; in popular parlance, this is called 'dumping.' Frequently, affects deplete when they are introjected, when one carries the affective burden of another, either by a straightforward transfer or because the other's anger becomes your depression" (6). But what is dramatized in *The Bluest Eye* is more complex; Cholly can project his hatred onto her, but he can't rid himself of his humiliation because he himself is the recipient of the hatred of the white men.

7 Today of course many people pop pills to relieve their depression, with our consumer culture selling happiness in the form of Prozac and other antidepressants. Swallowing other people's resentments and contempt is a form of what I call emotional pollution. In Dorothy Allison's wonderful novel *Cavedweller* an instance of this is dramatized; two young girls grow up with their grandmother, "swallowing her sour resentments and seething distrust of anything she could not bleach or scrub or bury in lye" (95).

8 In *The Bluest Eye* there are exceptions to this rule, the most significant being the three women—China, Poland, and Marie—who live in the apartment right above the Breedloves. Working as prostitutes, these worldly, smart women allow no one to intimidate them. They are described with admiration by Morrison as women who "hated men, without shame, apology, or discrimination" (47). Although a novel is open to multiple interpretations, it is a contained world. Thus I do not want to be misunderstood as insisting that *The*

Bluest Eye is paradigmatic of the experience of racial shame. Of the myriad accounts that present counternarratives I will refer here only to one, which is drawn from the work of the critical race theorist Patricia Williams. In *The Alchemy of Race and Rights* she recounts an incident that enraged her (she was not buzzed into a store in New York's Soho during the Christmas shopping season by a young white male salesclerk). "I was enraged," she writes. "At that moment I literally wanted to break all the windows of the store and *take* lots of sweaters for my mother. . . . I am still struck by the structure of power that drove me into such a blizzard of rage. There was almost nothing I could do, short of physically intruding upon him, that would humiliate him the way he humiliated me" (45). Her rage, she writes, "was admittedly diffuse, even self-destructive, but it was symmetrical" (46). Thus, like Barbara Macdonald, the sequence of emotions is shame-rage (or more precisely, humiliation-rage)—a rage that becomes a wise anger.

9 In the case of Pecola and Cholly shame is gendered along predictable lines. Here the work of the psychoanalyst Michael Lewis on emotional substitution in terms of gender is helpful. He argues that shame, when it is not acknowledged, is likely in women to find expression in depression; in men, in anger and rage.

10 See Linda Dittmar on the politics of form in *The Bluest Eye*.

11 In *Quiet as It's Kept: Shame, Trauma, and Race in the Novels of Toni Morrison*, J. Brooks Bouson, drawing incisively on the opening of *The Bluest Eye* and on Morrison's own view of her novel as "the public exposure of a private confidence," argues that the reader is potentially drawn into traumatic shame (26); my emphasis is not on identification but rather on the elegiac tenor of the prose itself; both of us share an interest in the narrative structure of *The Bluest Eye*. Morrison's words can be found in an interview with her by Mel Watkins in 1977. See also Jill Matus's excellent chapter on shame and anger in *The Bluest Eye* in her book *Toni Morrison*.

12 In "Black Writing, White Reading: Race and the Politics of Feminist Interpretation," Elizabeth Abel correctly cautions white feminists to be self-conscious and self-critical in relation to reading African American texts and to African American criticism of them. What is the fantasy (if there is one) that is played out in my essay? I would say it's the fantasy of understanding, one that underwrites what is generally understood, and often vilified, as a liberal politics. Consider also Barbara Ehrenreich's thoughtful comments on shame in *Nickel and Dimed: On (Not) Getting By in America*; it is shame, not guilt, that people should feel in regard to the scandal in our country of those who are called the "working poor" not being able to make a living wage. As she writes, "The appropriate emotion is shame—shame at our *own* dependency, in this case, on the underpaid labor of others" (220–21).

13 I thus bypass what was misleadingly referred to as the Monica Lewinsky story. See Juliet Flower MacCannell, "Politics in the Age of Sex: Clinton, Leadership, Love."

14 See Jennifer Steinhauer, "Agent Sherri Spillaine: Marketing the Controversial," *International Herald Tribune*, 12 April 1995.

15 See Ron French, "*Jenny Jones* Witness Lays Out a Chilling Tale as Trial Begins," *The Detroit News*, 15 October 1996.

16 See Frazier Moore, "Television Talk Shows Face a Key Question: Have They Gone Too Far?" *Milwaukee Journal*, 12 March 1995, A1, 23.

17 See Dina Al-Kassim's essay "Resistance, Terminable and Interminable," which deals with political resistance and the humiliation of being captured by the media.

18 The ACLU praised Jewell's testimony as powerful. See "ACLU Joins with Richard Jewell in Calling for Investigation of FBI's Handling of Atlanta Olympic Park Bombing," news release dated 30 July 1997. From the Web site of the American Civil Liberties Union (visited 12 September 1997).

19 See Bailey's introduction to *The Truce*, 10, 11.

four

LIBERAL COMPASSION, COMPASSIONATE CONSERVATISM

An earlier version of this chapter appeared as "Calculating Compassion" in *Indiana Law Journal* 77.2 (spring 2002): 224–45.

1 Linda Diebel, "No Miracles for Bush in TV Debate," *Toronto Star*, 16 October 1982, A1. See also Nancy Mathis, Greg McDonald, and Tony Freemantle, "Campaign '92," *Houston Chronicle*, 16 October 1992, A16.

2 The rhetorical history of presidential pain and empathy has also repeated itself. In the 6 March 2006 edition of the *New York Times* the columnist Paul Krugman, under the heading "Feeling No Pain," had this to say about President George W. Bush: "We're living in a time when many Americans are feeling economically insecure, but a tiny elite has been growing incredibly rich. And Mr. Bush's problem is that he identifies so totally with the lucky, wealthy few that in unscripted settings he can't manage even a few sentences of empathy with ordinary Americans. He doesn't feel your pain, and it shows" (A25).

3 "On the Trail," *Atlanta Journal and Constitution*, 31 October 1992, A6. While George Bush might not have won the election on the platform of compassion, he was nonetheless known as a man who was often moved to tears. See Mary Chapman and Glenn Hendler, "Introduction," *Sentimental Men: Masculinity and the Politics of Affect in American Culture*, 1.

4 This is clearly seen in five cartoons published in the *New Yorker* between November 1995 and June 2001: Mick Stevens, "We used to feel your pain, but that's no longer our policy," *New Yorker*, 20 November 1995; David Sipress, "Well, I guess this means we'll have to start feeling our own pain again," *New Yorker*, 22 January 2001; Mick Stevens, "Let me through. I'm a compassionate conservative," *New Yorker*, 9 August 1999; J. B. Handelsman, "I like that—

'compassionate predators,'" *New Yorker*, 1 November 1999; and B. Smaller, "Maybe the compassionate part will kick in during the second half of the Administration," *New Yorker*, 4 June 2001.

5   Bumiller, Elizabeth. "The Bawler in Chief: Real Men Can Cry." *New York Times*, 30 November 2003, 4: 2.

6   The rhetoric shifted from compassion to that of hope in George W. Bush's State of the Union address in January 2006, with the phrase "a hopeful society" providing a refrain. See the transcript of the address, as recorded by the *New York Times* on 1 February 2006 under the misleading title "We Strive to Be a Compassionate, Decent, Hopeful Society" (A20–21).

7   What Lauren Berlant writes in *The Queen of America Goes to Washington City* about the right-wing Reagan revolution, continued in the George Bush years, applies here: "This brightly lit portrait of a civic arm of sanctified philanthropists was meant to replace an image of the United States as a Great Society with a state-funded social safety net" (7).

8   Since the publication of Ann Douglas's *The Feminization of American Culture* in 1977 and Jane Tompkins's *Sensational Designs* in 1985, a fierce defense of the sentimental in literary and cultural studies, including film studies, has emphasized the association of the sentimental with the feminine, notwithstanding much research that has sought to explore the intersections of the sentimental with race and ethnicity. But recent scholarship has shown that the man of feeling has in fact a long history. See Mary Chapman and Glenn Hendler's *Sentimental Men*, a collection of essays that traces the antecedents of masculine displays of affect in various domains, including presidential politics. See also Julie Ellison's *Cato's Tears and the Making of Anglo-American Emotion*, where she brilliantly argues that we can understand the political attraction of today's sensitive men in terms of eighteenth-century male icons who displayed both sensibility and emotional reserve.

9   I greatly admire *Sensational Designs*, and it seems altogether apt to me, given my interest in professional affect and sequencing of the emotions, that Tompkins's impulse to write her book, as she tells us in *A Life in School*, was her experience of being moved to tears by *Uncle Tom's Cabin* and being angry that such feeling was proscribed in literary academic circles at the time. "Then and there," she writes, "I decided to fight for that book. To fight for my tears, and for the legitimacy of my reactions to literature all across the board. . . . It was this anger, the anger of someone whose intellectual position grew out of her own life—that enabled me to write a book that called for a changed canon of American literature" (107–8).

10   See the excellent collection of essays edited by Lauren Berlant under the title *Compassion: The Culture and Politics of an Emotion*.

11   See Martha Minow and Elizabeth Spelman's "Passion for Justice." See also the collection of essays edited by Susan Brandes under the title *The Passions of Law*. If in 1987 Lynne Henderson argued for the introduction of empathetic narratives in the courtroom, more have joined her in recent years. Indeed in

the very first sentences of the first paragraph of her introduction, Brandes refers to compassion three times and to sorrow twice.

12 Toni Massaro in "Empathy, Legal Storytelling, and the Rule of Law: New Words, Old Wounds" offers a sharp rebuttal to Henderson, arguing that the focus on empathy "represents a hope that certain specific, different and previously disenfranchised voices—such as those of blacks and women and poor people and homosexuals—will be heard, *and will prevail*" (2113).

13 *Parents Involved in Community Schools v. Seattle School District No. 1.* No. 05–908. Supreme Court of the U.S. Opinion IIA. Web site of the U.S. Supreme Court (visited 28 June 2007).

14 Although my primary purpose is not to critique Nussbaum, I do want to point to Megan Boler's excellent chapter "The Risks of Empathy" in *Feeling Power* where she takes up Nussbaum's essay (in addition to Nussbaum's book *Poetic Justice*), by making the strong point that the unwelcome implication of Nussbaum's model is that "fear for oneself" is the "agent of empathy" and that the reader is problematically positioned as the judge (159). Like Henderson, Spelman, and Berlant, one of Boler's main concerns is the relation between empathy and action; she theorizes a reading practice that would not be passive but rather inspire responsible action, one that is at minimum emotionally self-reflexive. In effect she argues for the cognitive edge of self-reflexive emotions. Like the narrator in Woolf's *A Room of One's Own*, she asks us to reflect critically on our own reading emotions and to analyze our own resistances to texts. As an example she offers "irritation," about which she suggests that it might "indicate the reader's desire to avoid confronting the articulated pain" (169).

15 With regard to this scene in *Incidents in the Life of a Slave Girl*, Elizabeth Alexander in " 'Can You Be BLACK and Look at This?' Reading the Rodney King Video(s)" makes this important point; the appeal to white women readers is for them to reject the perspective of a spectator and assume the position of a witness to injustice (89).

16 The scholarship in literary and cultural studies on sentimentality in American culture is vast. I single out two books here—Elizabeth Barnes's *States of Sympathy: Seduction and Democracy in the American Novel* and Shirley Samuels's edited collection *The Culture of Sentiment: Race, Gender, and Sentimentality in Nineteenth-Century America*—as well as the essay by June Howard entitled "What Is Sentimentality?" which offers a broad view of sentimentality by reaching back to eighteenth-century Great Britain and reaching out to other disciplinary perspectives on the emotions ranging from anthropology to neurology.

17 Berlant's essay "Poor Eliza" was published in the influential special issue of *American Literature* edited by Cathy Davidson and entitled "No More Separate Spheres!" As Davidson shrewdly points out, sentimentality is often "wielded as a weapon to control the expression of emotion, sometimes in women but

far more often in men" (456). The gendered binary of separate spheres is an example of what we could call retrospective emotional standards.

18 Although I have focused on texts by four women I don't mean to imply that men haven't contributed to the exploration of the power of the narrative of social suffering in moving people to fight for social justice. Consider the exemplary essay by the late Richard Rorty, "Human Rights, Rationality, and Sentimentality." His position is unequivocal. "We are now," he writes, "in a good position to put aside the last vestiges of the idea that human beings are distinguished by the capacity to know rather than by the capacities for friendship and intermarriage, distinguished by rigorous rationality rather than by flexible sentimentality" (18). How do we convince someone to do the right thing for another person? The best way, he counsels, "is to give a sort of long, sad, sentimental story which begins 'Because this is what it is like to be in her situation—to be far from home, among strangers,' or 'Because she might become your daughter-in-law,' or 'Because her mother would grieve for her'" (19). In keeping with Rorty's pragmatism, this is surely a pragmatic view of the moral deployment of what I have been calling the literary emotions, and it is one I endorse.

19 Qtd. in Marvin Olasky, *Compassionate Conservatism: What It Is, What It Does, and How It Can Transform America*, 219.

20 "Transcript of President Bush's Message to Congress on His Budget Proposal," *New York Times*, 28 February 2001, A14.

21 See the philosopher Karen Jones's essay "Trust as an Affective Attitude." Jones argues that trust has both cognitive and affective elements and that central to trust is the spirit of optimism, one that is akin to hope; her paradigm is interpersonal relations, one in which "trust is an attitude of optimism that the goodwill and competence of another will extend to cover the domain of our interaction with her, together with the expectation that the one trusted will be directly and favorably moved by the thought that we are counting on her" (4). See also Susan Miller's *Trust in Texts: A Different History of Rhetoric* in which she understands "the essence of persuasion" as the "willingness to cooperate"; "If understanding persuasion depends on reviving pre-Cartesian acceptance of emotion as always at its center, even if for some quite regrettably," she writes, "it further requires recharacterizing trust, our emotional consent" (146).

part two

STRUCTURES OF FEELING, "NEW" FEELINGS

1 In literary criticism today it is considered virtually axiomatic that changes in social structures will generate new feelings. See, for example, Sianne Ngai's *Ugly Feelings* where, taking the twentieth century as her canvas and philosophical aesthetics as her guide, she writes that "the nature of the sociopolitical

itself has changed in a manner that both calls forth and calls upon a new set of feelings—ones less powerful than the classical political passions, though perhaps more suited, in their ambient, Bartlebyan, but still diagnostic nature, for models of subjectivity, collectivity, and agency not entirely foreseen by past theorists of the commonwealth" (5). Ngai focuses on what she calls dysphoric affects, including irritation, envy, and paranoia, and although she insists they have a diagnostic dimension, she doesn't stress the cognitive nature of these feelings which have little in common with anger, for example, often linked with politics and action. What she calls affects have more in common with what I refer to as intensities rather than to psychological emotions. "My assumption is that affects are *less* formed and structured than emotions, but not lacking form or structure," she writes, referring to them also as "ambient affects" (27).

2   Although outside the scope of this book, I would be remiss if I didn't mention the provocative genealogy of feeling Alan Liu traces in *The Laws of Cool: Knowledge Work and the Culture of Information*—the industrial feeling of the Ford era of automation, the postindustrial feeling of service-with-a-smile, and the feeling of "online cool" associated with what he calls the age of networking. "Cool on the Web," he writes, "is a heady brio, gusto, rush, thrill, *feeling* of information" (231). But paradoxically, as he observes, there seems to be so little feeling in the feeling of information. "The heart of the problem lies in determining whether the cool 'feeling of paradox' is in fact a structure of feeling at all rather than, equally intuitive, a *lack* of feeling" (231).

five

SYMPATHY FOR NONHUMAN CYBORGS

An earlier version of this chapter appeared as "A Feeling for the Cyborg" in *Data Made Flesh: Embodying Information*, edited by Robert Mitchell and Phillip Thurtle (New York: Routledge, 2004), 181–97.

1   Consider *Wetwares: Experiments in Postvital Living* by the inimitable Richard Doyle. It virtually pulses with rhetorical life. Arguing that the oppositional boundary line between organisms and machines (with alife—artificial life—being one of his prime examples) has been definitively "smudged" (121), Doyle identifies several nonsubjective affects including panic, surprise, and anticipation. But his mordant wit is leavened by a comic good nature, and in the chapter "Simflesh, Simbones: At Play in the Artificial Life Ribotype" Doyle casts himself in the role of the "attentive and caring electronic biologist" who is linked affectively to SimLife alife creatures through play characterized by "frustration, surprise, and especially laughter" (53). On anticipation, Doyle writes: "While 'anticipation' is, of course, an affect that has been available to hominids for some time, uploading seems to install discursive, material, and social mechanism [sic] for the anticipation of an *externalized* self, a technosocial mutation that is perhaps best characterized as a new capacity to be

affected by, addicted to, the future" (134). See also Brian Massumi's *Parables for the Virtual* where he singles out the boredom that may be experienced following hyperlinks on the Web, writing that it "often comes with a strange sense of foreboding: a sensing of an impending moreness, still vague" (140). He contrasts this activity with Web surfing, which "like its televisual precursor, zapping, is oddly compelling" (141).

2   In "Notes on the Technological Imagination" Michel Benamou divides what I call the first wave of technocriticism in the 1960s and 1970s into technophobes (desperate and anxious, with Jacques Ellul as an example) and technophiles (happy and hopeful, with Marshall McLuhan as an example). See also Pierre-Yves Pétillon, who writes that in "American fiction, all the way down to the rocket, one is faced with that two-fold aspect of the machine: thrill and fear—heralding what: a new dawn or the crack of doom" (45). With regard to cyberspace, Sue-Ellen Case in *Performing Lesbian at the End of Print Culture*, similarly writes, "Critics swing between articulating the wish for ecstatic transcendence and crying doom" (233).

3   Here is McClintock describing her work with chromosomes, as quoted in Evelyn Fox Keller's *A Feeling for the Organism*: "I found that the more I worked with them the bigger and bigger [they] got, and when I was really working with them I wasn't outside, I was down there. I was part of the system. I was right down there with them, and everything got big. I even was able to see the internal parts of the chromosomes—actually everything was there. It surprised me because I actually felt as if I were right down there and these were my friends" (117); her feeling for the organism she describes as "real affection" (117).

4   A wealth of prose fiction narratives and science fiction films could constitute the archive for this chapter. I have purposely chosen two texts that continue to be well-known cultural references up to the present day (*A Space Odyssey* and *Do Androids Dream of Electric Sheep?* along with *Blade Runner*) as well as two lesser-known texts, one a film (*Silent Running*) and the other a recent novella (*Like Beauty*).

5   As Hartwig Isernagen observes in "Technology and the Body: 'Postmodernism' and the Voices of John Barth," "The borderline between the animate and the inanimate has obviously fascinated the Western imagination for ages. It is particularly the borderline between the machine and the human that has during the last three centuries become permeable in both directions, as the power of machines was allegorized as (quasi-)human or even (quasi-)divine at the same time that animals and humans were treated as or even actually reduced to (quasi-)machines. The robot, which has straddled the threshold all this time, has most recently fueled this fascination in extraordinary ways, as it has metamorphosed itself into the computer" (563). I would add that the computer is metamorphosing again into the robot.

6   See John Johnson's superb essay "A Future for Autonomous Agents: Machinic *Merkwelten* and Artificial Evolution." We have reached a point, Johnson insists,

when "research in evolutionary robotics seems to be readying itself to leap over the 'complexity barrier,' as von Neumann called it. When it comes, this leap will not only initiate a new phase in the evolution of technology but will mark the advent of a new form of machinic life" (474–75). Like others, Johnson places the emphasis on cognition. Such a development, he writes, "would allow us not only to evolve robots that could walk out of the laboratory to pursue their own agendas, but also to understand how cognition itself is an evolutionary machinic process, distributed throughout multiple feedback loops with the environment" (475). In *My Mother Was a Computer* Katherine Hayles notes the developments in affective computing—what she calls "emotional computing," a term I much prefer—although she does not expand upon this theme; "with the advent of emotional computing, evolutionary algorithms, and programs capable not only of learning but of reprogramming themselves (as in programmable gate arrays), it no longer seems fantastic that artificial minds may some day achieve self-awareness and even consciousness" (191–92).

7   This is a notable instance of what J. P. Telotte in *Replications: A Robotic History of the Science Fiction Film* finds in many science fiction films. "Nearly every image of the robot, android, or cyborg as menace or monster," Telotte writes, "seems balanced by similar figures cast in harmless, helpful, and most recently, even *redemptive* roles. . . . In these films that 'primal urge to replicate' . . . ends not calamitously but with an affirmation of the human spirit and a suggestion that our technological likenesses are not so much our *replacements* as our *extensions*, not really our *mismeasure* but in some way an *expansion* of the human measure" (190). The computer HAL, of course, plays both roles over the course of *A Space Odyssey*.

8   Haraway, qtd. in Mark Dery, *Escape Velocity: Cyberculture at the End of the Century*, 252.

9   Isabelle Stengers, "Les généalogies de l'auto-organisation," 99, qtd. in Jean-Pierre Dupuy, *The Mechanism of the Mind*, 154. See Dupuy's book for an excellent account and critique of the development of cognitive science.

10 There is a vast literature dealing with Dick's classic text that takes up some of the themes I deal with here. See Alice Rayner's excellent "Cyborgs and Replicants: On the Boundaries," where she privileges the ability to develop critique, not the development of the emotions in *Blade Runner*. In *Feeling in Theory: Emotion after the "Death of the Subject*," Rei Terada, whose concern is to offer readings of poststructuralist accounts of emotions (this is simplifying her complex study), concludes her book with a short commentary on *Blade Runner*, in which she understands the role of the emotions far differently than do I here. For her, emotions in the replicants are precisely a sign of the understanding that subjectivity—that is to say, a unified subjectivity—is an illusion, but that emotions exist nonetheless. As she writes of one of the replicants, "We assume she has had feelings before, but reserving the sight of her tears for this occasion dramatizes the fact that destroying the illusion of subjectivity does not destroy emotion, that on the contrary, emotion is the sign of the

absence of that illusion" (156–57). In *Wetwares* Richard Doyle devotes a few pages to *Blade Runner*; needless to say, they are priceless (123–24).

11 The action takes place in 2021 in the novel. *Blade Runner*, the film, is set in 2019. The human capacity for empathy is one of the themes of the science fiction writer Octavia Butler's *Parable of the Sower*, where it takes the form of the syndrome she calls hyperempathy.

12 See Kenneth Ford, Clark Glymour, and Patrick J. Hayes, eds., *Android Epistemology*, xi. Herbert A. Simon in his essay "Mind as Machine" in *Android Epistemology* explicitly makes the point that affect and cognition interact. Indeed as early as the 1960s Simon had insisted that cognitive models of mind needed to include the emotions; see his "Motivational and Emotional Controls of Cognition."

13 In this the film departs sharply from the novel. I can only speculate that between 1968 when the book was published and 1982 when the film was released, a cultural shift occurred, thereby rendering more acceptable the representation of replicants as indistinguishable from humans on emotional grounds.

14 Qtd. in Fred Kaplan, "A Cult Classic Restored, Again," *New York Times*, 30 September 2007, 5: 12.

15 David Nye argues that the technological sublime is "one of America's central 'ideas about itself'—a defining ideal, helping to bind together a multicultural society" (xii-xiv).

16 *Speaker for the Dead* was originally published in 1986; Card's "Introduction" was published in the edition released in 1991.

17 See Deborah Lupton's "The Embodied Computer/User" in which she also notes that "the ascribing of emotions to PC's is a discursive move that emphasizes their humanoid nature" (105). "The overt reason for portraying computers as human," she writes, "is to reduce the anxieties of computerphobia that many people, particularly adults, experience" (107). A decade later "computerphobia" is a thing of what seems the distant past.

18 Sony's Aibo Entertainment Robot, a dog-like machine, was discontinued in January 2006. This was, Eric Taub reported in the *New York Times* on 30 January 2006, "sad news" (C4). Aibos can bark and walk; the latest version can recognize some one hundred words and has a vocabulary of one thousand words. "I love them," a person who owns forty of them is quoted as saying; "I think of them as dogs" (C4).

19 See Horst Hendriks-Jansen's "In Praise of Interactive Emergence, or Why Explanations Don't Have to Wait for Implementation" where he pointedly draws on the interaction between a mother and her baby to suggest another model—one of situatedness and interaction—of artificial life. See also Steven Johnson, *Emergence*.

20 See Norimitsu Onishi, "In a Wired South Korea, Robots Will Feel Right at Home," *New York Times*, 2 April 2006: A4.

21 See the philosopher Don Ihde's *Technology and the Lifeworld* where he elabo-

rates a theory of a phenomenological account of human-technology relations. "The relationality of human-world relationships is claimed by phenomenologists to be an ontological feature of all knowledge, all experience," he writes (24). "Whatever else may enter the analysis of human-technology relations," he insists, "I wish to retain the sense of materiality which technologies imply. This materiality correlates with our bodily materiality, the experience we have as *being* our bodies in an environment" (25).

22 Similarly, in his discussion of uploading and anticipation, Richard Doyle in *Wetwares* remarks that "this may seem to be a literary affect provoked by an overdose on science fiction"; provocatively, he concludes that "the frenzied encounter with a contingent future" is resonant with "new markets and forms of finance capital" (134). See also Robin Marantz Henig's "The Real Transformers," *New York Times Sunday Magazine*, 29 July 2007, 28ff, in which she describes her socialization to sociable robots through literature, film, and television.

23 Cynthia Breazeal, "The Art and Science of Social Robots," Simpson Center for the Humanities, University of Washington, 2 March 2007. See also her essay, coauthored with Rodney Brooks, "Robot Emotion: A Functional Perspective."

24 Breazeal, qtd. in Beryl Korot and Steve Reich's *Three Tales*, a documentary digital video opera on three twentieth-century decisive technological developments.

25 In the words of Hershman Leeson, qtd. in *The Art and Films of Lynn Hershman Leeson*, edited by Meredith Tromble, "*Agent Ruby* is a self-breeding autonomous artificial intelligence Web agent shaped by encounters with users. She is thereby part of both the real and the virtual worlds. Ruby converses with users, remembers their questions and names, and has moods corresponding to whether or not she likes them" (92). All of the films I have discussed are gendered predominantly male. Hershman Leeson's marvelous films *Conceiving Ada* and *Teknolust* are gendered female.

26 Sandra Blakeslee, "Cells That Read Minds," *New York Times*, 10 January 2006, D1, 4.

27 V. S. Ramachandran, "Mirror Neurons and the Brain in the Vat." Interestingly, Ramachandran remarks that research has shown that children with autism don't possess a mirror neuron system, which may account for some of the symptoms of autism, including a lack of empathy.

six

BUREAUCRATIC RAGE

An earlier version of this chapter appeared as "The Bureaucratic and Binding Emotions: Angry American Autobiography" in *Kenyon Review* 17.1 (winter 1995): 50–70.

1 There are of course memoirs portraying experiences of the bureaucratic emotions—specifically with regard to illness—that are written from the first-

person point of view. See, for example, Eric Michaels's *Unbecoming*, an AIDS diary edited after his death. During his illness Michaels is hospitalized in Australia, showing that the United States does not have a monopoly on such experiences.

2 As Goodnight explains in "The Personal, Technical, and Public Sphere of Argument: A Speculative Inquiry into the Art of Public Deliberation," "'Sphere' denotes branches of activity—the grounds upon which arguments are built and the authorities to which arguers appeal. Differences among the three spheres are plausibly illustrated if we consider the differences between the standards for argument among friends versus those for judgments of academic arguments versus those for judging political disputes" (216).

3 I am writing predominantly from the point of view of those "outside" a bureaucracy. But what I call bureaucratic rage has also been leveled by businesspeople at the government at tax time. As noted in "Squaring Accounts with Uncle Sam," a piece by Jill Fraser that appeared in the *New York Times* on 10 April 1994, "For successful businesspeople, tax filings generate a wealth of emotions—much more often than not the negative ones. . . . If some executives respond with rage, however, others say they are simply resigned" (3: 29).

4 Ralph Blumenthal, "Finding Meager Help in a Sex-Complaint System," *New York Times*, 27 November 1992, B7.

5 See Christopher Dandeker, *Surveillance, Power, and Modernity: Bureaucracy and Discipline from 1700 to the Present Day*, 2.

6 See Jean-François Lyotard's *The Postmodern Condition: A Report on Knowledge*, 46.

7 See the sociologist Andrew J. Weigert's book *Mixed Emotions: Certain Steps Toward Understanding Ambivalence* for a consideration of ambivalence as a structure of feeling (although he does not use Raymond Williams's term) that characterizes the institutions of modernity as well as, more generally, the condition of modernity. In his cogent reflections on bureaucracy, he writes from the point of view of someone inside, not outside, the institution. Drawing on the work of Robert Merton and E. Barber, he observes that "in large-scale organizations, the contradictory demands of regularity and creativity can result in a kind of bureaucratic pathos. The unrequitable demands for empathic personal concern versus rational universalistic detachment pose acute problems and generate deep tensions" (41). Consider this anecdotal case. In a piece in *Time* magazine titled "Officers on the Edge" that appeared on 26 September 1994, the journalist Nancy Gibbs reports on the suicide of a police officer. A twenty-year veteran of the Los Angeles Police Department is quoted as saying, "Dealing with the bad guys is why I became a cop. What gets you down is the bureaucracy." Gibbs provides this context: "In his office in the L.A.P.D.'s Northeast division, which includes the grimiest stretch of Hollywood Boulevard, the computers are antique, the shotguns routinely fail during practice and the cars in the lot are monuments to budgetary restraints: the odometers read 132,000 miles, 136,000, 148,000" (62).

8   See "Final Take," *New York Times*, 7 January 2006, B5.

9   As with my consideration of statistical panic, I am here placing the accent on negative impersonal encounters. We can all point as well to the good Samaritans that populate bureaucratic institutions.

10 N. R. Kleinfeld, "More Than Death, Fearing a Muddled Life," *New York Times*, 11 November 2002, A1, 17.

11 See Vivian Sobchak's "Beating the Meat/Surviving the Text, or How to Get Out of This Century Alive."

12 See Paul de Man's influential essay "Autobiography as De-facement" (1979). De Man's insistence that the distinction between autobiography and fiction "is not an either/or polarity but . . . undecidable" (921) was intended to produce the effect of collapsing autobiography into fiction (and decidedly not the other way around).

13 The notion of the "autobiographical pact" we owe to Philippe Lejeune, for whom it is critical that the name of the author be "linked, by a social convention, to the pledge of responsibility of a *real person*" (11). Lejeune is preeminently clear that autobiography is related both to a practice of writing as well as to a practice of reading; "It is a historically variable *contractual* effect" (30). Thus for him trust is a key effect of autobiographical reading. This may help explain the media furor that erupted in the United States in January 2005 over the revelation that James Frey, the author of *A Million Little Pieces* (a book marketed as a memoir) had fabricated many of the details of his story. In *But Enough About Me*, Nancy Miller deftly sums up the reasons for our culture's voraciousness for the memoir: "It's the well-worn culture of 'me,' given an expansive new currency by the infamous baby boomers who can think of nothing else; it's the desire for story killed by postmodern fiction; it's the only literary form that appears to give access to the truth; it's a democratic form, giving voice to minority experience in an antielite decade; it's a desire to assert agency and subjectivity after several decades of insisting loudly on the fragmentation of identity and the death of the author. It's voyeurism for a declining, imperial narcissism. It's the market" (12).

14 Thomas Couser also makes this point in *Recovering Bodies: Illness, Disability, and Life Writing*, 9.

15 Couser makes a distinction between autobiographical illness narratives, which are first-person accounts, and illness memoirs, which are second-person accounts. Writing about AIDS diaries, Chambers refers to these second-person memoirs as "dual autobiographies," for "the writer who records another's death from AIDS is himself infected and may go on to record his own living out of the same scenario" (7).

16 "Most anthropological studies of death eliminate emotions by assuming the position of the most detached observer," Renato Rosaldo notes, telling us that his own personal experience of loss was required for him to come to an understanding of the powerful rage that the Ilongots described as central to

their grief out of loss (15). In his essay "Grief and the Headhunter's Rage" Rosaldo also takes up the question of positionality by elaborating in particular on the category of age.

17 See Miller's *But Enough About Me*, 2.

18 See Joseph Cady's essay "Immersive and Counterimmersive Writing About AIDS: The Achievement of Paul Monette's *Love Alone*," which is a companion piece to *Borrowed Time*. As Cady writes, "*Love Alone* is dominated by explicit, intense, and unembarrassed statements of painful personal feeling, which, in both their frequency and intimacy, are perhaps the book's most powerful literal representations of the devastation of AIDS" (247).

19 I am deliberately emphasizing the impersonal nature of the institution of the hospital. But if Monette unleashes his contempt for interns, he is lavish with his praise for others—the technicians and the receptionists—and he astutely understands how reciprocity builds hope. "Even on bad days," he writes, "we tried to be up for them, the receptionists and technicians, for their morale was as much at stake as ours, and we had to help each other" (276).

20 In the introduction I observed that in the second half of the twentieth century in the United States we see a general redistribution of the emotions in terms of gender. In *Borrowed Time* grief, explicitly identified with women, is appropriated by Monette as his natural emotional habitat. In several telling passages he identifies with the grief of women. On a cross-country flight he looks up to see Anne Bancroft in the film *Garbo Talks* and he breaks into tears. "Supermarkets are bad for grief; any widow will tell you," he remarks elsewhere (93).

21 In "Paul Monette's Vigilant Witnessing to the AIDS Crisis," Lisa Diedrich discusses this scene and the "affective force" of the address of Roger to Paul as well as Paul "to" Roger, a scene also elaborated in *Love Alone* as well as in *Last Watch of the Night*.

22 Jane Gross, "Prevalence of Alzheimer's Rises 10% in 5 Years," *New York Times*, 21 March 2007, A14.

23 When Roach goes to the bookstore to see what she can find on Alzheimer's disease, there was nothing there. Today we can point to many doubled-over autobiographical narratives, including John Bayley's *Elegy for Iris* and Elinor Fuch's *Making an Exit* as well as Deborah Hoffman's wonderful film *Complaints of a Dutiful Daughter* (1994).

24 I refer here to Elizabeth Bruss's influential *Autobiographical Acts: The Changing Situation of a Literary Genre*.

25 See Felicia R. Lee, "Raising Reality-TV Stakes, Show Plans to Offer Medical 'Miracles,'" *New York Times*, 17 January 2006, B1, 8.

26 See Carmen DeNavas-Walt, Bernadette D. Proctor, and Cheryl Hill Lee, *Income, Poverty, and Health Insurance Coverage in the United States: 2005*.

27 See Robert Pear's "Health Care, Vexing to Clinton, Is Now at the Top of Bush's Agenda," *New York Times*, 29 January 2006, A1, 18.

seven
STATISTICAL PANIC

An earlier version of this chapter appeared as "Statistical Panic" in *differences* 11.2 (1999): 177–203.

1 See Justine Coupland's "Ageist Ideology and Discourses of Control in Skincare Product Marketing."

2 The counterpart of this would be statistical hope. A couple having difficulty conceiving a child who are "given" a 3 percent chance of succeeding may imaginatively count themselves among that lucky 3 percent. Similarly, many of us speak of winning the lottery, which is a statistical improbability of astronomical proportions (not to mention an impossibility when one doesn't actually buy into the pool).

3 See the section "Statistical Persons" in Mark Selzer's *Bodies and Machines*, where he understands the correlation between the visible and the calculable in terms of a model of realism and naturalism. Selzer's emphasis, unlike mine, is not on statistics as a science of probability.

4 See Anne Kavanagh and Dorothy Broom's excellent study "Embodied Risk: My Body, Myself?" in which they distinguish "corporeal risk"(that is, who a person *is* rather than what they *do* or what is *done* to them) from environmental risk and lifestyle risk (442). It is the notion of corporeal risk that I discuss in this chapter through the narratives of cancer and Huntington's disease. For Kavanagh and Broom corporeal risk is located in the body and presents different kinds of challenges, including "the simultaneous presence of disease now and possibly in the future; the necessity for medical surveillance; a tendency to exacerbate the Cartesian split between body and self" (443).

5 See Sandra Gifford's important essay "The Meaning of Lumps: A Case Study of the Ambiguities of Risk" in which she distinguishes "two distinct dimensions" of risk in a medical context: "a technical, objective or *scientific* dimension and a socially experienced or *lived* dimension" (215), with the clinical context bridging the two. As she explains: "To the patient, risk is rarely an objective concept. It is internalized and experienced as a state of being. These different dimensions of risk as understood and experienced by epidemiologist, clinicians and lay women—further blur the already ambiguous relationship between health and ill-health. This ambiguity results in the creation of a new state of being healthy and ill; a state that is somewhere between health and disease and that results in the medicalization of a woman's life" (215). In this episode of *Chicago Hope* the kind of ambiguity that Gifford so discerningly identifies is not represented.

6 In 1999 the Mayo Clinic released a study that reported on the results, thus far, of what is called a bilateral prophylactic mastectomy in 639 women. It was concluded that the drastic operation reduced their chances of dying from breast cancer by 90 percent. Out of that figure eighteen women's lives were saved—but that means that 619 women had the operation performed need-

lessly! See Christine Gorman, "Radical Surgery," *Time*, 25 January 1999, 83. In 2000 the *New York Times* reported the findings from a long-term study that included women with genetic defects in the genes BRCA1 and BRCA2, which constitutes the highest risk for developing breast cancer (56 to 85 percent); it was found that a bilateral prophylactic mastectomy reduced their risk by 90 percent. See Denise Grady, "Removing Healthy Breasts Found Effective in High Cancer-Risk Group," *New York Times*, 4 April 2000, D7.

7 Note that the character from *Chicago Hope* was in fact shopping for a surgeon. As Robin Bunton, Sarah Nettleton, and Roger Burrows argue in their introduction to *The Sociology of Health Promotion: Critical Analyses of Consumption, Lifestyle and Risk*, "At a cultural level 'healthism' has become a central plank of contemporary consumer culture as images of youthfulness, vitality, energy and so on have become key articulating principles of a range of contemporary popular discourses" (1). Consider this example. In 1997 it was reported that a recent study revealed "cholesterol-lowering drugs could help even healthy middle-aged people with ordinary cholesterol levels reduce their risk of heart trouble by more than one-third" ("Cholesterol Drugs Shown to Cut Healthy Group's Risk," *New York Times*, 13 November 1997, A13). The drug, named Mavacor, costs about $100 per month. Who paid for the research? Merck and Company, the maker of the drug. See also Jackie Orr's powerful analysis in her chapter "Panic Xanax" in *Panic Diaries* (213–74) of the collapsed relation between research regarding the presumed medical condition of panic disorder and the global marketing of a drug in the 1980s and early 1990s by the company Upjohn. The medical model of psychiatry, one driven by statistical predictability based on huge data sets—and thus on huge markets that are created in the process—underlies the emergence of the category of panic disorder.

8 Melodrama is, as Lynne Joyrich shows in *Re-Viewing Reception: Television, Gender, and Postmodern Culture*, "a privileged forum for U.S. television, promising the certainty of clearly marked conflict and legible meaning even as it plays on the closeness associated with a feminine spectator-consumer" (64).

9 Most women will never get breast cancer. As Jane Brody summarizes in "Coping with Fear: Keeping Breast Cancer in Perspective," *New York Times*, 12 October 1999: "The '1-in-8 women' statistic is accurate, but only if you live to 85. And as you get older and remain free of cancer, the 1-in-8 figure starts dropping because you have already lived out many of the at-risk years. If, for example, you are now 70 and still cancer-free, your chances have dropped to 1 in 20" (D6).

10 See Mary Russo's powerful essay "Aging and the Risk of Anachronism" in which she discusses Gillian Rose's work, in particular *Love's Work: A Reckoning with Life*, in the context of aging.

11 I am alluding to a silly short piece that appeared in the *New York Times Sunday Magazine* on 8 August 1999. Under the title "Living Dangerously: The Odds," a list of nine different risks are taken from Larry Laudan's book *Danger Ahead:*

The Risks You Really Face on Life's Highway. We learn that the odds that we will crush our finger with a hammer are one in 3,000, that our doctor is really not a doctor are one in fifty, that our next meal will come from McDonald's is one in eight, and so on.

12 See Matthew Wald, "F.A.A. Seeks to Reduce Air-Turbulence Injuries," *New York Times*, 30 December 1997, A12. See also David Patch's ominously titled story "Invisible Streams of Danger Can Lurk above the Clouds," *Pittsburgh Post-Gazette*, 30 December 1997, A7.

13 Within the domain of the market, predictability is itself a commodity. Uncertainty itself has a price, one that is attached to what are called securities; more predictability means less risk. But within the domain of our own lives the calculus of risk can produce not security but panic. There is also an erotics of risk—namely the desire to test oneself and to succeed against the odds, to beat the statistics, as in sports, for example, or in gambling. On the banal level of everyday life, there is the hope that we (meaning "I") will win the lottery. There is a romance with risk. See also Adriano Sofri's essay "On Optimism." As he writes, "If Pangloss were living today, he would be a professor of statistics. This confirms the irresistible tendency of statistics to optimism. Because figures, even sad ones, are consoling. If they promise happiness and progress, they regard me. If they point to misfortune, pain, and death, they do not regard me. They are averages, precisely, hence abstractions, hence they always leave room for an exception for someone—that is, for me" (767).

14 See Diane M. Stuart's statement before the U.S. Senate on 19 July 2005.

15 Michael Power discusses what he has termed the "audit society" in terms of affect. "The audit society," he writes "is the *anxious* society in which perceived regulatory failure must be continually overcome and the mission of regulation re-affirmed. In the context of this permanent dialectic, audit is a crucial political technology. The 'fact of audit' reduces anxiety or, more positively, produces comfort. . . . And yet, paradoxically, the audit society is also one in which visible failure of audit is the norm and in which there are extensive investments in audit activity irrespective of their demonstrated substantive effectiveness" (307). Power submits that "the 'audit explosion' has occurred at the threshold between the traditional structures of industrial society and an emerging 'risk society' " (307) and that the audit "is part of the new 'cosmetics of risks' " (313). I would suggest that while the audit is a social practice performed by various regulatory agencies, individuals have learned to audit themselves in terms of what I have been calling their financial and epidemiological futures; the auditing of our individual statistical futures has been internalized. See also the work by Ulrich Beck as well as Mary Douglas and Aaron Wildavsky's *Risk and Culture: An Essay on the Selection of Technical and Environmental Dangers.*

16 The train has often been taken as the exemplar and embodiment of the emerging culture of urban modernity. See Leo Marx's *The Machine in the Garden: Technology and the Pastoral Ideal in America* and Wolfgang Schivel-

bush's *The Railway Journey: The Industrialization of Time and Space in the Nineteenth Century.*

17 Elizabeth Goodstein offers a genealogy of boredom in her brilliant study *Experience Without Qualities: Boredom and Modernity.* She argues that the boredom that emerged in the nineteenth century was associated with a malaise in the wake of the loss of foundational meaning, one that registered "the *democratization of skepticism in modernity*" (10), while today boredom is associated with the body, as I myself suggest in this chapter on the statistical body. If as Goodstein shows, the boredom of modernity is "a form of reflective distance that becomes a new attitude toward experience altogether" (3), that reflective distance is collapsed, I would suggest, in postmodern media culture. Goodstein remarks that the feeling of boredom that circulated in nineteenth-century Europe is "less a new feeling than a new way of feeling" (3). This is how I understand sympathy for nonhuman cyborgs, bureaucratic rage, and statistical panic—less as new feelings than as new ways of feeling those feelings or as new sites for those feelings.

18 I am indebted to Patricia Mellencamp's *High Anxiety: Catastrophe, Scandal, Age, and Comedy* for calling attention to this passage in Simmel's essay "The Metropolis and Mental Life." See *High Anxiety* for a brilliant and often hilarious discussion of the ways in which television is a machine for producing anxiety. If the processes of calculating and quantifying are critical to the modern mind, as Simmel insists, we should not be surprised that a learning disorder, named decalculea, has been identified for those who have difficulty learning how to deal with numbers.

19 Similarly, in *Accounting as Social and Institutional Practice* Peter Miller makes the point that accounting, a predominant means of quantification, is itself a technology.

20 In "Accommodating Merchants: Accounting, Civility, and the Natural Laws of Gender" Mary Poovey argues that women, whose writing was deemed unruly and excessive to the order required by a smoothly operating commercial system, were systematically excluded from participating in the work of double-entry bookkeeping. See also her *History of the Modern Fact: Problems of Knowledge in the Sciences of Wealth and Society.*

21 Importantly, in *The Taming of Chance* Hacking distinguishes between the ways in which the attitudes toward and uses of numerical data differed in eastern Europe (citing Prussia) and western Europe (citing France and Britain). Hacking traces the sea change between the statistical fatalism of the 1830s to statistical indetermination in the 1930s, a shift due in great part to developments in quantum mechanics.

22 Mary Ann Doane has argued that statistics and early cinema were responses to the contradictions of modernity at the end of the nineteenth century and the turn of the twentieth century; as she writes, "Statistics . . . constitutes a form of reconciliation of law and contingency, as well as of the individual with the increasing centrality of a concept of the masses" (129).

23 As Ann Kaplan and Susan Squier point out in *Playing Dolly: Formations, Fantasies, and Fictions of Assisted Reproduction*, risk-management discourse "is a new expert discipline that cordons off any real response to risk by authorizing as acceptable only those risks that lie within the parameters of scientific rationality. Disciplinary limits and expert systems with clear borders thus actually function to keep things running as they were before: the processes of modernization that gave us risk can continue unshaken" (5).

24 See David Zimmerman's *Panic! Markets, Crises, and Crowds in American Fiction*, a study of financial panic as a contagious mass feeling from 1898 to 1913, one that was both analyzed by writers and incited by mass reading. As he writes, panic novels "encouraged readers to see the market as a sentimental community comprised of individuals linked by grief or guilt" (8).

25 Theodore Porter refers to the probabilistic revolution in his conclusion to *Statistical Thinking: 1820–1900* (318).

coda
INEXHAUSTIBLE GRIEF

1 The scholarship on the *fort-da* is immense, and I have found the philosopher and psychoanalyst Jonathan Lear's thoughts on it in *Happiness, Death, and the Remainder of Life* to be especially provocative (90–98). He reads the narrative that is the *fort-da* through Aristotle as a prototype for the development of the ethical virtue of courage, one that requires both repetition and creativity.

2 On D. W. Winnicott's concept of holding, an experience that begins with the mother holding the infant, see Thomas H. Ogden's "On Holding and Containing, Being and Dreaming." Ogden argues that holding is for Winnicott primarily an ontological concept, one that has to do with the experience of being and the experience of time. With maturation we internalize the experience of being held by the mother. In "At the End of the Line" holding is externalized, with the son caring for the mother.

3 See Pontalis's "The (Generalized) Game of the Bobbin" in *Windows* (58–61).

4 On the string game, see D. W. Winnicott, "Playing: A Theoretical Statement," in *Playing and Reality* (38–52). "To control what is outside one has to *do* things, not simply to think or to wish, and *doing things takes time*. Playing is doing," he writes; play is universal and "belongs to health" (41).

5 Here are two more examples from narratives about older children whose mothers are afflicted with Alzheimer's disease and are now living in assisted-care facilities. In Michael Ignatieff's novel *Scar Tissue*, this is the very first detail he offers when the son takes his mother to "the institution": "In the lobby, there were some old people in wheelchairs with bibs round their chins watching television" (98). In Elinor Fuchs's memoir *Making an Exit*, her wry tone of dark high spirits, one inspired by her mother Lil's very theatricality, offers us this scene: "We return to find that the behemoth of a TV console has been rolled to the center of the common room. A ragged circle of the de-

mented has assembled around it in chairs and wheelchairs. The room has been darkened for this special event. I find an additional chair and make room for Lil amid the group, which in soft chorus is variously moaning, babbling, and crying out. . . . I pull up a chair for myself. I seem to be the only one aware that there's a movie on" (177).

6   See my essay "Telling Stories: Aging, Reminiscence, and the Life Review" in which I write about the positive valence of the feeling of reminiscence and what I call "prospective reminiscence."

7   Consider the difference between the feeling-tone of "At the End of the Line" and Freud's "A Disturbance of Memory on the Acropolis." Freud's mood of unease reflects the breakdown of connection between a son and his father (although, of course, the emotion of guilt testifies to Freud's attachment to his father as well). Freud's mode is ruminative but ultimately analytical as he searches for the key to this emotional puzzle.

8   As Bollas writes in "Moods and the Conservative Process," "When a mood serves to release a conservative object for experiencing, it differs from ordinary affect experience in that the true self is allowed an unusual freedom of expression precisely because of the dissociative feature of a mood as an allowed for, and therefore unintruded upon, right" (112). In "At the End of the Line" the conservative object here would be the memory of their intimate dinner together.

9   As Winnicott explains in his important essay "The Capacity to Be Alone," "Although many types of experience go to the establishment of the capacity to be alone, there is one that is basic, and without a sufficiency of it the capacity to be alone does not come about; *this experience is that of being alone, as an infant and small child, in the presence of mother.* Thus the basis of the capacity to be alone is a paradox; it is the experience of being alone while someone else is present" (30). In "At the End of the Line" we could say that the mother retains the capacity to be alone because her son is present to her.

10 Similarly, in writing about the *fort-da* in *Windows* Pontalis confesses that he wanted to describe it, not comment on it; he also is uncertain as to his point of view, not sure whether he was inhabiting the *fort-da* from Freud's perspective or from his grandson's perspective (59). In "Dream as an Object," which was written over thirty years ago, Pontalis argues that if we attach ourselves to our dreams as objects, ultimately we must give them up, detach ourselves from them, and regard them analytically. There he was writing as an analyst. But in "At the End of the Line" he writes as a son, creating a dream that is an object in more ways than one.

BIBLIOGRAPHY

Abel, Elizabeth. "Black Writing, White Reading: Race and the Politics of Feminist Interpretation." *Critical Inquiry* 19.3 (1993): 470–98.

——. *Virginia Woolf and the Fictions of Psychoanalysis*. Chicago: University of Chicago Press, 1989.

Achenbaum, W. Andrew. "Toward a Psycho-History of Late-Life Emotionality." In *An Emotional History of the United States*, edited by Peter N. Stearns and Jan Lewis. New York: New York University Press, 1998. 417–30.

Adamson, Joseph, and Hilary Clark, eds. *Scenes of Shame: Psychoanalysis, Shame, and Writing*. Albany: State University of New York Press, 1999.

Al-Kassim, Dina. "Resistance, Terminable and Interminable." In *Derrida, Deleuze, Psychoanalysis*, edited by Gabriele Schwab. New York: Columbia University Press, 2007. 105–41.

Alexander, Elizabeth. " 'Can You Be BLACK and Look at This?' Reading the Rodney King Video(s)." In *The Black Public Sphere*, edited by Black Public Sphere Collective. Chicago: University of Chicago Press, 1995. 81–98.

Administration on Aging. U.S. Department of Health and Human Services. *A Profile of Older Americans: 2006*. Washington: GPO, 2006.

Ahmed, Sara. "Affective Economies." *Social Text* 22.2 (2005): 117–39.

——. *The Cultural Politics of Emotion*. New York: Routledge, 2002.

Allison, Dorothy. *Cavedweller*. New York: Penguin Putnam, 1999.

Anderson, Perry. *The Origins of Postmodernity*. London: Verso, 1998.

Appadurai, Arjun. *Fear of Small Numbers: An Essay on the Geography of Anger*. Durham, N.C.: Duke University Press, 2006.

Armstrong, Nancy. *How Novels Think: The Limits of Individualism from 1719–1900*. New York: Columbia University Press, 2005.

Arrival of a Train at the Station. Dir. Auguste Lumière and Louis Lumière. 1895. DVD. Kino Video.

Asimov, Issac. *I, Robot*. 1950. New York: Bantam Books, 2004.

Baier, Annette. *Moral Prejudices: Essays on Ethics.* Cambridge, Mass.: Harvard University Press, 1994.

Bailey, Paul. "Saving the Scaffolding." Introduction to *If This Is a Man/The Truce,* by Primo Levi. London: Abacus, 1987.

Barnes, Elizabeth. *States of Sympathy: Seduction and Democracy in the American Novel.* New York: Cambridge University Press, 1997.

Barthes, Roland. *A Lover's Discourse: Fragments.* 1977. Translated by Richard Howard. New York: Hill and Wang, 1978.

Bartky, Sandra Lee. "In Defense of Guilt." In *"Sympathy and Solidarity" and Other Essays.* Lanham, Md.: Rowman and Littlefield, 2002.

——. "Shame and Gender." In *Femininity and Domination: Studies in the Phenomenology of Oppression.* New York: Routledge, Chapman, and Hall, 1990. 83–98.

——. "Sympathy and Solidarity: On a Tightrope with Scheler." In *Feminists Rethink the Self,* edited by Diana Tietjens Meyers. Boulder, Colo.: Westview Press, 1997. 177–96.

Basch, Michael Franz. "The Concept of Affect: A Re-examination." *Journal of the American Psychoanalytic Association* 2 (1976): 759–77.

Bates, Joseph. "The Role of Emotion in Believable Agents." *Communications of the ACM* 7 (July 1994): 122–25.

Bateson, Gregory. *Steps to an Ecology of Mind: Collected Essays in Anthropology, Psychiatry, Evolution, and Epistemology.* New York: Ballantine Books, 1972.

Baudrillard, Jean. "What Do We Do After the Orgy?" *Artforum* 22.2 (1983): 42–46.

Bauman, Zygmunt. *Liquid Modernity.* Cambridge: Polity Press, 2000.

——. "Survival as a Social Construct." *Theory, Culture and Society* 9 (1992): 1–36.

Bayley, John. *Elegy for Iris.* New York: St. Martin's Press, 1999.

Beasley-Murray, Jon, and Alberto Moreiras, eds. "Subalternity and Affect." Special issue of *Angelaki* 6.1 (2001).

Beck, Ulrich. "From Industrial Society to the Risk Society: Questions of Survival, Social Structure, and Ecological Enlightenment." *Theory, Culture and Society* 9 (1992): 97–123.

——. *Risk Society: Toward a New Modernity.* Translated by Mark Ritter. London: Sage, 1992.

Benamou, Michel. "Notes on the Technological Imagination." In *The Technological Imagination: Theories and Fictions,* edited by Teresa de Lauretis, Andreas Huyssen, and Kathleen Woodward. Madison, Wisc.: Coda Press, 1981. 65–75.

Benin, David, and Lisa Cartwright. "Shame, Empathy, and Looking Practices: Lessons from a Disability Studies Classroom." *Journal of Visual Culture* 5.2 (2005): 155–71.

Benjamin, Walter. "The Storyteller" (1936); "Theses on the Philosophy of History" (1939). In *Illuminations.* Edited by Hannah Arendt. Translated by Harry Zohn. New York: Harcourt, Brace and World, 1968. 83–109; 255–66.

Bercovitch, Sacvan. *The American Jeremiad.* Madison: University of Wisconsin Press, 1978.

Berlant, Lauren, ed. *Compassion: The Culture and Politics of an Emotion.* New York: Routledge, 2004.

———. "Poor Eliza." *American Literature* 70.3 (1998): 635–68.

———. *The Queen of America Goes to Washington City.* Durham, N.C.: Duke University Press, 1997.

Blade Runner. Dir. Ridley Scott. Warner Bros., 1982.

Blade Runner: The Final Cut. Dir. Ridley Scott. Warner Bros., 2007.

Blau, Herbert. "The Makeup of Memory in the Winter of Our Discontent." In *Memory and Desire: Aging—Literature—Psychoanalysis,* edited by Kathleen Woodward and Murray Schwartz. Bloomington: Indiana University Press, 1986. 13–36.

Boler, Megan. *Feeling Power: Emotions and Education.* New York: Routledge, 1999.

Bollas, Christopher. "The Evocative Object"; "Psychic Genera." In *Being a Character: Psychoanalysis and Self Experience.* New York: Hill and Wang, 1992. 33–46; 66–100.

———. "Moods and the Conservative Process"; "Normotic Illness"; "The Spirit of the Object at the Hand of Fate." In *The Shadow of the Object: Psychoanalysis of the Unthought Known.* New York: Columbia University Press, 1987. 99–116; 135–36; 30–40.

Borch-Jacobsen, Mikkel. *The Emotional Tie: Psychoanalysis, Mimesis, and Affect.* 1991. Translated by Douglas Brick and others. Stanford, Calif.: Stanford University Press, 1993.

Bouson, J. Brooks. *Quiet as It's Kept: Shame, Trauma, and Race in the Novels of Toni Morrison.* Albany: State University of New York Press, 2000.

Boym, Svetlana. *The Future of Nostalgia.* New York: Basic Books, 2001.

Brandes, Susan, ed. *The Passions of Law.* New York: New York University Press, 1999.

Breazeal, Cynthia. "The Art and Science of Social Robots." Simpson Center for the Humanities, University of Washington, Seattle, 2 March 2007.

Breazeal, Cynthia, and Rodney Brooks. "Robot Emotion: A Functional Perspective." In *Who Needs Emotions? The Brain Meets the Robot,* edited by Jean-Marc Fellous and Michael A. Arbib. New York: Oxford University Press, 2005. 271–310.

Breitwieser, Mitchell. *American Puritanism and the Defense of Mourning: Religion, Grief, and Ethnology in Mary Rowlandson's Captivity Narrative.* Madison: University of Wisconsin Press, 1990.

Brennan, Teresa. *The Transmission of Affect.* Ithaca, N.Y.: Cornell University Press, 2004.

Briggs, Jean L. *Never in Anger: Portrait of an Eskimo Family.* Cambridge, Mass.: Harvard University Press, 1970.

Bruss, Elizabeth. *Autobiographical Acts: The Changing Situation of a Literary Genre.* Baltimore: Johns Hopkins University Press, 1976.

Bukatman, Scott. "The Artificial Infinite: On Special Effects and the Sublime." In *Visual Display: Culture Beyond Appearances,* edited by Lynne Cooke and Peter Wollen. Seattle: Bay Press, 1995. 255–89.

Bunton, Robin, Sarah Nettleton, and Roger Burrows. "Sociology and Health Promotion: Health, Risk and Consumption under Late Modernism." In *The Sociology of Health Promotion: Critical Analyses of Consumption, Lifestyle and Risk*, edited
by Robin Bunton, Sarah Nettleton, and Roger Burrows. London: Routledge,
1995. 1–12.

Burgess, Ernest. "Aging in Western Culture." In *Aging in Western Societies*, edited
by Ernest Burgess. Chicago: University of Chicago Press, 1960. 3–28.

Butler, Octavia. *Parable of the Sower*. New York: Four Walls Eight Windows, 1993.

Butler, Robert N. *The Longevity Revolution*. New York: Public Affairs Press, 2008.

Cady, Joseph. "Immersive and Counterimmersive Writing about AIDS: The Achievement of Paul Monette's *Love Alone*." In *Writing AIDS: Gay Literature, Language,
and Analysis*, edited by Timothy F. Murphy and Suzanne Poirier. New York:
Columbia University Press, 1993. 244–64.

Campbell, Sue. *Interpreting the Personal: Expression and the Formation of Feelings*.
Ithaca, N.Y.: Cornell University Press, 1997.

Card, Orson Scott. *Ender's Game*. New York: Tom Doherty Associates, 1991.

——. *Speaker for the Dead*. New York: Tom Doherty Associates, 1991.

——. *Xenocide*. New York: Tom Doherty Associates, 1991.

Carroll, Noel. "Moral Realism in the Age of Postmodernism." In *Ethics and Aesthetics: The Moral Turn of Postmodernism*, edited by Gerhard Hoffmann and Alfred Hornung. Heidelberg: Universitätsverlag Carl Winter, 1996. 87–95.

Caruth, Cathy, ed. *Trauma: Explorations in Memory*. Baltimore: Johns Hopkins
University Press, 1995.

Case, Sue-Ellen. *Performing Lesbian at the End of Print Culture*. Bloomington: Indiana University Press, 1996.

Chambers, Ross. *Facing It: AIDS Diaries and the Death of the Author*. Ann Arbor:
University of Michigan Press, 1998.

Chapman, Mary, and Glenn Hendler, eds. *Sentimental Men: Masculinity and the
Politics of Affect in American Culture*. Berkeley: University of California Press,
1999.

Cheng, Anne Anlin. *The Melancholy of Race: Psychoanalysis, Assimilation, and Hidden Grief*. New York: Oxford University Press, 2000.

Chodorow, Nancy J. *The Power of Feelings: Personal Meaning in Psychoanalysis, Gender, and Culture*. New Haven, Conn.: Yale University Press, 1999.

Christian, Barbara. "The Race for Theory." In *The Post-Colonial Reader*, edited by
Bill Ashcroft, Gareth Griffiths, and Helen Tiffin. New York: Routledge, 1995.
457–60.

Clarke, Arthur C. *2001: A Space Odyssey*. New York: New American Library, 1968.

——. *2010: Odyssey Two*. New York: Ballantine, 1982.

——. *2061: Odyssey Three*. New York: Ballantine, 1987.

Clayton, V. P., and James E. Birren. "The Development of Wisdom across the Life
Span: A Reexamination of an Ancient Topic." In *Life-span Development and
Behavior*, Vol. 3., edited by P. B. Baltes and O. G. Brim Jr. New York: Academic
Press, 1980. 103–35.

Clough, Patricia Ticineto, with Jean Halley, eds. *The Affective Turn: Theorizing the Social*. Durham, N.C.: Duke University Press, 2007.

Code, Lorraine. *Ecological Thinking: The Politics of Epistemic Location*. New York: Oxford University Press, 2006.

Cohler, Bertram J. "Aging, Morale, and Meaning: The Nexus of Narrative." In *Voices and Visions of Aging: Toward a Critical Gerontology*, edited by Thomas R. Cole, W. Andrew Achenbaum, Patricia L. Jakobi, and Robert Kastenbaum. New York: Springer, 1993. 107–33.

Cohn, Jonathan. *Sick: The Untold Story of America's Health Care Crisis—and the People Who Pay the Price*. New York: HarperCollins, 2007.

Cole, Thomas R. *The Journey of Life: A Cultural History of Aging in America*. Cambridge: Cambridge University Press, 1992.

Complaints of a Dutiful Daughter. Dir. Deborah Hoffman. Women Make Movies, 1994.

Coupland, Douglas. *Microserfs*. New York: HarperCollins, 1995.

Coupland, Justine. "Ageist Ideology and Discourses of Control in Skincare Product Marketing." In *Discourse, the Body, and Identity*, edited by Justine Coupland and Richard Gwyn. New York: Palgrave Macmillan, 2003. 127–50.

Courtivron, Isabelle de. "Mid-Life Memoirs and the Bicultural Dilemma." *Sites: The Journal of Contemporary Twentieth Century French Studies* 4.1 (2000): 159–70.

Couser, Thomas. *Recovering Bodies: Illness, Disability, and Life Writing*. Madison: University of Wisconsin Press, 2007.

Crimp, Douglas. "Mourning and Militancy." *October* 51 (1989): 3–18.

Cristofovici, Anca. *Touching Surfaces: Speculative Photography, Temporality, Aging*. Amsterdam: Rodopi, forthcoming.

Culley, Margo, and Catherine Portuges, eds. *Gendered Subjects: The Dynamics of Feminist Teaching*. Boston: Routledge and Kegan Paul, 1985.

Cunningham, Michael. *Specimen Days*. New York: Farrar, Straus and Giroux, 2005.

Cvetkovich, Ann. *An Archive of Feelings: Trauma, Sexuality, and Lesbian Public Cultures*. Durham, N.C.: Duke University Press, 2002.

——. *Mixed Feelings: Feminism, Mass Culture, and Victorian Sensationalism*. New Brunswick, N.J.: Rutgers University Press, 1992.

Damasio, Antonio R. *Descartes' Error: Emotion, Reason, and the Human Brain*. New York: Putnam, 1994.

Dandeker, Christopher. *Surveillance, Power, and Modernity: Bureaucracy and Discipline from 1700 to the Present Day*. Cambridge: Polity Press, 1990.

Davidson, Cathy N., ed. "No More Separate Spheres!" *American Literature* 70.3 (1998): 443–63.

DeJean, Joan. *Ancients Against Moderns: Culture Wars and the Making of a Fin de Siècle*. Chicago: University of Chicago Press, 1997.

DeKoven, Marianne. *Utopia Limited: The Sixties and the Emergence of the Postmodern*. Durham, N.C.: Duke University Press, 2004.

De Man, Paul. "Autobiography as De-Facement." *Modern Language Notes* 94 (1979): 919–30.

DeNavas-Walt, Carmen, Bernadette D. Proctor, and Cheryl Hill Lee. *Income, Poverty, and Health Insurance Coverage in the United States: 2005*. U.S. Census Bureau. Washington: GPO, 2006.

De Sousa, Ronald. *The Rationality of Emotion*. Cambridge, Mass.: MIT Press, 1987.

Derrida, Jacques. "Of an Apocalyptic Tone Recently Adopted in Philosophy" (1983). Translated by John P. Leavey. *Oxford Literary Review* 6.2 (1984): 3–37.

Dery, Mark. *Escape Velocity: Cyberculture at the End of the Century*. New York: Grove Press, 1996.

Dick, Philip K. *Do Androids Dream of Electric Sheep?* 1968. New York: Ballantine Books, 1996.

Didion, Joan. *The Last Thing He Wanted*. New York: Knopf, 1996.

———. *The Year of Magical Thinking*. New York: Knopf, 2005.

Diedrich, Lisa. "Paul Monette's Vigilant Witnessing to the AIDS Crisis." *Literature and Medicine* 23.1 (2004): 112–27.

Dillard, Annie. *The Maytrees*. New York: HarperCollins, 2007.

Dittmar, Linda. " 'Will the Circle Be Unbroken?' The Politics of Form in *The Bluest Eye*." *Novel: A Forum on Fiction* 23.2 (1990): 137–56.

Dixon, Thomas. *From Passions to Emotions: The Creation of a Secular Psychological Category*. Cambridge: Cambridge University Press, 2003.

Doane, Mary Ann. *The Emergence of Cinematic Time: Modernity, Contingency, the Archive*. Cambridge, Mass.: Harvard University Press, 2002.

Douglas, Ann. *The Feminization of American Culture*. New York: Knopf, 1977.

Douglas, Mary, and Aaron Wildavsky. *Risk and Culture: An Essay on the Selection of Technical and Environmental Dangers*. Berkeley: University of California Press, 1982.

Downey, Gary Lee, Joseph Dumit, and Sarah Williams. "Cyborg Anthropology." In *The Cyborg Handbook*, edited by Chris Hables Gray. New York: Routledge, 1995. 341–46.

Doyle, Richard. *Wetwares: Experiments in Postvital Living*. Minneapolis: University of Minnesota Press, 2003.

Dreyfus, Hubert. *What Computers Can't Do: A Critique of Artificial Reason*. New York: Harper and Row, 1972.

Dupuy, Jean-Pierre. *The Mechanization of the Mind: On the Origins of Cognitive Science*. 1994. Translated by M. B. DeBevoise. Princeton, N.J.: Princeton University Press, 2000.

Egan, Maurice-Francis. "The Last Half of Life." Review of *Senescence*, by G. Stanley Hall. *New York Times Book Review and Magazine* (28 May 1922): 7.

Ehrenreich, Barbara. *Nickel and Dimed: On (Not) Getting by in America*. New York: Henry Holt, 2001.

Eisenberg, Lee. *The Number: A Completely Different Way to Think About the Rest of Your Life*. New York: Free Press, 2006.

Elias, Norbert. *Power and Civility*. 1939. Translated by Edmund Jephcott. Vol. 2 of *The Civilizing Process*. New York: Pantheon, 1982.

Eliot, T. S. *Four Quartets. The Complete Poems and Plays*. New York: Harcourt, Brace, and Company, 1952.

Elliott, Carl. *Better than Well: American Medicine Meets the American Dream*. New York: Norton, 2003.

Ellison, Julie. *Cato's Tears and the Making of Anglo-American Emotion*. Chicago: University of Chicago Press, 1999.

Emmeche, Claus. *The Garden in the Machine: The Emerging Science of Artificial Life*. Translated by Steven Sampson. Princeton, N.J.: Princeton University Press, 1994.

Eng, David L., and Shinhee Han. "A Dialogue on Racial Melancholia." In *Loss: The Politics of Mourning*, edited by David L. Eng and David Kazanjian. Berkeley: University of California Press, 2003. 343–71.

Erikson, Erik H. *Insight and Responsibility: Lectures on the Ethical Implications of Psychoanalytical Insight*. New York: Norton, 1964.

———. *The Life Cycle Completed: A Review*. 1982. New York: Norton, 1985.

Felman, Shoshana, and Dori Laub. *Testimony: Crises of Witnessing in Literature, Psychoanalysis, and History*. New York: Routledge, 1991.

Felski, Rita. "Nothing to Declare: Identity, Shame, and the Lower Middle Class." *PMLA* 115.1 (2000): 33–46.

Ferguson, Kathy. *The Feminist Case Against Bureaucracy*. Philadelphia: Temple University Press, 1984.

Filmer, Paul. "Structures of Feeling and Socio-Cultural Formations: The Significance of Literature and Experience to Raymond Williams's Sociology of Culture." *British Journal of Sociology* 54.2 (2003): 199–219.

Fisher, Berenice. "Guilt and Shame in the Women's Movement: The Radical Ideal of Action and Its Meaning for Feminist Intellectuals." *Feminist Studies* 10.2 (1984): 185–212.

Fisher, Philip. "Democratic Social Space: Whitman, Melville, and the Promise of American Transparency." In *The New American Studies*, edited by Philip Fisher. Berkeley: University of California Press, 1992. 70–111.

———. "Thinking About Killing: Hamlet and the Path Among the Passions." *Raritan* 11.1 (1991): 43–77.

———. *The Vehement Passions*. Princeton, N.J.: Princeton University Press, 2002.

Fleissner, Jennifer L. "Obsessional Modernity: The Institutionalization of Doubt." *Critical Inquiry* 34.1 (2007): 106–34.

Ford, Kenneth, Clark Glymour, and Patrick J. Hayes, eds. *Android Epistemology*. Menlo Park: AAAI Press/MIT Press, 1995.

Fraser, Nancy. *Unruly Practices: Power, Discourse, and Gender in Contemporary Social Theory*. Minneapolis: University of Minnesota Press, 1989.

Freud, Anna. "Adolescence." *Psychoanalytic Study of the Child* 13 (1987): 255–78.

Freud, Sigmund. *The Standard Edition of the Complete Psychological Works of Sigmund Freud* [*SE*]. Translated and edited by James Strachey. 24 vols. London: Hogarth and the Institute of Psycho-Analysis, 1953–74.

———. *Civilization and Its Discontents*. 1930. *SE* 21: 64–145.

———. "Delusions and Dreams in Jensen's *Gradiva*." 1907. *SE* 9: 7–93.

———. "A Disturbance of Memory on the Acropolis." 1936. *SE* 22: 238–48.

——. *Five Lectures on Psycho-Analysis.* 1910. *SE* 11: 7–55.

——. *Group Psychology and the Analysis of the Ego.* 1921. *SE* 18: 67–143.

——. *Inhibitions, Symptoms and Anxiety.* 1926. *SE* 20: 77–175.

——. *The Interpretation of Dreams.* 1900. *SE* 4–5: xi-338, 339–627.

——. "The Moses of Michelangelo." 1914. *SE* 13: 211–36.

——. "Mourning and Melancholia." 1917. *SE* 14: 239–58.

——, with Joseph Breuer. *Studies on Hysteria.* 1895. *SE* 2: 1–309.

——. *Totem and Taboo.* 1913. *SE* 17: 1–161.

——. "The 'Uncanny.'" 1919. *SE* 17: 218–56.

——. "The Unconscious." 1915. *SE* 14: 159–215.

Frey, James. *A Million Little Pieces.* New York: Doubleday, 2003.

Friedan, Betty. *The Feminine Mystique.* 1963. Harmondsworth, U.K.: Penguin, 1965.

——. *The Fountain of Age.* New York: Simon and Schuster, 1993.

Fuchs, Elinor. *Making an Exit: A Mother-Daughter Drama with Alzheimer's, Machine Tools, and Laughter.* New York: Henry Holt, 2005.

Fuller, Henry B. "The Last Half." Review of *Senescence,* by G. Stanley Hall. *Nation* 115.2979 (9 August 1922): 150–51.

Gallop, Jane. *Anecdotal Theory.* Durham, N.C.: Duke University Press, 2002.

Garber, Marjorie. *Academic Instincts.* Princeton, N.J.: Princeton University Press, 2001.

Gibbs, Anna. "Contagious Feelings: Pauline Hanson and the Epidemiology of Affect." *Australian Humanities Review* (December 2001): 1–9.

Gifford, Sandra. "The Meaning of Lumps: A Case Study of the Ambiguities of Risk." In *Anthropology and Epidemiology: Interdisciplinary Approaches to the Study of Health and Disease,* edited by Craig B. Janes, Ron Stall, and Sandra Gifford. Boston: D. Reidel, 1986. 213–46.

Gilbert, Sandra M. *Death's Door: Modern Dying and the Ways We Grieve.* New York: Norton, 2005.

Gilleard, Christopher, and Paul Higgs. *Cultures of Ageing: Self, Citizen and the Body.* Harlow, U.K.: Prentice Hall, 2000.

Gillis, Stacy, and Rebecca Munford. "Harvesting Our Strengths: Third Wave Feminism and Women's Studies." *Journal of International Women's Studies* 4.2 (2003): 1–6.

Gilmore, Ruth. "The Politics of Abandonment: The Prison Industrial Complex after Twenty-Five Years." Simpson Center for the Humanities, University of Washington, Seattle, 25 January 2007.

Goffman, Erving. *Presentation of Self in Everyday Life.* Garden City, N.Y.: Doubleday, 1959.

Goleman, Daniel. *Emotional Intelligence.* New York: Bantam, 1995.

Goodnight, C. Thomas. "The Personal, Technical, and Public Sphere of Argument: A Speculative Inquiry into the Art of Public Deliberation." *Journal of the American Forensic Association* 18 (spring 1982): 214–27.

Goodstein, Elizabeth S. *Experience Without Qualities: Boredom and Modernity.* Stanford, Calif.: Stanford University Press, 2005.

Gordon, Andrew. "Shame and Saul Bellow's 'Something to Remember Me By.'" *Saul Bellow Journal* (1995): 52–63.

Grasso, Linda M. *The Artistry of Anger: Black and White Women's Literature in America, 1820–1860.* Chapel Hill: University of North Carolina Press, 2002.

Green, André. *The Fabric of Affect in the Psychoanalytic Discourse.* 1973. Translated by Alan Sheridan. London: Routledge, 1999.

——. *On Private Madness.* London: Hogarth, 1986.

Greer, Germaine. *The Change: Women, Ageing and the Menopause.* Harmondsworth, U.K.: Penguin, 1992.

——. *The Female Eunuch.* London: MacGibbon and Kee, 1970.

——. *The Whole Woman.* New York: Knopf, 1999.

Gregg, Melissa. *Cultural Studies' Affective Voices.* New York: Palgrave Macmillan, 2005.

Grossberg, Lawrence. "Postmodernity and Affect: All Dressed Up with No Place to Go." *Communication* 10 (1988): 271–93.

Gruman, Gerald J. "Cultural Origins of Present-Day 'Age-ism': The Modernization of the Life Cycle." In *Aging and the Elderly: Humanistic Perspectives in Gerontology,* edited by Stuart Spicker, Kathleen Woodward, and David D. Van Tassel. Atlantic Highlands, N.J.: Humanities Press, 1978. 359–87.

Gullette, Margaret Morganroth. *Declining to Decline: Cultural Combat and the Politics of the Midlife.* Charlottesville: University Press of Virginia, 1997.

——. "Midlife Discourses in the Twentieth-Century United States: An Essay on the Sexuality, Ideology, and Politics of Middle-Ageism." In *Welcome to Middle Age! (And Other Cultural Fictions),* edited by Richard A. Shweder. Chicago: University of Chicago Press, 1998. 3–44.

——. "On Dying Young." *Salon.com* 2 November 2001 (visited 10 March 2006).

Gunning, Tom. "An Aesthetic of Astonishment: Early Film and the (In)Credulous Spectator." *Art and Text* 34 (spring 1989): 31–45.

——. "The Cinema of Attraction: Early Film, Its Spectator and the Avant-Garde." *Wide Angle* 8.3–4 (1986): 63–70.

Gutmann, David. *Reclaimed Power: Toward a New Psychology of Men and Women in Later Life.* New York: Basic Books, 1987.

Hacking, Ian. *The Taming of Chance.* Cambridge: Cambridge University Press, 1990.

Halberstam, Judith. "Shame and White Gay Masculinity." *Social Text* 23.3–4 (2005): 219–33.

Hall, G. Stanley. *Adolescence: Its Psychology and Its Relations to Physiology, Anthropology, Sociology, Sex, Crime, Religion, and Education.* 1904. 2 vols. New York: D. Appleton-Century, 1937.

——. "Old Age." *Atlantic Monthly* 127 (1921): 23–31.

——. *Senescence: The Last Half of Life.* 1922. New York: Arno Press, 1972.

Hansen, Mark B. N. *New Philosophy for New Media.* Cambridge, Mass.: MIT Press, 2003.

Haraway, Donna. *The Companion Species Manifesto: Dogs, People, and Significant Otherness.* Chicago: Prickly Paradigm Press, 2003.

———. "A Cyborg Manifesto: Science, Technology, and Socialist-Feminism in the Late Twentieth Century." In *Simians, Cyborgs and Women: The Reinvention of Nature*. New York: Routledge, 1991. 149–81. Originally published as "Manifesto for Cyborgs: Science, Technology, and Socialist Feminism in the 1980s." *Socialist Review* 80 (1985): 65–108.

Harding, Jennifer, and E. Deidre Pribram. "Losing Our Cool? Following Williams and Grossberg on Emotions." *Cultural Studies* 18.6 (November 2004): 863–83.

Hardt, Michael, and Antonio Negri. *Multitude: War and Democracy in the Age of Empire*. New York: Penguin, 2004.

Hartman, Saidiya. "The Time of Slavery." *South Atlantic Quarterly* 101.4 (2002): 757–77.

Havel, Václav. *Disturbing the Peace: A Conversation with Karel Hrizdala*. Translated by Paul Wilson. New York: Knopf, 1990.

Hayles, N. Katherine. *My Mother Was a Computer: Digital Subjects and Literary Texts*. Chicago: University of Chicago Press, 2005.

Heilbrun, Carolyn G. "Virginia Woolf in Her Fifties." In *Virginia Woolf: A Feminist Slant*, edited by Jane Marcus. Lincoln: University of Nebraska Press, 1983. 236–53.

Helal, Kathleen M. "Anger, Anxiety, Abstraction: Virginia Woolf's 'Submerged Truth.'" *South Central Review* 22.2 (2005): 78–94.

Heller, Agnes. *A Philosophy of Morals*. Oxford: Basil Blackwell, 1990.

Hemmings, Clare. "Invoking Affect: Cultural Theory and the Ontological Turn." *Cultural Studies* 19.5 (September 2005): 548–67.

Henderson, Lynne N. "Legality and Empathy." *Michigan Law Review* 85 (June 1987): 1574–1653.

Hendler, Glenn. *Public Sentiments: Structures of Feeling in Nineteenth-Century American Literature*. Berkeley: University of California Press, 1999.

Hendriks-Jansen, Horst. "In Praise of Interactive Emergence, or Why Explanations Don't Have to Wait for Implementation." In *Artificial Life IV: Proceedings of the Fourth International Workshop on the Synthesis and Simulation of Living Systems*, edited by Rodney A. Brooks and Pattie Maes. Cambridge, Mass.: MIT Press, 1994. 70–79.

Hennessee, Judith. *Betty Friedan: Her Life*. New York: Random House, 1999.

Hennessy, Rosemary. *Profit and Pleasure: Sexual Identities in Late Capitalism*. New York: Routledge, 2000.

Hertzberg, Hendrik. "Consumption." *New Yorker* (17 April 2006): 25–26.

Hillman, James. *Emotion: A Comprehensive Phenomenology of Theories and Their Meanings for Therapy*. Evanston, Ill.: Northwestern University Press, 1972.

———. *The Force of Character and the Lasting Life*. New York: Random House, 1999.

Hjort, Mette. "The Theater of Emotions." In *The Strategy of Letters*. Cambridge, Mass.: Harvard University Press, 1993. 160–95.

Hochschild, Arlie. *The Managed Heart: Commercialization of Human Feeling*. Berkeley: University of California Press, 1983.

hooks, bell. *Killing Rage: Ending Racism*. New York: Henry Holt, 1995.

——. *Wounds of Passion: A Writing Life*. New York: Henry Holt, 1997.

Howard, June. "What Is Sentimentality?" *New Literary History* 11.1 (1999): 63–81.

Hunt, Lynn. *Inventing Human Rights: A History*. New York: W. W. Norton, 2007.

Ignatieff, Michael. *Scar Tissue*. New York: Farrar, Straus and Giroux, 1994.

Ihde, Don. *Technology and the Lifeworld: From Garden to Earth*. Bloomington: Indiana University Press, 1990.

Isernagen, Hartwig. "Technology and the Body: 'Postmodernism' and the Voices of John Barth." In *Technology and the American Imagination: An Ongoing Challenge*, edited by Francesca Bisutti De Riz and Rosella Momoli Zorzi. Venice: Supernova, 1994. 563–70.

Jacobs, Harriet A. *Incidents in the Life of a Slave Girl*. 1861. New York: Oxford University Press, 1988.

Jacobs, Joseph J. *The Compassionate Conservative: Assuming Responsibility and Respecting Human Dignity*. Oakland: ICS Press, 2000.

Jacobus, Mary. *The Poetics of Psychoanalysis: In the Wake of Klein*. New York: Oxford University Press, 2005.

Jacoby, Henry. *The Bureaucratization of the World*. 1969. Translated by Eveline L. Kanes. Berkeley: University of California Press, 1973.

Jaggar, Alison M. "Love and Knowledge: Emotions in Feminist Epistemology." In *Gender/Body/Knowledge: Feminist Reconstructions of Being and Knowing*, edited by Alison M. Jaggar and Susan R. Bordo. New Brunswick, N.J.: Rutgers University Press, 1989. 145–71.

Jameson, Fredric. "Culture and Finance Capitalism." *Critical Inquiry* 24 (autumn 1997): 246–65.

——. *The Geopolitical Aesthetic: Cinema and Space in the World System*. Bloomington: Indiana University Press, 1995.

——. "Postmodernism, or The Cultural Logic of Late Capitalism." *New Left Review* 146 (1984): 59–92. Later published as "The Cultural Logic of Late Capitalism" in *Postmodernism, or, The Cultural Logic of Late Capitalism*. Durham, N.C.: Duke University Press, 1991. 1–54.

Johnson, John. "A Future for Autonomous Agents: Machinic *Merkwelten* and Artificial Evolution." *Configurations* 10.3 (2002): 473–516.

Jones, Karen. "Trust as an Affective Attitude." *Ethics* 107 (1996): 4–25.

Joyrich, Lynne. *Re-Viewing Reception: Television, Gender, and Postmodern Culture*. Bloomington: Indiana University Press, 1996.

Kaplan, E. Ann, and Susan Squier, eds. *Playing Dolly: Technocultural Formations, Fantasies, and Fictions of Assisted Reproduction*. New Brunswick, N.J.: Rutgers University Press, 1999.

Katz, Solomon. "Secular Morality." In *Morality and Health*, edited by Allan M. Brandt and Paul Rozin. New York: Routledge, 1997. 297–330.

Kavanagh, Anne M., and Dorothy H. Broom. "Embodied Risk: My Body, Myself?" *Social Science and Medicine* 43.3 (1997): 437–44.

Keller, Evelyn Fox. *A Feeling for the Organism: The Life and Work of Barbara McClintock*. New York: W. H. Freeman, 1983.

Kennedy, Gwynne. *Just Anger: Representing Women's Anger in Early Modern England.* Carbondale, Ill.: Southern Illinois Press, 2000.

Kittay, Eva Feder. *Love's Labor: Essays on Women, Equality, and Dependency.* New York: Routledge, 1999.

Klein, Melanie. *The Selected Melanie Klein,* edited by Juliet Mitchell. New York: Free Press, 1986.

Kleinman, Arthur. *Illness Narratives: Suffering, Healing, and the Human Condition.* New York: Basic Books, 1988.

Kleinman, Arthur, Veena Das, and Margaret Lock, eds. *Social Suffering.* Berkeley: University of California Press, 1997.

Korot, Beryl, and Steve Reich. *Three Tales.* Presented by the Whitney Museum of American Art, Kaufman Astoria Studios Film and Video Gallery, New York. 4–15 October 2006.

Kristeva, Julia. *Black Sun: Depression and Melancholia.* 1985. Translated by Leon S. Roudiez. New York: Columbia University Press, 1987.

——. *New Maladies of the Soul.* 1993. Translated by Ross Mitchell Guberman. New York: Columbia University Press, 1995.

Laplanche, Jean, and J.-B. Pontalis. "Affect." *The Language of Psycho-analysis.* 1963. Translated by Donald Nicolson-Smith. New York: Norton, 1973. 13–14.

Lash, Scott. "Information Is Alive" (interview with Nicholas Gane). In *The Future of Social Theory,* by Nicholas Gane. New York: Continuum, 2004. 91–108.

Latour, Bruno. *Aramis, or the Love of Technology.* 1993. Translated by Catherine Porter. Cambridge, Mass.: Harvard University Press, 1996.

Lazarre, Jane. *Wet Earth and Dreams: A Narrative of Grief and Recovery.* Durham, N.C.: Duke University Press, 1998.

Lear, Jonathan. *Happiness, Death, and the Remainder of Life.* Cambridge, Mass.: Harvard University Press, 2000.

LeDoux, Joseph. *The Emotional Brain: The Mysterious Underpinnings of Emotional Life.* New York: Simon and Schuster, 1996.

Lejeune, Philippe. "The Autobiographical Pact." 1973. In *On Autobiography.* Translated by Katherine Leary. Minneapolis: University of Minnesota Press, 1989.

Levi, Primo. *If This Is a Man/The Truce.* Translated by Stuart Woolf. London: Abacus, 1987.

Lewis, Helen B. *Shame and Guilt in Neurosis.* New York: International Universities Press, 1971.

Lewis, Jan, and Peter N. Sterns, eds. *An Emotional History of the United States.* New York: New York University Press, 1998.

Lewis, Michael. *Shame: The Exposed Self.* New York: Free Press, 1992.

Lewis, Myrna I. *A Proactive Approach to Women's Concerns: Women's Longevity Groups and Funds.* New York: International Longevity Center–USA, October 2005.

Liu, Alan. *The Laws of Cool: Knowledge Work and the Culture of Information.* Chicago: Chicago University Press, 2004.

Lupton, Deborah. "The Embodied Computer/User." *Body and Society* 1.3–4 (1995): 97–112.

Lutz, Catherine. *Unnatural Emotions: Everyday Sentiments on a Micronesian Atoll and Their Challenge to Western Theory.* Chicago: University of Chicago Press, 1988.

Lyman, Peter. "The Politics of Anger: On Silence, Ressentiment, and Political Speech." *Socialist Review* 11.3 (1981): 55–74.

Lynd, Helen Merrell. *On Shame and the Search for Identity.* New York: Harcourt, Brace, 1953.

Lyotard, Jean-François. *The Postmodern Condition: A Report on Knowledge.* 1979. Translated by Geoff Bennington and Brian Massumi. Minneapolis: University of Minnesota Press, 1984.

MacCannell, Juliet Flower. "Politics in the Age of Sex: Clinton, Leadership, Love." In *Trauma and Its Cultural Aftereffects,* edited by Karyn Ball. Special issue of *Cultural Critique* no. 46 (2000): 241–71.

Macdonald, Barbara, with Cynthia Rich. *Look Me in the Eye: Old Women, Aging and Ageism.* San Francisco: Spinster's Ink, 1983.

Mairs, Nancy. *A Troubled Guest: Life and Death Stories.* Boston: Beacon Press, 2001.

———. Review of *The Fountain of Age,* by Betty Friedan. *New York Times Book Review* (3 October 1993): 1, 28.

Manheimer, Ronald J. "Wisdom and Method: Philosophical Contributions to Gerontology." *Handbook of the Humanities and Aging,* edited by Thomas R. Cole, David D. Van Tassel, and Robert Kastenbaum. New York: Springer, 1992.

Marcus, Jane. "Art and Anger: Elizabeth Robins and Virginia Woolf." 1978. In *Art and Anger: Reading Like a Woman.* Columbus: Ohio State University Press, 1988. 122–54.

Martin, Emily. "The Rationality of Mania." In *Doing Science + Culture,* edited by Roddy Reid and Sharon Traweek. New York: Routledge, 2000. 177–96.

Martin, Randy. *Financialization of Daily Life.* Philadelphia: Temple University Press, 2002.

Marx, Karl. *The Economic and Philosophic Manuscripts of 1844. The Marx-Engels Reader,* edited by Robert C. Tucker. 2nd ed. New York: Norton, 1978. 66–125.

Marx, Leo. *The Machine in the Garden: Technology and the Pastoral Ideal in America.* New York: Oxford University Press, 1967.

Massaro, Toni M. "Empathy, Legal Storytelling, and the Rule of Law: New Words, Old Wounds." *Michigan Law Review* 87 (August 1989): 2099–127.

Massumi, Brian. "Fear (The Spectrum Said)." *positions* 13.1 (2005): 31–48.

———. "The Future Birth of the Affective Fact." *Proceedings of the Genealogies of Biopolitics/www.radicalempiricism.org* (October 2005): 1–12.

———. *Parables for the Virtual: Movement, Affect, Sensation.* Durham, N.C.: Duke University Press, 2002.

Massumi, Brian, ed. *The Politics of Everyday Fear.* Minneapolis: University of Minnesota Press, 2003.

Matus, Jill. "Shame and Anger in *The Bluest Eye.*" In *Toni Morrison.* Manchester: Manchester University Press, 1998. 37–54.

McLuhan, Marshall. *Gutenberg Galaxy: The Making of Typographic Man.* Toronto: University of Toronto Press, 1962.

——. *Understanding Media: The Extensions of Man.* New York: McGraw-Hill, 1964.

McPherson, Tara. *Reconstructing Dixie: Race, Gender, and Nostalgia in the Imagined South.* Durham, N.C.: Duke University Press, 2003.

Mellencamp, Patricia. *High Anxiety: Catastrophe, Scandal, Age, and Comedy.* Bloomington: Indiana University Press, 1992.

Menzel, Peter, and Faith D'Aluisio. *Robo Sapiens: Evolution of a New Species.* Cambridge, Mass.: MIT Press, 2000.

Merton, Robert K., and Elinor Barber. "Sociological Ambivalence." In *Sociological Theory, Values and Sociological Change,* edited by E. A. Tiryakian. New York: Free Press, 1963.

Michaels, Eric. *Unbecoming,* edited by Paul Foss. Durham, N.C.: Duke University Press, 1997.

Miller, Nancy K. *Bequest and Betrayal: Memoirs of a Parent's Death.* Bloomington: Indiana University Press, 2000.

——. *But Enough About Me: Why We Read Other People's Lives.* New York: Columbia University Press, 2002.

——. *Getting Personal: Feminist Occasions and Other Autobiographical Acts.* New York: Routledge, 1991.

Miller, Nancy K., and Jason Tougaw, eds. *Extremities: Trauma, Testimony, and Community.* Urbana: Illinois University Press, 2002.

Miller, Peter. "Accounting as Social and Institutional Practice." Introduction to *Accounting as Social and Institutional Practice,* edited by Anthony G. Hopwood and Peter Miller. Cambridge: Cambridge University Press, 1994. 1–39.

Miller, Susan. "Coda: Fundamentals of Authorship." In *Assuming the Positions: Cultural Pedagogy and the Politics of Commonplace Writing.* Pittsburgh: University of Pittsburgh Press, 1998. 254–91.

——. *Trust in Texts: A Different History of Rhetoric.* Carbondale: Southern Illinois University Press, 2008.

Miller, William Ian. *The Anatomy of Disgust.* Cambridge, Mass.: Harvard University Press, 1997.

——. *Humiliation: And Other Essays on Honor, Social Discomfort, and Violence.* Ithaca, N.Y.: Cornell University Press, 1993.

Minsky, Marvin. *The Society of Mind.* New York: Simon and Schuster, 1986.

Minow, Martha L. "Partners, Not Rivals? Redrawing the Lines between Public and Private, Non-Profit and Profit, and Secular and Religious." *Boston University Law Review* 80 (October 2000): 1061–94.

Minow, Martha L., and Elizabeth V. Spelman. "Passion for Justice." *Cardoza Law Review* 10.37 (1988): 37–76.

Mitscherlich, Alexander, and Margarete Mitscherlich. *The Inability to Mourn: Principles of Collective Behavior.* 1967. Translated by Beverley R. Placzek. New York: Grove, 1975.

Monette, Paul. *Being a Man: Half a Life Story.* New York: Harcourt, Brace, Jovanovich, 1992.

——. *Borrowed Time: An AIDS Memoir.* 1988. New York: Avon, 1990.

Moody, Harry R. *The Five Stages of the Soul: Charting the Spiritual Passages That Shape Our Lives*. New York: Anchor, 1997.

Morris, Meaghan. *Identity Anecdotes: Translation and Media Culture*. London: Sage, 2006.

———. *Too Soon, Too Late: History in Popular Culture*. Bloomington: Indiana University Press, 1998.

Morrison, Toni. *Beloved*. New York: Penguin, 1987.

———. *The Bluest Eye*. New York: Washington Square Press, 1970.

———. Interview with Mel Watkins. *New York Times Book Review* (11 September 1977): 48–50.

Muecke, Stephen. "The Archeology of Feeling." *UTS Review* 5.1 (1999): 1–5.

Munnichs, J. M. A. "A Short History of Psychogerontology." *Human Development* 9 (1966): 230–45.

Muñoz, José Esteban. "Feeling Brown: Ethnicity and Affect in Ricardo Bracho's *The Sweetest Hangover (and Other STDS)*." *Theatre Journal* 52.1 (2000): 67–79.

MURDER and murder. Dir. Yvonne Rainer. Zeitgeist Films, 1996.

National Institutes of Mental Health. U.S. Department of Health and Human Services. *Post-Traumatic Stress Disorder: A Real Illness*. Washington: GPO, 2005.

Negroponte, Nicholas. *Being Digital*. New York: Vintage, 1996.

Ngai, Sianne. *Ugly Feelings*. Cambridge, Mass.: Harvard University Press, 2005.

Nussbaum, Martha C. "Compassion: The Basic Social Emotion." *Social Philosophy and Policy* 13.1 (1996): 27–58.

———. "Narrative Emotions: Beckett's Genealogy of Love." *Love's Knowledge: Essays on Philosophy and Literature*. New York: Oxford University Press, 1990. 286–313.

———. *Poetic Justice: The Literary Imagination and Public Life*. Boston: Beacon Press, 1995.

Nye, David E. *American Technological Sublime*. Cambridge, Mass.: MIT Press, 1994.

Ogden, Thomas H. "On Holding and Containing, Being and Dreaming." *International Journal of Psychoanalysis* 85.6 (2004): 1349–364.

Olasky, Marvin. *Compassionate Conservatism: What It Is, What It Does, and How It Can Transform America*. New York: Free Press, 2000.

———. *The Tragedy of American Compassion*. Washington, D.C.: Regnery Gateway, 1992.

Opening Night. Dir. John Cassavetes. Faces Distributing Corporation, 1977.

Orr, Jackie. *Panic Diaries: A Genealogy of Panic Disorder*. Durham, N.C.: Duke University Press, 2006.

Parisi, Luciana, and Steve Goodman. "The Affect of Nanoterror." *Biopolitics*, edited by Melinda Cooper, Andrew Goffey, and Anna Munster. Special issue of *Culture Machine* 7 (2005). 12 January 2008.

Paster, Gail Kern. *The Body Embarrassed: Drama and the Disciplines of Shame in Early Modern England*. Ithaca, N.Y.: Cornell University Press, 1993.

Pétillon, Pierre-Yves. "With Awe and Wonder; or, a Brief Heliocoidal Overview of American Technological 'Mirabilia' through the Rocket, as Reflected in American Writs, Holy and Otherwise, 1829–1929/1969." In *Technology and the Ameri-*

can Imagination: An Ongoing Challenge, edited by Francesca Bisutti De Riz and Rosella Mamoli Zorzi. Venice: Supernova, 1994. 38–57.

Petro, Patrice. "After Shock/Between Boredom and History." In *Fugitive Images*, edited by Patrice Petro. Bloomington: Indiana University Press, 1995. 265–84.

Pfau, Thomas. *Romantic Moods: Paranoia, Trauma, and Melancholy, 1790–1840*. Baltimore: Johns Hopkins University Press, 2005.

Pfeil, Fred. "Postmodernism as a 'Structure of Feeling.'" In *Marxism and the Interpretation of Culture*, edited by Cary Nelson and Lawrence Grossberg. Urbana: University of Illinois Press, 1988. 381–403.

Pfister, Joel. "On Conceptualizing the Cultural History of Emotional and Psychological Life in America." In *Inventing the Psychological: Toward a Cultural History of Emotional Life in America*, edited by Joel Pfister and Nancy Schnog. New Haven, Conn.: Yale University Press, 1997.

Phillips, Adam. "Just Rage." In *The Beast in the Nursery: On Curiosity and Other Appetites*. New York: Vintage, 1999.

Picard, Rosalind W. *Affective Computing*. Cambridge, Mass.: MIT Press, 1997.

Pifer, Alan, and Lydia Bronte, eds. *Our Aging Society: Promise and Paradox*. New York: Norton, 1986.

Pinch, Adela. *Strange Fits of Passion: Epistemologies of Emotion, Hume to Austen*. Stanford, Calif.: Stanford University Press, 1996.

Pontalis, J.-B. "At the End of the Line." 1986. In *Love of Beginnings*. Translated by James Green, with Marie-Christine Réguis. London: Free Association Books, 1993. 166–71.

———. "Dream as an Object." Translated by Carol Martin-Sperry and Masud Khan. *International Review of Psycho-Analysis* 1 (1974): 334–62.

———. "Perdre de vue." *Perdre de vue*. Paris: Gallimard, 1988. 275–98.

———. *Windows*. 2000. Translated by Anne Quinney. Lincoln: University of Nebraska Press, 2003.

Poovey, Mary. "Accommodating Merchants: Accounting, Civility, and the Natural Laws of Gender." *differences* 8.5 (1997): 1–20.

———. *A History of the Modern Fact: Problems of Knowledge in the Sciences of Wealth and Society*. Chicago: University of Chicago Press, 1998.

Porter, Theodore. *The Rise of Statistical Thinking: 1820–1900*. Princeton, N.J.: Princeton University Press, 1986.

Post, Emily. *Etiquette in Society, in Business, in Politics, and at Home*. New York: Funk and Wagnalls, 1922.

Power, Michael. "The Audit Society." In *Accounting as Social and Institutional Practice*, edited by Anthony G. Hopwood and Peter Miller. Cambridge: Cambridge University Press, 1994. 299–316.

Probyn, Elspeth. *Blush: Faces of Shame*. Minneapolis: University of Minnesota Press, 2005.

Rainer, Yvonne. MURDER and murder (screenplay). *Performing Arts Journal* 55 (1997): 76–117. MURDER and murder (film). Dir. Yvonne Rainer. Zeitgeist Films, 1996.

Ramachandran, V. S. "Mirror Neurons and the Brain in the Vat." *Edge: The Third Culture* (2006) (visited 4 July 2007).

Raphael, Lev. *Edith Wharton's Prisoners of Shame: A New Perspective on Her Neglected Fiction.* New York: St. Martin's Press, 1991.

Rawls, John. *A Theory of Justice.* Cambridge, Mass.: Harvard University Press, 1971.

Rayner, Alice. "Cyborgs and Replicants: On the Boundaries." *Discourse* 16.3 (1994): 124–43.

Reddy, William R. *The Navigation of Feeling: A Framework for the History of Emotions.* New York: Cambridge University Press, 2001.

Reeves, Byron, and Clifford Nass. *The Media Equation: How People Treat Computers, Television, and New Media Like Real People and Places.* Stanford, Calif.: CSLI Publications and Cambridge University Press, 1996.

Retzinger, Suzanne M. *Violent Emotions: Shame and Rage in Marital Quarrels.* Newbury Park, Calif.: Sage, 1991.

Roach, Marion. *Another Name for Madness: The Dramatic Story of a Family's Struggle with Alzheimer's Disease.* Boston: Houghlin Mifflin, 1985.

Robinson, Mary. Foreword to *Human Rights and Older Persons.* Geneva: United Nations, 1999.

Rorty, Richard. "Human Rights, Rationality, and Sentimentality." *Yale Review* 81.4 (October 1993): 1–20.

Rose, Gillian. *Love's Work: A Reckoning with Life.* New York: Schocken, 1997.

Rose, Phyllis. *A Year of Reading Proust: A Memoir in Real Time.* New York: Scribner, 1997.

Rosaldo, Michelle Z. "Toward an Anthropology of Self and Feeling." In *Cultural Theory*, edited by Richard A. Shweder and Robert A. Levine. New York: Cambridge University Press, 1984.

Rosaldo, Renato. "Grief and a Headhunter's Rage." In *Culture and Truth: The Remaking of Social Analysis.* Boston: Beacon Press, 1989. 1–21.

Roszak, Theodore. *America the Wise: The Longevity Revolution and the True Wealth of Nations.* Boston: Houghton Mifflin, 1998.

——. *Longevity Revolution: As Boomers Become Elders.* Berkeley, Calif.: Berkeley Hills Books, 2001.

Russo, Mary. "Aging and the Scandal of Anachronism." In *Figuring Age: Women, Bodies, Generations*, edited by Kathleen Woodward. Bloomington: Indiana University Press, 1999. 20–33.

Samuels, Shirley, ed. *The Culture of Sentiment: Race, Gender, and Sentimentality in Nineteenth-Century America.* New York: Oxford University Press, 1992.

Santa Ana, Jeffrey J. "Affect-Identity: The Emotions of Assimilation, Multiraciality, and Asian American Subjectivity." In *Asian North American Identities: Beyond the Hyphen*, edited by Eleanor Rose Ty and Donald C. Goellnicht. Bloomington: Indiana University Press, 2004. 15–42.

——. "Feeling Ancestral: The Emotions of Mixed Race and Memory in Asian American Cultural Productions." *positions* 16.2, forthcoming.

Santner, Eric. *Stranded Objects: Mourning, Memory, and Film in Postwar Germany.* Ithaca, N.Y.: Cornell University Press, 1990.

Sartre, Jean-Paul. *Being and Nothingness: An Essay on Phenomenological Ontology.* 1943. Translated by Hazel E. Barnes. New York: Philosophical Library, 1956.

——. *The Emotions: Outline of a Theory.* 1939. Translated by Bernard Frechman. New York: Philosophical Library, 1948.

Scheff, Thomas J., and Suzanne M. Retzinger. *Emotions and Violence: Shame and Rage in Destructive Conflicts.* Lexington, Mass.: D.C. Heath, 1991.

Scheman, Naomi. "Anger and the Politics of Naming." In *Women and Language in Literature and Society,* edited by Sally McConnell-Ginet, Ruth Borker, and Nelly Furman. New York: Praeger, 1980. 174–87.

——. "On Waking Up One Morning and Discovering We Are Them." In *Pedagogy: The Question of Impersonation,* edited by Jane Gallop. Bloomington: Indiana University Press, 1995. 106–16.

Schivelbush, Wolfgang. *The Railway Journey: The Industrialization of Time and Space in the Nineteenth Century.* Berkeley: University of California Press, 1986.

Schwab, Gabriele. "Words and Moods: The Transference of Literary Knowledge." *SubStance* 26.3 (1997): 107–27.

Sedgwick, Eve Kosofsky. "Queer Performativity: Henry James's *The Art of the Novel.*" *GLQ* 1 (1993): 1–16.

——. "Shame, Theatricality, and Queer Performativity: Henry James's *The Art of the Novel.*" In *Touching Feeling: Affect, Pedagogy, Performativity.* Durham, N.C.: Duke University Press, 2003. 35–65.

Sedgwick, Eve Kosofsky, and Adam Frank, eds. *Shame and Its Sisters: A Silvan Tomkins Reader.* Durham, N.C.: Duke University Press, 1995.

Seltzer, Mark. *Bodies and Machines.* New York: Routledge, 1992.

Shamir, Milette, and Jennifer Travis, eds. *Boys Don't Cry: Rethinking Narratives of Masculinity and Emotion in the U.S.* New York: Columbia University Press, 2002.

Shields, Stephanie A. *Speaking from the Heart: Gender and the Social Meaning of Emotion.* Cambridge: Cambridge University Press, 2002.

Silent Running. Dir. Douglas Trumbull. Universal Pictures, 1972.

Silver, Brenda R. "The Authority of Anger: *Three Guineas* as a Case Study." *Signs* 16.2 (1991): 340–70.

——. *Virginia Woolf Icon.* Chicago: University of Chicago Press, 1999.

Simmel, Georg. "The Metropolis and Mental Life." 1903. Translated by Edward A. Shils. In *On Individuality and Social Forms,* edited by Donald N. Levine. Chicago: University of Chicago Press, 1971. 324–39.

Simon, Herbert A. "Mind as Machine." *Android Epistemology,* edited by Kenneth M. Ford, Clark Glymour, and Patrick J. Hayes. Cambridge, Mass.: MIT Press, 1995. 23–40.

——. "Motivational and Emotional Controls of Cognition." *Psychological Review* 74 (1967): 29–39.

Simpson, David. "Raymond Williams: Feeling for Structures, Voicing 'History.' " *Social Text* 30 (1992): 9–26.

Small, Helen. *The Long Life.* Oxford: Oxford University Press, 2007.

Smith, Joseph H. "On the Structural View of Affect." *Journal of the American Psychoanalytic Association* 18.3 (1970): 539–61.

Sobchak, Vivian. "Beating the Meat/Surviving the Text, or How to Get Out of This Century Alive." *Body and Society* 1.3–4 (1995): 205–14.

——. *Screening Space: The American Science Fiction Film.* New Brunswick, N.J.: Rutgers University Press, 1997.

Sofri, Adriano. "On Optimism." Translated by Lydia Cochrane. *Critical Inquiry* 30 (summer 2004): 739–70.

Solomon, Andrew. *The Noonday Demon.* New York: Scribner, 2001.

Solomon, Robert. *The Passions.* New York: Anchor, 1977.

Spelman, Elizabeth V. "Anger and Insubordination." In *Women, Knowledge, and Reality: Explorations in Feminist Philosophy,* edited by Ann Garry and Marilyn Pearsall. Boston: Unwin Hyman, 1989. 263–73.

——. *Fruits of Sorrow: Framing Our Attention to Suffering.* Boston: Beacon Press, 1997.

——. *Repair: The Impulse to Restore in a Fragile World.* Boston: Beacon Press, 2002.

Spurlock, John C., and Cynthia A. Magistro. *New and Improved: The Transformation of American Women's Emotional Culture.* New York: New York University Press, 1998.

Srivastava, Sarita. " 'You're Calling Me a Racist?' The Moral and Emotional Regulation of Antiracism and Feminism." *Signs: Journal of Women in Culture and Society* 31.1 (2005): 29–62.

Stauffer, Andrew M. *Anger, Revolution, and Romanticism.* New York: Cambridge University Press, 2005.

Stearns, Carol Zisowitz, and Peter N. Stearns. *Anger: The Struggle for Emotional Control in America's History.* Chicago: University of Chicago Press, 1986.

Stearns, Peter N. *American Cool: Constructing a Twentieth-Century Emotional Style.* New York: New York University Press, 1994.

Steedman, Carolyn. *Dust: The Archive and Cultural History.* New Brunswick, N.J.: Rutgers University Press, 2002.

Steinem, Gloria. "Doing Sixty." In *Moving Beyond Words.* New York: Simon and Schuster, 1994. 249–83.

Stengers, Isabelle. "Les généalogies de l'auto-organisation." *Cahiers du CREA* 8 (November 1985): 7–104.

Stevens, Wallace. "Adagia." In *Opus Posthumous,* edited by Samuel French Morse. New York: Knopf, 1957. 162.

Stewart, Kathleen. *Ordinary Affects.* Durham, N.C.: Duke University Press, 2008.

Stowe, Harriet Beecher. *Uncle Tom's Cabin or, Life Among the Lowly.* 1852. Edited by Ann Douglas. New York: Penguin, 1981.

Stuart, Diane M. U.S. Senate Committee on the Judiciary, Department of Justice. *Reauthorization of the Violence Against Women Act Hearing.* Washington: GPO, 2005.

Swados, Elizabeth. *The Four of Us: The Story of a Family.* New York: Farrar, Straus and Giroux, 1991.

Tavris, Carol. *Anger: The Misunderstood Emotion.* Rev. ed. New York: Simon and Schuster, 1989.

Taylor, Charles. *Sources of the Self: The Making of Modern Identity.* Cambridge, Mass.: Harvard University Press, 1989.

Telotte, J. P. *Replications: A Robotic History of the Science Fiction Film.* Urbana: University of Illinois Press, 1995.

Terada, Rei. *Feeling in Theory: Emotion after the "Death of the Subject."* Cambridge, Mass.: Harvard University Press, 2001.

Thomas, Sandra, ed. *Women and Anger.* New York: Springer, 1993.

Tisseron, Serge. *La Honte: Psychanalyse d'un lien social.* Paris: Dunon, 1992.

Tomkins, Silvan. *Cognition: Duplication and Transformation of Information.* New York: Springer, 1992. Vol. 4 of *Affect, Imagery, Consciousness.* 4 vols. New York: Springer, 1962–92.

———. *The Negative Affects: Anger and Fear.* New York: Springer, 1991. Vol. 3 of *Affect, Imagery, Consciousness.* 4 vols. New York: Springer, 1962–92.

Tomlinson, Barbara. "Tough Babies or Anger in the Superior Position." *Cultural Critique* no. 39 (1998): 151–88.

Tompkins, Jane. *A Life in School: What the Teacher Learned.* Reading, Mass.: Perseus, 1996.

———. *Sensational Designs: The Cultural Work of American Fiction, 1790–1860.* New York: Oxford University Press, 1985.

Trillin, Calvin. "Alice, Off the Page." *New Yorker,* 27 March 2006, 44.

Tromble, Meredith, ed. *The Art and Films of Lynn Hershman Leeson: Secret Agents, Private I.* Berkeley: University of California Press, 2005.

Turkle, Sherry. *Life on the Screen: Identity in the Age of the Internet.* New York: Simon and Schuster, 1995.

2001: A Space Odyssey. Dir. Stanley Kubrick. Metro-Goldwyn-Mayer, 1968.

Varela, Francisco J., Evan Thompson, and Eleanor Rosch. *The Embodied Mind: Cognitive Science and Human Experience.* Cambridge, Mass.: MIT Press, 1991.

Walker, Margaret Urban. "Picking Up the Pieces: Lives, Stories, and Integrity." *Feminists Rethink the Self.* Boulder, Colo.: Westview Press, 1997. 62–84.

Weigert, Andrew. *Mixed Emotions: Certain Steps Toward Understanding Ambivalence.* Albany: State University of New York Press, 1991.

Weil, Simone. *First and Last Notebooks.* 1956. Translated by Richard Rees. London: Oxford University Press, 1970.

———. *The Need for Roots.* 1949. Translated by Arthur Wills. 2 vols. London: Routledge and Kegan Paul, 1956.

Weisman, Mary-Lou. "Golden Daze" (review of *The Fountain of Age,* by Betty Friedan). *New Republic* (11 October 1993): 4949–51.

Wexler, Alice. *Mapping Fate: A Memoir of Family, Risk, and Genetic Research.* New York: Random House, 1995.

Wexler, Nancy S. "Genetic 'Russian Roulette': The Experience of Being 'At Risk' for Huntington's Disease." In *Genetic Counseling: Psychological Dimensions,* edited by Seymour Kessler. New York: Academic Press, 1979.

Wharton, Edith. *The House of Mirth*. 1905. New York: Charles Scribner's Sons, 1933.

Williams, Bernard. *Ethics and the Limits of Philosophy*. London: Fontana Press, 1985.

——. *Shame and Necessity*. Berkeley: University of California Press, 1993.

Williams, Patricia. *The Alchemy of Race and Rights*. Cambridge, Mass.: Harvard University Press, 1991.

Williams, Raymond. *Politics and Letters: Interviews with New Left Review*. London: New Left Review, 1979.

——. "Structures of Feeling." In *Marxism and Literature*. Oxford: Oxford University Press, 1977. 128–35.

Winnicott, D. W. *The Maturational Processes and the Facilitating Environment: Studies in the Theory of Emotional Development*. New York: International Universities Press, 1965.

——. *Playing and Reality*. London: Tavistock, 1971.

Woodward, Kathleen. *Aging and Its Discontents: Freud and Other Fictions*. Bloomington: Indiana University Press, 1991.

——. *At Last, the Real Distinguished Thing: The Late Poems of Eliot, Pound, Stevens, and Williams*. Athens: Ohio State University Press, 1980.

——. "Grief-Work in Contemporary American Cultural Criticism." *Discourse* 15.2 (1992–93): 94–112.

——. "Late Theory, Late Style: Loss and Renewal in Freud and Barthes." In *Aging and Gender in Literature: Studies in Creativity*, edited by Anne M. Wyatt-Brown and Janice Rossen. Charlottesville: University of Virginia Press, 1993. 82–101.

——. "Telling Stories: Aging, Reminiscence, and the Life Review." *Journal of Aging and Identity* 2.3 (1997): 149–63.

——. "Tribute to the Older Woman." In *Images of Aging: Cultural Representations of Later Life*, edited by Mike Featherstone and Andrew Werrick. London: Routledge, 1995. 79–96.

Woolf, Virginia. *Jacob's Room*. 1922. New York: Signet, 1998.

——. *A Room of One's Own*. 1929. New York: Harcourt, Brace and World, 1957.

——. *Three Guineas*. 1938. New York: Harcourt, Brace and World, 1963.

Worsham, Lynn. "Emotion and Pedagogic Violence." *Discourse* 15.2 (1992): 119–48.

Wyatt-Brown, Bertram. *Southern Honor: Ethics and Behavior in the Old South*. New York: Oxford University Press, 1982.

Zhang, Yanhua. *Transforming Emotions with Chinese Medicine: An Ethnographic Account from Contemporary China*. Albany: State University of New York Press, 2007.

Zembylas, Michalinos. "Witnessing in the Classroom: The Ethics and Politics of Affect." *Educational Theory* 56.3 (2006): 305–24.

Zenk, John L. "Advant Rx-Joint Health: An Arthritis Breakthrough." *Total Health* 23.2 (2001): 64.

Zettel, Sarah. *Fool's War*. New York: Warner, 1997.

Zimmerman, David A. *Panic! Markets, Crises, and Crowds in American Fiction*. Chapel Hill: University of North Carolina Press, 2006.

INDEX

Ahmed, Sara, 22, 247 n. 14

AI (film), 143

Aibo Entertainment Robot, 263 n. 18

AIDS: illness memoirs and, 5, 177–80,
191, 218, 264–65 n. 1, 267 n. 18, 267
n. 20; literal deaths of writers and,
174; mourning, activism, and, 29

airline industry, 210–11

Alchemy of Race and Rights, The
(Williams), 252 n. 35, 254–55 n. 8

Alexander, Elizabeth, 258 n. 15

"Alice, Off the Page" (Trillin), 195, 196

Al-Kassim, Dina, 256 n. 17

Allison, Dorothy, 254 n. 7

Alzheimer's disease, 138, 173, 180–84,
191, 219, 224, 267 n. 23

Amedure, Scott, 102–3

American Cool (Stearns), 16, 18

America the Wise (Roszak), 248 n. 4

Anatomy of Disgust, The (Miller), 63,
249 n. 9

Ancients Against Moderns (DeJean), 241
n. 29

Anderson, Perry, 137

android epistemology, 148

Android Epistemology (Ford, Glymour,
and Hayes), 263 n. 12

Anecdotal Theory (Gallop), 240 n. 26

anger: anthropology and, 19–20, 240
n. 25, 245 n. 4, 266–67 n. 16; autobiographical experience of, 7; chafing emotions and, 33; clarity of, 52;
cognitive dimension of emotions
and, 46, 49, 57, 237 n. 10, 246 n. 12,
252 n. 34; consciousness raising and,
49–50, 247 n. 14; containment of,
30, 42–43; cultural right to, 51–57,
247 n. 15; emotional sequencing of,
85, 253 n. 2, 254–55 n. 8; epistemological aspect of, 7; feminism and
analysis of, 30, 34–35, 45–51, 77,
252–53 n. 37; feminist, 8, 23, 48–52,
247 n. 14; gendered perspectives
and, 30, 51, 111, 245 n. 6, 247 n. 15;

guilt and, 30, 43–45, 52, 246 nn. 9–
11; hysteria and, 4, 34–38, 245 n. 6;
moral authority of, 73–78; oppressor-oppressed paradigm and, 54–55;
as outlaw emotion, 30, 31, 47, 54, 75,
80; as personal emotion, 50; politicization of, 49, 246 n. 12; racism-in-
feminism accusations and, 56, 248
n. 22; rage and safeguarding, 77,
184; self-reflexive thought, 57, 79–
80, 248 n. 23; shame and model of,
83–85, 253 n. 2; statistical panic
countered by, 26; women and, 34,
48, 51, 58, 245 n. 6, 248 n. 1; Woolf's
dramatization of, 46–49, 53–54, 57,
175, 247 n. 13, 247–48 n. 21

"Anger and Authority" (Culley), 55

"Anger and Insubordination" (Spelman), 49, 52

"Anger and the Politics of Naming"
(Scheman), 49, 52, 170

"Anger, Anxiety, Abstraction" (Silver),
247–48 n. 21

Another Name for Madness (Roach), 138,
180–84, 191, 219, 224

anthropology, 19–20, 240 n. 25, 245
n. 4, 266–67 n. 16

anxiety: age anxiety, 63; doubling of,
92; Freudian theory of, 45, 204–5;
retailing of, 167

Appadurai, Arjun, 210

Archive of Feelings, An (Cvetkovich), 29

Aristotle, 59, 118, 272 n. 1

Armstrong, Nancy, 22

Arrival of a Train at the Station (film), 213

*Art and Films of Lynn Hershman Leeson,
The* (Tromble), 264 n. 25

artificial life, 154

Asimov, Isaac, 143

Assuming the Positions (Miller), 242
n. 34

"At the End of the Line" (Pontalis), 19,
219–33, 272 n. 2, 273 nn. 9–10

audit society, 270 n. 15

258 n. 14; statistical panic and, 218. *See also* empathy; liberal compassion

tics of, 2, 7, 235 n. 3; diminution of, 16; dominant tradition and, 4; dreams and, 6; epistemological privilege of, 47, 97; as evolutionary strength, 145; expansive, 33; Freud on, 3–4, 33–47, 49–54, 244 n. 2, 246 n. 8; histories of, 8; literary, 7, 20, 95, 124, 232–33, 259 n. 18; meta-emotion, 248 n. 23; narrative and, 32, 118, 124–25, 240–41 n. 28; neoliberal concept of, 23; oscillation of, 138; ownership of vocabulary for, 1, 3, 24, 148, 233; philosophers' works on, 2, 7, 235 n. 1, 237 n. 10; poetics of, 3, 9, 11, 19, 98, 123, 135, 153; prosthetic, 136, 139–40, 160, 263–64 n. 21; quiet, 33; rapid circulation of, 8; regret of, 18; self-reflective, 258 n. 14; sequencing of, 30–31, 85–87, 238–39 n. 16, 253 n. 2, 254–55 n. 8; social construction of, 73; social and historical context of, 10–11, 20–22, 241 n. 29, 242–42 n. 31, 242 nn. 32–33; standards of, 61–62; strong, 33; structures of feeling and, 12, 237 n. 12, 237–38 n. 13; study of, 2, 235 nn. 1–2; techno-artifacts and, 136, 163–64; theory of, 3–4; transmission of, 50–51

emotional correctness, 110

emotional exercise, 67

emotional experience, 3, 219

Emotional History of the United States, An (Lewis and Sterns), 62

emotional illness, 18

emotional labor, 21, 23, 241–42 n. 31

emotional loss, 2–3, 180, 192, 235–36 n. 4

emotional pollution, 94, 254 n. 7

empathy, 71, 110, 113–17, 118, 146–48, 185, 192, 218, 242 n. 33, 256 n. 2, 258 n. 12. *See also* compassion

"Empathy, Legal Storytelling, and the Rule of Law" (Massaro), 258 n. 12

Ender's Game (Card), 156

Eng, David L., 235–36 n. 4

Erikson, Erik H., 249 n. 5, 251 n. 24

Etiquette in Society (Post), 1–2

"Everyone's Protest Novel" (Baldwin), 122, 123

evocative object, 27, 233

"Evocative Object, The" (Bollas), 229

expansive emotions, 33

Experience without Qualities (Goodstein), 271 n. 17

Extreme Makeover (television program), 190

Extremities (Miller and Tougaw), 18

fear, 243–44 n. 44

Feeling for the Organism, A (Keller), 141, 155, 261 n. 3

Feeling in Theory (Terada), 262–63 n. 10

"Feeling No Pain" (Krugman), 256 n. 2

Feeling Power (Boler), 235 n. 2, 237–38 n. 13, 247 n. 13, 247 n. 18, 258 n. 14

feelings: aging and, 69; archive of, 29; bureaucratic, 136–37, 167–73, 265 n. 7; critical phenomenology and, 135; defined, 26; histories of, 8; narrative and, 19–27; new sites and, 135–38; power of, 219; social and historical context of, 7, 10–11, 20, 240 n. 25; study of, 2; thought and, 234

feeling trap, 97

Felman, Shoshana, 247 n. 18

Feminine Mystique, The (Friedan), 68, 250 n. 21

feminism: anger and, 30, 34–35, 45–52, 77, 243 n. 13, 243–44 n. 14, 247 n. 14, 252–53 n. 37; guilt and, 106–8; oppressor-oppressed paradigm and, 54–55; pedagogy and, 54–55, 247 n. 18, 247–48 n. 21; periodic reinvention of, 60; politicized groups and, 49–51, 247 n. 14; racism

Gallop, Jane, 240 n. 26

Garbo Talks (film), 267 n. 20

Garden in the Machine, The (Emmeche), 154

gender: aging and, 64, 68–69, 249 n. 13, 250 nn. 19–20; anger and, 30, 34, 35–36, 46, 51, 111, 245 n. 6, 247 n. 15; compassion and, 110–11, 127; cyborgs and, 264 n. 25; double-entry bookkeeping and, 271 n. 20; display of grief and, 8, 111, 233, 267 n. 20; history of statistics and, 216, 271 n. 20; private sphere and, 111; public sphere and, 110–11; textual violence and, 245 n. 6

Gendered Subjects (Culley and Portuges), 55

Germany, 235–36 n. 4

Gibbs, Anna, 243 n. 42

Gibbs, Nancy, 265 n. 7

Gifford, Sandra, 204, 268 n. 5

Gilbert, Sandra M., 233–34

Gilleard, Christopher, 180

Gillis, Stacy, 56

Gilmore, Ruth, 136–37

Glymour, Clark, 263 n. 12

Goffman, Erving, 200

Goleman, Daniel, 147

Good Housekeeping, 196

Goodnight, C. Thomas, 168, 265 n. 2

Goodstein, Elizabeth S., 271 n. 17

Gordon, Andrew, 268–69 n. 6

Gore, Al, 110

Grasso, Linda M., 55–56

Gray Panthers, 75

Green, André, 92, 104

Greer, Germaine, 58–59, 68, 75, 248 n. 1, 250 n. 22

Gregg, Melissa, 240 n. 27

grief: capacity to be alone and, 273 n. 9; diaspora and, 235–36 n. 4; fantasy of place and, 219, 230–32, 273 n. 10; feeling, 4–5, 24; financial panic and, 272 n. 24; *fort-da* and, 222–23, 227–28, 230, 272 n. 1, 273 n. 10; gendered perspectives and, 8, 111, 233, 267 n. 20; *Hamlet* and, 242 n. 32; holding onto, 4; managing one's, 181, 234; media and, 25; mood as affective space and, 26–27, 228–32, 244 n. 45, 273 n. 8; mother-child connection and, 227–28; nostalgia and, 229, 232–33; ownership of, 1, 24, 148, 233; reactions to, 2–3; separation vs. connection and, 219–27, 272 nn. 1–2; universal experience of, 233–44

"Grief and the Headhunter's Rage" (Rosaldo), 266–67 n. 16

Griffiths, Paul, 73

Grossberg, Lawrence, 26–27

Gruman, Gerald J., 73–74

guilt: feminism and, 106–8; Freud on anger and, 30, 34, 43–45, 52, 80, 245–46 n. 7, 246 nn. 8–11

"Guilt and Shame in the Women's Movement" (Fisher), 79

Gullette, Margaret Morganroth, 63, 74, 252–53 n. 37

Gunning, Tom, 212, 213

Hacking, Ian, 195, 211, 216, 271 n. 21

Halberstam, Judith, 254 n. 5

Hall, G. Stanley, 60, 63–68, 249 nn. 14–15

Han, Shinhee, 235–36 n. 4

Hansen, Mark B., 140

Haraway, Donna, 1, 19, 139, 141, 142, 145, 252 n. 31

Harding, Jennifer, 237–38 n. 13

Hardt, Michael, 241–42 n. 31

Hartman, Saidiya, 235–36 n. 4

Havel, Václav, 78

Hayes, Patrick J., 263 n. 12

Hayles, N. Katherine, 139, 154, 261–62 n. 6

health: genetics of mental illness and, 192; mania and, 138; normotic ill-

Reddy, William R., 241 n. 29
Reeves, Byron, 156–57
reading unconscious, 124
Reich, Steve, 264 n. 24
remembrance, 4–5, 226–27, 273 n. 6
Replications (Telotte), 262 n. 7
repressed desire, 3–4
"Resistance, Terminable and Interminable" (Al-Kassim), 256 n. 17
Retzinger, Suzanne M., 102, 246
n. 8
Re-Viewing Reception (Joyrich), 269 n. 8
Rich, Adrienne, 51
Rich, Cynthia, 77
Rise of Statistical Thinking, The (Por-
ter), 217
risk society, 174, 203, 211, 270 n. 13
"Risks of Empathy, The" (Boler), 258
n. 14
Rizzolatti, Giacomo, 164
Roach, Marion: *Another Name for Mad-
ness*, 138, 180–84, 191, 219, 224, 232;
on health care system, 191; illness
memoirs and, 176; on impacts of ill-
ness, 192; literature on Alzheimer's
disease and, 267 n. 23
Robinson, Mary, 74
Robo Sapiens (Menzel and D'Alui-
sio), 162
robots. *See* cyborgs
Robot Stories (film), 143
Roe v. Wade, 114
Romantic Moods (Pfau), 244 n. 45
Rorty, Richard, 259 n. 18
Rosaldo, Michelle Z., 19–20, 171, 240
n. 25
Rosaldo, Renato, 176, 245 n. 4, 266–
67 n. 16
Rose, Gillian, 208
Rose, Phyllis, 199, 208
Roszak, Theodore, 248 n. 4
Rules of Sociological Method, The (Durk-
heim), 22

sadness, 253 n. 2
Samuels, Shirley, 258 n. 16
Sartre, Jean-Paul, 81–85
Scar Tissue (Ignatieff), 272–73 n. 5
Scenes of Shame (Adamson and Clark),
253 n. 1
Schadenfreude, 212
Scheff, Thomas J., 102
Scheman, Naomi, 49–50, 52, 54–55,
170, 235 n. 1, 247 n. 14
schizophrenia memoirs, 176, 184–89,
191, 192
Schmitz, Jonathan, 102–3
Schwab, Gabriele, 244 n. 46
science fiction, 136, 141–42, 261 n. 4
Screening Space (Sobchak), 146–47
Sedgwick, Eve Kosofsky, 85–87, 236–
37 n. 9, 253–54 n. 4
self, as object, 136
self-analysis experiences, 6–9. *See also*
illness memoirs; narratives
self-reflexive thought, 57, 79–80, 248
n. 23
Seltzer, Mark, 268 n. 3
Senescence (Hall), 60, 63–68, 249
nn. 14–15
Sensational Designs (Tompkins), 112,
257 nn. 8–9
sentimentality, 112–14, 121–23, 257
nn. 8–9, 258–59 n. 17. *See also* compassion
Sentimental Men (Chapman and
Hendler), 257 n. 8
September 11 attacks, 14, 61, 210
sequencing of emotions, 30, 31, 85–87,
238–39 n. 16, 253 n. 2, 254–55 n. 8
Shadow of the Object, The (Bollas), 16
shame, 79, 81; anger and, 83–85, 253
n. 2; commercialization of, 100–
104; compassionate conservatism
and, 30; confusion and, 95–97, 106;
defined, 80; emotional sequencing
of, 85, 86–87, 253 n. 2; ethical model
of, 81–83; as free radical, 86; Freud

on, 80; gender and, 82, 84, 254 n. 5, 255 n. 9; liberal, 108; liberal compassion and, 30, 32, 124; as outlaw emotion, 87, 97; as psychological emotion, 31; queer identity and, 85–88, 253–54 n. 4, 254 n. 5; sexual orientation and, 82; as social emotion, 31, 246 n. 8; studies of, 253 n. 1; transformational model of, 85–88, 253–54 n. 4

"Shame and Gender" (Bartky), 94–96

Shame and Its Sisters (Sedgwick and Frank), 139, 236–37 n. 9

"Shame and White Gay Masculinity" (Halberstam), 254 n. 5

Shapiro v. Thompson, 114, 115

Shields, Stephanie A., 248 n. 23

shock, 32, 138, 212–17

Sick (Cohn), 191

Silent Running (film), 142, 149–51, 154, 261 n. 4

Silver, Brenda R., 48–49, 247–48 n. 21

Simians, Cyborgs and Women (Haraway), 252 n. 31

Simmel, Georg, 203, 214, 271 n. 18

Simon, Herbert A., 263 n. 12

Simpson, David, 237 n. 12, 237–38 n. 13

situated knowledge, 75

Smilow, Stanford, 173

Smith, Joseph H., 236 n. 8

Sobchak, Vivian, 146–47

Social Security, 61, 249 n. 6

social suffering: compassionate conservatism and, 117–18, 131; liberal compassion and, 32, 114–17, 123, 257–58 n. 11, 257 n. 12, 259 n. 18

Social Suffering (Kleinman), 131

Society of Mind, The (Minsky), 160

society of the spectacle, 100, 102, 190, 211

society of the statistic, 197, 199–200, 205, 208–12, 268 nn. 3–5, 269–70 n. 11, 270 n. 15

Sociology of Health Promotion, The (Bunton, Nettleton, and Burrows), 269 n. 7

sociology of human-technology interaction, 142–43, 155–59, 263 nn. 17–18, 264 n. 22

Sofri, Adriano, 270 n. 13

Solomon, Andrew, 17, 218

Solomon, Robert, 75

Space Odyssey, A (Clarke), 141–42, 144–46, 154, 261 n. 4, 262 n. 7

Speaker for the Dead (Card), 156, 263 n. 16

Speaking from the Heart (Shields), 248 n. 23

Specimen Days (Cunningham), 19

Spelman, Elizabeth V.: "Anger and Insubordination," 49, 52; on compassion, 109, 110, 113; *Fruits of Sorrow*, 120–21, 124; on hysteria, 245 n. 6; philosophers' works on emotions and, 235 n. 1; on politics of emotion, 49

Spielberg, Steven, 143

Spillane, Sherri, 101

"Spirit of the Object at the Hand of Fate, The" (Bollas), 231

Spurlock, John C., 62

"Squaring Accounts with Uncle Sam" (Fraser), 265 n. 3

Squier, Susan, 272 n. 23

squiggle game, 227

Srivastava, Sarita, 33, 56, 248 n. 22

States of Injury (Brown), 247 n. 14

statistical body, 195–96

statistical hope, 268 n. 2

statistical panic, 8, 135; action to convert, 215; as affect, 24; airline industry and, 210–11; anger and, 26; author's experience of, 9–10, 237 n. 11; boredom and, 14–15, 25, 138, 212–16; breast cancer risk and, 198, 201–4, 268 nn. 4–5, 268–69 n. 6, 269 n. 9; calculus of risk and, 211,

Weisman, Mary-Lou, 251 n. 25

Wetwares (Doyle), 260–61 n. 1, 262–63 n. 10, 264 n. 22

Wexler, Alice, 10, 13–14, 200, 205–8, 217

Wexler, Nancy S., 206

"What Is Sentimentality?" (Howard), 258 n. 16

Whole Woman, The (Greer), 58–59

Williams, Patricia, 252 n. 35, 254–55 n. 8

Williams, Raymond: *The City and the Country*, 237 n. 12; *Marxism and Literature*, 11, 21; *Politics and Letters*, 14; structures of feeling and, 11, 14, 53, 135, 163, 237 n. 12, 237–38 n. 13

Windows (Pontalis), 222–23, 229, 234, 273 n. 10

Winnicott, D. W., 223–24, 227, 272 n. 4, 273 n. 9

wisdom, 31, 59, 62, 64–65, 71–72, 74–75, 251 n. 24, 251 n. 26, 251–52 n. 29, 252 nn. 30–31

"Wisdom and Method" (Manheimer), 251–52 n. 29

witnessing, 99, 112

"Witnessing in the Classroom" (Zembylas), 247 n. 18

women: anger and, 8, 34, 48, 51, 58, 245 n. 6, 248 n. 1; emotions becoming feminist and, 78; grief and, 267 n. 20; hysteria and, 4, 34–38, 245

n. 6; private sphere and, 111; repressed desire in, 4; TV melodramas seen by, 198, 269 n. 8

Woodward, Kathleen, 63, 251–52 n. 29, 273 n. 6

Woolf, Virginia: anger dramatized and analyzed by, 7, 46–49, 53–54, 57, 175, 247 n. 13, 247–48 n. 21; *Jacob's Room*, 33, 57; models of shame and, 83–85; *A Room of One's Own*, 7, 12, 23, 46–48, 53, 83, 85, 175, 240 n. 26, 247–48 n. 21; on social and historical context of emotions, 11, 34; *Three Guineas*, 48

"Words and Moods" (Schwab), 244 n. 46

writing unconscious, 6

Xenocide (Card), 156

Year of Magical Thinking, The (Didion), 1, 5, 6, 26

Year of Reading Proust, A (Rose), 199

"You're Calling Me a Racist?" (Srivastava), 33

youthful structure of the look, 79

Zembylas, Michalinos, 247 n. 18

Zenk, John L., 196

Zettel, Sarah, 163

Zhang, Yanhua, 253 n. 2

Zimmerman, David A., 272 n. 24

KATHLEEN WOODWARD is a professor of English and the director of the Simpson Center for the Humanities at the University of Washington. She is the author of *Aging and Its Discontents: Freud and Other Fictions.*